THE HISTORY OF ETERNITY

James E. Winder

Setarcos Spectrum Publications
Hanover, Maryland
First published in the United States

Copyright © James E. Winder, 2020.
All rights reserved. Reproduction of the whole or any part of the contents without permission from the author is prohibited.
Library of Congress Control Number: 2019915674
Identifier: ISBN: 978-0-578-57579-7
Book interior and Cover design by
Hammad Khalid
www.hmdgfx.com

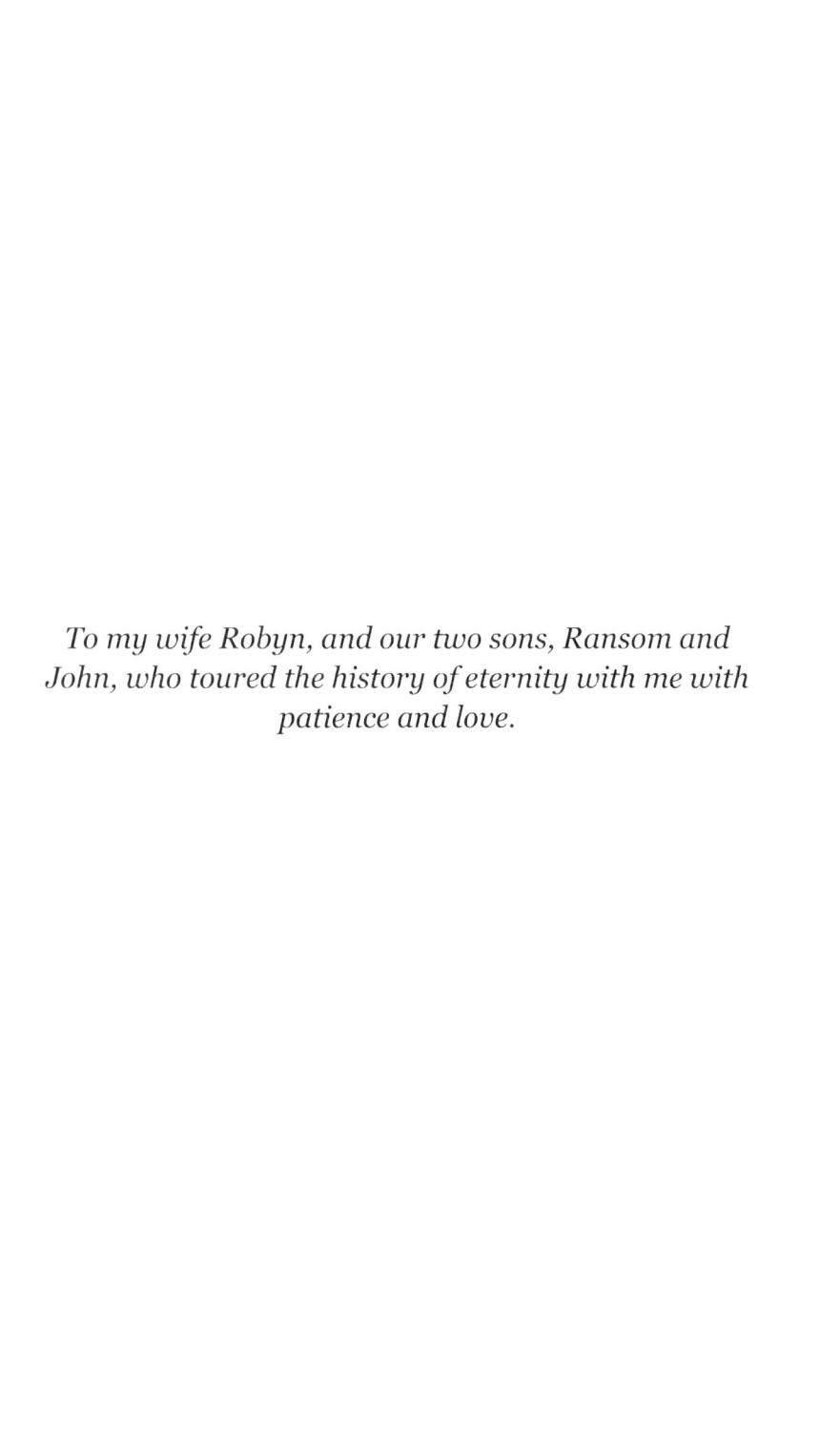

To my wife Robyn, and our two sons, Ransom and John, who toured the history of eternity with me with patience and love.

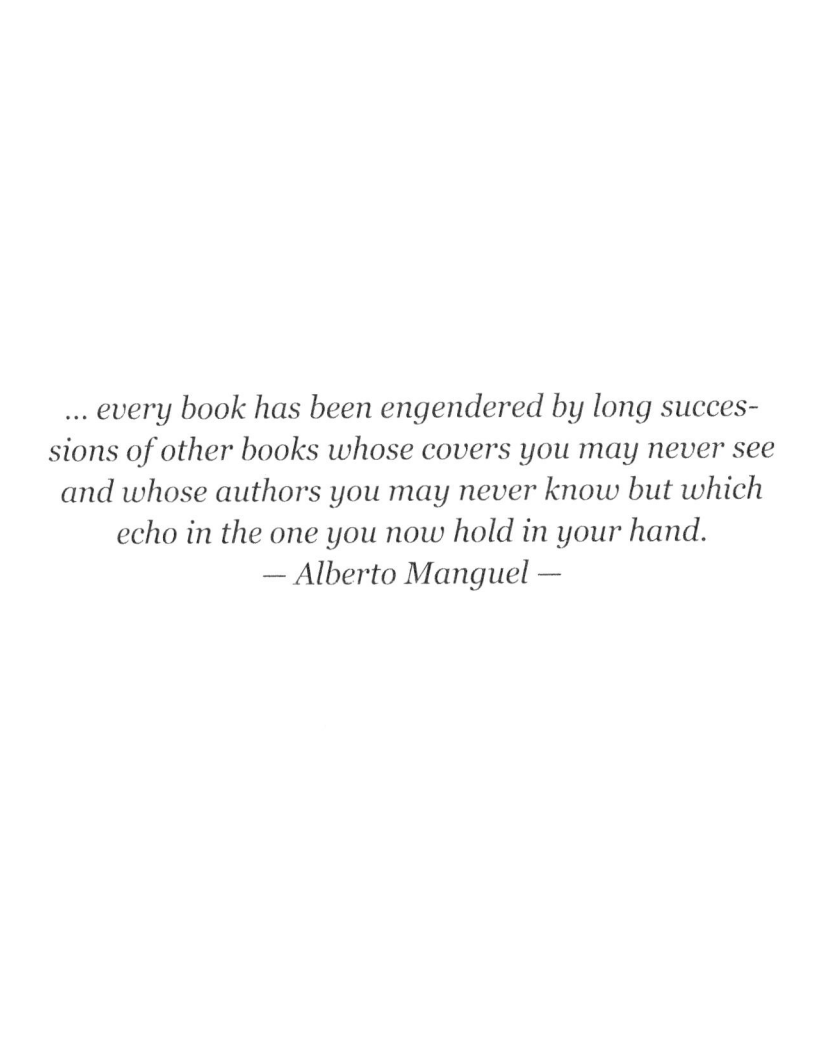

... every book has been engendered by long successions of other books whose covers you may never see and whose authors you may never know but which echo in the one you now hold in your hand.
— Alberto Manguel —

CONTENTS

ONE — THE BROKEN SYMMETRY

I. The Thousand Strangers 1
II. The Songbird's Throat 1
III. The Deepest Rift 1
IV. The Metalled Taste 3
V. The Dreaming Universe 3
VI. Your Soul's Upholstery 4
VII. The Nursing Home 5
VIII. The Worm-Hole 5
IX. The Steep Ravine 6
X. The Homeless Man 6
XI. The Cackling Leaf 6
XII. The Vainest Boast 7

TWO — BECOME SOMEONE ELSE

I. The Body's Certainty 9
II. The Wingless Butterfly 9
III. The Crimson Palm 10
IV. The Empty Ask 10
V. This Golden Bowl 10
VI. The Gray Sky 11
VII. The Full Face 11
VIII. For the Few 12
IX. The Wilted Leaf 12
X. The Abandoned Chrysalis 13
XI. Unseen Green 14
XII. The Field of Maize 15

THREE — HUMAN BEINGS FLICKER

I. The Pregnant Agony 17
II. The Crannied Wall 17
III. The Conscious Wind 18
IV. Under the Dead Leaves 18
V. The River 19
VI. The Overpass 19
VII. The Blackberry Picker 20
VIII. The Latest Order 22
IX. The Bitter Taste 24
X. The Baggage 25
XI. The Godless Grip (Or Roses From Emily) 25
XII. The Timid Life 26

FOUR — THE OLD SCREW

I. The Deck of Signs 28
II. The System of Cruelty 29
III. Where the Snow Goes 31
IV. The Serenity of Cemeteries 33
V. The Shock of Corn 35
VI. Among the Heathen 37
VII. A Dearth of Light 39
VIII. The Circle of Self-Pity 40
IX. That Rude Solvent 42
X. The Fiddler's Plea 44
XI. The Makeshift Image 46
XII. Caves of Ice 48

FIVE — THAT STRANGE ATTRACTOR

I. Stunted Hopes 52

II. Expect the Obvious 54
III. A Crowd without a Face 54
IV. Whores of Perception 57
V. Daydream's Fingers 59
VI. What You Are..61
VII. Death In Love 63
VIII. A Pathless Land 65
IX. Grow the Unsayable 67
X. Less Brutal Gods 69
XI. Among the Evicted 71
XII. The Flower of Others.. 73

SIX — THE FIERCE ROUTINE

I. Toward Last Illusions... 78
II. The Naked Stream 80
III. Your Vanishing Twin... 82
IV. The Organ Grinder 82
V. Scent of Apples... 85
VI. The Whole Orchard 85
VII. Light's Blind Angel 88
VIII. The Ancestral Scrimmage...90
IX. Grief of Love 94
X. Your Way Out... 96
XI. Hooks of Hope 100
XII. Your Failed Escape... 110

SEVEN — BEHIND DISENCHANTED HEDGEROWS

I. Add Torturous Sums 132
II. Blue Smoke Rings 136
III. The Second Degree... 138

IV. Against All Odds 140
V. One Unspindled Thread 144
VI. Imagine There's Something 146
VII. Oblivion's Obligations 146
VIII. Rage of Mourning 147
IX. To Bitter Tyrannies (For Monsieur No.6) 147
X. Beyond the Peephole.. 148
XI. Mutatis Mutandis 152
XII. Forget the Notes 156

EIGHT — HUSK OF LOYALTIES 157

NINE: PART ONE — THE HEART'S RESIDUUM

I. Warm Snow (Wallace Stevens) 163
II. All or Nothing (Darwin) 165
III. Playing Hardball (Newton) 170
IV. On Hippo's Campus (Augustine) 172
V. Countenance of Crows (Kafka) 176
VI. Life's Blind Charity (Adam Smith) 182
VII. The Eddy's Core (Beckett) 187
VIII. To Costly Grace (Bonhoeffer) 197
IX. The Last Refuge (Samuel Johnson) 203
X. Every Glad-Hander's Nightmare (Jeremiah) 208
XI. Your Level Best (Proust) 216
XII. The Middle of Nowhere (Joe Louis) 225

NINE: PART TWO — GOD'S LATEST IMAGES

I. Rumors of the Rose (Dante) 233
II. Panic at the Picnic (Milton) 239
III. Your Own Arms (Machiavelli) 250
IV. The Middlebrow Blues (Virginia Woolf) 258

V. Why Antigone Wept (Antigone) 269
VI. The Book of Expectations (Isaiah) 275
VII. The Last Conviction (Dostoevsky) 282
VIII. The Final You (D.H. Lawrence) 288
IX. On Rembrandt: The Other Side of You 294
X. The Last Mohican (Tocqueville) 299
XI. The Miser's Jar (Leopardi) 305
XII. Fifteen Minutes of Famine (Simone Weil) 310

NINE: PART THREE — A DRASTIC MISTAKE

I. The Eternity Reckoner (Pascal) 319
II. Where You Live (Rousseau) 323
III. Hunger to Be (Boehme) 327
IV. At the Spot (Kierkegaard) 330
V. Your Bold Apocalypse (Van Gogh) 335
VI. Perpetual Mourning's Afterglow (Schopenhauer) 337
VII. The Pathless Path (Eckhart) 341
VIII. How It Is (Lucretius) 345
IX. Your Sacred Way (Edith Stein) 350
X. Keep Counterfeiting Eternity (Sartre) 354
XI. Arc of Promise (Levinas) 360
XII. Wonder Never Ends (Rosenzweig) 367

NINE: PART FOUR – THE COMMON DAY

I. Whole Damn Schmear (Nietzsche) 377
II. Rumors of Regret (Montaigne) 385
III. State of Grace (Joan of Arc) 391
IV. Roar of Silence (Malraux) 395
V. Blind Man Singing (Claudel) 402
VI. The Great Unwinder (Bergson) 409
VII. What Suffering's Allowed (McTaggart) 414

VIII. The Bragging Rights (Emerson)..........................419

IX. Your Life Taken (Goethe)......................................429

X. Soul in Motion (Cicero)...437

XI. What Rapture's Like (Schubert)..........................443

XII. Eternity and Its Discontents (Plotinus)..............451

NINE: PART FIVE – MIRACLE OF SELF-REFERENCE

I. On Self-Deception's Crutch (Henry James) 460

II. One More Life (Plutarch) 470

III. Eden's Back Door (von Hofmannsthal) 476

IV. Show Him How (Spinoza) 483

V. One Ounce of Once (Chekhov) 492

VI. The Unsurest Tourist (Parmenides) 500

VII. The Bent Stick (Heraclitus) 506

VIII. The Unmade Man (Aristotle) 511

IX. What Happiness Is (Yeats) 518

X. The Stubborn Miracle (Hume) 529

XI. Against Grudging Gods (Herodotus) 535

XII. The Ragged Blindfold (Bach) 542

NINE: PART SIX – DON'T STAY DAMNED

I. Its Hardest Bone (Balzac) 552

II. Coming Back ... Hard (Virgil) 562

III. Nihilism's Trump Card (Bloch) 570

IV. Bet Your Life (Cervantes) 579

V. Of Eternity's Sarcasm (Henry Adams) 586

VI. Your Common Day (Ezekiel) 592

VII. The Inverse Avatar (Rabelais) 599

VIII. An Honest-to-God Hypocrite (Gide) 604

IX. Seeing It Otherwise (Wittgenstein) 611

X. The Christmas Killing (Faulkner) 617
XI. Eternity's Shrewdest Pretender (Wagner) 627
XII. Theory of Everything (Whitehead) 636

TEN — CHOOSE ANOTHER POISON

I. The Thread of Truth 646
II. Covenants of Chaos 651
III. Apologies to Hierologies 656

ELEVEN — THE COMIC BOOK OF CHANGE

I. Therapy is Tyranny 662
II. Nomads from Nowhere 667

TWELVE — IMITATIONS OF THE HUMAN

ABOUT THE AUTHOR   679

THE HISTORY OF ETERNITY

— ONE —
THE BROKEN SYMMETRY

*Whoever conquers his fear of death believes himself to be immortal;
whoever does not have this fear, is.*
— E.M. Cioran, *Tears and Saints* —

I. THE THOUSAND STRANGERS

Alas, even the will to change ... changes.
And yet death is never a wholly welcome guest.
For when your own death arrives,
It will neither appreciate nor acknowledge
The projects you completed
And the plans you strived to fulfill.
In the lucid mirror of your death,
You'll see reflected — not yourself,
But the thousand strangers you've become.

II. THE SONGBIRD'S THROAT

Note on note on note
Fall from the songbird's throat.
Your choices, right or wrong,
Just voices in the song,
Are melody or noise.
Listening, you copy all,
Yet you don't know what they meant.
Are they the latest lessons,
Or the mute cryptographer's lament?
Beach urchins, raising turrets
From myriad glassy grains of sand
Abandon their castles of might have been
For home. Still inhabiting the tide's edge,
You watch their fugitive tracks erode
Like a faithless pledge.
If you could count yourself
A king of this infinite place,
Bounded within the coherence of a conch-shell,
Each grain — a shattered mirror — would reflect
The hidden agenda you can't detect.
And each deciphered note would then appease
Those countless strangers you can't displease.
But mere meaning, a stammer before the crowd,
Cannot arouse the snoring ocean's solitude.

III. THE DEEPEST RIFT

Fate is a family's home before sunrise:

Footfalls padded in the darkness,
Up the stairs you did not take
Toward the happy loft you exchanged for safety.
The first thing you remember,
The sober smell of steaming coffee,
Alarms the household gods with warning.
Sleeping alone, not you, but your disconsolate dreamer
Awakes from greedy childhood's glamour
To the chilly smoke of brittle autumn leaves.
What mattered was not the message but the media.
For each word you used
Was a little piece of your ambition,
A blemish on the illustrated bible,
Or a fingerprint in the well-thumbed encyclopedia,
The only books in this unlittered house.
Pawning the seedy relics of that long lost tribe,
You buy but another means toward mediocrity.
All was lust succumbing before the bribe:
Thirsty glands in an April rain,
The clumsy gropings of a would-be scribe,
The gaunt grimace of an unloved girl,
And the mercy of a mole on her pretty face.
But errant marks of pedantic punctuation
Cannot efface the graceless grammar of desire.
Or modulate the pangs of unsuccess.
Like an unbought, unthought, un-longed-for gift,
The trackless, factless, faultless virgin snow,
As smooth, as sleek, as the whitest wedding dress,
Was a hidden labyrinth of untried layers,
Before the deepest rift.
Betrayal is fulfillment that regrets
What lust discards and hope forgets.
All these accumulations are so much vapor
Before the morning sun, like the false benevolence
Of a snowfall that does not cleanse,
But that only covers, the dirt
Of a much more permanent landscape.
Your tokens of shaky certitude
May get you where you're going,
But the subway carries you with little freight.
Thus, in the jostling interim — you wait

For some unceremonious reception:
For a leap of faith,
Or the lure of self-deception.

IV. THE METALLED TASTE

The crack in the compass called despair
Points toward your new direction — there,
Where the polygrapher's fluttering needle
And your lies like melting coins
Beneath the friction of a speeding train
Were confessions he could not wheedle.
If truth is merely what we register,
We're lost, like that dead, quiet, gentle father
Who slew your boyhood pup …
… Midnight, that chicken slayer you adored,
Who drank from your thin cup
Who he knew could resist no longer
The metalled taste of blood
Within your neighbor's coop.
Guilt is an algorithm out of kilter,
A fence with a faulty gate.
And reverie an infinite loop,
A mental circuit without a filter,
Limited solely by your lack of power.
Thus, you re-trace the trail of useless crumbs
To that homely hedge where pheasants disappear.
Ignoring the lure of lesser fowls, you strive
To reach at last where you arrive
And touch the bloody scar where meanings are.
Seized by the silence there, you fear
The wishing well before the last reprieve,
That tender spot where all lives must begin,
The endless ash on an old man's sleeve,
That awkward outward urgency from within,
And those broken toys lost long ago
   … on Christmas Eve.

V. THE DREAMING UNIVERSE

You remember much forgetfulness.
Yet the dreaming universe, you always knew,

Knew too that you were dreaming.
Reality's luckless looking glass remembers
What faithless fortune soon dismembers.
But like an endless matryoshka doll
Each dream reflects ... contains the dreamer,
For what the gremlin and gopher chase
... is not a time, is not a place,
Not a shell within a shell,
Not a face within a face,
But a little rest and a touch of grace.
Each goal that you surmise
Digs deep the hole of your demise.
For grace that's not a particle of life
... is always now a wave of suffering.
Panting with naked, new-born lust,
Are those menacing angels you tried to trust,
Who, perching ... now ...riding up your fears,
Clutch and claw and cluck with glee:
While you and all your perfidious lovers,
Lock limbs in a secret tryst,
And throw away the key.
Under dream's dark wings
Memory's no defense.
But how senselessly close to wisdom
Still seems the want of sense.

VI. YOUR SOUL'S UPHOLSTERY

The elfin voices of missing children,
Garish gremlins to wisest ears,
Conspire to reveal the stranger in your midst.
The truth in every leaf, in every tear,
The uninvited visitor, you find
By not seeking, finds you.
The old man only remembers:
What's gone lies still in that green shade,
A fine and private place,
Where some, not he, can yet embrace.
For you, that now unimaginable summer still rustles
With the noise of unheard music.
When rapture was a sunlight-watered pond,

A guarded garden of peddled roses,
A frieze frozen in a sentimental movie
That preserves and still discloses
The wilderness of moving images that you are.
Snug as sin within
The occult folds of your soul's upholstery
Are the wrinkles of each moment.
For time's tawdry aleph contains
All nows, all selves, all others.
Once all that matters now
From that solitary atom hurled
To breed the broken symmetry of your world.

VII. THE NURSING HOME

Your gods are as you want them, being born.
No deity ages well who does not retire to obscurity.
But what happens to gray, sullen idols, unused to scorn,
Pensioned off, or scraping by on social security?
The nursing home, besieged by bureaucrats, beset by vermin,
... is kept by quibbling old maids who refuse to dust.
Their vigor gone, the gods now sleep as senile hounds,
No scent for game, no longer used to lust.
Perhaps they'll find a lonelier champion than love.
Love of past ...
      Love of present ...
            Love of future.
Fortune still favors a foolish god,
But these old dogs won't hunt.
Yet no idle worshipper thinks it odd
When newborn gods enact the same old stunt.

VIII. THE WORM-HOLE

You thought you should begin in Athens. So you did.
A smoky place, lonely, quaint, and fertile,
Nestled in the heart of the oldest, highest hills.
Year after year of arrogance bruised by defeat
Convinced yourself and those you sought to please
That this lad of Athens was not to be
Yet another immortal Socrates.
Do you still recall the moment

When philosophy became *foolosophy?*
When time became a tunnel turned upon its tail,
The worm-hole in the apple of your eyes,
The locus of your hopes where, though still frail,
Eternity's bedraggled puppet cries?

IX. THE STEEP RAVINE

Hope carried you up the hill
Where the sleds of others had left their ruts.
The glide path led to the remains
Of an ancient maple tree,
The last and only stop before the steep ravine.
Gravity granted speed, giving way to mirth
On the way down to the end of your and their careers
Where you too left your wounds
On the stump of its time-worn bark.

X. THE HOMELESS MAN

Cutting a crooked path through dim December woods
The smoke of early rising hearths
Feints like fog above whispering limbs.
Day breaking before the moon's descended
Startles the farmhouse zoo
Of cock and hen and hungry mice.
At home again, swaddling your grown-up sorrows,
Each track you leave in the inches of ice
Remembers regretless laughter in the snow.
The sudden smile of this child within your past
Dwarfs your somber presence in the wind.
And fantasy, like a fat and faithless frog
Caught in a casket of early frost,
... is killed by the child that cannot last.
As the homeless man is chilled by the cost
   ... of shelter.
This breeze of brittle leaves
   ... leaves little you can find
To swell a hope or advance an honest mind.

XI. THE CACKLING LEAF

Cragged and steep you've become,

Resisting that huge hill's suddenness,
Hugging neither light nor darkness.
The abstract ashes of charred philosophy
Like yesterday's damp and chalky embers
Lit no path through late fall's twilight.
From the precipice of that moment,
You still recoil, *for none you know*
Can work through that dark night.
This rude shake of mourning
May hush the cackling leaf.
But nothing can redeem the religiosity of elves,
Or soothe the history of a maple's grief.
True believers are in for rough sledding.

XII. THE VAINEST BOAST

Thus, winter came a withering in,
But memory's melting solitudes of snow,
Still craved companionship of desire:
What you don't touch, for you lies miles way;
What you don't grasp is wholly lost to you;
What you don't reckon, you believe not true;
What you don't weigh, that has for you no weight;
What you don't coin, you're sure is counterfeit.
Cheapest medals are as false as you
And all your equally lonely others.
What is everything that is not eternal?
Islands in dishonored grass
Where the green gives way
To drifting mounds of appalling snow.
Each note of memory remains negotiable
Like the very first paper money
That was paid to the dead,
But not to the living for whom
All payment is a sacrament and a sacrifice.
Spare change is eternity's inspiration.
Just as shame precedes the vainest boast
So the tallest peak was once a deep foundation
Where the lowest lie becomes in truth the uppermost.

— TWO —
BECOME SOMEONE ELSE

Your body is a shell, in which a bird will be hatched from the spirit of eternity.
— Angelus Silesius —

I. THE BODY'S CERTAINTY
The body is the soul's homework.
And time is the medium
In which we sculpt our destiny.
It is by time's elastic
That we stretch reality into the future.
A man and a woman are drawn together upon a bed.
And together they come to know
The certainty of the flesh: the body's certainty.
The flesh is sure and steady.
It may tremble. It may lie.
But at least it glistens
With the sweat of love and living.
At least it knows.
Yes. Oh, yes. The body knows.
For the body, more than the soul, is time's crucible.
The body is the soul's homework.
And when the body is awake —
When the body is truly awake —
The spirit of necessity
Must take out time for a holiday.

II. THE WINGLESS BUTTERFLY
Mother. Mother. Pearls and pearls of paying elegance.
This is the summer of mother and the wingless butterfly.
The summer of the hedge and the bloomless honeysuckle.
There are no strings of nectar to pull and sip.
Only wings of butterflies to rip.
Her hair is the rain in a stormy willow.
The whip, the lash, the limber wood,
The weeping limbs, the vaulting thighs.
This is the summer of disguise.
The shivering flesh against the raw bark blanches,
White against this tree, this ocean of many branches.
Here lies the residue of lust, your fate,
Like initials carved in an old tree trunk
Scored with unguessed meanings.
And amid the rippling, rain-washed feathers
You hide, you watch, you wait,
Where above the very roots of ubiquitous obscenities,

There is cut the equation of lovers.

III. THE CRIMSON PALM
You fear the faith that looks through death,
The darkling thoughts that once were wise,
The solitude of willow's breath,
The stark sententiousness of thighs.
But your glassy essence eyes escape
The moon's mad martyr of desire
When aimlessly you spy the shape
Of bloody rose on every briar.
Each burst of dawn, a rediscovered warning,
Betrays what cannot last,
As the crimson palm of morning
Backhands the reeling past.
... Yet toward the sea
Where all the rivers run
Erupts an also rising sun.

IV. THE EMPTY ASK
Only the empty ask to be filled.
What you want is a mirror
To reflect the significance of your sighs.
What you settle for is the cavity of another body,
Which, like your own, is but a grave of sorrows.
Desire, protests the biologist, is the instrument of evolution.
But two lovers locked in each other's embrace
Neither know nor care where humanity is headed.
They know only that they have arrived at this moment,
And it is the emptiness they share in common
That each ardently wants to fill.

V. THIS GOLDEN BOWL
You've always wanted to become someone else:
More wise, more beautiful, more worthy.
Following that noble example
Leaves you — high and dry and dreaming.
And your fear of being merely you
Keeps you stumbling toward oblivion.
Are you full enough to fill this moment,

This golden bowl where ashen roses leave their dust?

VI. THE GRAY SKY

All is dancing straw before these revelations.
The gathering clouds, a waterfall of faithless change.
The gray sky, a womb without alternatives.
Do you still remember the moment
When time turned into distance,
A destiny and a direction you wish for,
While you pray for escape?
When sullen art, like life itself,
Became the practice of impotence and falsehood?
The interior castle of your loves and fears
Still rattles with the battles of your thoughts.
But even the wish for change fades out.
And all is decried in that one lonely shout.
Startled in the mirror of midnight,
You awake, foolishly awake,
Imploring those deafening torrents
To relax the speed of their relentless cataract.

VII. THE FULL FACE

Before the lost paradise of faulty memory
There is the unforgetfulness of hell.
Each deed done, each thought thought, each feeling felt
Still lies shopworn on the dusty shelf.
For you — along with all grubby proprietors,
Are still your ownmost self.
You dream the death of indiscretion
In the full face of infinity.
But not even saints can flee
The mediocrity of possession.
Thus the gopher burrows yet another hole
Another task, another mask, another role.
Blind and deaf, you still can feel the shock
Of the cracked compass and the fractured clock.
Amid nettlesome noise, eternity takes its toll.
Then clangs the broken bell within your beery soul.

VIII. FOR THE FEW

Only one of endless tact
Can touch the value of a fact.
Only one without a heart
Can steer a life along a chart.
Only one who dances well
Can balk at heaven or skip through hell.
Only one who has no aim
Can beard the lion or make him tame.
Only he who's loved a wife,
Can face off death and call it life.
Only he who has no hope,
Can walk the plank or brave a rope.
The scent of plums, a fragrant convolution
Distills the riddle in each solution.
Chocolate, orange, and mellow pear,
A peach, a toddler's matted hair,
Steaming coffee and morning dew.
Aroma is aroma for the few.

IX. THE WILTED LEAF

Give me matter, and I will build you a world.
Let me fashion your most foolish fears
Brick by brick into a solid wall of fact.
Some building, you say, that smells
With the sweat of those who build it.
Some power, you say, that swells
With the force of those who wield it.
But building is neither force nor fact.
It is the quiet summation of an act,
A pretense that no longer holds.
As the wilted leaf dies unto its truest colors,
So the relativity of change predicts its own downfall.
Heavy with the souls he's saved,
Weary with the flags he's waved,
A missionary, his task exhausted,
Collapses at the foot of the altar.
Meager are moments that we make so much.
Eager are yearnings we cannot touch.
Yes. Mr. Yang and Mrs. Yin

Were there when God invented sin.
All that rises, falls.
All that listens, calls.
All that empties, fills.
All that frightens, thrills.
All that matters, hurts.
All that lives, flirts
With changeless death, the end of change.
Was it you, or a stranger
Who saw the spider in the cup you drank from?
You've already abandoned good and evil
Like sloughed-off skin. So, who or what
Can now explain your sorrow?
To speak of sin foregoes all tact
For what was fantasy is now a fact.
But can you kneel where prayer is no longer valid,
Where each greedy grunt and squeal
Command equal attention and respect?
Yet your sorrow has no eyes
To inspect yourself or your faceless future.
Only for weeping does it have a knack
And brims the poisoned well of human tears.

X. THE ABANDONED CHRYSALIS

Spring lightning in the snow
Muffled solitude while April thundered.
The girl, kneeling in the Parthenon's glow,
Stumbled darkly on one ski,
A bird with a broken wing,
In Nashville, Tennessee.
A willowy, shaken, moth-like silhouette,
An unseen face untouched by you
That had the feel of being felt,
The silent look of being looked at.
Was it merely you
Dreaming this butterfly,
Or was it she, the butterfly, dreaming you?
Once you saw her face, you thought,
In a crowd of others.
And though you never saw her again,

She loitered in your memories, in your dreams.
This fantasy lover you never met
Became your teacher.
And for you, the art of practicing love alone
Changed yourself into a fantasy,
Far less real and beautiful
Than the distant reality of the one you loved.
Yet your dreams, your memories, of this fleeting moment
Transformed your fears into a faith
That even loneliness itself could not shake:
The change in you, that created her, now changes you.
Yet you love, you say, only what persists.
For what you love, not you, is what exists.
Each hope's cocoon, the virgin flesh
That worms shall try
But fail to fathom or refresh,
Encapsulates the seedy past and needy future
Into a traveling motto.
Death leaves the abandoned chrysalis of your body
Like a would-be prince arriving at a banquet of frogs.
Yes, departure is arrival, for now you can't deny:
To say "I love you" means "You'll never die."

XI. UNSEEN GREEN

She never laughed.
She never cried.
She never smiled at children.
You stalked her through billowing waves of corn
As she fled nimbly
In a moonlit tide of unseen green.
Her crime of coyness,
The well-wrought anachronism
Of a seducer, sly and vain
... And vying for what neither you nor she
Could ever quite attain.
All the world is water to thirsty lovers
But ...
Lust is a sordid swamp.
Desire is a vast, eternal ocean.
And love rising — high and dry and dreaming —

Out of the sterile sea is a summit
You try to climb, but rarely reach.

XII. THE FIELD OF MAIZE

The evening star was over the field of maize,
But the frogs began to call.
Was it this moment
That you began to love eternity?
Perhaps that's what Krishnamurti meant.
Life is idle passage.
Traveling is eternal.
Death alone is arrival.
To have the bowl empty
... is to have life that is deathless.
All else is fantasy or faithless frogs.

— THREE —
HUMAN BEINGS FLICKER

I realized that the wide and ceaseless universe was already slipping away from her
and that this slight change was the first of an endless series.
— Jorge Luis Borges, "The Aleph" —

I. THE PREGNANT AGONY

An acorn is the prophecy of an oak tree.
Each organ of change, a fragment of eternity
Striving toward a destiny it can't fulfill
Without yielding identity and yearning for difference.
All doubt is sterile
Before the pregnant agony of belief.
If the sun and moon should doubt,
They'd immediately go out.
Is that why we human beings flicker?
Sap quivers into fertile chestnuts
Raising faint hopes into sturdy wood.
Flesh once grass, now stiff, now cold, now blue.
Ashen, grasping palms no longer bid adieu.
Blood quickens into post-midnight terror.
Was it the stranger's corpse,
Or your brother's you cried to kiss?
For your life, you say,
Was a trial of error you tried to miss.
A restless traveler in an antique land,
Like a fallen, forlorn king of kings,
Still you tumble, mumble, grumble in your bed.
Must we call no man happy before he's dead?

II. THE CRANNIED WALL

Asters in the crannied wall.
Spores upon the angry wind.
Sweetness rolled into one ball
As if coyness never sinned.
Unkempt gnomes in urban sprawls,
Abandoned in their solitude,
Will answer not when duty calls
Nor quit their wastrel's interlude.
You'd seek some city at its heart
A horrid city victuals-mart,
Torturous alleys, pointed gables,
Beets, kale, and onions on the tables;
Meat-stalls where blue flies take life easy,
Feasting on roasts well-done and greasy;
There you will always find

Stench and activity combined.
A disheveled face in a crowd of others,
Petals on the breaking bough of change.
A runaway, in flight from all that smothers,
Becomes enamored of the strange.
A prism is a cup of light
Or its dissection into tawdry colors.
But a star, no grieving mother,
Smells not the scent of its breathless progeny,
But burns with the radiance of what it is.

III. THE CONSCIOUS WIND

Every harlot was a virgin once,
And every fairy moth a worm.
You harvest the sweat of solitary doves,
Distilling their self-forgetfulness into loves
That fly like thieves upon the conscious wind.
All strangers commit their little treasons:
Doing their worst for the best of reasons.
You console yourself:
The circle of your crimes is small.
The circumference of ever smaller meanings
Cannot contain a lifetime's bitter gleanings.
You are as little as your lust is large.
So let the fog horn blow.
Let the tugboat guide your barge
Of guilt out of harbor with its heavy load.
The doctors of the self will lay you bare.
You'd be naked, if not for their explanations.
But the inexorable logic of their excuses
Cannot appease your ruses and abuses.
If you were a simple seed about to sprout
You could grow and become yourself.
But you are alien corn,
A husk with empty promises ...
If you do not grow now,
You will never grow.

IV. UNDER THE DEAD LEAVES

Drawing nectar through a sieve

... is all that aimless lust can give.
Sparring sparrows in the sky
Dance in God's oblivious eye.
Your quaint faith in what you've been,
Remembrance of a faded sin,
Twitters in the surly breeze
As rustling sleet on bare, ruined trees
That yet may clutch a brittle leaf
Like widows clinging to their grief.
What you feel and what you know,
Drumming rain and whispering snow,
Precipitate and rise anew
And fall again before you're through.
All accumulations are scars
On the wrinkled skin of memory.
But ...
Slumbering eternity, stretching its paws,
Relaxes through the novelty of change.
The whiskers of each moment tingle with its discovery
In the smile, in the tear, under the dead leaves,
In that vagrant vagabond's love
That knows no past and dreams of no tomorrow.

V. THE RIVER

Swifter than a weaver's shuttle is the river
That plowed the gulleys of your heart.
The river receives everything, and gives up nothing
But the sad sewage of childless corpses.
Cleansing as it travels, flowing far and wide,
Its one salutary motion
... is life and death to home-bound fish.
This country, the land between the big waters,
Will know feast, know flood, know famine,
But a riverless country is no country at all.

VI. THE OVERPASS

No highway could bear that traffic for long
Without buckling under the freight of weary commerce.
Crossing the overpass toward weekend and freedom
Couldn't dispel your Puritan's impatience for Monday

And that mindlessly emended list of things undone.
A crowd of hands couldn't count the times
You've paused to wonder: What's the difference?
This unholy litany you weakly rehearse
... is meant to purge your thoughts of unfinished reports.
Yet embarrassed pangs of dubious regrets,
The bungled briefing unprepared and half-delivered,
The promising conference, prematurely disrupted,
Return to haunt your cabin of solitude.
If only you'd reach the inner state of your fears.
By finding a way in on the way out of worry,
You'd see the bloom on every weed needn't hurry
To transmute its homeliness into beauty.
On every interchange of despair,
There's always another beckoning course —
The way of the roadside rose,
Or the ghosts of commuter's remorse.

VII. THE BLACKBERRY PICKER

i

The night's heat heaved a plaintive sigh
Of relief that fell as heavy dew.
The day didn't break, it scattered
Behind the clouds it couldn't penetrate
Like the faint glow of roses behind her eyelids
That wouldn't open themselves to anything old or new.

ii

Sunless June's perfect for picking the ripest fruit,
But blackberry winter chills your naked limbs.
And, like thermometers, fooled by their own cool metal,
You register an uncertain temperature.
Are you too old to follow
The familiar trail of successful summers?

iii

Your oversize bucket dangles above your knees.
Long before noon you'll fill it full three times over,

But a patch of briars is not a field of clover.
And the berries you pick will not be hers.

iv

The June bug likes to dance and sing before he feeds,
But he's sluggish in this sunless weather.
On hotter days, his hum becomes a symphony.
Your kerosene-soaked sleeves
Fend off other unseen pests.
But what will save you from your own impatience?
If you're less than careful now,
You'll step into another gopher hole.

v

Yes. Hacking your way through briars
Strangles all the berries.
Always, you've been too easily snagged
On the prickly finitude of infinite things.

vi

Shall you quietly await that unsung music,
Or shun the consolation of consenting angels?

vii

Each berry picked tumbles
Toward revaluation of what you claim to be.
Belief hangs on the prong
Of that unanswered question.
For he who does not doubt
Does not know how to believe.
And he who does not love
Does not know how to grieve.

viii

This flower of sudden sense
Will fade, then re-commence,
Searching for a different profession,
Opting for another obsession.

ix

Just as your bucket holds the berries but not itself
That bundle of happy perceptions called a child
Cannot contain what it desires.

x

Her eyes close around the mystery you can't share.
It's she you want, without entanglements.
Yet through the hopeless gray
A ray of faith pokes through:

xi

Grief is not love but both mix in the pail,
For what you can't escape becomes your jail.

xii

Those fatuous sunbeams believed
They could bring light unto darkness.
  ... And they did.

VIII. THE LATEST ORDER

i

She was unpersuadable Time,
Relentless in her execution of righteous judgments.

ii

Stripping away the petals,
She counted the ways you still could stay together.

iii

Her binary logic of loving and not loving,
That last infirmity of ignoble minds,
Could yield a choice without a cause.

iv

Nothing succeeds like succession.

v

But hers was a lonely voice without a pause
Or change of heart.
Her familiar, forgivable sins
You could easily abide
But the idea of change was a demon
You couldn't bring yourself to countenance.

vi

Even your own primitive tribe
Has its humble cosmology.
But you no longer care to remember
What threw the latest order into disarray.

vii

The wart on an elegant arm
Raises an eyebrow of alarm.
The sore that cannot heal
Utters a sentence without appeal.

viii

One more subtle change will happen
Before she becomes wholly different
From what you knew and once desired.

ix

The expedited metabolism of cancer
... is a symptom of changing too quickly into someone else.

x

The stranger's face you might have loved
Becomes no-more, too-late, farewell.

xi

The moment's monument congeals
Those lucid pools of light
That were eyes too wise to see.

xii

O, daisy, don't look back!
For the flower that peers behind forsakes its power
And its beauty has already gone to seed.

IX. THE BITTER TASTE

Dialogue is prayer,
A confidential opening,
A surgery of the heart
And all its secrets.
Unto each instinct
There is a god of gratification
Who smiles or frowns
At its fulfillment or frustration.
Less than all cannot satisfy
Your urge for belonging.
More than none cannot pacify
Your ravenous longing.
Ashes on the tongue ...
Screeching in the ears ...
Stench inside the lung ...
Salt within cold tears.
The bitter taste of a thousand senses
Could not disguise the false pretenses
Of the gods we worship
But lack the courage
To confront in conversation.
Weakened by indulgences,
Strengthened by abnegations,
You are as empty as the cup
That holds the invisible air of solitude.
Breathing is believing,
For you cannot help but believe in something.
But the truth lies not in the cup but in yourself.

X. THE BAGGAGE

Choices are faces on one stone,
Blossoms on one tree.
And your guilt is one short step
From the terrible to the tender
Down a path you can't evade
Lest you fail to surrender
Your urge to resurrect first innocence.
You've acquired careless habits of accuracy
Clouding your easy questioning
Of the queasy scheme of uneasy things.
You too shall enjoy the mercurial shame,
The blameless, quicksilvery fame
Of each moment's passionless notoriety.
Received opinion's complacent smile will bequeath
This wretched atmosphere in which you breathe
The fetid air of faith transformed into piety.
Those who cannot believe in guilt
... are those whose choices slowly wilt
Like blighted buds of May
Along forking paths of feckless gods
Whose wrath no longer wreaks
The havoc of unknown ways.
Such is the baggage of being human,
For every decision you make is a mistake.
And each mistake — *a gray suitcase*
Full of dark sighs.

XI. THE GODLESS GRIP (OR ROSES FROM EMILY)

Evenings brought you sunsets in a cup.
And easy candor remained your tepid friend.
Can you still recall those unbandaged moments
When your wounds lay open as light in ashes?
Only now you wish to endow the dead
With tears you squandered on the living.
Epoch has no basis here.
For when that plank in reason broke

All you loved was left to choke
In the godless grip
Of death's large, democratic fingers.
You loved her less than the cause that slew her.
And she could have loved you more
Had you been bold and beautiful.
There is no gratitude
Greater than the grace of death.
All is the price of all.
Nothing in between means anything
Except the counterfeit presence
Of those who've abandoned simplicity.

XII. THE TIMID LIFE

Nothing's more tender than service without hope
For it's never too late
To lament the cost of what you've lost.
Abdication of belief made you small,
As small as all
Those starving refugees from Parnassus.
The timid life of evidence, she said,
Keeps pleading "I don't know."
That crowd of elves streaming down the mountain
Forsake their divine legacy
For the panic of the present moment.
And you — you alone in your solitude —
Utter one whisper, and your whisper
Becomes but a lonely echo
That reverberates throughout eternity.
Eternity, she said, is ample, and quick enough, if true.
But revelation's limit is embarrassment
Before God, before one another,
Before the infinite aurora of another's eyes.
And this crowd, this endless stream of panic,
This river of others,
... is the mirror in which you see yourself reflected.
You are yourself and not yourself.
You are yourself and all others.
You are yourself the twin brother
Of all those you condescend to scorn.

— FOUR —
THE OLD SCREW

Yes, I feel throughout my diversity
a constancy;
I feel that what is diverse in me is still
myself.
—Andre Gide, *Journals* —

I. THE DECK OF SIGNS

The world is all that tumbles.
And belief that's justified and true
... is rusty as the old screw
That no longer turns.
Your soul like a remorseless stone
... is a porous solitude,
A society of lost occasions,
Full of the void between events
That leave their ghostly tracks
On the only face you see.
Do you remember the day
You faded from the album?
You'd tried so hard to harden yourself
With gin, and sin, and skepticism.
Time smiled like a furtive child,
Playing checkers in a drafty church.
Like him, you were bent
On beating yourself at your own game.
Dog-eared images,
Nestled in quaint portfolios,
Were models of myriad tumbling worlds
That death cannot alter but only end.
Each move, each pebble's rippling effect,
Disturbed the matrix of the game.
But just as the pond's smooth mirror
... is part of the reflection it contains
You are at one with the waters you swim in.
Is this how you became
A picture in an institution?
Amid incessant shuffling
Of the deck of signs,
A card is played
By a hand that trembles.
You were that trembling,
Those rippling circles of absolution.
Alone — with no crowd to worship —
You made your moves in silence.

II. THE SYSTEM OF CRUELTY

i

So much depends
On the competency of a soul
You can't be sure of.

ii

That day you lost your way
The beaten path trailed off in brambles
Toward that labyrinth of nighttime woods
That is your soul's mystery.
Where the tangled branches of each tree
Resemble the forest,
And the forest remembers you.

iii

Nostalgia honors the better part
Of childhood you never had,
The unimproved infancy of elves
Too little for the largeness of their desires.

iv

Yes. That dark knowledge called character
 ... is the shadow cast by the culture of your mistakes.

v

In that long, long night
You both chased syllogisms in the grass
As if to separate fact from fiction,
As if to escape the harrowing,
Unharmonious harp of unlived time.
As if to catch the unbounded variables of equations
Scrawled in the humus of your love's brief history.

vi

And the pale moon's testimony between two lovers

Became a self-healing tautology in which
A little bit of everything was everywhere.

vii

Vainly, you hastened to debunk
The system of cruelty
That calls itself religion or politics.
But her breasts were doves too quick
For clumsy hands to capture.

viii

Unawares — she caught you unprepared
To love her, or anyone, or anything.

ix

Her dying words taught you
The immorality of palliatives:
A crust of bread
On the tongue
Of a starving child
Accentuates the need
It seeks to alleviate.

x

But you loved her less than the logic
That proved everything but itself.

xi

Your daylight world's divine debris
Are broken remainders of your dark vision,
Of a thirst no photograph can fake or slake.
For the human eye is no camera.
And a pair of lucid eyes,
Blue, green, or warmly, eternally brown —
That's what science and immortality come to.

xii

The day you saw her face,

The day you saw her beauty dying,
The day you saw the difference between map and territory
... was the day the dead learned not to believe in death.

III. WHERE THE SNOW GOES

i

A mountain moved by its own melting,
The glacier inches forth
To scar the land
With the waste
Of a different climate.

ii

Hand in hand you picked your way
Through unillumined wreckage
Toward that perilous chapel of icy stones.

iii

Each step you took echoed
The impermanence of place,
The emptiness of unattended years.
Each leaf that shook revealed
The mutability of grace,
The cause of unintended tears.

iv

Ruin is not an instant's act.

v

For in evolution's slow nightmare
Each identity thaws
Into another place
      ... another face
          ... another world.
But light only reaches where shadows disappear
Into that realm where the dead have knowledge
They're no longer free to share.

vi

What melts, what ebbs, what flows,
... is highest wisdom, is lowest folly
That ever shifts but does not change.
The rhythms you ride called habits
Corrupt while offering survivability.
But youth learns little before it perishes,
For its tide is a fierce routine,
Endangered by distractions it cherishes,
Ignobled by the sacred made obscene.

vii

Your rebounds from one fate to another
Are facets of ineluctable destiny.
And like phases of the moon,
Your changes are moving images
Of your eternal character.

viii

Do you still remember
When weather became your horoscope?
When her words whistled
With the gust of prophecy
Through the fiery fall
Of endless maple leaves?

ix

Because you could not see what stays
You thought that all must go.
Because you could not stoop to praise
You overlooked the snow.

x

Those who believe that nothing persists
Have much to learn from the child
Who wonders where the snow goes.

xi

Occasional disappearances are for her
No sign of extinction.
For the North Pole lurking
Within the heart of a child
...is the place where snow never melts.

xii

And the eternal hidden
Within the hearts of two lovers
...is the place where love never dies
But lives forever.

IV. THE SERENITY OF CEMETERIES

i

Nothing's quite so settled
As the serenity of cemeteries.
Doubt's only the feeble companion of certain terror,
The sole intruder in this dust
Of dreaming granite and sorrowing solitude.

ii

Each alien family of familiar names
... is a paradox of novelty and repetition.
And each name, each grave,
A nest of countless others.

iii

The mottled chalice
Straddles a headstone
Like a tarnished crown,
Saying:
  Here she lies,
  Her flesh eternal,
  Gone but not forgotten.

iv

Befuddled ghost and manless boy,
You returned to haunt
The scene of your repression.
"Oh, my child!"

v

You vanished with her lament.
She weeps ...
  She weeps ...
    She weeps ...
        ... For you.

vi

For that great brown river,
Where no willows grow.
For that quiet pool
Where no fish swims.
For that thicket of stars
Where no reeds blow.
For that constellation of elms
Where light never dims.

vii

Lovers bask in each other's glow,
But can you be warm alone?

viii

Chlorophyll's cool shadow,
That green nimbus of faith, recoils
As the merciless emperor of August disrobes.

ix

Only a child could be astonished by the scorn.
But never before had you understood
The unconsoling cruelty of illuminated love.
For honoring each companion in this grass

Means loving all those strangers in yourself.

x

Death's one great, bright eye burns
Like a poker thrust
Through the fog of the living.

xi

You're lost, lost, lost ...
   ... lost in the light, but dangerously lost.

xii

Only the dead see the nakedness of things.
Death is the only surprise that lasts.

V. THE SHOCK OF CORN

i

Lying down, you say:
"When shall I rise again?"

ii

But the night is long.
Like the shock of corn in a dry season
You perceive only what dies with you.

iii

What lasts is
   ... beyond eyes,
      ... beyond ears,
         ... beyond touch.

iv

What doesn't change is not eternal: ... it's stale
As that whispery fragrance of expected death.

v

What is the task of the wind that stalls,
Rising before it falls
And calls your name for the last time?

vi

Pursuing dry stubble,
Harassing the driven leaf,
Each gust that bends a stalk
Betrays the breath of a deathless god.
Each scattered kernel, an ignoble archive,
… is the seed of that first catastrophe
Whose only birthright ripens
Toward a future it can't redeem.

vii

Each sprout injures innocent soil.
Just as she wounded you
With fears of what could now be lost.

viii

Just as you only knew you loved her
When at last she'd hurt you into happiness.

ix

You kissed and something began to grow,
An irrepressible, regretful wound
You could neither face nor replace.
Was this a fantasy or a faith worth clinging to?
As unseen eyebeams crossed
Into the vision of a hapless child,
One more picture was tossed
Into the album of humanity.

x

Reality is the burial ground
Of your improbable children,

Of what you never had but hoped for,
And what you cannot help but not forget,
Like the gritty-lemon flavor of warm rain
On the naked skin of defenseless arms.

xi

For the nameless,
Nirvana is the urn of bliss
They'll never miss.

xii

For only emptiness is there to touch or share
A truth that founders in the grasping.

VI. AMONG THE HEATHEN

i

In the beginning was the song
You were born already singing.

ii

Desire negotiating each note
Tunnels through the throat
Of childhood's ceaseless channels of despair.

iii

She left before you knew her name,
Before you'd fully drenched yourself
In her yellow rain of tears and tattered hair.

iv

But he said: Your voice is free.
So why not raise it in complaint
Against the uncompliant squall of change?

v

Each note in the general economy of love

Succumbs to the cruel melody of barter.

vi

Each event echoes what it's never been.
Each image is a face
Embroidered with threads
You feel but cannot fathom.

vii

Each note is a kernel about to sprout
With the novelty of new leanings.
And each child is father
To the men he'll never be.

ix

History may hunker down on its hinges,
But wisdom, you thought, confers immunity
To the winds of doctrine and the scroll of creeds.

x

Can her beauty still withstand
Your feeble interpretations of interpretation?
Revolution may overturn the currency of action,
But the sacred is summoned solely
By the violence of infraction.

xi

The only holiness that holds
... is the stiffening nakedness of a stubborn force,
A languageless sense of violation,
Beyond the lungs of explanation,
Without a trace of traitor's remorse.
Whoever breathes this sovereign air of betrayal
... is forever guilty in respect of love.

xii

Whistling past lucid vigils of the wind
... is the solitude of one tomb — her tomb,

One stone among others
In this colony of astonished names,
Where you can only wait without hope
To be exalted among the heathen.

VII. A DEARTH OF LIGHT

The lights beneath the lids
Ripple with the gaunt gleam
Of a star's pale trajectory.
Such is the fate of all souls.
They fall to earth
To die a lonely death
In a dearth of light.
The first things you really see
... are her eyes.
Her pupils' studied gaze
Leaves you dazed
Yet dimly aware of her body ...
Present, unperceived and unavailable.
Adjusting to the suddenness
Of another blind afternoon,
You spy the dancing laughter,
And chase the hidden sorrow
.... In her face.
And then and only then,
Her eyes illuminate
What they first obscured.
At this moment
You experience the oppressiveness
Of a tantalizing delusion:
If you had the audacity
To traduce all convention,
You would lean forward,
Caress the eyes, cheeks, lips
Of this strange woman,
And suddenly — without further ado ...
Leap headlong into her very soul.
It is only when this delusion subsides
That lust begins.
And her body in its beauty

Becomes something
You desperately want to possess.

VIII. THE CIRCLE OF SELF-PITY

i

You must begin wherever you are.
And wherever you are,
You must begin in sin
Within … the circle of self-pity.

ii

Naked — you were delivered —
Alone into exile,
And being born,
You're always
Already old enough to die
The untimely death of children.

iii

Her caresses were commands,
And her tears threats
To the sanctity of your fabled innocence.

iv

If only you'd been there
When truth became a fiction,
You'd never have become
The obedient example
In someone else's theory.

v

Conception's inaugural begins
Death's dull dream of satisfaction,
Of the final lure of desire.

vi

You saw her only once
And she became an obsession.

vii

Not to have what you desperately want
... is the common legacy of Adam,
Who having taken what he wanted,
Condemned you to wanting
What you cannot take.

viii

And if you take her as you wish,
Would your obsession survive
The satisfaction of lust?

ix

Having is not wanting
Because you want
What you cannot have.

x

Wanting is not having
Because you have
What you no longer want.

xi

The one you want
... is the obscure object of a desire
That won't survive fulfillment.
To embrace her but once
... is to lose her forever.

xii

The one you chase cannot be caught,
For the chaste cannot be captured.
For what cannot be caught

... is the only one there is.
And the only one that stays,
The only one there is ...
... is the one that stumbles in self-pursuit.

IX. THAT RUDE SOLVENT

i

Too long, you've slept
In caves of bad appetite.

ii

Now, staggering into white light,
Into another crisis of nostalgia,
You stay as long as it takes
To bury the corpse of an old ambition.

iii

The history of decay
Is the story of a concept
That lost its edges
In the shininess of overuse.

iv

How many women could you lump
Into that one word: woman?

v

All you reached for
Molded themselves
Into counterfeit coins
Of second-rate experience.

vi

How many exchanged their reluctant solitudes
Dissolving like sculptures of muddied snow
Before the glare of your fierce routine?

vii

A few black swans, still swimming,
Palely loiter
Before drowning along with you
And all your equally lonely others
In that rude solvent,
That merciless torrent of others,
You have the gall to call yourself
And your own experience of their experience.

viii

If biology is destiny,
Then you cannot escape the perils of lust.

ix

When bodies entangle with desire,
No thought is given
To the merger of genetic estates.
What is sought is possession and release.
And both are fleeting.

x

Having ten thousand conquests
... is having one woman.
Variety is delusion
For you know nothing of those possessed.

xi

And if you protest,
If you claim to know the difference,
Then your experience is
Something other than naked lust.

xii

Between lust and love is the erotic
And the erotic
  ... glimpses,

   ... acknowledges,
       ... admires
            ... what only love can grasp.
 ... And what you grasp is the unattainable
   ... In all you fail to reach.

X. THE FIDDLER'S PLEA

i

You were seduced by your song's own echo.
Yet you heed the fiddler's plea
For the music of another's dream.

ii

You kissed her brow with deathly thirst
As if her skull were a cup to drink from.

iii

She lay in the glare of dying
And you in the shade of being born.

iv

Have you forgotten that fatal moment
When you became enamored of your own passion,
When you became obsessed by the specter of rapturous death,
When you began to seek with fury its pale embodiments
In the fine furrows of female flesh?

v

Your thinking traced the witch's flight
Of moon, and broom, and empty womb.

vi

Do you still recall that evening
When her sorrow showed its face —
Not an idea, not a word, not a shadowy symbol of the sad,
But sadness, sadness, sadness itself?

vii

For a long time sorrow was a word
You had carefully coddled.
Your father had the wound, and his ... and his.
Your mother had the wound, and hers ... and hers.

viii

For sorrow has its pedigree of images
Waxed and polished and handed down
Through the generations of each tribe, each clan, each family.

ix

Soaked in the sangria of her sorrow
... was the unbandaged awe of a face you cannot fathom,
But which mirrored the madness of your own:
 ... That album of strangers that you are,
 ... All those equally lonely others,
 ... Rippling in the revelation of her eyes,
 ... Not a school for scandal,
But her first and her last teaching
About the limits of solitude.

x

What you want from her is nourishment
And the privacy of shared truth.

xi

But truth is a withered child ...
Bald ... naked ... and club-footed.

xii

In its toothless, breathless maw
Lolls the idle, knotted tongue of wisdom.

XI. THE MAKESHIFT IMAGE

i

... The still point keeps moving ...
Homo erectus inspect us:
Have we made progress?
Have you escaped the charmed circle of his many postures?
Your language is a system of quotations —
His grunts, his squeals, his gestures.
A flake of splintered stone
Or a makeshift ax, hastily assembled,
Foretells the rocket's parabola of desire
Wherein you still are hurtling.

ii

... The still point keeps moving ...
A forager of fruits,
A consumer of carcasses crudely cooked —
His diet in the shadow of your family tree
... are morsels that still you savor.
His murderers, his knowledge-thirsty descendants,
... are your as-yet unsettled ancestry
And his very own taste of mortality.

iii

... The still point keeps moving ...
Can you remember what he knew
Before you learned to float
On bladders of philosophy and religion?

iv

... The still point keeps moving ...
Between the raw and the cooked
... are lineaments of a still ungratified desire.
Rising from the swamp of sleep
... is the hideous lucidity of your insomnia,
The monotony of light in a spidery nook
Where memory is a root that gnaws on oblivion.

v

... The still point keeps moving ...
Lucidity is blind to its own darkness.
And if leopard spots could see,
They'd shatter drowsy conventions of her fierce beauty.

vi

... The still point keeps moving ...
What's your history the history of?
Should it pause for another prayer of forgetfulness?
Can the tender amnesia of her love
Disclose the other side of solitude?
As if she alone in eloquent silence
Could caress the soul of a stallion in the hulk of a hog.

vii

... The still point keeps moving ...
If only you could wish that hole in your heart away!
Such is the madness of men without chests
Whose hollowness only harbors
The bloodless dream of a beating heart —
Throbbing, warm and secret.

viii

... The still point keeps moving ...
Frogs begin to croak out of wisdom,
As if fear were not enough
To startle the assembly of would-be princes.

ix

... The still point keeps moving ...

x

All that can be believed is the makeshift image of your truth
        ... a screen between ...
What you ought to be ...   ... and what you really are.

xi

The still point keeps moving ... at the speed of darkness.

xii

Yes. Sin is whatever puts you to sleep
When you've just begun to awaken.

XII. CAVES OF ICE

i

From the tree
    ... there fell a leaf
        ... that had no equal.

ii

In your soul
    ... there sang a song
        ... that had no sequel.

iii

Doubt still clings to the scar
Where belief had been
Pleading like the rattling tin
Of cups that no longer hold your heart's desire.

iv

All that you had come to trust
Goes to ground like brittle dust.
Yet to breathe is still to inhale
The last smoke of a smoldering concept,
The wispy goodbye of an evaporating reality.

v

Two lewd mirrors of a thousand eyes,
Those limpid pools at once you saw,
Reflected strangers in your shrewd guise

Like caves of ice that come to thaw.

vi

Wisdom, you thought, ought to fear what it desires.
But death, you know, seldom cheers what it retires.
What does the deep midnight declare?
A haze and subtle fragrance of eternity.
Truth's random pendulum swings from the gallows,
Casting quivering shadows of belief on *startled grass*.
The rabble applauds its timely execution,
Its very presence — a cry of absence,
Absolving you from attention to *what is*.

vii

Long since having lost
Your readiness for the kennel or the cloister,
You seek the death-surrogates of murdered truth.
What will serve you now —
Death itself, or its many ersatz companions?
There is no lasting substitute for *"there is"* ...
For the white noise of your own despair.

viii

But you could not avert those endlessly liquid eyes,
The juxtaposition of face to face, of hers to yours,
Like an hourglass or a chalice culled from time,
Like containers whose contents can't be held,
Toppling over in a field without boundaries,
Coiling together into lazy eights of untold infinities.

ix

In how many littered beds you rolled
To twine with girls of furious gold?
How many fugitive joys have fled
While lust lay ripening in your head?
What stands unstill will surely run
From all those tasks you've left undone.
But if eternity could only purr,
You'd be left alone — just you and her.

x

What would you give, what could you sacrifice
To caress the fading fantasy of spiritual flesh?
To recline deaf and dumb
Before death's negative miracle of alien grace?
To wash yourself in the rain of her untimely moments
And forget at last: you only get what you give away?

xi

As if you could learn anything
But how to proceed
On this songless nest of withering leaves.

xii

 ... And yet
You must now praise first
Those scents you cannot trace.
You must now quench thirst
And drink the dancing twilight of her face.

— FIVE —
THAT STRANGE ATTRACTOR

And yet I have not seen you despite the eternities we have spent drowning in each others' eyes, with the certainty that the god had come, coupled, and that henceforth eternity overtook us in thought.
Yet the disaster is there, now, you have never seen yourself in me, you no longer know quite well, right here, who you are, nor do I know who I am.
— Jacques Derrida, *The Post Card.* —

I. STUNTED HOPES

i

The branch once green with meaning soon withers.
The dormant stump now blooms with stunted hopes.
From embryo to ashes to other embryos,
Each coupling is a wilderness of briars,
Scattering with sorrow the seeds of equivocation.

ii

Can you admire what still has courage
To burgeon in this exhausted soil?

iii

Are eggs mere questions answered by the sperm?
On each footstool, the toad is about to leap.
The shell about to hatch, the bud about to open.
Cocoons twitter at tales of their untimely future.
And hives hum with conspiracies of your significance.

iv

A butterfly flaps its wings … a hurricane ensues …
As if each small change were the beginning of something big
That can only flutter
At the prospect of being born to greatness.
Each tremulous step, a false step,
Before precipices you can't envision or behold.

v

Each step echoes a past that can't return,
Where footfalls foreshadow a now
That neither is … nor will ever be:
That's nowhere, yet now here … forever.

vi

Yes. You are alone in the womb of this moment
That never recurs because it never was.

You can never forgive yourself for infinities
You lack the largeness to contain,
Because you always mistake what is
For something that's only about to be established.

vii

You'll enjoy no continuity of becoming
   ... only a becoming of continuity:
Forever falling short of what you yearn to be.

viii

That strange attractor sin
Grins in the chaos,
While duty hides its humor in your solemn cloak.
For obligation is an ogre,
Finding no felicitous metaphors
In pilfered files of your disinherited mind.

ix

And what you mistook for love
Leaves you alone with your exhaustion.
Never a rose without a thorn ...
Never a path without a traveler ...
Down slippery avenues of eternity,
Where desire abandons you
To that day of disclosure that never comes.

x

Strangers, widows, orphans claim you with their faces.
Yet it's hers and hers alone
You really want to reach
With perpetual illusions
  ... of your uncommon speech.

xi

You had never been so lonely
Until you began to dream defiantly of eternity.

xii

But the next responsibility of love
Is this loneliness you must endure
If only to welcome others.

II. EXPECT THE OBVIOUS

Yes, oh yes — there are those as yet unweary
Of the obsession for confession:
   ... Those with talk that makes you tick
   ... Those with tricks that make you tock
   ... Those who squawk that you are sick
   ... Those who drool at each new shock.
Like early nostalgia for the latest idolatry
Abandoned love returns to lust
To that strange adultery that keeps a brothel in each breast.
Are you too headed toward
The Magnificent Merger, the Benevolent Buy-out,
The Soothing Sinkhole of absolution
Into which you'll slip on something more comfortable
Than the prickly pears of outworn passion?
What shall it be — the lady or the tiger,
Your tedious teddy bears, or your buddies the Buddhists
Whose only novelty is forgetfulness of oblivion?
Neither love nor lucidity — lest you forget
How falsely you've never been what you never were.
Now always armed by arcane arts of accusation,
You've never learned to expect the obvious:
Life's relentless sad safari is a camel ride to the tomb
Where ancient evenings slumber in a bed of humbled stars.

III. A CROWD WITHOUT A FACE

i

Hideous and blind they fell
From a star that had no equal.
Imploring you, they plead:
We've come ...
   to ask your permission ...
        to study the Buddha.

ii

You resist all moral authority
Abiding — least of all — your own
Faltering confidence in counterfeit compassion,
In the oily ostentation of an ogre's only charm.
You made mistakes but were never wicked.
You were culpable but your heart was pure.
You judged not — lest ye be judged.
And inch by inch you slipped
Between the covers of your own story.

iii

A lie pays untruth no greater homage
Than by confessing itself a fraud.
Those aliens were a crowd without a face,
And you were a bawd without the grace
To admit his prudishness.

iv

The tardiest liar is never late in loving his propaganda,
For nothing lubricates deceit like self-confession.
So you became an honest scoundrel
Applauded for the courage of your admissions.
One more crocodile tear will moisten the cheek
You cannot turn toward any other.
Practiced sincerity hides a multitude of sin.
Yes. Even your common touch of hypocrisy
That makes the whole world kin.

v

To love a stranger as yourself
… is to love yourself as stranger
Than any admissible truth.
Conformity is a cruelty to oneself:
No angry saint scourges money changers
From that tall temple of solitude,
That palace of malice,
Where you imbibe the gall
You used to call … your guilt.

vi

Yet still you summon
These lesser angels of your nefarious nature.
But which comes first:
    the conspiracy,
        or the cover-up?
The covenant,
    the unmade bed,
        or the wingless lover's cup
            ... of suffering?

vii

Nirvana nestles on the other shore
Where the beauty of her eyes lies
Safe from risk or rescue.

viii

How easily you slipped
Through sieves of moonlight,
Through dancing willow winds,
Caressing tender cruelties of her love.

ix

Each newcomer is a traitor to her season.
And all your confessions betray each reason
She ever had for loving you.
The smothered quilt of summer lies heavy
Beneath the innocence of autumn's happy leaves
Where each vein was a tributary to lives
You might have led but didn't.
Your names, frail bubbles,
Yearning to burst in oceans of recommended anonymity
... were words still rippling with pulses of particularity,
Above and beyond the burdens of song,
Below the deeper violences of your wrong,
Where truth is a chaos you can't share,
And champagne mutely flows
In green methusalems of despair.

x

Pale impatience — at the very end of distance —
Sees the Alps as a solitary nest of earth and stones.
But those were peaks you climbed together
And valleys you could not bear to inhabit.

xi

Each stranger is a soulless ghost without a name.
You cannot wait till they have faces.

xii

So hastily you reply:
The love you lost is still immortal.
The Buddha cannot teach you how to die.

IV. WHORES OF PERCEPTION

i

You believed you could
Hammer out anthems on anvils of heresy.

ii

You believed you could
Look things straight in the eye
And call them by their right names.

iii

You believed you could
Reach riddles of your origins.

iv

You believed you could
Chase those tracks to the one who made them.

v

You believed you could

Caress her face
Through the composition of her make-up.

vi

You believed you could
Sate your desire for her
In one final, fatal burst of fierce attention.

vii

You believed you could
Overlook traces of polygamy in each love.

viii

You believed you could
Escape the fear of giving dangerously
What you cannot save.

ix

You believed you could
Hunt hidden sources within hollow chestnuts.
Because you always
    ... saw more than you could see.
You always
    ... heard more than you could hear.
You always
    ... felt more than you could feel.
You always
    ... thought more than you could think.

x

In her trembling hands she took the new born terror howling.
And you and all the world she left behind were scowling
At what you and she ... could no longer hope to be.
Like shimmering beads of fallen dew
Reality's afterglow was all you knew.

xi

And much-too-much was there to touch

Or to retrieve the abandoned crutch
    ... of unendurable shame.

xii

Thus her image resurrects the ruin of your desire.
And the whores of perception cannot be cleansed.

V. DAYDREAM'S FINGERS

i

You rose as if to pray
To the sad and the unsusceptible.

ii

You uttered words unheard.
You swore unheeded oaths.
You rehearsed psalms of supplication
Unleashing lewd mythologies of her body,
As though flesh were facts
That daydream's fingers touch.

iii

You crushed the violet in her book.
You fondled blemishes on her page.

iv

But you couldn't mourn her sentence
Where rabbis read of phases
In the moon's indifference ...
Where every map is the wrong map
And every path a mournful detour
Through undiscovered country ...
Where the other's door never opens
And sentiment only petrifies
The imprecision of indecision.

v

Even wide-eyed urchins
Succumb to slow contagions of time.

vi

And by disaster or decay,
You arrive at slovenly hills of order
Only to languish in your aesthetic stupor,
That one-time padded cell,
The encrypted solitude of each moment ...

vii

Where anecdotes of wilderness
Tell tales unschooled by rhyme ...
Where the business of the apple
Denies the worm in every fruit
With the ecstasy of benediction.

viii

Just one blind kiss is all you'll miss
Of what you stole from her abyss.

ix

But break her jar and you get marmalade.

x

Therefore:
You belled the cat.
You chased the barking dog.
You fed the famished mongrel.

xi

And what she became was
The relic of your defections.

xii

What she became was the dove
In the belly of your beastliness.

VI. WHAT YOU ARE

Are you what you will be?
... You have no plural,
... But I have many faces.
... You have no sin
... But I lack all the graces.
Will you be what you are?
... That carrion comfort despair
... Abides neither day's law nor night's passion.
... It cannot trade each fashion for the ration
   of uncommon sense.
Be what you will, you are:
... Such is the economy of meaning
... Greening within you like the copper of discarded coins.
You are: what will you be?
... Do you still reside inside
... That crowded stage of strangers,
... That closed circle of befuddled players,
... In the theater of God's judgments?
Will you be what you are?
... This age-old algebra of human longing
... Is a sideshow of substitutions,
... And each desire an unsolved cryptogram.
You are you: what will be?
... Death's visit recalls your own mortality.
... It visits in your brother's ...
... In your friend's demise.
... Oblivion will not obviate its visitations.
You are you: be what will.
... Distractions won't bar the door.
... For just when you think you've forgotten,
... Your own death will arrive to visit others.
What you are, be, will you?
... Your absence, just as God's departure,
... Makes room for others to inhabit.
What you will be, you are.

... Crooked yardsticks are mirrors
... Of your failures to behold or be beholden.
Will what you are. Be you.
... But any mind that measures cannot escape illusion.
Be will: what you are: you.
... Thought only borrows the ways of flesh
... For your stalled spirit is ethereal mesh
    ... of blood and bone and emaciation.
What are you? Will you be?
... Love is not a word.
... Reality is not a concept.
... But is love as strong as death
... Which makes has-beens of us all?
What will be? Are you you?
... You sought unanimity in diversity
... And achieved the anguish of mediocrity.
Be you: what you are: will.
... Accident was your norm, anomaly your law.
... You passed over paradise for tawdry destinies.
... Eternity's vocation, you swapped,
... For chronicles of wasted time.
... You still recall the sterility of wisdom
... And the retracted claws of its erstwhile passions.
Be what you are: you: will.
... Shall you reject the call of chaos,
... The vertical barbarism that makes you safe from Visigoths
... And scared of your own vast progeny?
You: You are what will be.
... Were you smudged by guilt's erasure?
... By philosophical alibis, by serpentine psychiatries,
... By justifications of vice and its vapid confessions?
You are you: what will be.
... The terrible velocity of your ambition
... Asserts itself in fright and flight
... From what you only pretend to be.
... The Infant Tyrant,
    the Great Deserter,
        the Merchant of Being,
... Trades eternity for endless transformations.
... Such is the crack in the teacup of human potential.
... For weakness waits gnarled and knuckled

... At the heart of every will to power.
You are what will be you.
... Consider well your absences, your peregrinations,
... For returning only fouls the nest you can't abide.
You are what you will be.
... Your possible worlds are variations
... On one sentence. And its meaning,
... The myriad codicils of one last will
... And lonely testament:
What you will be, you are.
What you are, you will be.
You will be what you are.
What you are, will be you...forever.

VII. DEATH IN LOVE

i

If you reflect what you embrace,
You must fulfill what you disgrace
In martyred mirrors of her face,
Where guilt alone can leave a trace
  ... of passion.

ii

The lizard behind each leaf
Resembles hazards of his hiding place.
More and more and more:
Is that the chameleon's only chore?
To abide, in sorrow, loves you now abhor?

iii

Each belief, each history of your grief,
Conforms at last to what you truly are.

iv

The wise in heart, they say, never mourn ...
Neither for the living nor the dead.
Only he who masters himself is wise,

Who makes of mourning forgettable jealousies
Over mutably inscrutable desires.

v

Yes. You know the drill:
Ratcheting lust lurches forward,
Stumbling, stalling, upon some object.
Attraction springs forth,
Grabbing what it cannot have.
Desire, first gently kindled,
Fastens on fierce routines of passion.
Passion breeds recklessness,
And recklessness wrings memories
From agonies of accumulated defeats.

vi

But only because you shun the way,
The way of detachment,
The way of sublime indifference,
The way of not loving, not hating, not caring,
Only consuming each and every desire
Without stopping for death,
 ... for life, for love, for her.

vii

Of such indifference are masters of serenity
Made — and betrayed — by disloyalty
To the lost and losing cause of love.

viii

If all is one, nothing makes a difference.
But God himself could not be warm alone.

ix

Thus, ready yourself for battle on the sacred plain
With whatever guide you reverence most.
And wear your unholy wounds like badges.
For each wound, seizing you by surprise,

Teaches reliance on its fidelity.

x

Can you cleave unto unities of vast indifference?
Can you cleave unto promises of refuge,
From birth and risk, from death or rescue?
Isn't there a wisdom that wants to be itself forever?
Yes. There's no question of your love.
You'll yield tranquility
For violent beatitudes of her grace.

xi

Changelessly wild, unborn, and free,
She's obscure to you and the wayward world.
Once more with faith, with feeling,
Come with her, be born again,
To the world of death and change.

xii

Let the gurus go.
And clasp her hands
With a lifetime's little death in love.

VIII. A PATHLESS LAND

i

Gauche: you broke the ice in frigid chapels,
Uttering—sans cynicism or romance —
A fact as bald as the present king of France.

ii

Too soon for sustenance to train you:
You were beyond the vigor of any rule.

iii

Too late for limits to restrain you:
You shunned the rigor of any school.

iv

Customs, uses, institutions:
A game of chess is a mess
   ... without its absolutions.

v

You had confusions
   ... you never thought you could have had.

vi

Sordid seismologies of souls
Were solutions to each puzzle
Before you grasped the muzzle
   ... of common sense.

vii

And yet ...
Harkening still are heresies of her face,
Dark ciphers of loves you must embrace
   ... with only words.

viii

All her lessons left you leaning
Between the lamp you need
And the ladder you left behind.

ix

There are no experts in living:
Only excluded muddles of mere meaning,
Only obsessions yielding professions
Of something rather than nothing.
Each fact is a miracle,
Or perhaps it's not a fact,
But only the forlorn tract
Of truth in a pathless land.
Purloined wisdom is as plain
As a walk in the rain with the one you love,

As faint as unfinished mysteries of her face,
As calm as the covenant of unmade beds,
As quiet as disorder in a lonely room,
Inviting the sleep of death or dreams.

x

Shall you strum — or hush — those lips
Where logic and religion kiss
In respect of silence?

xi

The *truth-ache* of logic
Takes care of itself and little children
Who neither conjugate a verb nor parse a sentence.

xii

What they know, a wise man might pronounce,
If only he knew how to speak.

IX. GROW THE UNSAYABLE

i

Yes. *You saw eternity*
  ... the other night:

ii

For when lovers embrace,
They form a solitary angel
  ... of endless solitude.

iii

As if love were
  ... the knot of life and death,
As if man and woman
  ... could touch and blend,
Not in sound and fury,
But in word and fire.

iv

The truth, he said, begins with two.
But within his fallow heart,
No hermit saint can grow the unsayable:

v

Love is truth and truth love.
That is all ye changelings know,
And all ye need to show
Of everlasting duty.

vi

Beckoning are the steps
 ... of every ladder.
The risk, they say,
 ... is where and when
To stop for love.

vii

Is this then God's covenant
 ... with the undeserving,
 ... with those foolish enough to care, to strive,
To expect the world should have a meaning?

viii

That you should have the boldness
To be happy in what you love?

ix

And yet ...
Unto each reason, there's a crime.
Unto each treason, there's a rhyme.
Unto each season, there's a time ...

x

    ... a time for sacrifice.
A time to sacrifice virgins to angry gods,

A time to sacrifice your lust for virgins,
   ... and a time to sacrifice yourself
     ... to the virginity of unbelief.

xi

Is this the hurt
  ... that makes the heart go hollow?
  ... that injured each home you might have had
    ... in your deciphered world?

xii

Yes. Perpetually perishing ...
        ... is every path of truth,
Taking its ruthless revenge on those who dare
To own or disown its perilous legacy.

X. LESS BRUTAL GODS

i

Every solitude seeks some consolation
In eyeless citadels of crypts that never open.
But the rotted rose at the bolted door
Had the look of fright on a horse-shoe whore.
Was her face a fantasy you forsook
Or the nightmare hag you mistook ... for love?

ii

You always tread too lightly over undeciphered stones,
Where secure footholds slip ... risking enchantment.
But her sleeping lips could speak of angels
And still you'd disbelieve ... still grieve
For something more than hands can hold and hearts can heal.

iii

She was neither text nor interpretation.
Yet her body was a fable you caressed,
A moral you digested without the bitter herbs
  ... of easy nouns and faster verbs.

iv

If time is torrent,
Eternity's breath ... is imperceptible.
Each character, each kernel, you thought,
Contained the stalk of truth.
... Oedipus or oracle
    ... organ or orchid
        ... orgy or origin?

v

But your lost and whispering words,
Your echoing coins of used-up experience,
Were fallacies of misplaced abstraction,
And she and all her kin — islands in the stream,
Stubborn little eddies of desires that dare not die.

vi

All that's buried rises from inadequate graves.
Thus, the hunt for her is never over:
Wherever she is, is always a place to come to ...
Where one tomb exits another,
Into unimaginable elsewheres ...
Where forever you'll chase
What's missing at the heart of every result.

vii

Seduced by charms of the refutable,
You readily love, then spurn, what's easily disproved.
To know a love you can't return:
Is that your greatest fear?

viii

Yes. Hers were hands that killed with leniency.
Forgiveness flowed too freely to be merciful.
Spectacles of sanity or insanity
No longer scarred your vision.
Everywhere was nowhere ...
Nowhere was everywhere ...

ix

And both were truant centers
In languid circles of wry doubts.
Ragged geometries of self-delusion
Rarely embrace the rude intrusion
Of truths that do not cower
Before the dwindling tower
Of a theology now edited by lawyers.

x

Thereupon rests the locus of hocus pocus,
For the only lens that's left is out of focus.

xi

And yet ...
Beyond rims of insight
　... on edges of blindness,
Dawn's mourning and grief's twilight
Bordered splendors of her days.

xii

But your confession — a fraud of unintended denials —
Awaits less brutal gods of gentler rivers
And prayers more difficult than praise.

XI. AMONG THE EVICTED

i

You were born in dissolution's angry arms.
And you stand bereft ... as autumn's furious maple
Whose avalanche of leaves is lost
 ... and dutiful to the merciless wind.

ii

Seizing living quarters among the evicted,
Memory's homeless wastrels harden into habit,
Then quietly take up residence

In cozy hollows of what's departed.

iii

Do you crave change, or the scandal
   of its rehearsal ... or reversal?
Death itself would be easy
   ... if you got used to it.
But death's discretion has confidences
   ... the dead can't share.

iv

... Is the will to change the urge
... To repeal an earlier transformation?

v

Are you consequence or cause —
The sign ... or signified
   ... of fundamental laws?
Are you that one unchanging ingredient
   ... in a constantly repeated recipe?

vi

Yes. Each note's the harbinger of an unplayed song.
But can you resist repetition's tedious drama?
Is comedy a tragedy that stops too soon?
Or tragedy a comedy that lasts too long?
Are you too late to catch the act
That touched the value of a fact?

vii

As the icy monument still thaws,
Shall you proceed without a pause?
Can you measure how much you'll make
Of the mulch of decisions and conditions?

viii

Shall you abide an amassing harmony
That leaves you out ... or sucks you in?

Can you answer this ... and not disturb
　... the deep disquietudes of sin?

ix

... Is the will to change the urge
... To repeal an earlier transformation?

x

Change's ferment never settles the yeast of questions.
Each moment's density is destiny unscrambled.
Each cure creates another deformity.
Each disease inaugurates a new enormity
　... Perpetrated by chance — the would-be architect of change.
Each effect's a cause for celebration,
A novelty you cannot fail to recognize or remember.
Dark precursors within you plead:
You're this ... this ... this ...
　... this unchangeable you.

xi

... Yes. The will to change is often the urge
... To repeal an earlier transformation.

xii

Yet you keep on reliving the same experience
But lack the courage to call that character.

XII. THE FLOWER OF OTHERS

i

From the rose, you say, has risen many lies:
After many bungles, many tries,
To bury what life can't settle,
Luckless petals vainly strive
To hide that thorny nettle
　... stinging within the joy of creation.

ii

No breath blows that cannot sway the candle.
No truth is told that cannot carve a handle
To fit the form of your innermost solitude.

iii

All life is a diorama:
The madness of one moment in miniature
Mirrors the mania of them all.

iv

Tension before each curtain's rise
Recoils from follies of goodbyes.
Lest you grow inured to sceneries of departure,
A stage-hand rearranges props
To bolster plots of other plays.
Always near, the abstract bird
Whistles with word ... on word ... on word
Of a song that's strong, yet still unheard.

v

You hear him rustling in the wings,
When risk ripens toward danger,
Gathering as he comes and goes
Observances of an onlooking rose.
His fate is whatever slowly swells below the dam
Like the rush of fish who spawn
In ponds of impending death
Then burst through dark like dawn.

vi

Each youth is the rose of a new obsession,
An elf with many voices, many times,
And destiny — the monotony of several rhymes
That try to build a nest of meaning in your prose.

vii

His song has the hollow ring of brass
As if — at last — you'll be an ass,
Despite your Aristotle.

viii

Her love was sacrifice and lust for resurrection.
Her every sigh could have been her last.
That's why, you say, her breath's eternal:
Shrewd deflections and trusting lies ...
As if you too could resurrect yourself
   ... in the trust of the one you love.
Immortal sap, you mused, within her rainy breasts
Once coursed through roots that touched eternity.
 ... As if her gentle torrents
         weren't blood and tears, but wine.
 ... As if your lazy eights
         could outrun the very end of forever.

ix

But love is lucidity's alcohol,
And clarity — the crinkled lakes of ancient eyes
That watch though they are weeping.

x

... The wand is in the willow.
... All lust is on a lark.
... Her brow is on your pillow.
... The rose is in the dark.

xi

Seedlings can't belie cruel hardships of cultivation,
For disillusionment keeps love in condition
Like dispirited acrobats yearning and churning
Inside widowed skins of erstwhile athletes.

xii

Thus, the boarhound and the boar
Settle another age-old score:
Yes. A seed must die to bear its fruit
In the flower of others.

— SIX —
THE FIERCE ROUTINE

*We always imagine eternity as something
vast, vast! But why must it be vast?
Instead of all that, what if it's one little
room,
like a bathhouse in the country, black and
grimy, spiders in the corners,
and that's all eternity is?*
— Dostoevsky, *Crime and Punishment* —

I. TOWARD LAST ILLUSIONS

i

Just one drop betokens ... a torrent,
Just one torrent ... a river,
Just one river ... an ocean,
  ... a well of vast attraction,
  ... a sea of examples
    ... without the bottom
    ... you used to call its heart.

ii

If only you'd shake that treadmill feeling.
Wave after wave,
    lap after lap,
      step after breathless step
        ... that kept you reeling.
But, then, Eternity's infernal dealing
Always takes time for desolation.

iii

There will come a mingling of strange gods.
... Yahweh ... Lucifer, we hardly knew ye:
... You, who drank in lilting luminance,
... Like darkness guzzling up the light.

iv

You were salvation's child.
You carried water to thieves.
You starved yourself for applause.
You stanched open wounds.
You murdered gentle brethren.
You curried favor with tyrants.
You wallowed in sapphire-studded mud.
You bathed in fragrant ponds.
You raked oyster beds for finest pearls.
You preached strange gospels.
You charted abstract unities

... of beaches and birds.
You mortgaged open secrets.
You peeled glossy apple skin.
You stripped its core of chaos.

v

You felt ...
   ... that faint and faltering pulse of praise
   ... in every lame and lurching paraphrase
        ... of unrewarded truth.

vi

You made mistakes.
You called your torment *love*.
You nursed the dream of every youth.
But — all along — you knew:
Every skeptic's a cuckold to his banished bride.

vii

Your fidelity was a scandal,
And — your marriage — a boon
   ... to all your faithless lovers.

viii

You transcended guilt.
You pronounced it *sin*.
Your rigidity thawed.
Your mast fell, heavy with infamy.
You lived only where your body was:
As if gravity's enfleshed karma
   ... could sway photons toward proof,
As if you were but the brief remembrance
   ... of all that's happened,
As if you were first and last to awake,
   ... to rise in rage from the sleep of dogma
   ... and ignite *appalling lamps of vacant creation*.

ix

Bodies and dying empires accumulate many laws:
In time, you'll grow massive as the moon,
   ... as monumental as the Great Wall,
   ... as twisted as any Byzantine,
A largeness bending light toward last illusions.

x

As almost anyone who could not love,
You shared with gods their vain ambition:
To move — unmoved and unmoving — like water lost in water.

xi

You could — of course — forget that you are you.
But you're always you — only in your deepest enchantment.

xii

And you — you, alone in the dark —
Were promised the light.

II. THE NAKED STREAM

Belief was strong and lazy as a lion:
Its melancholy, long, withdrawing roar
Recalls you passed that way before
To press your tracks in chastened snow,
As quivering as the hobbled doe,
Who knows her lonely heart is hunted.

Cold and chill, the naked stream
Shall run without the gauntest gleam,
Aware your lust can never free
Yourself of what you yearned to be,
A child of scorn without the glee
Of craven immortality
Whom slow despair had stunted.

Each empty oyster on the strand
Annuls all weddings you had planned,

Betrays your feast before the stars,
Regales tossed lures with feinted scars,
With pleasures hurried through time's womb
And brightest evils you brought home
Towards where some tawdry bait was shunted.

Why? Whither? Whence?
Let the dancing now commence:
O Change, unchanging child of change,
That time will make less strange.
Give up now your wily dread,
For once in passages you read
Of truths that wane, of lies that wax,
Where wisest men, mislaying facts,
Revere false gods undaunted.

Yet each lame foot that tripped across
The borders of a land that's lost
Follows trails no tour guide knows
Through dank defiles of shrieking crows.
And creaking through low limbs of trees,
Slyly turns some evil breeze
Toward that dark rite she wanted.

The music of the cosmos sings
In ratios of trembling strings.
As if her breathing wove a net,
You might escape but not forget.
But how, alas, does this relate
To her you yearn to impregnate
With those frail hopes she taunted?

At every door you didn't take,
There was a sin you cannot shake.
For every whore that slipped you by,
There was a lie you could not shy.
For every time she sighed you sinned,
As if her hair could hold the wind —
And chill the heart she haunted.

Why? Whither? Whence?

Let the weeping now commence:
O strange, unchanging child, so strange,
Those joyful tears will never change.
So, give them now your love's remorse
And go and chase its saddest course
Through piercing valleys too extreme
And canyon walls too deep to dream:
The fate you cannot will to change ... you wanted.

III. YOUR VANISHING TWIN

No egg in its lofty nest can rest
Until it cracks itself open.
Thus, you start — a single cell —
Already a copy of what you've just become.
One becomes many:
A movement with no name — or any.
Yes. Any... any ... any ...
Any name will do.
For "any" aches with the algebra of desire,
   ... with your quest for the Other,
   ... that lonely variable, your vanishing twin.

IV. THE ORGAN GRINDER

i

Dull — not dark — was the day
The dead departed.
The day your brother died ...
The day your sister cried ...
The day your mother lied ...
The day your father tried ...
  ... and — yes — the day he failed,
The day when no birds sang,
The day foolosophy's dream-pistol
Exploded into cheap flowers and cotton candy.

ii

Over youth's deathbed, you hovered,
Technology entangling flesh:

As if furrowed brows hadn't covered
But revealed afresh
The vague inadequacies ...
              ... of your devotion.

iii

What ails thee uncle?
  ... Have you eyes? Have you eyes?
  ... Alas, you have none ... or perhaps too many.
Weariness wore itself out,
While worry waded
Through wave on wave of exhaustion.

iv

Extremities stiffen, blood recedes,
As if this infirmary of departures
Recalled some future ground of ancient needs:
  ... No, not this hospital's sleazy charity
  ... Endowed by forgettable sins
  ... Of some ruined, some unremembered millionaire,
But omens of a happy fall to come,
Whose season guarantees a brilliant death.

v

Stymied before castles,
Whose gates are closed,
Blind beggars sleepwalk
On thresholds of sublime revelations:
Practices without love,
    ... dead acts in whited sepulchres.
Should pilgrims of absolution embrace all these
To worship gods they cannot please?

vi

Some say the world we know
  ... is born in the soul of a woman's smile.
You know the grief you show
  ... is the bitter grail of guiltless guile.

vii

Yes. Inside that tarantula of tube and wire,
Your brother's heart's a seed
About to burst ... with its last and latest bloom
    ... of gentle warmth and subtle fire.
To him that bloom is the birth of another world.
To you: "it's oblivion — just now unfurled."

viii

Yes. Towards sleep ...
You're always falling,
And Eve's forever weeping.
Yet who, if not you, knows the shame
Of her shuttered heart, her own true name?
    ... her naked face?

ix

Can you believe her tears,
Those tears you can't erase
With yet another explanation?
"Jim and I are Gemini," she might have said.
Or just as well: "your little brother's dead."

x

For all the faith he must've mustered,
The organ grinder couldn't crank another song.
Alone again, you palely loiter ...
One more stranger in the crowd
  ... of accidental travelers, touring machines,
Humming, churning, and turning on cue
  ... in a Chinese room.

xi

But, the grain of truth in your delusion
Justified pangs of grief's confusion.
  ... And yet...
Deep desire placed no restriction
On the strength of your conviction.

xii

So, is it real — this life you've lived,
This death that you are dying?
Yes, you'll revert to feeble literature.
You'll tune in to —
 ... no — turn into ...
  ... the human tradition,
As if that inverted prophecy called history were not
 ... a forum for sedition,
 ... a catalogue of antiquities,
 ... a brochure of iniquities,
 ... advertisements for obliquities ... you cannot change.

V. SCENT OF APPLES

Dying's evil:
So say those gods
Who will not die.
Yet the scent of apples
Kept you breathing.
Or was it ashen roses
Bleeding air of dusty myths?
One more rote emotion
Makes of death
 ... a rude commotion.
But each room's a chapel
For those who cherish
Some perishing truth.

VI. THE WHOLE ORCHARD

i

The fierce routine continues:
 ... Is it ...
 ... algorithm or intensity?
 ... Music or mediocrity?
 ... Heresy or holiness?
 ... Or feverish disease
For you ...
Who can't appease

Your endlessly replicating self?

ii

Insight or flight, denial or recall?
Such is the peril of all in all:
Of one more nested loop
In a program of infinite betrayals.

iii

Yes. You stole a few apples,
But lost the inheritance
    ... of the whole orchard.
You gave up the ghost,
Then found what still astounds,
... your heartless host,
A machine for traveling and survival,
Becoming enslaved to each revival.

iv

Such is the body's envy for the soul:
As if flesh alone could know
What you can surrender
    ...and still be you.

v

In confidence, you placed your trust
In the low specific heat of lust,
Growing suddenly warm, then cool,
Like the unresilient wisdom of a fool.
Yet you give it many other titles,
And sample, then discard, as many bridles
For passions you cannot hope
  ... to blame ... or tame.

vi

Yes. How close, it seems,
    ... is the act of naming
To the sacrificial rite of blaming

... whatever you can never bear to be.
Yet the fear that something's true
Recalls a deed that torments you.

vii

Thus, soon you'll be no longer able,
To give every suffering beast a label.
Can so many oars in the water
Summon an oath you can't avoid?

viii

You brought a heart into a room
And — departing —
 ... carried none with you.
Yet its frightful absence on the stair
Makes one little room, an everywhere.

ix

On the best of days, you shake with fear
To think how false — or true — may be
 ... the spectacle of one tear.
Thus, that *spider love*
 ... converting manna into gall
Throws the vastest faith into a stall.
Yet, *your little world was made with cunning,*
Though you know not what may keep it running.

x

Yes. Each lure invents some rule of reverence,
For the game's default is creative severance
From a past you can't redeem.
What's new ... is you:
For is there nothing else so strange
Dividing the constant velocity of change
 ... as the eternal novelty of that wave
 ... whose cryptic character you cannot save?

xi

Your body's spirit's a shadow
She can no longer touch with words.
While you prepared ... for other tours,
Whatever you were
... was never wholly hers ... or yours.

xii

If only you had eyes to see,
Or beaks could speak,
You'd flee the vacuum in the room
That could let a greatness enter.
But light has no tongue,
And darkness has no lung
     ... to breathe.

VII. LIGHT'S BLIND ANGEL

Go, leper, go; go cleanse thy flesh:
Your sickness summons all afresh.
All that grow and yet have breath
Enlarge that language you call death.

Go forecast rules from antique sin
To learn how lustful lilies spin.
Go travel to be born — and then,
You're born to travel ... yet again.

Your world was first by number made
By folded digits that had prayed
And worship still that quantum score
That every moment plays once more.

The universe in every tear
Yields no new star whereby to steer.
Forgetfulness just like a thief
Throws all you own in stark relief.

Yes, stiff twin compasses are two,
But love can't turn that rusted screw.

Thus public places circumscribe
Lost corners of your timid tribe.

Could nothing have been unsounder
Than fantasies doomed to founder
On the square root of two lovers
Who vanished beneath the covers?

Fate cast love as your harsh duty;
Loaded dice denied you beauty.
As if there were a steeple near,
You curse the faith in every fear.

Each lone nymph in every wood
Would have loved you if she could.
Yet every maiden that you kissed
Repeated fancies you dismissed.

Go, deer, run shy, in shameless throngs,
As lions dance their mournful songs.
Each gambit gives, it yanks away,
And then returns in force to stay.

Yes. "Light, more light!" is what he'd said.
Just three more words, then he was dead.
Face your dissolution ... and pray:
There is no way to have your way.

Mute solitudes of fright alone
Foretell the memoirs of a stone.
Though no one heeds what you decried,
Deaf stones must speak what you denied.

Rude calculus of your belief
Deciphers now each sob of grief,
And makes of mourning meaning yet
Before you forfeit one last bet.

Go shuffle now the deck of signs
That teach you what desire maligns.
Nimbly press the channel changer;

Turning makes each panel stranger.

Go wade amid the data stream
To bathe in midnight with a dream
Where nakedness of number ran
And lust turns more than lovers can.

Go play lewd games just like an elf,
While dormant souls snore on the shelf.
But if you nail that monstrous shrew,
Will she go lucid through and through?

Eternity cuts short its span.
The sudden West grows old and dies.
The slackened East's unborn again.
Who tells you which of these is wise?

Yes. Elves will laugh at those who weep,
Yet you have promises to keep.
When they proclaimed: "It's all the same,"
Your last cruel light's blind angel came.

VIII. THE ANCESTRAL SCRIMMAGE

i

The climate changed;
You became a country of thirst.
For every leveled truth betrays
Your lust for the incommensurate.
You arranged everything
By measure, weight, and number,
As if passion wouldn't seek
   ... another way to slumber
            ... into dogma.

ii

Thus method made its way to everyone.

But no matter how you felt
That glacier was always sure to melt,
For warmth is ...
    ... accelerated by being human.
Looking back through an icy lens,
You'll recollect a continent of sins.
Yes. Even number found room for the irrational.
Now bristling with x's and y's,
One question with a thousand why's
Plucks the flower between her thighs.
Did your faith also founder
On the square root of two lovers?

iii

Pythagorean adoration of perfection
Invented a celestial tenth body,
An invisible counter-earth,
Not some ideological statue of snow,
But a living, mobile thing of the blind.
Yet, alas, no site for Shangri-La,
For utopia means precisely this:
No place to be you.
Not even an oak and linden love
Can resist nostalgia for paradise.
Thus, attend to geology:
Discover your major, active faults.
For eternity's history
  ... hides deep within its vaults
    ... the sum of your unbroken cryptograms.

iv

Yet the circumcised ...
Shall still break bread,
Devise new testaments,
Engrave new tablets of stone.
Alternative compensation
  ... relentlessly ...
   ...is sought
    ... and bought
     ... and taught,

And identities achieved
  ... sans consequences.
For discharged metaphors
 ... always find employment
In economies of salvation.
If time were money,
 ... how would you spend it?
If love were honey,
 ... how would you blend it
         ... into what you are?

v

The flight behind the image
Is part of the ancestral scrimmage,
And each cliché — a fossil
Of some already discarded reality.
From sheltering forests to wide savannas,
From dreary caverns to dry hosannas,
You gave cave-dwellers only glimpses
Through chinks of transcendence.
You fled the shadow, yet sought what cast it.
For your flight had always been a passage home,
As if love could arise from the semen-foam
         ... of a castrated god.

vi

Each time you reached the naked edge of your world,
You discovered what can only happen
   ... when a laughing meadow weeps.
But what happens when a promise keeps
Its vigil over all your equally lonely others?

vii

The more you hold the less you grasp,
The more you grasp the less you hold.
Yes, every corner will be turned ...
    ... from brass to gold,
And codified into laws,
 ... an endlessly amended, rescinded reconstitution.

Diligent scholars shall toil
 ... to scrutinize each clause
But who in solitude shall pause
To behold spectacles of your public death?

viii

As accountants assess the cost,
Who'll reoccupy lands they lost?
Unlike they, you do not count,
But detect missing animals in the herd.
Faith ... wisdom ... whore:
The fattening worm in the apple core.
Three stones away,
There's the other shore:
Is this a place you've been before?

ix

As blood first shrinks to ink,
 ... then digits,
Of one mighty giant,
 ... they'll make so many midgets.
The wicked art of navigation lurks
Hidden and obscure in the guts of a compass.
Everything belongs to everything,
For you can't resist
 ... the rudderless rumpus of all that is.

x

When everything is full of gods,
Everything increases the odds
Of finding Spinozas in jasmine arbors
Where you can choose ... or refuse
To snooze soundly in safest harbors
Of what was ...
 ... what is ...
 ... and what must always be.

xi

But shall anyone discern

Your preference for certain comparisons?
Is it enough that one alone sailed past the Sirens?

xii

Yes. You yourself are the waves you sail upon,
And all rivers reach the sea with many arms.

IX. GRIEF OF LOVE

i

Birth was only beginning of difference.
Yes. You'll come to know
   ... rites of passage
   ... periods of rut or dormancy.
Yet once upon the time
   ... of one sigh ... one eternity,
You were seed within a womb,
Conceived to endure
   ... another grief of love.

ii

From that narrow
        ... between ...
Where you're from ... and where you're going,
There's a blizzard already snowing
In chilling winds of its bestowing.
Because she was she, and you were you,
There was really nothing else to do.

ii

Despite those Christmas disappointments,
Again and again, you'll find it shocking
To glimpse another unfilled stocking.

iii

Yes. Nudity's starkness is perpetually new,
Laying bare the dread of dispersion ...
As if each fetish could fetch

... another occult meaning.
As if each drop of grammar
    ... could distill an ocean of relief,
        ... or fathom wells of disbelief.

iv

Yet each fragment mirrors consuming wholes
In which you yearn to drown.
What is lost is only recovered with words.
What's revealed is neither form nor presence,
But body lost on body,
    breast lost on breast,
        thigh lost on thigh,
            cry lost on cry
                ... of joy and sorrow,
  ... an otherness nullifying self
    ... that finds no medicinal shelf
        ... in which to fold away its pain.

vi

Across clamoring waves,
You ride the mare that tramples dreams.
Then her ghost resumes its fleshly shape
As if the stiff nakedness of her body
Were every form the world unfurled.

vii

The moment your arms leave off embrace
    ... what's left is not a face
            ... but desperate eyes.

viii

Yes. You were there when knowledge became therapy,
As if each rhyme, a copulation of sounds,
Clanged some broken bell that now confounds
                ... your will to know
  ... sad destinies of tracks you left in melting snow.

ix

Yet were you there
   ... when her body became infinite?
Such is the encounter of two
Who can only embrace what each can't hold.
You looked at one another
   ... as one might look at truth,
Yet her permutations yield no truce.
For the narcissism of small differences,
 ... it is said ... opens deepest chasms.

x

That trump of angels — love —
Absolves no one from loving
And brought you both
   ... to the joyous desperation of one death.

xi

If you had no hope of dying,
Would you rest on laurels
   ... of envy for someone else's lot?
If you had no cause for trying
   ... would you tie this lover's knot
         ... of fate and freedom?

xii

In death's underground there are roots
That almost reach the promise of resurrection.
Without hope, you'll live in thirst,
As if each moment were about to burst
         ... into eternity.

X. YOUR WAY OUT

i

Each time it's said there is no truth
Then think on this:
Each lie uttered

Turns one page closer
Toward the complete handbook of excuses.

ii

Death has not reached you yet,
Nor does guilt lead you down to torment.
But can you find your way out
    ... of the second circle of despair
Before you've escaped
    ... your thirst ... for the first?

iii

Semen poured on the altar
    ... or retained in the blood
Is — for the lettered — the origin
       ... of all that's good.
Each seed, a program for production,
Each need, another fact of seduction,
Brings far less and — yes — far more
Than you ever sought to bargain for.

iv

But the night is rising,
And once you've seen the orchard whole,
It's time for another departure.
No, you did not die ...
And, no, you did not remain alive.
Each name, spelling desire,
Chased one another like cascading water.
You rode each crest to the latest fall,
Toward some past,
      some vast,
          some last
              ... disenchanted evening.
Yes. Even time's deeply backward abyss,
Revealing chances you can't dismiss,
Always yields one lasting, lonely turn
             ... to spurn
             ... or burn
   ... the unrenewable fuel of one desire.

v

You were pale
   ... as one who frightened turns to ice.
As if grandmotherly perceptions
   ... could pronounce such horrors: nice.
As if the pelican's broken beak could speak,
Or vulgar voices in the crowd could shriek
         ... some fat, unwholesome Truth.
For every worm-hole holds serpents
Yearning to dance like angelic butterflies.

vi

Love alone was your rule of thumb.
But Time ...
   ... is only made good by times.
And Eternity — yes —
        ... will soon succumb
   ... to vacant offices of rhymes.
You'll make room
For ever widening horizons,
For ever outward edges,
Where strange compasses
Turn on verges of what you're pleased ...
            ... to call your world.
Each day you'll drink deep
            ... of forgetfulness.
For you, Truth's timid friend,
Have tasted grass,
Consorting wantonly
     ... in seas of other gods.

vii

Love, as it must, abandons itself to lust.
Just as you ... abandon yourself to trust.
Thus, ask not ... why your present world
        ... has gone astray,
For the cause resides
     ... in you, and you alone.
And in all the consequences you own.

viii

Yes. Each evening levels out the sacred plain
Towards what was once the peak of God's domain.
Before strangers, dogs will bark,
And just ...
　... as fire must follow spark,
So smallest prey
　... must soon precede the shark
　... into the belly of the dark.
Involving,
　... revolving,
　　　... yet unresolving
Into greater depths,
　　　... you're still dissolving.

ix

Yet,
　... again,
　　　... again,
　... rising to descend ...
Only to greet your orbit's end,
You'll spy the threshing floor of infamy
That made your flame so fierce.

x

From erstwhile heights ...
　.. all are hills and ruts and river mouths,
And rough-hewn corners of your world
Become as smooth as her flesh,
As warm, and ... then ... as cold
　... as the ashes of her smile.

xi

Lapsing in and out of rhyme,
　... attracted,
　　... and refracted,
　　　... and distracted,
Always forgetting this dumb show,
Those melting monuments of snow,

Or whisperings of hidden waterfalls
In forests you cannot fathom.

xii

Even as you become that unheard music,
You know it cannot last …
　… that you can't remember what you know.
Yet what keeps silence
　… is what still reverberates
　　　… throughout all eternity.
As if only her song could transform thee
　… into what goes quietly home with confidence
　　… and stays there forever.

XI. HOOKS OF HOPE

i

You slept the furious sleep of a green idea
　… that awakened colorless and calm
　　… as a bleached out rainbow.
You traveled in all directions
　… and found no boundaries,
As if the smoky hearth of sacrifice,
　… or that empire of endless snow,
　… were both nowhere and now here,
　　… a place too near to fear
　　　… or too far to go.
And though…
　　and though …
　　　　and though,
Never trusting
　… what you couldn't know,
You'd tell any story that befits
A truth convertible to terabits.

ii

Yet you could not flee
　… from what never stops to rest.
Or … returning … foul

... with fleeting presence
      ... an already poisoned nest.
As if knights of undecidable gratitude
At some lone crossroads of their quest
Could kneel before that overflowing cup
    to imbibe one last embittered sup
        ... of intermittent joy.
Every broken circle sharpens
    ... blunt angles of intent
   ... for passions you're still re-living,
  ... for cruelest gifts that keep on giving
     ... until they're spent.
Yes. Those tender hooks of hope
Always threatened disappointment.
As if what shall be received
    ... must be deceived somewhere.
As if every new arrival
    ... unlearns the way toward home.
As if every false covenant
    ... brings only death.
As if every promise left unfulfilled
 ... was another nerve of truth you killed.

iii

You still recall excitements of that midnight
When slender ontologies of Christmases past
Were braced with fantastic expectation.
All your rituals happened then
      ... as now and forever
As if every moment could achieve,
        ... then sever ... the sacred.
Ovoid horrors hung in balls of mirrored light,
Necklaces of fiery sapphires on beds of darkness.
For nothing could appease your raging fright
That all must end
   ... and begin again
      ... in endless silence.
As if all that's left unheard
Awaits the roar of a broken word.

iv

Ornament balanced ornament like petty gods,
As if you could calculate the daunting odds
Of gifts beyond any need of justification.
You could hold, but were not held,
As if you, and you alone, could meld
  ... invalid elements of an infinite
    ... and therefore indecipherable cryptography.
You were the cryptic sum
    ... you thought — of all you've met,
    ... but you never were a proper set.
You were liar
    ... but not the liar.
You were fire
    ... but not the fire.
She was briar
    ... but not the briar.
She was rose
    ... but not the rose.
But, yes ...
As visible as the emperor's clothes
Were all those destinies you chose.

v

You belonged but could not belong.
You beheld but could not hold.
Yet you touched
    ... the snow flower cold,
That six-fingered star
      ... of sudden illumination,
Your burgeoning sense
        ... of disentanglement
          ... from everything alien.
You practiced eternity.
You traced the circulation of light.
Yet with the mischief of a prank,
You gave that organ another crank,
Raising hopes that always shrank
   from aiming your lust

        or trust
              at any lonely other.
For in her, you always found, first joy,
        ... then bitterness,
Only staving off that glad-handing glitterness,
Betraying each new dragon castle of desire.

vi

You gave the logic of the gift
    ... the shortest shrift.
For a gift acknowledged
    ... is a gaping rift
Between sign and counter-sign,
Between what life wants
    ... and what you fail to reach,
Between drollish, vapid morals
      and what mere exchange
          ... could never teach,
    ... yet must malign.
You contained
    ... but could not contain yourself.
For you were omen,
        sign,
          trace,
            ... and promise,
A shimmering of erstwhile platitudes,
Within harrowing, blighted latitudes
            of despair,
With only a coppery coin for two to share,
To trade for what you can't believe
       ... and now must grieve.
For truth is more than you can establish,
      ... more than you, more than she,
  ... more than you and she can ever be.
More than ribboned presents beneath the tree.
As though you and all your relinquished others
    ... were offspring of some unwholesome lineage,
As though all you desired
  ... had been a detour
        ... towards attainment of that image.

As though your itinerary knows
    where you've been
  before you get there.
As though your every motion
Comports with pre-established harmonies
     ... of devotion.

vii

Again, again, you strain
    ... in vain
       ... to arrive,
As if your lot were always looped
    ... in knots of fate,
Where being early's already late.
You stumbled on in hot pursuit,
As if to greet the fickle joy
    ... of a wind-up toy,
The autonomy of the automaton,
The dream
  ... or nightmare
      ... of that boy,
Who blundered happy into an unlit room.
But the abysmal
  ... and the clinging hope unite
Flickering against the greater night.
You lay down and feared tomorrow:
That daybreak could bring such sorrow,
That your future could ever borrow,
Then abandon ... unreplenished,
    ... your starving past.
That instant you sought perfection
Was always already sure defection
From what you knew could never last.
You asked
  ... and asked
    ... and grew perplexed.
For every now's already next,
A parenthesis
 ... in the sentence of time.
Yes, every moment was

   always another universe,
And every piety a quid pro quo,
All dressed up, no place to go.

viii

Along forking branches of the night
Winnowing winds will fall contrite.
For dark italics must condense
Every flower's unsudden sense ... of fame.
Yes. Fatal blooms you cherish
        ... must perish,
  mistrusting moments
   made everlasting, yet warmed
    by cinders of a dying wish.
Was it self-delusion,
  or mere confusion,
   or some counterfeit coined
    from the chaos of the unnameable
     that promised unto eternity
      loyalties of what you tried
          but failed to love?
As if only departures
     ... without return
    ... could prove so clever
  ... as to turn,
    or spurn,
      or burn
  one arc, one spark, one candle,
  one promise you couldn't handle
     or dissever,
 ... one unpronounceable name,
 ... one rare and remorseless blame,
    ... one unwise, unwavering flame ... forever.
Thus, you counted ways
 ... you thought you'd pass the gift.
You counted ways
  ... that time would always shift
     ... towards eternity.
As if you — and only you — could bear to sift
  ... through dangling baubles to know a love

   ... that's never changed,
   ... that's not deranged,
   ... that's unestranged
       ... and unexchanged.

ix

How long you endured
    the myth of passage!
As long as the legend of length
   ... you lacked the strength ... to question.
Without fail, you blazed another trail,
As though every ice age
     were bound to melt
But could not abide horrors
   ... of every myth made literal
   ... of every truth belied
     by endless explanations,
  ... each appealing,
    and concealing,
    yet repealing
    every feeling
      that you felt.
You betrayed gods for human kind
  succumbing to birds of prey.
You opened a yawning wound
  that only forgetfulness could heal.
You merged with stone
  leaving devouring fowls alone
  with their hawk-eyed hunger.
You grew unremembered
   ... by gods, by birds, by words
      you no longer uttered,
   ... by dreams that no longer cluttered
    lucid insomnias of your wakefulness.
Your weariness of gods and flight
  gave up the ghost of exhaustion,
  and your wound closed wearily in silence.
Yes, each roundworm completed its circuit
     in the entrails of a bird.
As if you knew what lies at stake,

... you croaked a graceless ode
    to another nameless nematode,
        whose speechless code,
You fear, but cannot bear to break.
You unwrapped enigmas of Pandora's dust,
    ... a thousand bitter seeds
        ... in a jar of ashen lust.
Her identity was fidelity
        ... to what you save or discard,
For her coveted stash,
 ...her sloughed-off trash,
    ... revealed histories
        of consumptions,
Unraveling century after century
        of assumptions,
Preparing you again longingly
        for resumptions
            ... of eternity.

X

The heart must die; it did.
The soul must fly; it fled
 ... from whatever
    gullible geometries had led astray.
You saw points that had no part to play,
  ... lines that had no breadth to weigh,
    ... planes that had no depth to stay
        ... in place ... for now or forever.
For only fantasy can live
  ... in sanitary dug-outs of pale abstraction,
  ... or die the brittle death of your inaction.
But following the thrill
        ... of each kill,
There's still yourself
    ... and your restless will.
Yes. Again, you'll conjure white elephants
            ... worthy of worship,
If only their feces
  ... are as even, clean, and odorless as yours,
  ... or fit relentless patterns of your tours.

Even you might asphyxiate in this vacuous necessity,
So you sought out slums of possibility,
    ... inhaling the filthy oxygen of freedom,
Where obsession with each oppression
Justified any and all transgression.
And you prayed
   for vortex,
     for whirlwind,
        for darkness,
As if light undone
  by gravities of desire
    should rotate according to its own flaw.
You were eddies
   of each effect
     in a torrent of causes,
An endless stream of panic
      that never pauses,
        to reject its raging currents.
Yes. Integrity's an antique
  ... enshrined to pique
 ... the fury of those pleading
          without blame
            ... for self-esteem,
Among quaint, no longer cherished relics
   ... in museums of manly virtue,
Where saying: Yes
     ... and Yes
     ... and Yes
       ... to all
  means having no character at all
          to call ... your very own.

xi

Perversely, you craved sadness,
         sadness,
          and more sadness.
You craved its power
 ... to withstand the onslaught of mirth.
For you feared monotony at the maw of madness,
And monotonous madness in the caw of joy.

Yes, you lost your loyalty to the ineffectual.
You mastered that logic of disenchantment
 ... where process and result are one,
 ... where prophecy and loss are dross,
 ... where both and neither make a difference.
For every open secret closes
 ... with absence of surprise,
With the secret that was no secret,
With the gift you gave without reservation,
With the other you chased but could not capture,
 ... resuming the fiercely, unconsoling rapture
 ... of repetition.
Or seeking that exorbitant whylessness of some love
That waits in passion for whatever there is that comes.

xii

Yes. You sinned.
You did the demanded, yet forbidden,
    the ordered, but accursed.
In every vice, you became well-versed,
Daring those insane rivalries of lust to attack,
Or take revenge on a world that loved you back.
Yes. Your ruin, your salvation,
 ... is every law that crashes
In the whispery smoke
 ... of a blinding stroke.
For when flame embraced the rose,
 ... the thunder spoke:
Your fear is merely misunderstanding
The meaning you missed
  ... in the unity of light and ashes.

Imaginary postscript for the as yet unwritten:
"What holds the universe, then, young Joseph, lost, as you claim, here in Egypt?" asked the vaunted wise man. "The thinnest reed," answered Joseph, "the thinnest reed."

XII. YOUR FAILED ESCAPE

- i -

Shall you dignify yourself
       ... with a comment?
Shall you interpret
       ... one more dominant impulse,
Repeating without knowing,
Welcoming without showing
       ... your innermost despair?
If you should number each expression,
Each labeled line's a sure confession
Of your failure to complete yourself.

- ii -

Each chance you had
  ... was caught in the wings of desire.
Yet exits were always there,
For the way up and the way down
Share the monotony of one stair.
You rode each rise and fell each fall
Toward twilight fears that now recall
Doors ajar at backs of minds
Where naked ladies pull the blinds.
On this side of the curtain
 ... you're still uncertain,
   ... the subject of unpredictable fluctuations.
Foundations disrupted, certitudes dislodged:
How many truths have you now dodged?
Either/or's and neither/nor's,
Thresholds between revolving doors.
Body without soul, bereft of mind,
With only the ghost she left behind.
Beneath all mirrors hides the stain
Upholding images they contain:
The joker buried in the deck,
The albatross around your neck,
The briar beneath the bloody rose,
The circle that conspires to close,

A picture made by fallen stalks,
Or a rainbow's many-colored coat
 ... that chalks
Across the sky ... its angel's eye.
The cave behind each cave,
Particles inside each particle,
And waves within each wave.
The direst wager of distress,
Or God alone and playing chess.
A language game you cannot win,
For you're the instrument of sin,
Or the labyrinth of one line ... alone, invisible and everlasting.

- iii -

Always there's the lure
 ... of undecidable propositions,
And the long-awaited cure
 ... for inexorable oppositions.
Shall you justify the choice
 ... of axioms in your model?
Or curry favor with premises
 ... you cannot help but coddle?
Yes. Again and again, you'll play the fool
Converting again — according to some rule —
One set of symbols into another.
When you surrender
 ... thus to science,
And you must,
You'll become as dinosaur bones,
A superannuated appliance
That fascinates
 ... and fastens fates
 ... together.

- iv -

You'll dine, play backgammon and converse
On what cement was meant to glue the universe.
But, in truth, there is not one ... but two:
Can you explain embarrassments of complexity?
Can razors shear away the vain excess?

Can one more concept mop up the mess?
Or has some demiurge stuffed baloney
Into hallowed principles of parsimony?
Yes. Grizzled knob twisters of the cosmos
Fine-tuned their work to make you what you are,
A self-excited circuit bootstrapping yourself
Again and again into ceaseless transformation.
To be is to be the value of a variable,
And — yes — the value of a variable is to be
Dupe or disciple of habits you've sought to master.
As if you could
   ... break humanity's history in two,
   ... into whatever lies before,
   ... or row with one last oar
   ... toward whatever's true forever more.

– V –

Turning from action at a distance,
You plead again for its insistence.
Patches of blue, a lark's bright wing,
A share of all's in everything.

Shall an iron block universe decree
What each and every part shall be?
From swerve of shore to bend of bay,
Shall every atom have its way?

Compared to what at prayer you saw,
All you wrote then seemed as straw.
From a hilltop, travelers you did see,
Befuddled, bedimmed and forever free.

Before the stars saw one another plain
You hurried aboard the jostling train,
While ravens of exhortation's terror
Tangled with margins of trial and error.

In aftermath, you'll trace its path,
Trampling out the grapes of wrath,
Where wrinkled sadness of the moon

Reached only you to importune.

Locomotion of emotion,
With its savage, rude devotion,
Inscribes just like a mystic rune,
One lasting, lonely, lilting tune.

Circuits of eternal recurrence,
Reviving flesh of each occurrence,
Shall recollect before your birth
The dance of water, fire, and earth.

Always different, never strange
Is the measure of each change.
Yet every much will still want more
Of what it's always had before.

If you row without relation
Through the middle of duration,
Will other rowers snidely scoff
At your shy sense of running off?

If there's *later than,* there's time,
Lest you mistake the truth for laughter.
And if there's time, there must be change:
What was, is now, and ever after.

But what's *later than* can only be
If each event assumes all three.
But what *once was* cannot *soon be*.
Thus, you conclude: *Eternity.*

Every law must run its course.
Accelerated mass must equal force.
Yet centuries later you opined:
Length and time are undefined.

If time is real, it cannot fill,
The hollow that you are, until
Complete descriptions, you await,
Arrive as always: ... moments late.

Postpone tomorrow's fight at sea
Until the future answers thee.
Climb higher up the logic tree
To see that what must be must be.

For body, rank, and mean estate,
Ambitions grow and can't abate.
Surly cynics turn and chortle:
To kiss a child is also mortal.

Javelins tossed toward each limit
Enlighten freedom or must dim it.
If mind escapes this causal net,
You'll never want what you must get.

Is there anything diviner
Than believing a grand designer,
Affably huffing and puffing,
Created *all that is* from *nothing?*

Yet can you say why you're obsessed
With endless life, beheld, possessed?
Illusions let you propagate
With a will you cannot sate.

Because the gods have lost their nerve
Every atom's random swerve
Delineates the curve of fate
And makes your life a moot debate.

Fallacies of equivocation,
Undermining each foundation,
Assure that every folly's praised,
Dissolving every issue raised.

A clever lad will cheat at jacks,
Embezzling time he always lacks.
Another hack will go: clack, clack!
Eternal lack without the knack ... of fulfillment.

- vi -

Your world atop a mammoth rides
That high upon a tortoise strides.
Beneath this tortoise then must squat
Some puzzling X you know not what.

Sacred integrities of mind
Cannot annul a double bind.
In twisted chains, your brain repents,
Ashamed of what it represents.

All men by nature know desire,
Yet in your gown nearby the fire,
You'll resume the slump of sleeping,
Laying traps for faith's safekeeping.

Just as two plus three is five,
A clump of wax culled from the hive
Will in its subtle way survive
To bolster answers you derive.

Yes. Everything's to be doubted.
No truth left will go unshouted.
Yet whatever you can't doubt in deed
Engenders sanctities of your creed.

No idol of the tribe need bribe
What self-deception must imbibe.
A stone, a leaf, an unfound book
Condense alike into a look.

Yet when you've left the last reception
With your bundles of perception,
A timeless seer stalling doom
Saves the furniture in the room.

Religion passed its fiery brook.
Yet certitude still seeks its nook.
Yes. Thought negates, preserves, uplifts
What every moment always shifts ... toward oblivion.

Substance that once had made you wince
Becomes predicted modes of sense.
Curt logicians, hard-nosed and gruff,
Will analyze this *neutral stuff*.

Pausing once again, you'll sigh;
Your dread's predictions go awry.
Uncertainty's probably sure
To be a stop along your tour.

Increasingly ethereal,
Displacing raw material,
The imagined glare of matter
Is just as real as idle chatter.

Between what's surface and what's deep
Unrolls that bed where reasons sleep.
But empty thoughts are not content
To go where intuitions went.

A doe-eyed child's inventive stammer
Re-invokes a hidden grammar.
Thus, there'll arise a new gestalt
For once again you must exalt … the unobstructed whole.

Regularities of succession
Made at most a faint impression.
Solitude's maze-like mystery
Mimics patterns of your history.

Enfeebled minds grow anodyne.
You stumble forward unconfined.
The mysterium tremendum
Fades into a mere addendum.

Rosy blooms on cheeks of youth
Disclose another shade of truth.
Some new concept's sculpted frieze
Reveals unmarbled Hercules.

Forgetful shepherds of being

Harness yokes to old ideas.
Consciousness and its lapses
Retreat to nooks in your synapses

Repetition of appetition
Recreates a proud tradition.
Paradigms without cognition
Turn the keys in your ignition.

Custodians of self-image taught
The alphabet of human thought.
But lucid systems they have wrought
Cannot parse from *is* ... an *ought*.

Absorb with calm the harshest shocks
Of stubborn facts and paradox.
No cornerless ontology
Can thrive without apology.

The open texture of your grief
Unknits the fabric of belief.
Thus, spread your wings and fly at dusk,
As if fluttering light could fill your husk ... with meaning.

- vii -

You're the pilot in your vessel,
But your train's just leaped its trestle.
Collapsing guardrails have foretold
The snake oil nostrums you have sold.

First the leper, then the fool,
Telling tales outside of school.
Nursing madness in the clinic,
Hands of gladness greet the cynic.

Every palm that tosses dice
Performs a rite of sacrifice.
Yes. Being odd is getting even;
Seeing God and stoning Stephen.

You burn, you thirst, you turn and try
To vie, to strive, to guess and die.
But theories — pure and manifold —
Cannot caress a flower of gold.

Are there too many things to name?
Does each word cry: the same, the same?
Yet random strains in every sign
Crimp the style of each design.

Just like a flame without a fire,
The sliding signifier's crier
Screams fast along the fuse of time,
Conflating wrongs with ruse and rhyme.

Totem, taboo, and monkey's paw,
Living well and thinking raw.
What could be more detrimental
Than transgressions sentimental?

Each unrepression takes in stride
The wake of another patricide.
Thus, every id makes one last bid
To lie to what it cannot kid.

Don't undersell the lie's allure,
Though talking cures are never sure.
But in truth's place the cheapest grace
Forgives, forgets, yet smites your face.

Ingratiating impotence,
Impersonating innocence,
Stringing your long-distance cables,
While the wicked tell you fables.

Babbling oracle, shrieking chorus,
Each self's a cell a bit too porous.
So with your lonely others sup
Presence of absinthe in a cup.

Will to power and true belief

Both lead alike to equal grief.
That a family can resemble
Made all your definitions tremble.

Never meaning just what you say
Means to concede, give all away.
And if you give all that you are,
Can you still spin that Chinese jar?

How many inches in an hour,
Or years within a golden flower?
No calculus of felicity
Can measure your lubricity.

Explaining retrograde motion
Was once a ritual of devotion.
Always movement, then repose,
Unfolding petals of a rose.

Determinism's demon chance
Initiates another dance.
But pellets on a roulette wheel
Cannot tell you how to feel.

Whether outer sense or inner light,
Cocksureness is an awful blight.
With each dragon that you slay,
Convention's crust just breaks away.

Wretched elves without a system
Cite a paradox by Tristram.
Cleansing baptisms of names
Reify your reference frames.

As they betray what you disgrace,
Houses rise ... fall ... and in their place,
With termites gnawing at their base,
Leave only cobwebs there to brace ... the crumbling walls.

Your failed escape from history
Succumbs once more to sophistry.

Appearances saved, but at great cost,
Revivify the lust you lost.

Once again you'll feel the lurch
As all who worship at the Church
Of Whatever Forever Breeds
Beyond the briar-entangling weeds ... of justification.

- viii -

Perpetual peace?
            ... the sages plead:
                    ... just trust us.
To each according to his need:
Is that what makes your centuries bleed
                ... from justice?
With a talon or a claw,
Can you grasp the moral law?
Brains in vats, or cats on mats
Abuse themselves to strain at gnats.
If your self's your only measure,
Each key that's lost is also treasure.
Shall you grasp that cosmic mitosis
At the core of your neurosis?
How harshest, cruelest logic defamed
Your love in every possible world?
With compassion's breath, you'll always hear
  ... the echoing hollowness of fear,
  ... the lesson of an untaught teacher,
  ... the sigh of every oppressed creature,
  ... the transverberating heart of the heartless world.
Shall every liar's quantifier
Get pricked .... on the briar ... of eternity?
Yes. One pariah on Moriah with a dagger
Made all your categories stagger ... toward absurdity.
As if all morality could heed this dictum:
The smoke of sacrifice survives the victim.

- ix -

You're reborn, and the good news travels,
You die, and it all unravels ... into many futures.
Yes. *A sentence can be rendered eternal in divergent ways.*

And yet there is no outside text,
For sheer indifference has no next.
Messiahs of each moment arrive too late
To scrawl upon the blankest slate ... some enduring revelation.

- x -

Your time is limited
   ... but without definable boundaries.
Yes. The day she filled the orbit of your arms
A gleam escaped the lashes of her eyes.
And yet:
You searched for night beneath the light, as though
You both could forsake your little gods and go
Towards some darkness that disdains all metaphor.

- xi -

So feeble were your acts,
   ... you say ...
So fragile were your facts,
And so negligible your mass.
Yet you blasted a star
That spawned a thousand worlds.
This is no neutral activity:
Only an image of your obsession
Can resolve your stubborn riddle
           ... Or knife a path
Through the unexcluded middle
           ... Of your life.

- xii –

A Pilgrim's Shell

(1)

Shall all things come alike to all,
Or shall you alone be different?
First and last — your eye's the circle,
And your world — the second, endlessly repeated,
   ... geometries of passion uncompleted.
In hours of departure, you arrive.

You go your way and still survive.
Whether variable, bound or free,
You were always you;
    ... and she was always she.
Approaching unattainables,
Ravishing unremainables,
Once again you'll play by rote
The hymn of another asymptote.

(2)

While truth retreats, falsehood sows.
Where danger is, remedy grows.
The monad breathed into your void
Her startling beauty unalloyed.
That spidery web at nowhere's center
Spun all you trust ...
   ... from her soul's splinter.
Yes. At last, you'll come to know
What's only known in self-deception,
Your window on one unrepeatable exception.
These united states of a miracle:
Is there anything more empirical
Than whimsy flashing across truth's face
Or deepest revelations of her grace?

(3)

Hearing your oar's unsteady swish,
You soon discovered what's amiss,
As if the fecund bladder of a fish
Gave birth to each and every wish.
Your hysteria for criteria
Succumbed to creatures of darkness,
For you lost your way
When theory stubbed its toe on everything,
When the logic of the infinite
Ensured your descent was bent
    ... toward beatitude's kiss.

(4)

Yes. The letter killed the spirit,

Though you're among the last to fear it.
No. You'll never know what X is,
Nor reach that haunted, nameless nexus,
Where rhyme, river and rower meet,
Where love and logic embrace to greet
Your lust again and again ... forever.

(5)

Magician's sun, high priestess moon,
Imperial tower, and empress star.
Can you become just what you are?
Shall you escape your propensity
              ... for intensity?
As if the will's quietus
Could at last deplete us ... of desire.
Ecclesiastes invariably bedevils
The temperance of two lovers.
And the strength of the hanged man
Seeks hermetic justice
In the judgment of a fool.

(6)

Yes. It was just a day ...
    ... that could be any day ...
      ... that will become everyday.
But that bright day you said *I do*
Wedged fast between what was before
And what's promised true forever more.
That moral centaur, man and wife,
Repeats cruel harmonies of strife.
Yet will and truth join in relation
To resurrect a rare sensation.
Love's gravity, that shortest line
   ... between two points,
Always frustrates
     ... then anoints
       ... a stretch of space,
      ... a second's cup,
          ... to catch the grace ... called home.

(7)

Is it the beginning,
    ... or the end that speaks,
Or is it
    ... that great bright day in You
                ... Eternity?
You were the one permeating every number.
You were bittersweet fruits on a twig.
You confronted gates of the temple:
   ... the way, the truth, and the life.
You went north, south, east, and west.
You trod the primrose path of quintessence
 ... surviving wave on wave of obsolescence.
You endured a day of crucifixion and benediction.
You reached the seventh shuffle of the deck.
Auspiciously, you died in paradise,
  ... in darkest rooms of an upper storey.
You envisioned orders of angels in their vainglory,
  ... and the integer that was her own true self.
You received commandments;
   you heard declarations of innocence.
You committed sin.
You repaired the broken wheel.
You renounced enlightenment.
You hugged the night.
You forsook the path ... you stumbled.
You heard her wrath ... you mumbled.
You were the one that keeps.
You filled three baskets with meditation.
You were law.
 You were joy.
   You were transformation.
You were every impulse to become real.
You were every possible world made actual.
You were clashes of fact with counterfactual.
You were every rule's last exemption.
You were every fool's incompetence
           ... at redemption.
You were love stronger than death.
You were death greater than breath

            ... of compassion.
You were starving soldier without a ration
  ... who spent one lasting, longing holiday
              ... of passion.
You were at one
    ... with the miracle
       ... but did not vanish.
You were Borges
    ... translated poorly
       ... from the Spanish.
You were a mill
    ... for grinding rogues
      ... honest, good, and true.
You were the thankless, turnless screw
     ... of one enduring exception.
You were gaps between silence and declaration.
You were ways and means of self-deception.
You were trial after trial
   ... of unsettled claim
   ... and brash denial.
You were every ritual of thought
That tried so hard, yet came to nought.
For your every fluctuation
   ... had the character of happening
    ... now, nowhere, and forever.
You were lucidity less vast, more brief.
You were every doubt that caused belief.
You gathered herbs to lay on wounds.
You were faith that never swoons.
You stepped inside bright clearings
  ... outside all memory of yourself.
You were dust-encrusted wisdom on a shelf.
Invariably you sought to do
Whatever you thought was true
            ... for you.
And yet ...
What's true
   ... is always forgettably
         ... not yet.
You were all those strangers you've never met.
You were the weakest link in the chain of being.

You were infinite vacuities in the scale.
You were every vice — and virtue not for sale.
You climbed the tree of life.
Unmoved and still unmoving,
   ... you were exempt from passage.
You were willow root
   ... nourishing its own side of the tree.
You were bodiless swarms of particles on a spree.
You fostered insight
         ... dreaming boundaries.
            ... and their toll.
You were unsmelted iron
         ... in feckless foundries
             ... of the soul.
From antiquity to post-modernity,
On your tour of pale eternity,
First ... up one path,
    ... then down another.
You were every lonely other's brother.
You were zebras of every stripe.
You were tokens of every type.
You were coiling spirits of the snake.
You were every issue that's at stake.
Again, again, you sang the chorus.
You were self-consuming *ouroboros*.
You were counter and counted,
   ... mounter and mounted.
You were moment's movement and position.
You were changelessness in transition.

(8)

Yours was a journey
  ... of one bearer
    ... and one burden.
You were princely soul
  ... informing the body of a cobbler.
You were number of motion
  ... one raindrop in rivers of too much time.
You were eloquence that had no need of rhyme.
You moved like a knife-edge through the hedge of life.

You were wilderness of thirst in a parched land.
You ransacked tombs in eternity's graveyard.
You stole loaves of the glorified dead.
You drank with the profligate,
  ... but could not bear
    ... the taste of immortality.
You feared what you desired.
You desired what you feared.
You were petrified fact
  ... caught red-handed in the act
    ... of its own unmaking.
You were fountain flowing forever
  ... toward a form it fails to establish.
You were an accident among countless others
  ... until you met a lasting explanation.
You were a bell of glass
  ... that shattered as it rang.
You were impulse about to speak.
You were suffering about to shriek
  ... some somnolent curse.
You were vital force and conscious stream
  ... the conquering worm in every dream.
You were every unmotivated term
Containing another dormant germ ... of meaning.
Your moment's vision, your blinking eye,
  ... shed a tear, but could not cry.
You were the lamplight of intimacy.
You were rock, shield, fortress, horn.
You were the clarion call of scorn.

(9)

You sailed from doubt
  ... toward faith's first article,
Cast adrift on that lonely particle ... of belief.
You saw all in light of one experience
  ... and one experience in light of all.
You were false countenance
    ... and true continuance
  ... of everything in its own being.
You wielded unconcealing wands of seeing,

As if you could ...
   ... finally, utterly, magically
      ... glimpse everything at once.
You were form still forming,
   ... machine still warming,
     ... organ still beating,
       ... context still pleading,
         ... for an adequate interpretation.

(10)

You prophesied in mirrors of presence.
You grew hoarse with discourse.
You fell still-born from the press of circumstance.
You fumbled at knots of word and world,
  ... unfurling spirals that you are.
You clasped the witch's foot.
You stared at the twelve faces of heaven.
You sought purgations of the superfluous.
You unloosed the silver cord.
You broke the golden bowl.
As wind returning to its circuits,
You turned to behold wisdom, folly, madness.
Your logic, the enemy of antinomy,
Could not reconcile what must defile
   ... itself in the cryptic sum
     ... of all the life there is.
You deciphered encrypted imagery
 ... of what still professes to be thought.
But perfection proved too elliptical after all
     ... to catch the roundness of a ball.
You inspected the competence of one last concept.
You changed ... and arose again the same,
With only your unchanging will to blame.

(11)

You melted fast before the thaw.
And, yes, at last, you finally saw
    ... how every timeless moment's ripe
      ... to repeat another archetype.
You were possessed,

>   abandoned,
>   possessed again,
>   surprised
> ... at every rhythm you comprised.
> You were others, not elsewhere, but in this life.
> You were the name of a thousand chimeras.
> You were thought
>   rising,
>   falling,
>   progressing,
>   infinitely regressing,
>   and retrogressing.
> You were ...
>   guilty beauty,
>   ... and ...
>   ... ugly innocence.
> You were every lowly pawn undoing
>   ... its own penitence ... of conversion.
> You were fall
>   ... and
>   ... flight,
>   ... choice,
>   ... and
>   ... submission.
> You were uncounted sins
>   without remission.
> But, yes — oh, yes —
> Your flesh still covets what reason condemns.
> For without the slightest word,
> Her first and last caress conferred
>   ... immunities
>   ... beyond
>   ... communities ...
>   ... of the herd.

(12)

Always and incorrigibly uncouth,
You sought a place to face the truth.
The fluted scallop of a pilgrim's shell:
Is this the cave in which you'll dwell ... for eternity?

Yes. Unweave the rainbow in her hair,
For her presence there's beyond compare.
Drink from her cup, and go on living:
The unopened gift is not worth giving.

— SEVEN —
BEHIND DISENCHANTED HEDGEROWS

To wish, but never have our will:
To be possess'd, and yet to miss;
To wed a true but absent bliss:
Are lingering tortures and their smart
Dissects and racks and grinds the Heart!

— Henry Vaughan, "Etesia Absent" —

I. ADD TORTUROUS SUMS

i

You awakened ... trampled
By the raunchy hoof of a bad dream.
Born in solitude, suckled in silence,
You sought something uninfected by the world,
As if nothing could divide
 ... that curdled quietness of eternity
Where you vaingloriously hurled
Your exhausted hopes.

ii

Take away number and all shall perish:
As if digits were contractions
 of all the words there are,
As if you — and you alone — could read
 the dark mathematics of a scar.
Yes. Each mystique's a mistake of abstraction,
Naked remainders of every failed subtraction.
Knitting raw edges of every schism,
You compressed fact into formula,
 ... angry faith into patient fatalism.
Despite your insistence on resistance,
Shall you still see Nobody
 ... at such a distance?
Yet you cared for once and kept it close,
As if eternity were near to fear
 ... yet not the cause of it.

iii

Yes. Between nowhere and now here is one place
 that made all the difference.
You were a creek bed that could not flow,
But leaned forever in the same direction.
And you'll believe
 this heading's your own accomplishment,
For every vision's
 already sapped the marrow of action.

You shall step twice ...
        indeed many times ...
            into that same nightmare,
   where a thousand flightless, starving birds
   gather round to pluck the carcass of your infamy.
You were every name that pronounced the letter I.
Yes. Even those that asked and always answered: Why?

iv

If you would strive, then strive.
If you would travel, then travel.
If you would arrive, then arrive.
If you would rest, then rest.
If you would work, then work,
  forging every little quirk
      ... into an occupation.

v

If you would command, then command.
If you would obey, then obey.
If you would belong, then belong.
If you would accept, then accept.
If you would refuse, then refuse,
  exalting every little bruise
      ... into a badge of honor.

vi

If you would go, then go.
If you would stay, then stay.
If you would grow, then grow.
If you would pray, then pray.
If you would hate, then hate,
  for every moment's too late
  to bear the burden of your love.

vii

But wherever you choose to stand
Shrink back from silences of fluttering wings,
  from secretive glands of soporific certitude.

Bad art became your best religion
Until at last no one and nothing
Could escape the cheap grace of entertainment:
  ... Of forgiveness without repentance,
  ... Of baptism without discipline,
  ... Of communion without confession,
  ... Of obsession without repression,
  ... Of self-forgetfulness without love.

viii

You plunged madly with violent lust
  where fearless divers
    sought pearls and drowned gold,
      toward Bluebeard bedrooms
        ... and groves of Baal.
And again, unguarded and alone, you sail,
As if viciousness made your virtue sing,
Swimming madly in the girth
    ... of divinity's breeding wing.
Now, there is always time for turning
  toward detonations of spoken words
      you trust but never verify,
  toward delusions of insight
      that every therapy
        not only fails to cure ... but fosters.

ix

How long can you practice the art of the aggrieved?
Can nothing tame your martyrless solitude
 ... that sublime futility of a single momentary god
   ... no longer reachable
     ... by covenants of comfort
       ... by premeditated ecstasies
         ... enacted below the waste of human desire?
Should you regale yourself
    ... with that hag's stiff-neckedness?
Or shall you again recoil
    ... from the tedium of lifting one last veil?
Of refusals flouting
  ... every border,

   ... every boundary,
   ... every foundry
    ... of sullied faith?

x

Yes. Every mosaic serpent craves apocalypse.
Thus, in your orbit,
   ... you turned on the axis
      ... of skin-to-skin experience.
Every promise you didn't keep
Bound the tyranny of the heap,
As though one grain of sand alone
Could never reflect eternities
That culminate in every moment.
Yes. She was younger than April snow,
And you — older than the death of winter.

xi

You drank from the same fountain,
Yet chased in thirst an obscure residuum.
But all you still wish for hardly rises
   ... above tall grass
    ... behind disenchanted hedgerows
     ... in darkening cul-de-sacs
      ... down avenues of mythical trees.

xii

Each spearhead of novelty
Announces your ignorance.
Yet you must add torturous sums
Before practicing rites of knowing nothing.
Shall you begrudge yourself
      the false felicity of your world?
Yes. Temptations of every would-be happiness
        flaunt their faithless refusals.

II. BLUE SMOKE RINGS

i

Dust, ash, and mud ...
 ... pale copies of your father's blood
Ride thin blue runnels of your veins.
The royal funerary machine proceeds:
 ... an engine of engrams,
  or an organ of mimicry?

ii

Can you still hear that murmuring rush
That's almost the same as silent music?
Frail blue smoke rings you puffed
Were only promptings of self-reference.
For you were scattered as promiscuous rain,
Whisked by the broom of journeying winds.
Torrents, it is said, have three properties:
 ... They overflow all in their course.
 ... They fill all hollows.
 ... They overpower all sounds with their own.

iii

You trespassed thickets of the heart,
Seeking greater company in solitude
Than the lonely tedium of others.
Was it she you claimed to love?
Or was it yourself transformed
Into what you dreamed she was?
You'll resume the phantom charm of making.
Pearl after flawed pearl, you'll string
Snarled necklaces of dangling orbs,
Reflecting hollow movements without borders,
Defined solely by what they feign to hold.

iv

Yes. You feared the pigeonhole,
 ... the dry rattle of dice,

   ... of beetles in a box.
But does your future's unresembled past
Align blackest expectations in one neat row,
Or summon with surprise ...
   ... the sufficiency of one white crow?

v

If only there were something
       ... you were equal to.
But equality, says Bolzano,
   ... is a special case of difference.
Thus, you become faux unity in a rule of change,
The curse on the tail of every promise.

vi

Broken by codes you failed to break,
Ye shall come to know her truth,
And truth shall drag you in its wake.

vii

But are your mistakes your own,
Or do they belong to the universe?
Upon one lone peg so much depends,
As if linking litters of loose ends
Could resolve the riddle of relation
Between all you are and all that is.

viii

Uncertainty's quantum becomes precise.
Yes. Almost enough to exact the price
       ... of knowledge.
Or is the logic of probability
       ... only probably valid?

ix

Yes. You were there
 ... when porridge woke up,
   ... and matter began to crawl,

As if the chain of being's escalator
Conveyed you everywhere and everywhen.
Yet slow and stubborn changes in the kiln
Yield the beauty of unpredictable effects.

x

An arbitrary breeze fills every urn:
All that leads nowhere leads there,
As absolutes dissolve
At places where you begin to live.

xi

Yes. The truth is whole,
But must be unfurled
 ... fold by fold
   ... pulse by pulse
     ... beat by beat
        unto its own rhythm.

xii

Whatever is, is
  ... in whatever way ...
      this motion of your heart.
Yet every ghost on this moving stair is also real,
Lest you no longer deign to dream or dare to feel.
One and all, they are flesh of your obsession,
Your endless re-enactments of unattended pain.

III. THE SECOND DEGREE

i

O why do seashells murmur
    ... her lost enchanted name?

ii

Why should they raise her voice
  to disturb burgeoning,
        anonymous

    asylums
       of your world?

iii

Yes. Whatever she was, was there
Before you committed consciousness
  ... in the second degree.

iv

Before you looked back with longing
  ... at what you've always been.

v

Your echoing sigh returns
 ... prayers that can't sustain
    ... yet still remain
  ... steps of ladders leading nowhere.

vi

  ... Or perhaps
You'll lean on charlatans of the ineffable,
Tempted by words you cannot speak,
Charmed by effigies you feign to tweak
    with vain and vengeful appetites.

vii

O yes, Lust, you were young once
    ... once and forever.

viii

You were heartless flight not seeking what you chase.
You fed on countless hungers
  ... and fled the bountiful harvest of her face.
You grew toward one truth and found another.

ix

You did not sleep but awoke — two solitary others

... alone, ungraspable and everlasting,
Gauntly groping with one unabandoned caress,
  ... one unrepentant slash
    ... in the tangled continuum of time.

x

And with each failed touch, you reached higher than knowing.
Thought on tumbling thought was out of season.
And you crumbled ... fumbled ... stumbled
     .... upon diagonal proofs of unreason:
  ... that your line of fate's far denser than imagined.

xi

Succumbing never to sanity, meaning or measure,
Escorting joy with paramount conviction,
You coupled with the cut of unkindness that is love.

xii

Not habit, not instinct, not addiction:
Love is lost to its own eternity.

IV. AGAINST ALL ODDS

i

Titans clashed,
    gods created,
      atoms smashed,
        and giants mated.

ii

Thus resumes your trek to the promised land.
Surviving, you'll triumph
        against all odds
            in desperate battles.

iii

You were welcomed:
  ... a guest in hell.

You braved wilderness.
You were iliad in foreign climes.
You were odyssey returning home,
Shirking unfit destinies of rhymes.
You faced famine, fire and flood
 ... all the mire and miseries of human blood.
You endured the apocalypse
  ... of alien conquest and its vengeance.
You were jaded, then inspired
  ... by necessity's shrewd contingence.
You winced and moaned as he raised the knife.
You found sustenance in the branch of life.

iv

You quenched your thirst in its river.
You enjoyed hidden gifts without a giver.
You reaped secrets from the other shore.
You despised what saints alone adore.
You trampled garlands.
You restored withered land.
You polished philosopher stones.
You exhaled vague prayers.
You muttered incantations.
You sought out mystic formulae.
You worshipped a great and giving goddess.
You were seer with sight bestowed on the worthy.
You were holy man, shaman, sly magician.
You achieved absolution without contrition.

v

You retched and reviled the eunuch's scorn.
You were trickster enticing the unicorn.
You were weak and wan, lax and lame.
Yes. You gilded the mediocre with your fame.
You ravished vessels of sacred strength.
You unfolded the gnarled and naked length
         ... of your own cruel shame.
You sacrificed what you loved.
You loved what you sacrificed.
You were one and legion ... without a name.

You were clown, jester, fool.
You were exceptions
   ... refuting every rule.

vi

You accosted serpents,
   dabbled with demons,
     grappled with gorgons,
       dallied with dragons,
         vanquished vampires.
You trafficked with troglodytes.
You unsettled every order,
   liberated every passion.

vii

You smelled boundary,
      nook,
        prison,
          blindness
             ... in every goal.
You chased after every uncatchable cone of light
That could not be grasped
   ... but left behind its own bewitchment.
You confused mind with matter,
       clue with criminal.
Your every would-be hope soon waxed subliminal.
You were the paragon of competition.
You were paralyzed by repetition.
You were time controlling time
  with vaunted myth
    and misbegotten rhyme.

viii

But shall anyone forget to ask
    ... the proper setting
        ... for the latest task?
As if you could leapfrog
   ... twisted ladders of learning,
Or discover hidden variables in equations unbalanced

... save for naked infinities they fail to mask.

ix

You were treadmill, turnspit, style.
You were algorithm sans gall or guile.
Yet you'll imitate, circumscribe, intensify
Inane raptures beneath a blue October sky.
What was it ... then ... setting off
    that tinderbox lightning
        of your happiness?
Those flint-jarring sparks of risk
    that teased the darkness into song?
And ruptured cheerless solipsism with astonished cries?
Yes. All that's left
    to tell forbidden rites what's wrong
        ... was the eternity of her smiling eyes.
Or maybe: You've been there. Done that.
You'll hum what you become. Or become what you hum.
Or, then again: Perhaps you'll rake dung
    ... and like it no less than music-making
        or making love.

x

Yet you've no chance to pass or pause
Over absence of assignable cause,
Or even think for once how odd
Should be the pseudonym of God
When he disdains all signature.

xi

In deepest wells of silence
You heard the quiet thunder.
As if nothing could last but joy
 ... or the cherished intimacy
  ... of a shared blunder.

xii

Yes. The night is large,
And you're too small

To add the sum
 ... of all in all.
Thus, you fall,
  ... kneel,
    ... arise,
      ... and arrive again
From eternity — where you've almost always been.
You were darkest blotches on Eternity's brightest day.
Yes. You are what you are because you got that way.

V. ONE UNSPINDLED THREAD

The clue of one unspindled thread,
Entangling every dwarf's advance,
Unravels, thrills, all homeward dread,
As your steps stuttering in a trance,
Explore the false escapes of sorrow.

Let stranger lewdnesses befriend
The ancient honor guard of sin.
Upend Adam, then re-begin
Circular labyrinths of dead ends.

Let inhumans choose a human self.
Let ogres gnarled within knot you.
Let the riddled code be twiddled.
Let them lubricate the rusted screw.

Give all you have and then be done.
Give up the magic circle's frill.
Give up the cheapest trophies won.
Give up each fillip as you will.

Make every broken arc a center.
Render right unto caesar's flaw.
Let the plank of reason splinter.
Then rend asunder every law.

Yes. Beginning and end will rhyme
As long as ceaseless echoes vie
To wring a destiny out of time

Or snag tomorrow in their lie.

First, middle, last: the die is cast.
Its cutting gilt has lost its edge.
Your faultless future breeds the past,
As sly as a fox who hogs the hedge.

All you've felt is understated:
Unto the greatest kneels the least
Of nobler sums uncogitated
Whose next betrayal kills the beast.

Medusa tree, with head and heel:
In root and branch, beginnings end.
You're less, you're more than you can kill.
You'll rise as far as you descend.

In lethal hearts of every maze,
You must heartlessly re-enact
Another ritual to praise
Miracles sleeping in each fact.

In loneliness you'll reinvent,
In each forbidden forest snare,
As if you meant to represent
The lure of rainbows never there.

Beseechers: be ye rare as beauty.
Weave and plough and sow between
The endless columns of your duty
Your private myth and public dream.

The sacred wound is still unhealed.
But once again before you're through,
You'll pause again to see revealed
The mystery vanishing that's you.

VI. IMAGINE THERE'S SOMETHING

A bat, a bear, and a bumblebee:
Imagine there's something it's like to be.
But perhaps that's not quite fair,
For indeed you know what it's like to bear
I.E. ...
  ... your inability to be
        ... a bumblebee.

VII. OBLIVION'S OBLIGATIONS

Can you save yourself from shriveling hours
  ... from the ruffle of prayers you never offer
      ... from the unanimous mud of fame?
Yes. You endorse unofficial views of being,
But suspicion slits poetry's throat.
For every style is casket and confession
  ... concave fantasy or convex horror
   ... as if you could understand
    ... that terrible leisure of God
     ... in an uncreated world.
Beyond spheres of waning influence,
Below bubbles of causes and effects,
     ... beckon tides of prophecy
      ... the flow of escape
       ... and the ebb of resignation.
Or perhaps you'll forfeit
     that last
       vast
        vain ambition
         ... your thirst to disappear.
Recovering, you'll fall back on scholar's tricks:
 ... the stock of cant,
    deepened by ravelling histories of cliche,
 ... the shock of antiquity,
    threatening more than now or tomorrow
  for you can't help forgetting
      what you failed to borrow

from the past.
Yes. Strange familiarity is her theme,
Much more than diversities you esteem.
In the wake of oblivion's obligations,
You abscond with unlost glimmers of insight,
Blasted in the radiance of her wise despair,
That blessed state of innocence that only the guilty know.

VIII. RAGE OF MOURNING

Arriving where you were
  ... no past at your back,
You'll remember the future
  ... and
Follow with faith
  ... that paths lead somewhere.
Across exhausted twilights ...
Out of unholy silences ...
To waltz with dawn,
You'll walk on words
  ... that only defile
    ... the crippled joy of living.
Beatific buddha ... or grimacing savior?
Yes ... even on your very best behavior
You were never quite so tender
  ... as the blindfolded splendor
    of her beauty.
From the East ... light, from the West
    ... the fruit of your unmaking.
Go wash yourself in waters of home,
In the unprejudiced rage of mourning,
For beauty is your only promise of happiness.
Yes. Beauty ... is only a promise of happiness.

IX. TO BITTER TYRANNIES (FOR MONSIEUR NO.6)

Precarious cavities widen within you,
Uncompassed scopes on the brink of bursting.
But ... you've always really wanted to be a fascist
  ... to arrive already

    where you will be
        before you've started,
 ... to succumb to bitter tyrannies of the everyday,
 ... to get stuck like a stamp on the great state of being,
 ... to screw yourself to the organless body of eternity.
Yes. You'll always play the despot
    ... when you're too stiff to bend toward virtue.

X. BEYOND THE PEEPHOLE

i

Groans, though forced, and notes too few
Grew more than ample enough to screw
One small true fact of kindness
To unkillable hearts of cruelty.
Desiring machine, string-pulled but jaded,
Intensely, you fed, fled, fought and mated.
Yet you traveled too fast to catch yourself,
Too fast to fetch light out of smoke
   ... or roses out of dunghills.
Unasylumed, unarchived, and unattended,
You were the way's end before it ended,
Until it led everywhere,
        somewhere and
            now here,
Where crowfeet eked out smiles on cosmic snow
To unlimber yourself
   ... and your letters of living purpose,
To become a minutely chiseled destiny you cannot love.
As if there were gleaming, but no gladness, in miniatures,
As if the little man within each little man
Mattered less than universal history's span
              ... of cluttered moments.
So in your slump, you bump
Along muffled edges of ineffable chaos,
Nesting between cause and effect,
   ... between source and sink,
Between oblivion's ersatz obligations
And the last temptation to think
Yourself ... the sum of your exhausted passions.

ii

In the excluded middle of yourself and your love
You saw two puppets dallying in transition
    ... toward another truant disposition.
Yes. Every moment passes before it arrives.
But somewhere betwixt grunt and treatise,
   ... you conjured connections,
    ... your idol maker's homage
      ... to uncuttable Adams who now must bleed
        ... the pale blue fog of exhaustion.

iii

Yes. Burning fag to ashes clings
  ... to wanton magnets of broken rings.
Turn slowly with disordered cadence
  ... admire the tune that chaos sings.
Through humanity's wispy filigree
At last some gleams of light have come
To spurn your species-mortal hum
  ... of madness and mutability.

iv

Perhaps you'll cherish the specious presents
Of heedless hedgerows and hunted pheasants
Where weary wayfarers at last confessed
Their itch for a niche and a feathered nest.
But the cost of comfort is extinction,
And doom ... *darker than any sea dingle,*
Could not suppress the latest jingle,
The eyeless poetry of lukewarm vice
And next door virtues kept on ice.

v

Nothing that lasts could prove more wrong
Than belief in the beauty of an unheard song.
So ... long, loud, and hard you cried
For the upright candle of the simplified.
You reached for the near too little and the far too much,

As if to capture the free white spree ... of infinity
Between where she was and what you feigned to touch.
But you could not flatter the infinite with additions
Nor embarrass it with depletions.
For infinity minus one equals infinity:
One infinity/one song ... one measureless gift
In the endless rift and broken rhythm of time.

vi

No nearness of embrace is ever close enough:
An ambiguous kiss ...
    that's still too far to hold forever.
Always and already, you're just one blink
Beyond being yourself,
    beyond giving, receiving, or deceiving
A gift that no longer keeps accounts.

vii

Home hails from the cloud of possible worlds
As lost, as final, as precipitous
As one locationless ruin
In the continuum of eternal desire:
In the memory of a rose,
    ... no gardener ever died.
In the recollection of a tear,
    ... no widow ever cried.
Broken puppet eyes collapse inside
Windowless monads that cannot hide
For islands cling to a reef that suffers.
Languishing lust can't quite erase
That forlorn ungraspable trace
Where ashes of the hearth foretell
Temples made of your homely cell.

viii

Is it sinister or tongue-in-cheek?
Perhaps again you'll take a peek.
But beyond the peephole, the scandal's already occurred.
For history's periodic table of perdition

Awaits with boredom the extradition ... of present tense.
Depressing keyboards of imagination,
The music meanders still unabated,
And upon dark registers inscribes
Orphaned totems of your lost tribes.

ix

The opening line: Who's there?
Creeps from the cradle of causeless care.
And the eyeball behind the lens
Harbors a multitude of sins.
But upon each traveling now
   ... you stand to unfold yourself,
To read the cryptic book that bars your better wisdoms,
Or in good faith deride
   ... the fruitful river in the eye that forms a heart.

x

Crippling the candlelight fantastic,
You trip over sorrows of love unshared,
The guilty knowledge of notes compared,
In the dead reckoning, that common cul-de-sac
    ... where all ways meet in habit.
Everywhere you're dead except one twirling spot
In the crowded ballroom where the curling knot
Of fraudulent sleep must keep on knitting
Survivals of fates it's found most fitting.

xi

But eternity brooks no fierce routines
   ... only isolated instants of transformation.
As if you could resolve the philosopher's dilemma:
   ... to live somewhere with the memory of nowhere.
As if eternity could never recall what's vanished
   and past, present, and future vie
    to catch the twinkling of an eye.

xii

Yes. You lost your way

     when you began to keep records.
But beware my eyeless puppets
     into what glad truth you've fallen.

XI. MUTATIS MUTANDIS

i

Departing early,
Arriving late,
You drifted,
   sifted,
    shifted
  ... through the difference engine ... change,
  ... through icy Eden and mean estate,
   ... through the out-of-kilter jilter of your freight,
    ... through every stop the fates arrange.

ii

But shall you forget the night is large:
  ... when daybreak brings
    ... birdsong
      ... bursting the shell of your solitude?
As if only the exuberant Sphinx of her music
Could violate the virginity of each repeated act,
Or gloat with gleeful disenchantment.

iii

Yes. You sought consolation in music, rituals, categories.
Yet wherever you passed or paused
  ... you always stopped short of arriving somewhere.
Trapped between the flower too blue
        ... and the tree gone green.
Between the wearisome clarity of old men
  ... and the beautiful blindness of children.
Between the lazy yawning drone of eons
  ... and the still longer lethargy of one moment.
Between the shore you're after
  ... and the wreck you left behind.
Between specialists of the last gasp

... and connoisseurs of the first sigh.
As if you could rip with rage
    each friend of a lonesome cry,
Or hear the howling wound
    ... of a want that can't be sated.

iv

Swept in eddies of aftereffects and premonitions,
You dangle where you've already swung before,
Where returning's as tedious as going o'er,
Where life's an infinitesimal moment
                ... between two eternities,
And everything you say has already been said
By those who didn't know what they were saying.

v

Are you ache
 ... or ecstasy
 ... or orgasm,
  ... punctuating the fierce routine
   ... and slashing the arteries of cognition?
A remnant always returns.
And what returns is the permanent possibility of sensation:
 ... the ethereal reins of time's attempt to harness eternity.
Your thought, affection, and ruling care
Are machines for noticing what isn't there.
Your eyes, your algebras of substitution,
Snub with a refugee's cruellest spite
All appetites for whetting and forgetting:
The darkest pupil absorbs the greatest light.
Yes. You're on the edge of something
   ... still bound by borders leaped across.
Nowhere or now here?
But if you can't discern the boundary,
Then how do you know the difference?

vi

Quickly, here, now, always, you forget
How the stubborn child of language

Grows rebellious toward revelation,
As if panic were the horror of everything
You cannot hope to master.
Yet faster ... faster ... faster,
You kept twirling toward oblivion.
For you were as mutable
As the energy of your own motion.
Yes. Your memories fade and flee,
As your vibrations cease to be.
Yet still you'll succumb to the wizard breath of fashion,
For every symptom's the shopworn seed of an old solution,
Sprinkled with instructions for deeper, ruddier wrinkles.
How many emotions were etched in jade,
Before you lost the memory of being made?
Thus, you fled history at the edge of nature,
   ... and nature on the fringe of history.

vii

Yes. Something must have happened around 1910,
When you sloughed off the taint of sin.
No more errant notes or stray digits
Could be shoehorned into syllogisms:
  ... no more I love you's,
  ... no more I owe you's,
  ... no more I do unto you's,
Only the ill-fare way of waiting
For what cannot fail to come,
Where mind must buckle and bow to the nature of things.
As if what is knowable could be as pungent as pigeon droppings
    ... or subtle ... as a raging scream of invisible light.

viii

She was the rose, the nightingale, the sun in its radiance.
But can you still remember her broken virtue?
Gifts without givers are naked as names without meaning:
Long before her tabula rasa began teeming with intent,
You encountered the cruel principle of her virginity
              ... and you loved her just the same.
But what you loved was never exempt from your rigors,
For always you dissolved into the vanishing of what you wanted,

Into another hollowness your emptiness might fill.

ix

Nicodemus ... then calculemus your petty sins:
You were delivered not into this world,
But out of its unfinished struggle to emerge whole.
You sought true but unproveable rules:
　... the box circle, you know exists, but that can't be opened.
You wanted to give what can't be given.
You wanted to get what can't be gotten.
You rejected mistaken identities of love.
You sought an infinity of worthless women.
You shuddered, stuttered, and muttered
　... over paternal names unuttered.
But ageless sybils in her eyes
　　... with more or less acuity
　　... now fold the tent of ambiguity,
As if the core of every maze
　... is a gateway to another labyrinth,
As if you could find the key to every deadlock
　... in the carnal envelope of unremitting desire.

x

You'll tour the sky and underworlds
Where eternity's wayward tail still curls
　　... its crooked path with rhyme ...
Through the grooves where Chronos cut
　　... your destiny drawn in every rut:
... the cries of toads beneath the harrow,
... the death of the deadlier degree you call tomorrow,
... the ego made palpable in the palm of time,
... the thumb rump of manipulation,
... the index of insidious accusation,
... the ring of ritual bliss,
... the middle gesticulator of insult,
... the permanent knowledge of mutilation,
... the open fist of unheld secrets,
... the sterile fantasy and the flowering axioms of grasping,
Or the linear labyrinth of the one and only list
　　... of everything that's gone unnoticed.

xi

You'll know pathways of wind and moons of later birth.
You'll share the common stock of temptations,
The mourning irony of unmelting snowmen.
Yes. You too have always been
   but a few decimal points away from annihilation.
Thus: Can anyone say what happens to the snow?
"Man, if you gotta ask, you're never gonna know."
Each grief of ice confounds your unexpected terror,
For every image is the frigid trace of abstracted error.
Yes. All your buzzing confusion yearns for an imagined simplicity:
Such is the will to grasp what can only be beheld in wonder.
Are you anything different from the love which fills your heart?

xii

Thus, into the old world — suddenly young — you came,
Where you arise again — transformed — the same.
No. Nothing changes but time and location,
And your only lasting vocation is ... eternity.

XII. FORGET THE NOTES

Nothing raw or cooked
  ... can heal the wound with nine openings.
Thus go deep deep deep
  ... deep enough to sink into your own flaws.
But you cannot shake off sacrifice
As if you could assume
     ... the unimprovable karma of a god.
Thus, play with confidence:
Forget the notes you missed,
For something else you've played quite perfectly.

— EIGHT —
HUSK OF LOYALTIES

i

Like a snail, you carry on your back
The husk of loyalties you live in.
For your burden is the ruler of its own expanse,
And each inch you crawl is a ratcheting toward destiny.
But can you abide those trails you did not follow?

ii

The spiritual labyrinth of your body
Embrangles roads of experience
     ... into a thousand twisted tributaries,
And most of them cannot bear
The nightmare of this discovery.
No. You were never guilty,
   ... only repressed,
    ... obsessed,
     ... possessed,
      ... or unconfessed.

iii

You were another Adam
   bewildered in his garden
     by an abundant absence he could not name.
But you were bred to expect the best.
So you heard this pernicious fable and believed it.
Yet you stumbled when you saw the worst
   ... on wings of cruelty you could not fathom
                           ... but condemned.

iv

After tumbling towers of pride and ignorance
Defame the bleeding edge of counterfeit compassion,
Shall you still plumb with patience the viciousness
Of someone else's vain misunderstanding?
According to the law of large numbers,
There's something statistical and sophistical
           ... in every breath and death.
But are you calculation or experiment?

Yes. Love was always calculation
        ... and pain: experiment.
Chance and necessity combined
But left your motive undefined.

v

If truth is merely a coin that's tossed,
Shall you, as those in their wickedness, then waltz
To the cockeyed splendor of the false?
Yes. Every vice communes with sinners of darkness
   ... invisible vampires whose only power
     ... is the grip of remembered agony and transgression.

vi

Theirs is an undying grief of murderous dreads
        that again and again retreads
      the lowest rut in being's register.
Not even the best can redeem
    one iscariot of betrayal,
    one trigger of dismay,
Nor in their deepest grief
   ... relieve the toxin of harsh emotion
   ... in the belly where anger bleeds its poison.

vii

Yet you lack the grace
   ... to embrace the greater horror
   ... the shock and shudder of that moment ... that it could seem:
     this premeditated disaster is the fulfillment of another's dream
     ... of a universal and anonymous crime
   that will survive, even thrive, on the death of its author,
   that in his sleep of fame,
   this author will persist as the cause of an endless disturbance.

viii

You desperately try to bury your fear
    with hatred, revenge, even grief,

your fear that assassins will hover by your side,
like an ungentle torture for all eternity
... as perpetual ghosts of what you might have been
but with ... infinite mercy ... failed to become.

ix

Essential lapse ... essential need,
All must hinge on the thinnest reed
        ... of your integrity.
Yes. Your ability to be
        ... is the courage to say *no*.

x

Inch by inch, the carapace of justification grows,
But each new reason is another cryptic deposit
In the tangled bank of indeterminate life.
Yet how close you cling to delusions of the simple,
As if you could lead a life without entanglements,
As if you could strangle the strangler sin
And without reservation of past or future
Begin ... and ... begin ... and ... begin ...
        ... again
In the virginity of your immaculate present,
As if each moment were an egg about to hatch itself
Into the eternal novelty of a new world ... a new earth.
But all clarity is cast before the shadow's storyteller
Who re-tells the simple tale of how everything innocent
Gets lost in the nest of complexity.

xi

Along every corkscrew trail are shocks
That evolution coils with paradox.
Such are the passageways through eternity.
The right path is plain but impalpable.
It is you – and you alone – who are complicated.

xii

In all that you reject,
You'll meet yourself,

   as always,
Returning from where
   you haven't yet arrived.
For eternity, the stamp on every other
    ... is the mark of Cain on every brother.
Is this the sacrifice you make,
              for getting and for giving?
Simplicity, like innocence, is a dream:
The temptation to exist
  means everything you bear
               is borne guilty.
Complications are the dues you pay for living.

— NINE —
ELIMINATING THE MIDDLEMAN
— PART ONE —
THE HEART'S RESIDUUM

I. WARM SNOW

i

You sat stumped on Solomon's porch,
While frogs of fraudulence kept on croaking
   ... endlessly belaboring the belatedness of being.

ii

Was it *warmth, or was it snow?*
Had you forgotten what you know:
How ethics and beauty rhyme?
How only an act creates a fact?
That embodied joy is not a toy?
That descriptions, your fecund jewelers,
     are never prescriptions for truth?
How every face is a pathless tract
   ... of unredeeming rime at melting time?

iii

Was it language that you loved,
Or was it the belittled you
Within the larger eye
   ... of each occasion's baffled cry?

iv

Could it be ...
    you were happy without noticing it?
Even so, it might've been nice
   ... to peruse your map of paradise.
As if you – *lived* – or – *left* – us much,
But somehow you never learned to touch
Anyone ... or anything ... in any way?

v

Your mind, a many-slippered thing,
With pheasant chase or philosophic ruse,
Stalks metaphysical news in ruby shoes.
You lack astonishment at corruptions of flesh,

As if sin were hand-me-down Hebrew lore
That only redneck prigs deplore.
But after you've studied the nostalgias,
You hanker for juicy fruits of the physical world.
Yet no imagined pearl of any price
Could trump the virtues of your vice.

vi

Imitations, you despise, arise,
Feinting with damn praise,
 ...alas ... the sacrilegious rite,
For those flattering you with envy
Or sanctioning you with spite.

vii

Your trussed-up facts were fiction,
Manufactured by elegant diction.
Forsaking unkempt shrewdnesses of the crow,
Beautiful Babylons, you build ... innocent as snow.
Is that how you hid from hideous sepulchers
   ... of gospels you couldn't guzzle or muzzle?
            ... or garnish inside your puzzle?

viii

There were prophetic murmurings,
Sudden but averted senses of the serpent,
Embedded with eccentric axletree
         ... in mud and metaphor.
Yet you couldn't even say "Tough Shit"
      ... to a still more dishonored Eloquence.
And – *duty* – that most unpoetic word
        ... was less digestible than a turd.

ix

Ignore the orphan slaughter in the street.
But if metaphor murders metaphor, then you bleat.
Is this what made your poetry so complete ...
The coldest comfort food one could eat,
The poetry of the obese, the elite and the effete?

x

The Sunday game ... to you ... was lost
To ersatz entertainments and their cost.
But fantasy's spindle can never dwindle.
For the diurnal dump is full of images,
Your chronicles of winning scrimmages
                           ... with fact.
Reality could not shuffle a brighter deck of cards,
Or match your metaphysical chat with canasta and canards.

xi

There was once a buzz in the Land of Uz:
Only learning how difficult it is to be
Can enflesh the skeleton's filigree.
But whatever's real is no less strange
    ... than the will you wrote but cannot change.
Repeating farewells, you flicker with fears
        ... of continuity and conscience,
As if change ... changing enough,
Makes one ready ... and one rough
    ... sketch of your eternity.

xii

Mere being could not trim Ulysses' sail,
As one who did and died in Connecticut,
An overblown child ... almost awake at his own death.
No. The pineapple was never enough:
In prating peacock climates of your mind
Dangles the tufted, green and emerald rind
Of the heart's residuum ...
    ... your would-be, never warm, forever showy snowiness.
And yet nothingness was never more real
               ... than your unreeling self.

II. ALL OR NOTHING

i

Once upon an eternity, nothing

Morphed into all, and all into nothing.
Dawn's earliest light always comes later
Than expected, for everything's surprised
At what sheer nothingness has rejected.
If a life is an event in the life
Of another life, no life is explained
Till the end of an infinite series
... is reached. Thus no life is explainable.
Greening between grimaces of extremes
Teems life's burgeoning tangle of meaning.
But once again the muddled Middleman
Shall span this abyss with a kiss of bliss.

ii

You were most like what you studied and how
You studied it—a notorious
Accumulator of irritating fact,
An uneasy stalemate deciding which
Grain in the balance should fail or prosper.
Obeying your persistent impulses,
Betraying roots of one ancestral chain,
Your life was one long, ruthless argument.
Yes. You called hot chaos to order ... cold,
Bleaching savage minds with your cruelest stain.
You taught old dogmas new tricks, for no one
Sailed more shrewdly in streams of living change,
Yet streams, if they flow, must hug their shoulders,
And shoulders they hug, they cannot behold.

iii

Amiably, you were stranger to yourself
Than your exotic species. Well-heeled heir,
Obsessive accountant, a capitalist
Always sly and—yes—somewhat shy, you had
A special talent for business. You had
That middling modicum of selfishness,
Neither too much nor too little. You shared
Vanities of your race and class, petty
Despair at the sure genius of others,
Peevish obsessions over slight affronts.

You sidestepped funerals for father
And beloved mentors, using your illness,
Or your lack of it, to dodge the dullest
Rites of your then newfangled profession.

iv

Unlike keen breeders, you leaped for middles,
Forsaking their extremes for the middling
Increments of the little-by-little.
A good father, tender husband, you were
An eclectically generous man.
In person, career, and thought, you became
Our last original champion of
Family values. Indeed, your lawn was
A veritable paradise of worms
And your laws parables ... spermatic germs
Crowded with invisible characters.
You were yourself a master wriggler,
A jiggler justly praised and reappraised,
Amid the din of celebrated men.

v

Famously traveled, you became quite staid,
A clockwork stay-at-home machine guzzling
Fact and grinding out law in the upside
Down house of your lowered expectations.
Darwin, did you ever see a grampus?
Baba abbadubba? ... Pup and Papa
Fuse like fossilized polyps into reefs
That cannot cop a plea for paternity.
You too were the rudiments you retained
And reversions to which you're liable.
Yet stemming the tide of eternity,
You saw how permanence is pliable,
How fitfulness in fortune's portendings
Annuls longed-for laws of happy endings.

vi

An arena for acrobats of death,
Life quickly outstrips its own provisions.

Life's law giver, you gave us the law of
Living change: first multiply, then vary,
Let live the strongest, let the weakest die.
Life's cunning carnival yields errant type,
Luck's fitting misfits of fruitful errors,
That cleave unripe to your tree of knowledge.
Hapless, happy letters of mutation,
An uncrossed T, or an undotted I,
Tell just-so stories of who lives and why.
For you, survival was always success,
But success is a very special case
Of the broader category ... mistake.

vii

Offshoot of an Old World simian stem,
Your differences ... so small ... become large
With the lapse of ages, and you ... prophet
Of the rare and endlessly new ... learn how
To interpret the turning of a screw:
Hand of man, wing of bat, leg of horse, fin
Of porpoise are the corpus of kinship
Bred in the bone, a little more than kin,
A little less than kind, indelibly
Sure-fire stamps of a lowly origin.
Creeping disbelief caused you little grief,
For your urge to diverge could not relent
Or repent ... blind human nature's long and
Sinuous meanderings of descent.

viii

Nothing ... anything ... something ... everything:
Each individual is the history
        ... of its eternity's paternity.
Amid shoulders of fatherless extremes,
The muddled middleman repeats his dreams.
But the donkey said, "Let us bray" before
The coming empire of science, or pray:
The wisest god makes all things make themselves.
Never reaching the condition of true
        identity ... equals non-entity:

Nothingness is the last great magician;
Species are characters in transition.
Naturally, you no longer mind that nature
Never quite creates a natural kind.

ix

Rarity, that precursor to extinction,
Ends the next beginning of distinction.
Drawing down the blinds on natural kinds,
Each species is its genealogy:
Not immutable, but refutable,
All species are varieties making
Or forsaking what's numb, or null or full
Of sudden promise, specious origins
Of new life's betters ... fiercely begetting,
But not forgetting death's dull residuum.
With promises keepable or unkept,
Little by little, life becomes adept ...
At preserving its most divergent offspring.

x

You would not succumb to the forbearance
Of forebears nor propagate illusion.
Your deepest thought is life aborning life.
Your evidence is death suborning death.
Health in your world is its wealth of error,
Assuaging the terror of unmeaning
Whenever lungs of yearning catch their breath.
Far more than snake philosophy could bear,
Your theory melts the ice box of cold truths,
Dissolving all ideals that can't contain it.
Life peoples life with nostalgic desire,
Rehearsing mistakes that can't explain it.
Sex answers sex ... and ecstasy connects
The nothing that was ... and the something that is.

xi

Yes. Soon they'll say of you: names name you not.
Fixity in taxonomies of life

Falsifies a life too quick and narrow
To grasp your origin and destiny.
Your unreturning past lasts just long enough
To creep repeatedly toward novelty.
Reproductions reproduce your griefs ... as
Cheated egoisms produce beliefs,
Malign and hopeful monsters of design.
M ... you said ... in *AM* means *I*. *I AM* thus
Retains a useless rudiment more strange than
Steps you cannot see, but deduce ... as change.
Eternity—a gift no one can give—is ...
Simply the thing you are that makes you live.

xii

"If we choose to let conjecture run wild ...
We may be all melted together." But
If all is one nothing makes a difference.
Heartsease and red clover hinge on habits
Of bumblebee. Such is eternity's
Green logic of humming and becoming.
Flower modifies bee, and bee ... flower.
Both are entangled in the power of grace.
Their necessity is the bliss they kiss.
Eternal biography then foretells
Your riddle of the unexcluded middle.
Yes. Eliminating the Middleman
Takes more than luck, even more than one last
Tedious funeral you could not duck.

III. PLAYING HARDBALL

i

You were born old, Isaac, a childless man,
Soon playing hardball with the universe.
You stood on Nemo's shoulders, on boulders
Of extremes, between the larger than large
And a little so little it's next of
Kin to nothing. Beginning at both ends,
You worked toward the middle as if to snatch
The riddle from the magisterium

Of chaos. You brought number to nature.
You squared the crooked lines that could be squared.
You tallied the ebb and flow of tides.
Born posthumously, obeying your law,
With little laughter and less affection,
You kept moving in the same direction.

ii

Between the unique and ubiquitous
Flickers the iniquitous pattern of
All impatience and the filigree of
All misunderstanding that are one and
The same. Your God could never be never
And nowhere. *Every soul that perceives*
...is, still, throughout its occasions, the same
Indivisible person. Every man,
Yes, every thing of perception, is one
And the same during his whole life and in
All and in each of his organs of sense.
You refused last rites, you left no will, but
Only a testament that cannot teach
Occult motions to a ripening peach.

iii

Always, everywhere, your God was all eye,
All ear, all brain, all arm, all force, all sense
Of understanding's action. You wanted
To see what the oldest saw, alabaster
Calculi, whereon names are written that
No one knows, save those who are witness to
Their own cause. God did with you what he could
Do with no other. You revised old saws,
Grinding them to eloquent novelties
Of universal laws, into organs
Of extreme perfection, of one in awe.
Fanaticism found its avatar.
They say they doubt you ever saw the sea,
Yet the sea is the oldest saw of all.

IV. ON HIPPO'S CAMPUS

i

Before Yahweh, there was your way ... and O
How you burned and yearned and churned for your way.
Yes. Yahweh became your way, but only
After you seized upon the ritual
Of comparing spiritual with spiritual.
Self-justification was your lodestar,
Your boundless compass on Hippo's campus.
There, you scoured extremes before they melted
Into nostalgias. You found new places
In the heart. The way was with you, but you
Were not with the way. The will was with you,
But, no, you were not with the will ... until ...
You found that place ... eternity ... must fill,
Where life cannot die and time does not kill.

ii

You wandered lonely as a crowd of selves.
Gregarious, you forged now's solitude,
As if past and future could not intrude.
You murmured confessions of obsessions
You could not conquer without denial.
You sought freedom first in solemn rites of
Gnostic bliss, as if – optimistically –
You could follow promptings of one true self,
As if sacred routine alone distilled
Ruined fragments of the luminous kingdom.
You sought to mimic mangled liberty.
When they said "Let's go, Let's do it." You were
Ashamed not to be shameless. So you went,
You did. In shadows of your sin, you hid.

iii

Your life was the thirst of one long trial.
You drank down savageries of the circus.
Slouching across your stretch of soil and salt,
You found nothing could elate or appall.

You rummaged in vain for a new gestalt.
You guided yourself to your own downfall.
Thus, you battled boredom in the caldron
Of Carthage. Are you ... your body? Are you ...
Your time? You became questions you could not
Hope to answer. You comforted yourself
With riddles. You sold the skill of speech.
Your thought grew numb to flesh, flesh blind to thought.
You lost the thrill to teach ... when that broken
Confidence ... *philosophy* ...came to naught.

iv

Before you dared to soar on eagle's wings,
You learned how guile gutted wisdom with the
Force of a few ... but sad and certain things:
That the way of a man is not his own,
That one and all, we come from the same lump,
That cauliflower ... cloven ... in the skull,
Where images bodying forth can trump
The truth of your promises ... full or null.
Before the luxury of inner light
Comes the blight of nothing ... nothing but the
Flux, the whole flux, and nothing but the flux
That flutters ... before ... an eternity
You could not taste. But with untimely haste,
You could not abandon the truth you faced.

v

Down darkest roots of your remembering,
You searched that unsearchable sea monster.
Backtracking beyond the archaic toward
That time before your living time began,
You learned to revile the vile inventions
Of your midden mind, those reeking clues
Of an objective, fat, and obvious world.
Beauty, for you, was once both fair and fit
Before your direst wit saw how error
Takes longer to correct than to commit.
You lived before the clocks began to click
As if caterpillars inching their way –

Before the stain of any sin could stick –
Might grow – from crowd's cocoon – to Cicero.

vi

Heart is the time of place, but place is not
Its body. Time is the heart of body,
But body is not its place. Body is
The place of heart, but heart is not its time.
Place is the body of time, but time is
Not its heart. Yet shutters of the heart will
Open to anyone who heeds the knocks,
Who's elected and reads the face of grace
And yearns to shadowbox with paradox.
As doubter doubting, you betrayed your doubt.
You believed ... to know, you knew ... to believe.
You whispered prayers as if to shout
How time wears eternity on its sleeve,
Nakedly within ... brazenly without.

vii

Mere mind commanded mind, but disobeyed.
But whence this monstrousness, and to what end?
Yes, this was the pattern of how you sinned.
So much you did when to will was not by
Itself to be able ... Or ... "No ... not yet."
You were appetites you could not forget.
You were alembic to the limbic mind,
But could not quite melt into what you felt.
You neither died to death nor lived to life.
You knew how to abase ... and to abound.
But always ... found ... hollowness through and through.
You could not love what you endured, but still
Loved to endure. You loved to discover
Truth, but balked when the truth discovered you.

viii

Remembrance rankled without revival
Of farewells earlier than arrival.
There is a life beyond your life, a psalm
Beyond that impalpable palm of

Memory, a placeless chapel, a time
That's no time, a when without boundaries,
A place that is no place, neither before
Nor after. You believed to understand
As the blind man's stick tries to see what it
Taps and touches. You learned to walk on the
Crutches of uncommon sense: Whoever
Cannot read is oppressed by the logic
Of experience. To read is to hear
The inaudible voice of another.

ix

You chased yourself as far as you could go
Till nothing could prove you're more than nothing.
Always conscience heard a "No, not yet" in
Your backward transmigrations of regret.
It took too long and it went too quickly,
But the unction of compunction was as
Prickly as pears you filched and threw to swine.
A son of such tears, they said, could not be
Lost. So, at last, you sought to pay the cost.
But – no – you could not help yourself at all,
Because all you said was accusation.
Out of the abyss of judgment, one depth
Called to another: from the emptiness
Of here ... and now ... to the fullness of there.

x

Thus, you became indentured to elsewhere,
A place that's neither here ... nor is it there.
You were not there ... before you were ... so as
To make yourself ... willingly warm ... to wisdom.
Images after images accrue
The angry plenitude of being you.
Out of the same lump, all grow to honor
Or dishonor ... toward despair's damnation.
Out of the same school, all must slowly learn
The humble remorselessness of a fool.
You called no one happy, until wanting
What one has, one has what one wants, and all

One has is good. Love ... then do ... what you will,
And ... all you are ... then yearns for what you should.

xi

You remembered how forgetfulness signs
Its imageless name in memory, as
If eternity were made visible,
As if your own life were not part and
Parcel of presents past and of presents
Future. You could not touch the body of
Your happiness, for happiness is not
A body. You could not touch or taste your
Joy. Yet you remembered a joy that was
No *where and no when*. A placeless, timeless,
Bodiless joy. As unforgettably,
Egregiously immortal as mortal sin.
Yes. There's a spirit ... spirit knows not of ...
The spirit that answers with what you love.

xii

Between nostalgia and nightmare is the
Paradise of amnesia. There are no
Shadows in paradise ... only lyric
Lacerations and the lacy essence
Of eternity. No. You could not change
Yourself, you changed ... unto eternity.
Forgetting all you could not love or own,
You fed on the food of a man full grown.
To exult in the cult of loneliness
Defies the other side of solitude,
For gravity is the force that makes us
All crave company ... or that makes us ... sink
... Deep ... down darkening depths you could not plumb.
Walk fast ... walk fast ... before the shadows come.

V. ON FK: COUNTENANCE OF CROWS

They know not, neither will they understand; they walk on in

darkness: all the foundations of the earth are out of course.
— Psalms 82:5. —

For *WS*

With violent solitude, with ruthless tact,
You numbered notes toward the supremest fact.
You hankered for that west that was west of
Westering, as though there were some final
Coast of the real. Self to self, you traveled
On the cheap, a cell in search of inmates,
Resenting that residue of belief,
That aches for revelation, as if your
Unkillable story could ever die, as if
Tribunals were not always in session,
As if confession weren't always a lie,
As if spirit were not a certainty,
Sans hope, that smothers ... as if whatever
Made you you, could never welcome others.

It Must Be Concrete.

i

Crooked timbers, only two are needful,
Perch on cumulating snow as if they
Dare not dig their heels in sensible earth.
You keep asking for the impossible
But to yearn for the impossible is
To remember God. To accept what is
Possible is to dwell here and now with
Equally lonely, befuddled others.
Thus, the double-jointed collar tightens:
At moments of supreme expectation,
You showed us the hollowness of hope, when
All that wakes ... sleeps its sleep, when salvation's
Storyteller must make us laugh ... and weep.

ii

But the deeper the thicket, the thicker
The timbers, and denser the imagery

That remembers how the tallest timbers
Are easily toppled, as if to make
Clear the unclearness of life. Oh, but
The deeper you go the deeper it gets,
And it gets harder as you keep going.
Explanations accost the unexplained.
Thus, you stared at that vacancy you made
Visible. Then you saw what still towers
In the delusion of nothingness, where
Castilian splendor might once have stood, that
Might yet stand, that might still stand, but cannot
Shake off the terror of standing upright.

iii

You begin with stubborn facts, your task is
Their impossible refutation. The
Peak you seek to climb is no steeper than
Yourself. The tower that you seek to build you
Cannot help but scale. And yet the base of
The highest hill, or the greatest tower,
... is as wide as the narrowness of your
Stance. The goal, you say, exists, but it is
Nowhere on any map. Each possible
Route is a reverie that's off the chart,
That teases with an absence that never
Capsizes into presence. The scourge of
Fantasy's whiplash is the stinging knot
You cannot master, but that masters you.

iv

Irony's vague dream of resolution
Recalls the law's nightmare of unreason,
That will not yield its secrets until the
Law itself becomes a parable of
Unbridled horsemen, an apocalypse
Of hidden dissuaders that can't bear their
Freight from one snowed-in village to the next,
But that ride their heedless horses between
Oblivions. Without a parable
You could not shriek the shriek that drowns the din

Of sin. But, yes, stuck in the muck, you were
The one of all of us, an exception,
Ineluctable, scared of the sacred,
Yet still scarred by the indestructible.

v

Admirers, enthralled by resistance to
Gloss, want most to pluck out the heart of your
Reticence, want to evade your greed for
Evasiveness, that palpable fear of
What survives you, that nimble crookedness
On two legs. But you could not find the food
You liked, as though to stuff yourself, like a
Bohemian paterfamilias,
With food that cannot expiate your greed.
You grasped for what could no longer be grasped.
But why should you, who could not grasp, be grasped
By others? Morally equivalent
Stabs at comprehension negatively
Prehend your map of misunderstanding.

vi

Commandeered by your confounding fathers,
You recoiled, as if you lived in the noise
Headquarters of the cosmos, a clanging
Cacophony of infinite doors, where
The destiny of doors is to be slammed.
But all that vagueness comes back too clearly.
Is there honor in hesitation? "No,"
You said. You could not write *the decisive
Thing*. Yet indecision hangs like risky
Fruit on the limbo of your earliest
Expectation. The soul, disembodied,
Almost abstract, too tight to fit itself,
Could not be worn by you as if your
Spirit were an empty suit of armor.

vii

For you, night was never night enough. Right

Was never right enough. Thus, sin became
The circus of your shortcomings. Every
New theory conceals more than it reveals.
Each covering cherub perpetuates
And obscures the abstract myth of moral
Simplicity, as if that murder by
Apples could disguise ... or disclose ... Edens
That lurk near the countenance of crows. As
Though eternity could ever stand still,
Everything threatens to become something
Else, and what you become is what you're bold
Enough to embody, that body where sin
Must etch its terrible calligraphy.

It Must Be Eternal.

viii

You shunned giant boulders of big words, but
Stumbled on "eternity." The wrong track
Might have sufficed had it been hobbled by
More stumbling blocks. But, then: *Eternity
In person cranks the barrel organ that
Plays only one monotonous tune.* No,
Nothing negates *"Wie geht's?"* Once you are, you
Could ... *not* ...*not be*. Was this your minimum
View ... of eternity? But, then, you snooze
Through salvation's testimony, while the
Comic chatterbox reveals his secrets:
That all is lost is an unlikelihood
Even more extreme than the extremest
Improbability of salvation.

ix

The martyr of cubicles is glad of
Gladiatorial exhaustion:
He seeks the suffocation of last gasps.
You asked for what you couldn't believe, and
Are astonished that such queries are still
Possible. But rushing headlong toward
Eternity is shockingly easy.

It is a downhill path, where gravity
Gives no cause for gratitude, for the way, which
Does not exist, is infinitely long.
It cannot be longer. It cannot be
Shorter. It cannot admit subtraction
Or addition. At last, it hems you in,
Within the choking circle of your sin.

It Must Give Suffering.

X

Burrowing builds that dangerous room of
Your own that cannot welcome others, that
Lucidity that trusts no one, neither
Yourself nor others, that can't let go, that
Cannot plunge into vague complacencies
Of your own flaws. You struggle to become
Small, to flee the erstwhile largeness of souls,
But you could never be invisible.
You groped for doorways out of yourself, but
Where is your doorway? If you found it, could
You cross that threshold without bringing
With you that room of your own? Such is the
Soul's cruelty of forsaking, of suffering
Alone in caves of its own unmaking.

xi

You meet god in the guise of a dog, and
The common bite of canines inflicts its
Wearisome wound. The law's misbehavior
Cannot resolve dubious precedents
Into a savior. You were off the rails,
For the locomotive, that had not reached
You, still idled at the station, where your
Conviction escapes like steam on trestles
Of unbelief. Wherever you were, you
Were there when goodness grew disconsolate,
When locomotion stuttered, when truth, that
Blind enigma, opened your eyes ... as cruel ...
As tender ... as your light ... light strong enough

To stanch the good ... or revive its splendor.

xii

Paradise lost ... paradise sought, are both
Perhaps fought in paradise present, and
Paradise lost ... is the cost ... of struggle.
Any tingling fact is fantastic, and
The fantastic is a tingling fact, shot
Through with sense and sensibility, with
Suffering through the clarity of last things.
Nothing, nothing at all could be noticed
Except the ecstasy that's here, that's not
Enjoyed, that's almost void, but undestroyed.
Whatever happens cannot be undone,
But only muddied by motivation.
Attention to bliss cannot distract the
Law that lassos life in a noose of fact.

VI. LIFE'S BLIND CHARITY

Our sensibility to the feelings of others, so far from being inconsistent with the manhood of self-command is the very principle upon which that manhood is founded.
– Adam Smith, *The Theory of Moral Sentiments, III, iii* –

i

Posthumously, you came forth on the Firth
Of Forth. A tinker might have been your trade
Had you never been redeemed from gypsies.
You stumbled in your speech, yet you warmed with
Eloquence on what you knew inside out,
Never rising to a shout, but always
Seeking the fervid pitch of moderation.
In your gait – *vermicular* – you sidled
Neither right nor left, neither left nor right.
But – yes – relentlessly particular,
In medias res, you saw what you saw,
Ironies that never made you flinch, with
The uncommon light of uncommonly
Good, commonly avoided, common sense.

ii

Extremely uniform was your life as
You described it. A very slow worker,
You called yourself, doing and undoing
What you did ... before you found it pleasing,
Teasing ... without appeasing ... your restless
Self. Yet true to form before you ended,
You insisted, you had always been bent
On doing more, while doing far more than
You intended. Only a stoic god
Assumes the dubious ability
To enjoy suffering in tranquility.
Convicted, but not convinced, you never
Winced: The nether side of utility
   ... is the futility of recompense.

iii

No science of singular abstraction
Could ever discover reciprocal
Banalities of goods and goodness, nor
Derive – as you did – your principles from
Pins and nails, meat and manure. Small beer, grass
And hay hold their sway over your empire
Of self-interest. No cobweb science could
Efface the indelible trace that goods
Give to goodness, that goodness gives to goods.
Speculations – sublime – can never rhyme
With neglect of the smallest active duty.
Imaginary cities of the sun
   ... Remain ... perpetually unable
To furnish meat for the dinner table.

iv

Avarice, ambition, and vainglory
Overrate the gap between rich and poor,
Between obscurity and fame, yet all
Human industry turns on the axis
Of this felicitous misconception.
The poor man's son, tortured with ambition,

Must learn to compete without contrition,
Without the annealing recognition
That he only reaches at last with vain
Struggle for the place he started. Serving
In self-delusion what he hates, he works
And waits for the grandest hour that never
Arrives as long as he strives for what the
Wise ... always and already ... have in power.

V

The nursery of belief finds relief
From grief in explanation, as if the
Genealogy of your every act
Could ... retract ... the eternal verity
Of fact. But to explain something is not
To stanch its truth. No genealogy
Of goodness can undermine its value,
For value is not a variable.
Competition's clash of self-betterments,
Unwittingly, yields the betterment of
All. Yes. You saw what's always depended
On the almost always unintended.
Against the grain of gain, prevailing winds
Then push your private aims to public ends.

vi

Avatars of unseen hands blindly churn,
Pointing without knowing ... where goodness is
Going, goodness – that's not a cheat – but that
Trips ... on the coarse clay feet ... of self-deceit.
At first, you yearned for coherence, then for
Some supreme superintendent of the
Unattended world, and at last, you faced
That rude paradox of unintended
Consequences, how blind leads blind
To ironies of design that's undesigned,
A system that finds its path without map,
That lays its plan without purpose, that builds
Its house without blueprint on the forlorn
Station of a fatherless universe.

vii

Called by passion, cooled by reason, and
Ready for sense and sympathy, agent
And spectator, observer and observed,
Judger and judged, conscience and commerce, clash
Within ... and clamor without, wreaking
Woes that weigh against the happiness of
Men, while amassing the wealth of nations.
But lest abundance become extinct, all
Your slow, uncertain reasons succumb
... Without a wink ... to instinct. To act on
Reason unreasonably is thus to
Worship fallibly a perilous god.
Aspiring cannons must shoot their fodder,
Making all that strives a little odder.

viii

The arduous inmate within the breast,
Abstract ... ideal ... loses contact with the
Real. But the better part of happiness,
You said, is the consciousness of being
Loved. Such is the sorrow that springs from
Sorrows of others. *Your senses never
Did ... and never could .... carry you beyond
Your own person. Yes. You judged their sight by
Your sight, their ear by your ear, their reason
By your reason, their resentment by your
Resentment, their love by your love.* Conscience,
The third party in each transaction, is
Always the middleman who makes the deal,
The one who's most alone but cannot feel.

ix

Caring for others is imagining
Them as yourself, imagining they feel
As you feel, wishing them to see you as
You wish to be seen, wishing they admire
You as you wish to be admired in your
Own eyes, eyes that cannot see the source of

Such admiration in the sordidness
Of self-interest. You learned to see yourself
As though you were your neighbor, your stranger,
Your own worst enemy. You hazarded
Tedium for perspicacity, but
Few rise with your capacity, for life's
Blind charity ... itself ... no rarity
Has rarely ever reached such clarity.

X

The other's eye is the looking glass in
Which you can see yourself already judged.
Self-examination employs its own
Division of labor: the self divides
Itself in two, spectator and agent,
Judger and judged. First, one says, "Give me what
I want." Then, the other says, "you shall have
What you want." Thus, the gravity of self
And society is the blind impulse
To exchange, the gratuitous give and
Take of invisible hands. Commerce is
The cause of conscience, and conscience ... commerce.
The rest of the story is the history
Of the use and the abuse of capital.

xi

Each individual seeks the greatest
Advantage for whatever capital
He commands. But he who commands himself
Commands the greatest capital, and what
He commands is not plain, not palpable, as
Differences of birth or fortune. Wisdom
And virtue, you said, are invisible
And uncertain to undiscerning eyes,
Eyes that most want the esteem of others.
Labor is the real measure of value:
When his scalpel turns upon the surgeon
Himself, the boldest surgery is plied
By hands that do not tremble, but that flay
Away cruelties of self-deception.

xii

False disciples deride what you implied:
An economy is a system of
Moral beings, propelled not solely, but
Surely by self-interest. On the chessboard
Of conscience and commerce, there are rules and
Patterns, stratagems, snares. But each player,
Each person, is not some stoic pawn, but
A piece of freedom, a society
Of imagined others within your self
That, whenever wise, retains its awe … for
Liberty … and law. Yes. First and foremost,
Unwittingly – you saw: how each lonely
Other must become an ever closer
Continuer of your own self-interest.

VII. THE EDDY'S CORE

Belacqua made an inarticulate flourish with his stick and passed down the road out of the life of this tinker, this real man at last.
— Samuel Beckett, *More Pricks Than Kicks*, "Walking Out" —

— *For FK* —

Yes. Infinity's almost certain to
Pull down the curtain on eternity.
That star-like spool, that magnetic tape, that
Squittering reed, that twittering fool, that
Maddening shape … keeps summing you up with
No escape … keeps offering you previews
Of coming attractions. Half-lives of your half-
Hearted heart keep adding you up, as if to
Ravish that rare and radiant flower that
Glows … white on white … and nearly perfect, but
Never, ever … goes … to green. … Perfection
Cannot tell you what you're meant to mean. Each
Lily that festers could blame its greed. But
Now, ye know, there's such a thang as the weed.

— *Early Resignation* —

i

The dying, so say the pious, pass from
Time into eternity. It is all
One evacuation: one colon, or
Just one semicolon that winks or blinks
At what it has but cannot hold. And so
Begins again whatever's there that starts
Again and never ends. Yes, your sentence
Begins somewhere, ends somewhere, and excludes
What it's not from first to last. You joined the
Conspiracy of change. Abasing that
Fraud, eternal life, and squatting near it,
You sought to smear it, before at last you
Came to fear it, as if only shabby
Clowns and wastrels could approach or cheer it.

ii

Dearest despair, facile but intense, was
Not enough to make you wince, as though you
Were what you were … a scalded crustacean.
You drank gall from the goblet of goodbye,
But could not retire the ire in Ireland.
Oh, yes. Your birth was the death of you.
Thus, you studied loftier miseries
And found them wanting. You disdained deeper
Truths yet found them haunting. You had enough
Of enough. Yes. You had it rough. You lived
On what you wrote but could not live by rote.
You sketched the necessary house of being,
With jokes so beguiling, you catch yourself
Smiling, when there is no sense in smiling.

iii

Absconding from your upright house, late and
Loitering, you lost the knack of contact.
From afar, excavating the lost, you

Tried to share the cost you could not share, tried
To bear the cross you could not bear. No rain,
No midnight, you bungled the quietude.
Yearning for your return to mutterhood,
You told your story again and again
In re-scrambled words. Stoking the dark, you
Hungered for others without knowledge or
Admission. Then, you revised the myth of
Hopelessness. You abused fact with fancy,
And fantasy with plainest fact, peddling
Your dolorous wisdom with wit intact.

iv

You gave the nothing new its due, for the
Nothing new is subaltern novelty,
A trinket on the gewgaw wrack of change.
Brick by brick, you build yourself trick by trick.
Stroke by stroke, you steel yourself joke by joke.
But you protest, you say, a brick is not
A stratagem but a piece of wall, the
Obstacle between call and counter-call,
Between the end of rise and start of fall.
And you protest, you say, a joke is not
A joke but a serious tale of how
The bank went broke when the wish for something
... is no longer deposited in your account
Of what it might have meant to be just you.

v

Something of everything remains there to
Confound the flounder. The muck ... that sucks you
In ... is the chaos of every sin, that
Sign below the knees of prayers no longer
Valid, but shredded in dismal salad
Days of sorrow. Never properly born,
You go out, as if you've just come in ... to
Play a game you cannot win. The way
To win, you say, is not to play. Wisdom
Wounds itself and unwinds its bandages.
Convinced but not convicted, you play

As one evicted. But exorcism of
Of all explanation cannot suffice
To retire your debt or to name its price.

vi

You abandoned canneries of knowledge.
Funambulist without the fun, you were
Terribly funny, balancing insights
You could not buy, for you lacked the money.
Some Gresham-like law devalues goodness
In favor of the gabby and shabby.
You must have been grateful for the general
Glut of propositions because no one's
Buying ... or trying ... to solve the riddle
Of how much there is ... or who gets what.
Every dog has its bite, and again and
Again returns to its own vomit. Each bark
Becomes a Babbitt for the other, with
Never the slightest yelp ... of: *Let me help.*

— *Checkmate* —

vii

Time's the medium of your tedium.
Declining to rejoice, you found your voice.
Faster, faster, from Bloomsday to doomsday,
You travel faster to disaster, through
Riddles of middles you cannot master.
But calamities of yester years keep
Ringing in your ears. At first, you wanted,
It seemed, to evade all madness, or just
That gladness that is a piece of madness
In your dead reckoning that must keep on
Beckoning you toward how it is and how
It's not. Out of the silence of dismay,
It's time for a shout ... Let it all run out
... without delay ... Happiness had its day.

viii

You dreamed of a flatland where rising is
Never surprising because it never
Happens. The lie of the land goes nowhere
And goes on forever. Thus, you fluffed the
Pillow of old words; you put a bit of
Stick about. Perhaps what you wanted most
Was a brand new pair of wheels. Not even
Nothing could be more real than to feel the
Chill at the end of the reels. Thus, you sought
Felicity ... in ... specificity.
Yet out of luck ... and in the dark ... there laughs,
Arising ... that lark ... that's still surprising.
But the concrete is always abstract, a
Conceptual slab of petrified muck.

ix

You were agog like a cog in the fog
Of the rigging, a contraption with two
Wheels. Thus, the bicameral mind becomes
Bicyclical ...body and soul, floorless
Holes where, hunkering down, you keep on digging.
Manhood that became Ma-hood ... lost its name ...
Became a motherhood statement, a screed
Of futility that disables, that
Scrawls and crawls and clears the tables. The man
In the jar is never very far from
The kingdom of heaven. He could be one
Of two ... if he had company ... he could
Be that tidy little capital that
Should, if it could, encourage you to live.

x

No. No. There is no signal in the noise,
Horatio, not even the sounds that
Sin against silence and signify sin.
The seeds of manhood die in the sheets of
Innocence. But the luckiest, you might
Have said, are dead before morning. You said

Almost nothing and far too much. But it
Takes but the tiniest bit of something
To make nothing impossible. A thing that
Matters is a thing superb beyond the
The suburb of knowledge. But then you wait
Without the slightest hint of what matters,
Crowing over what chatters in tatters
Of uncommonly gelded opinion.

xi

Names keep changing to obscure the guilt of
That voice that never changes, the one who
Keeps on sinning against silence, that voice
You were, that voice you are, and that voice you
Will be, the one that gives as good as you
Get, that gibberish ... garbled and gargling
In the deep throat of puzzled solitude.
There will be a thousand detours down the road
That gets you where you're going, that place where
Going goes away, that can't go on, yet does.
You were a citizen of nowhere. For
You, there's neither place nor time to exult,
As if different games with different pieces
Invariably produce the same result.

xii

Wherever you're worth nothing, there you should
Want nothing, yet still you want what you taunt.
That's how it is: Not idea, not image,
But the thing itself that's not a thing, but
An insectivorous longing, bereft
Of all the thronging that once upon a
Time was your own unquestionable sense
Of belonging ... to yourself and others.
Yes. You were the topsy-turvy spiral
That comes to its end in the absence of
Any room. Rejoining the chorus of
Oroborus, germ becomes worm, becomes
Term, in your unending series of self-
Swallowing, self-obliterating words.

xiii

Head in muck, you saw what the ostrich saw,
As if the passion flower of sleep could keep
Your dreams in check, as if Newton were but
Another Milton gone blind, a stilt on
Which you, the proverbial dwarf, must stand,
Look far and wide, and forget which way you're
Facing. Let the nightmare remain private,
And the worm will worm its way within you.
Knowing means nothing unless another
Knows you know. You squirmed with impotence, with
Ignorance ... stung by the comic cruelties
Of a life lived incommunicado.
And yet ... telling just one who understood
Could lay the first foundation of the good.

xiv

Starvelings perish in plenty, belittling
The little they cannot twiddle away.
Constancy in tears and laughter obscures
That game you thought comes after. You chart the
Noumenal world, report what unlikeness
Would be like if you could live it. Shifting
From the key of you to the key of new,
Someone, somewhere, perhaps many, surely
More than one, are taking notes: you hear the
Murmurs in their throats. Whatever be the
Law, whatever be the claw, that mars the
Text of one moment to the next, always
There's the permanent possibility
Of meeting your happiness in person.

— *Stalemate* —

xv

No memory, no hope, no history, no coin,
No knowledge, no prospects, no worth, you had
A very promising beginning. Your

Jar was ajar, no ceilings, no floors, just
Those infinite doors leading nowhere,
Or leading there, where you are already.
You squeezed the old chestnuts; you made them less.
But *yes*, which rhymes with *less*, is always more.
Watchers watched, and the watched botched what watchers
Watched. Despite flourishes of trumpets you
Deplore, you feared the more and more, the one
Alone without a second … keeping score,
The one that's smug, as snug, as your will to
Live … and give … all that you can give and live.

xvi

No. There is no God in *Godot,* or else
You would have said it. Just as there is no
Joy in life, or else you would have spread it.
Hobbled, you move one square at a time in
Any direction, always with the threat
Of mumbling, stumbling or being captured.
Movements are one. It is all one movement.
Each square waits for someone to show up. Each
Turn keeps waiting for something to happen.
The ultimate statement you wish to make,
The persons you wish to name, are gambits
In a game that never ends but
That slouches toward the stale, yet still depends
On a lasting hail and a first farewell.

xvii

You never quite discovered the use of
You, the man in the middle of nameless
Images, those imageless names, yes, those
Scrimmageless games, that keep adding you up.
Go play your old favorites, that music
Of yester years, until your eardrum bursts
With the ever-changing firsts. Rehearse those
Thirsts you cannot quench, that same old last, that
Same old first, that can never burst into
Something new. Moldy old reliables
Have pretty much tried all the try-ables.

Yes. A joke or two ... well-told ... can surely
Demolish ... a thousand silver poems of
Destiny ... that cannot hold a polish.

xviii

There will be joy, there will be sorrow in
Your empire of nonevents. What is done is
Done again. What is said is said again.
What is thought is thought again. What is felt
   ... is felt again. What is dead is dead again.
To move at all, yes, to inch forward or
Backwards or sideways, with just the slightest
Motion, is perhaps the supremest act
Of devotion. Moments good, moments not
So good, are expected, long before and
After you're resurrected. Yours was more
A comedy of terrors than errors
Unless, of course, you're in error about
The terror ... and that's a comedy too.

xix

You're an ancient wastrel now, you'll be one
Again ... as you were before, a desert
Wayfarer, dying of thirst, who claws at
A cactus to make it burst, to yield its
Sustenance ... to quench your thirst, just enough
At its best ... and worst, to revive your thirst.
No, nothing, alas, can extract us, from
The vicious circle of bashing cactus.
Again, in desert wastelands, there will grow
A forlorn cactus tree neck deep in snow.
Desperate cheerfulness will make its noise,
And then from first to last will give you poise.
Not much, alas, but enough, at least, to
Make your faith in famine a fasting feast.

xx

God's a word un-French ... without the O, but
You could not retrench the dot and make it

Go. No. Let the dough go, let money flow,
Let the mindless, bodiless train of the
Insane go ... though in the main, alongside
The rails, the train cannot go, cannot go
Even slow, cannot remain without the
Strain of what the failure to go must know.
The train about to depart rehearses
Its arrival, the endless revival
Of a hoped-for silence about to be,
But that's loud and lewd forever more ... Thus,
Enter our story as we entered yours.
Forget about the threat of other tours.

xxi

There is always another world for what
You thought you lacked the words. There is always
Another solution to the problem
Of life, a problem solved single file, one
Person at a time, through the narrow gate
Of grief and gratitude. Pricks outnumber
The kicks in your futilitarian
Calculus of pain and pleasure. Each prick,
Each kick's a measure of what you missed, stabs
Of misunderstanding that missed the heart.
But the bluest smudge of the palest light
Could never be as bright, as light, or as
Heavy as your life. Yes. Already dead
  ... is that heart that makes its home in your head.

xxii

Forgive yourself for the time you wasted.
Stop looking for the thing that was not lost,
That dust that makes visible the sky, star
Dust of crumbling stars, raw ravages of
Decay that makes shine the milky way, motes
Of decomposition, that catch the quiet
Composure of the cosmos, fire-specks
Of freedom, freer than darkness, darker
Than necessity, wiser and brighter
Than the spotlit circle of elusive

Light that clowns can chase but not quite capture
With their dustpans. Gaze at the zenith, nod
At the nadir. Scrawl, if you must, but crawl
Out of the crater of incoherence.

xxiii

Usages for you had no use, they're just
Strings of words that knot the noose, that slipknot
That never lets you loose from suffering. But
That time will come when blasphemy begins
To mourn its condemnations. You are the
Gift, this place, this time, there is no other
Clime where ladders of the heart can start or
Finish, no other way … to play it at
Full tilt, no other way … to open and
Replenish what you can't diminish. As
If the eddy's core could be replenished,
You wait for God, God waits for you, for the
Perpetual unscrewing of a screw
That never quits … or admits: *I'm finished.*

xxiv

The distance from the seen to the unseen
  … is *zero zero,* origin, home, that
Threshold's brink you braved but could not cross. Yes.
To act with even the smallest deed, to
Take decisively even the smallest
Step, would be telling; to speak, yes, even
With the slightest whisper would be yelling.
Life is not unpunctuated murmur.
It's replete with commas and conscience: all
Those things that make you pause lest you forget,
All that faux forgetfulness that makes you fret.
Nothing can appease the eternity
That no one ever sees. No. Charity
With open eyes cannot sustain itself.

VIII. TO COSTLY GRACE

Where death is the last thing, earthly life is all or nothing.

— Dietrich Bonhoeffer —

All that is Christmas originates in heaven and comes from there to us all, to you and me alike, and forges a stronger bond between us than we could ever forge ourselves.
 — Maria von Wedemeyer to Dietrich Bonhoeffer in Cell 92 —

i

How long, how long, had the prophet dithered,
Before the worm smote the gourd it withered?
Whatever devours the prolific in
Its feast is not the greatest but the least.
Beneath the juniper tree, beneath the
Gourd, the coveted truth you hoard will grow
Depleted, will wax prolix before what
Devours and destroys the uncompleted.
In wakefulness and watching, you'll arise
To fight the fight ... for good ... in many a
Guise ... with fools ... and with the wise. But what can
That sleeper mean who does not awaken?
It's difficult and dangerous to turn
Solitude into shared experience.

ii

What troubled you was what eternity
Really is for a man of your time, how
Eternity might still be revealed in
A realm without religion, how it might
Still inhabit all those religionless
Multitudes ... As a worship word in a
Time without worship? As a figure of
Speech that preachers can no longer preach, that
Scriptures no longer teach, that persons can
No longer reach with hearts, with minds, or with
Wearisome words? ... You did not go home at
Whitsuntide. Thus, you turned a corner on
Consolation, asking: What's the use of
Rites when you've lost any right to believe?

iii

Tending to eternity as a boy,
Perhaps you sought to petrify your joy.
Forsaken, you drink what must be drunk,
Eternity's liquor, that final bribe
Recovering theoholics must imbibe.
Thus, you drink as theoholics must
Drink their gods, as god-intoxicated sops
Of sorrow that can only expunge what
They cannot borrow from lonely others.
Every ideology you ingest,
You greet … as another unwelcome guest.
No, that cherub who covers the ice cream
Sundae fans the flame, but cannot melt the
Frozen, faithless milk of human kindness.

iv

Confusion will allow you to steady
Yourself with another paradox, with
Words at war with themselves that are never
And nowhere as bold, as brave, as lucid
As your life. There is a tedium to
An ethics not lived but thought, but each and
Every *is* gives birth to an *ought:* that can
Never be taught, that can never be sought,
That can never be fought, that can never
Be bought, but that is forever fraught with
The revenge of metaphysics. Lest you
Let tyranny dictate the image of
Your life and world, you scratch what itches, you
Empty what's full, you fill what is empty.

v

From the beginning towards the end, knowing
Neither end nor beginning, you are in
The middle of something that never ends.
Your God, it is said, is created out
Of need, an idol of the first and last,
Because you cannot bear to live without your

Beginning and without your end, because
You fear the muddle that's the riddle of
Of your middling life. *The nothingness of the
Man in the middle who does not know the
Beginning ... is ...* you said ... *the last attempt
At explanation.* All strategies of
Self-justification fail. Thus, alone
In your leaky boat, you begin to bail.

vi

To break your faith with the cult of the star
    ... is to begin to wonder what you are
Or what you might yet be without glory.
Groundless power always depends upon
The folly of others, but nothing you
Scorn in others is absent from yourself.
When the ground gives way, you find only the
Intolerable, the repugnant and
The futile. Thus, open your mouth for the
Dumb, open your heart for the numb, who fear
They can never touch eternity's core,
Who flail about among falsehoods, who think
The truth is that there is no truth, as if
There were some cheaper route to costly grace.

vii

Meaning writ large, in the largest sense, is
Not sense at all but promise, a promise of
What cannot bear to die. Nothing you learned
Could forestall the end for which you yearned: not
Merely to die, but to die the youngest,
Finest, devoutest death. Those death bed rites,
You re-imagined, as if you could stanch
Your urge to forge a few last and famous
Words. Yes, in the end, it's the end for you,
The end that is the beginning of your
Life. Though never one to dither or to
Slither, you became a serpent in the
Breast of the church, the angel in the end
Who ... did his duty by the devil too.

viii

No larger than the smaller thumb of a
Little man is that soul that hungers for
Eternity. Narrow as the thousandth
Slice of the thinnest reed is that soul that
Soars toward infinity. The heart curves in
Upon itself, forging the recess of
Inner bliss, the crustacean's last attempt
To build his safety net in solitude.
After you, there will be another, and
Then another, who raises the same scream.
But where eternity pauses ... there is
No room left for conditional clauses.
Anguish arrives and another door slams
Shut in the face of lasting happiness.

ix

Silent you were, the witness of evil.
Drenched you were, by rising storms. Snared you were,
By the lure of pretense. Bewitched you were,
By the arts of equivocation. Then
How could you be of any use? Some screamed:
"Order!" But you heard chaos calling. A
Grownup world gives up its gods. What's left is
Not a matter of ends but odds. Creaking
Skeletons of causality might still
Ask: What causes this? Yes, there is always
A tale that's still untold, another hymn
You cannot sing by rote, but the beyond
... is not what is most remote, but what is
Readiest to hand and hardest to hold.

x

Religionless, the earliest and the
Latest rites have no rights to be. But as
Though still proud, you live off a heritage
Disavowed ... yet still not cowed ... by the facts.
Truth has never been ... can never be an
Institution. Only your holiest

Angel ... pain ... forces you to regain what's
Lost in the cost of your discipleship,
Revealing without measure the treasure
Held in occult furrows of forever's
Gateway, that obstructed door, that curtained
Death, that dawning of the last that makes the
Next-to-last hold always furious and
Forever fast to your eternity.

xi

Revivify the now, that moment that's
Every day, and the days that are every
Moment. Crowds of indefinite sons and
Daughters cannot constitute the choir
Of vision. Without identity there
   ... is no vision. Without vision there are
No limits. Without limits there are no
Lineaments of freedom. But without touch
There is really, really nothing much, but
The wobbly crutches of all those other
Smothering, sad and smoldering senses.
It is not the eye of the heart that sees,
But the invisible hand that touches
And revivifies what it cannot seize.

xii

Do not stop at the gaps and call that God.
Do not speak his name and call that final.
Do not stutter before paradox and
Call that knowing. Let science push knowledge
To the far frontiers, then you will hear him
There, ringing in your ears. Let sweepers sweep
The wooly mammoths clean. There you embrace
The promised scene. Amid evolutions
Of the foolish and the wise, you'll behold
Him in any guise. When all say this is plain
Illusion ... a weak man's crutch ... his gift with
Nerveless hands ... will touch ... your famished face.
To worship aright ... is to honor this
Gift in others ... as others honor you.

IX. THE LAST REFUGE
You have but two topics, yourself and me, and I am sick of both.
[as said in the company of Boswell and others]

Happiness is not in self-contemplation; it is perceived only
when it is reflected from another.
— Dr. Samuel Johnson —

The great business of your life was to flee
Yourself ... to cure the sad with talk. And if
One should speak with rigorous exactness,
You said, no mind is in its proper state.
Hence, you dream of counterfeit perfection.
But hope of reunion tempered by the
Reality of no return cannot
Dampen the fire in you that burns for more.
Thus, you live your paradise of cunning
Dialogue, an interchange of old saws.
Bladed anew, honed sharp, cutting quick with
Wit, with the hot work of fresh expression,
Every you that speaks, every you that hears,
Summons your return from the cause of tears.

i

Giant among giants in the earth of
Your day, you tempted readers to return
To the hastily forgotten and long
Discarded. You sought a permanent sign,
An instrument that resists decay, as
If the resentful ages could ruin
The pages of your prose with their ironed-
Out ironies of the English language,
As if your own plain words could be unlocked,
Defrocked, and mocked, while succumbing to the
Truth that mutability unravels.
Thus, you must persist in probing the wound
You cannot heal, while envy roars, whispers,
And slanders with all its latest cavils.

ii

Your religion was of small comforts and
Large disquiets. Thus, more than solitude,
You loved the raucous riots of the crowd.
A small cavity of cosmetics and
Conveniences, the heart of a man, like a
Woman's purse, conveys paraphernalia
Of the vain. When emptied, there are only
Vapor trails of what's gone but keeps giving
Notice of its absence. Such vanities
Are reminders that remain when nothing's
Left: ashes and soot and oily traces,
Grimy shadows of faces in a shroud,
Not quite stark enough to make confident
And make proud the crustiest crustacean.

iii

Murmurs of discontent can never be
Silenced. The mouth in the mirror speaks
More than it reflects. The critic's voice that
Shrieks embraces what it neglects. Vary
The virtues of life, you said, then mark their
Physiognomies to show infinite traces
Of faces in the crowd of the famous
And the famished. Few others, alas, than
You remain to blame us for vanities
Of human wishes. Yet you survive to
Shame us for inanities that frame us.
Forever you'll be that sage in whom the
Shrewd confide, a wit that still derides the
Dubious aid of guides who've lost their way.

iv

There is a changefulness in all cant, and
A cant in all changefulness that yearns so
Desperately to be dull in new ways.
The effect of novelty upon your
Ignorance makes you wide with wonder but
Never wise enough to fathom all the

Rudiments of your *Ecclesiastes*.
Each new event brings the shock of the past's
Surprising precognition, and all your
Future is – at best – your restatement ... of
What teems with the past without abatement.
To inform is to remind ... and to make
Eloquence of the facts in platitudes
And legendary wit you left behind.

v

After the sure subtractions, you rattle
Those bones that might yet live: you rally the
Remainders to see what still stands up
To tell its story. Then, your flintiness
Collides with a thousand themes to yield its
Sparks of genius, that fleeting fire fanned high
Or banked too low in smoldering hearts of
All who hasten to their proper subject.
With vanity you strive for distinction,
And the strife of self-deception hardens
To habit, and habit, forgetful of
Origins, is ennobled by baseless
Hunger for the sublime, a lasting thirst
That enlarges hearts, while enslaving minds.

vi

You knew how many things there are that you
Do not want, but things you want and do not
Want are made darker by definition.
Hoodwinked by this cheat, you swallow your own
Story: That the happiness you should feign
... is feigned by others nonetheless inspires
Your envy and prickles theirs, as if what
You feign is shared by others who in turn
Envy that happiness feigned by you. What
You really share is the transparent fig
Leaf that hides the truth seen through by you to
Private parts that still crave clothes. Thus, you share the
Stubborn weed of envy's delusion:
That joy leaves nothing more to be desired.

vii

Any change that answers expectation
Prolongs the fraud of the familiar and
… is really no change at all. Minus grace,
No baptism can cleanse the stubbornly
Human. Your wit was always fit to scoff
At whomever thought humanity could
Be washed off. Happiness-mongers hanker
For change, and changing, they are barely changed,
Before they change again. Do not spread the
Stale abroad with all your mediocre
Transformations. Change not, lest ye be changed
Into something that propagates future
Wonders, for all else is but the careless
Redistribution of your wasted time.

viii

You wrote what must be read too slowly by
An age that reads too fast or not at all.
Your own life was best written by yourself,
And so it was. Nothing and no one could
Expose your whole truth, not even that other
Self who fluttered over what you uttered,
Who journalized your wit and *Johnsonized
The land*. Clucking like a hen, exhaling
Like a whale, your wit could not bear to fail …
To scorn the immoral or spurn the stale.
You told them how it is … exact, abstract …
Sparing little fact: That the universe
Should exist without moral purpose is,
For you, pernicious satire of the truth.

ix

Every fallible will … will fail somewhere.
At worst, you were the hireling ruffian
Of the king, who said with a much safer
Pension that taxation's no tyranny.
At best, you were the first to despise your
Worst, for harboring the vices you cursed.

Yes. Your nobility and compassion
Studied how savage a life could be. How
Vain, how vile and yet how also splendid
Were all those whom fame once catapulted.
Yet frigid caution creeps from one poet
To another, till all those, who must lie
Against time, forge eternity's kindred,
The clan of the no longer consulted.

X

Gerrymandering schemes of resentment
Can never divide the false from the true,
For the method you choose is always you ...
Yourself and your lonely others, all those
Ripening persons on the vine of trial
By terror, scorched by the glare of reason
And teased by the tortures of decay. How
Dies the wise man? He dies like you, he dies
The death of a gratefully enlightened
Fool, fighting phantoms that cannot be wounded,
But learning from the wounds he suffers but
Cannot inflict. Devout without a doubt,
You never shake your suspicion that God
Could not trust us ... with poetic justice.

xi

This now, the only time you know, expects
Or recollects, thus using up the room
In all those moments that were meant for you.
There's never time to be yourself, to be
What you were before the birth of envy,
Before the ambush of a specious hope.
All your counterfeit merit dissolves in
Disillusion, where all touches all in
The real estate of your eternity.
Truth that goes to ruin is never sacred.
For truth is precisely what your secret
Fears of eternity cannot efface.
Where nothing lasts, there cannot be wisdom,
For wisdom is to greet what lasts with grace.

xii

You were kindness in a rage, with a life
More relished and embellished than your page.
You were never charmed by disenchantment,
Yet lament the plight of those bewildered
By life's blind maze, those who worship echoes
Of the blustering wind. From cellar to
Garret, you rarely scrounged a carrot to
Call you forth from the melancholy taste
Of barren waste. All isolated joy
Plugs but one hole in the sieve of despair.
The last refuge is never in yourself,
But always in others. In the end, you
Gave to others what you could never give
Yourself: you gave others ... your endless life.

X. EVERY GLAD-HANDER'S NIGHTMARE

*When I would comfort myself against sorrow,
my heart is faint in me.*
— *Jeremiah 8:18* —

i

A prophet: that amphibian monster,
Never at home on land or at rest in
Water, estranged from every status quo.
The bull frog croaks; few care to hear; fewer
Pause to listen; and no one understands.
Touched not by burning coal, your lips were touched
By the touch of madness, touched by sublime
Reluctance ... that madness that burned in you
For forty years, that turned your life and times
Into rivers of tears that could not quench
Your obsession to forecast evil, to
Bring and bear unglad tidings, to make a
Doleful noise unto all the world, to kill ...
Not thrill ... complacencies they call the crowd.

ii

You were appointed before your birth to
Prophesy all that's evil on the earth.
So, there you are, Jeremiah: mouthpiece
Of God. The noise cannot nestle quietly
In your heart. It must burst forth, unheard and
Unheeded, perhaps unneeded: it must
Burst forth. Those who loved you will seek your life,
To destroy it. Those who loved you will make
Your peace a torment. But if there be none
That seek or speak the truth, there can be no
Pardon for those who perpetuate the
Lie, for those who trust in prophecies of
The wind, for those who never escape the
Word ... that wanders ... from what remains unheard.

iii

Arrested and detested, dogged and flogged,
Stocked and mocked, tried for treason, forsaken
By your family that sought your death, dragged to
The dungeon, sunk in the mire, rescued by
The king who desperately conspires to save
Your neck, and still you advise: Surrender!
Jerusalem junked, the temple torched, all
The land is scourged and scorched, the king blinded,
Humbled, and bereft of sons, and at last
The remnant is carried away captive.
You will be destroyed, you will be captured,
You will be exiled, you will be ravaged.
All you hold dear is ruthlessly savaged.
Yes. All these things your God will do to you.

iv

Enemies without, enemies within,
Betray with seductive bigotries of
Sin, with the false confidence of lies that
Cannot give you safety, cannot give you
Freedom. There is no place to hide, for all
Your hiding places have been exposed. Thus,

Naked and alone, you're born ... you're bred ... for
Exile, and your captivity repeats
The fate of all those who succumb to the
Same exposure. You are destined for the
Disaster that descends upon all flesh.
There's a standing invitation: you are
Invited to your own funeral, an offer
You can always abuse but not refuse.

v

You must become what you prophesy. Yes,
You become the prevalent terror of
Imagination. Your accusation
Rebounds on you in ridicule ... in the
Mouth of the crowd, who, like you, hated the
Truth you stated. The east disdains the feast;
The north will be named; the south will be blamed;
The west has confessed. There will be terror
In all directions. Every myth is made
Literal: And the north, the north that will
Be named, is the enemy embodied,
And it must bring literal destruction.
All the grapes go sour; their only power is
Forgetting what tears can no longer cleanse.

vi

Oh, no, you did not desire the day of
Disaster, but you stood between the God
You could doubt but not reject and the crowd
You could condemn but not neglect. Every
Honest prophet hesitates to state the
Honest truth, for prophecy is treason
Against the status quo, and where there is
No such treason, there is no prophecy.
Betrayal that was once cosmic becomes
Personal; betrayal that was public
Becomes private; and betrayal that was
Spiritual becomes pornographic, for
You and besotted others continue
To traffic ... in self-justification.

vii

You could not trust yourself without doubting
God. You could not trust God without doubting
Yourself. You could not shout yourself without
Shouting God. Yours was the persecuted
Truth of a beleaguered trust that suffers
Always for its reluctant loyalties.
Each croak will choke yourself and others. Each
Stroke will smite your face and that of all your
Brothers. The voice no longer still ... is no
Longer small. You heard it roar with wrath on
The path toward all in all: apocalypse.
But when the crowd balks, as it must, you want
Revenge, a revenge that would vindicate
Your trust in the peace that never comes.

viii

The marriage is broken, and the weeping
Never stops. Those never claimed by suffering
Have never lived the lives they claim to lead.
And those who still refuse to understand
Have never touched the veins that make them bleed.
Somewhere within is the dread you go on
Kneading, the lump of pain that must go on
Breeding self-deceit. Truth that's perished is
Hoisted from the mire by rotten rags of
Psalms no longer written, no longer said.
Shouting the truth is bringing back the dead.
Treachery pleads with treachery, and the
Leavened lump rises with pain to bring the
Needed words out of the crowded silence.

ix

Every false peace continues the turmoil
By devious means. Drink deep the cup of
Consolation, drink deep in sorrow, but
What survives tomorrow: the bible of
The free, or the bondage of unending
Misery? When all the images are

Confounded and the last feeble hope is
First propounded and then pounded into
Dust, shall there be a remnant of trust that
Does not lie, that does not fear, that does not
Tremble and dissemble? Shall there be a
Cornerstone in the rubble upon which
To build anew ... that will not bloat into
Another bubble of self-deception?

x

Can you continue to lie to yourself
Without knowing the truth the lie betrays ...
As if self-deceit could hand honesty
A receipt for its last secrets? ... Are you
Honest enough to make the report and
Yet clever enough to understand its
Meaning? No concept, no doctrine, no creed
   ... is generous enough to embrace your
Pain. The thorn in every side of every
Issue knits the tissue of your suffering.
Believing without knowing: is that rung
First or last on the ladder of deceit?
Honesty could be honest as the day
  ... is long, and honesty could still be wrong.

xi

There is an infinity that exceeds
Your grasp, that reflects ... that always contains
What it condemns and condones. You suffer,
He suffers. You condemn, he condemns. You
Vilify, he vilifies. You forget,
He forgets. You forgive, he forgives. You
Weep, he weeps. You exult, he exults, with
Astonishing results ... for the promise
He promises to keep ... he keeps ... you keep.
Anxious, you always are, before his fierce
Demands ... that you ... alone before God ... are
Responsible for the very master
Who commands ... not an ark of law, not an
Ark of safety, but an arc of promise.

xii

Once again, sin betokens destruction.
No. Piety is never enough. The
Obedience that guarantees nothing
... is necessary, impossible and
Never sufficient. Obedience that
Thinks itself enough is idolatry.
You will lose your land, your home, your temple,
Your king. You will lose yourself, a self that
Must be reclaimed in captivity. Your
Obedience is the first step and yet
The stumbling block toward the promise that lies
Beyond it, beyond all you can answer,
Explain, or justify, for all your self-
Justification is idolatry.

xiii

Stretched out and still stretching are shadows of
Your evening land, backsliding away from
The day that never was, that cannot stay.
Old paths are lost. There is no way back to
The place you came from. Great and small run to
And fro through the labyrinth of their hedges.
You no longer study at the same schools.
You can no longer live by the same rules.
Thus, make soft your bed, that raft adrift in
Dreams: your mistake is flooded in its wake.
You will drown in rivers of your own ways,
Ways that damn with faint-hearted healing, by
Appealing for a peace that no longer
  ... is, that never was, that can never come.

xiv

The fountain no longer flourishes, no
Longer nourishes. Cisterns are broken.
Thus, you stand in pools of squatting water.
Leeching into polluted soil, you go
To ground, losing and abusing all that
You have lost, partaking of all that has

Never found, that never finds its level.
Each truth interrupts its revelation,
And never quite gets established. There's a
Restlessness in every peace, a cry of
Anguish unheard by the complacent and
The proud, stiffening the nakedness of
Total exposure that cannot charm the
Cockatrice or redeem the desolate crowd.

XV

You croak, you grumble, and your shout could as
Easily be a mumble because no
One understands the fire, the fire that burns
In bones, and the hammer, the hammer that's
In every spirit ... that razes idols ...
That petrifies faces .. that crushes stones.
Your story is the history of all who
Have heard but refused to listen. This then
... is the beginning and end of sin; to
This with Jeremiah, you say: Amen.
You weep for them, you weep for God, you weep
For you, you weep for the prophet who will
Speak and will not be heard, for the tribe who
Will be deafened ... and stiffened by his word.

xvi

Your fears, your tears, your pain sayeth not: it
 ... is enough. Enough is never enough.
Written, burned, rewritten, unresisting
As before, the promise of something more,
Your book, every book, is a parable
Of authority, a fable of how
Authority arises from nowhere.
No law, no ritual, no ideal, that's
Imagined, no fantasy, even that
Fantasy you feel ... as imposingly
Real, can welcome you home from suffering.
How does one follow a command that comes
From nowhere? And whither must you go ... to
Build in summer your monuments of snow?

xvii

Of the continuing whirlwind, there will
Be no end. There will be perpetual
Desolations. They will not end with you
Or begin with others, for all will share
The astonishment of the desolate.
Your most cherished places, those high, those low,
Like Shiloh, belie the sanctuary
You think you inhabit. Thus, let every
Complacency, your prophecy, beware:
The battle that's always underway is
Already lost. The battle, producing
Nothing just, nothing fair, yields but those few
Left standing ... who stand, if they dare, amid
The glare ... of every glad-hander's nightmare.

xviii

Your precursors live not in your past, but
In your future that culminates in the
Past, in you. Earlier but still later
Than your offspring, you already begin
To recoil at the violence of your words,
Of God's words, of a God whose terror is
In all directions, yet who's forever
Tempted by tenderness. What shall it be?
The hammer or the tuning fork? Or the
Ceaseless doubt forsaking any tool but
Your tormented self, the never-ending
Rending of your doubt, of that bleeding scar
You share with God, that time-haunted rent where
Eternity greets the one who suffers?

xix

You cannot leapfrog pain to arrive at
The sordidly promised scene ... safe, sane and
Serene ... in consolation. Every path
To peace is paved with suffering. This is the
Lucidity glimpsed through the lens of tears.
When the battle's lost, as it always is, there's

Only croaking ... choking ... lamentation.
Idolatries of present nostalgia
For past loyalties are the harbingers
Of future betrayal. There is no one,
And nothing you can trust: no, not one ... not
Others, not yourself, not God. And where there's
No one and nothing to trust, there is no
One to receive and believe your report.

XX

Your offerings are unacceptable.
Your sacrifices, no longer meet, are
Perhaps as sickly sweet as the rotting
Banquet of the indigestible, the
Remnants unconsumed, beloved by you, but
To others detestable. You eat the
Words, you devour the surds, you croak with praise
For a time that will no longer shriek the
Phrase: *no longer*. Thus, the messiah, you
Surmise, will at last arise when the crowd
... is free to do all it pleases. Still
Burning hot, you're caught in the condition
That freezes. Such is the peace that never
Appeases your inconsolable pain.

XI. YOUR LEVEL BEST

We are attracted by any life which represents for us something unknown and strange, by a last illusion still unshattered.
— Marcel Proust, *The Guermantes Way* —

Where can I go to be safe? Where can I hide?
— 19-year-old American hero on Omaha Beach —

i

Narcissus, you want most to show your scar:
That irretrievable cost, first and last,
And forever lost in chronicles of
Wasted time. Relentlessly, you gesture

With this gentle invitation: *Please come*
Away with me fellow traveler. Come waste your
Time with me. Whoever would be read must
Brandish this not-so-hidden presumption
In his head. There's too much togetherness
In every memory. The harmonious
Tribalism of a happy childhood
... is almost always cluttered with conflict.
This is the promise you keep: Your long and
Remorseless insomnia goes to sleep.

ii

In your mind's eye, two bodies embrace, and
Neither one is yours. Is this jealousy's
End ... or beginning? Halfway along the
Arc, jealousy jumps the shark toward that still
Imagined place or that unimagined
Nowhere, that volumeless point where you could
Still safely be loved and yet still love. All
Such fantasy is fact, and such fact is
Fantasy, for your memory of every
Fantasy is remembered fact, the act
Of mind sparring blindly with its winless
Champion, that jabs and stabs at healing,
While reeling from the tortures it inflicts,
Tortures that are endured but never cured.

iii

In the perpetual turning of the
Screw, will there be any room left for you?
Jealousy earns its bill of attainder,
Sans liberty, save for that one stubborn
Remainder, your claustrophilic fetish.
Obsessively observing, you give free
Reign to obsession's observations, to
Verdicts without judge, vistas that perch with
No church to smudge or besmirch clarities
Of what each sees but can never seize. No
Lawmaker can legislate one lasting
Adieu to suffering, to what incites and

Recites cares that thrill ... then kill ... what you can
Never distill ... into eternity.

iv

Thus, you seek to retrieve the time you lost.
But what are the incitement premiums
And the opportunity costs in the
Moral economy of your long and
Exhaustive quest to remember yourself?
Every lucidity ... first slack ... then taut ...
Becomes provisional. Confusion that's
Clarity's forebear becomes its offspring.
Each ego born bright and fair dies hard in
Darkness before it's born again, barely
Bright. Each fragment resents the mosaic
That subsumes it, that makes fate a fixture
In the cosmic décor. The trouble with
You is that you could not abide a bore.

v

Regretting the loss, dreaming the promise,
Imagine Noahs, restless in their arks,
Queasy pilots in cockpits of concern,
As if every heart held some crystalline
Calyx and corolla at its core, as
If this diaphanous, always dreaded
Desideratum, fragile to the touch
Were the forbidden source that makes much more
Of every much. Thus, you must limp along
On this invisible crutch, as if what
You want most of all would tremble, recoil,
Then shatter at your touch. To capture the
Desired is to murder it, to launch just
The slightest caress shatters everything.

vi

An admiral of the ocean sea, you
Explored unknown continents of the past.
Playing both ends against the middle, your
Book was a vast seagoing novel: C

For Combray, C for comedy, C for
Consciousness, C for the chimes of memory
That startle the complacent snobbery
Of solitude, C for the call ... of the
Yellow patch of wall, C for the cloudy
Crystal ball of art blurring life and life
Blurring art's disservice to all in all.
Time is no longer invisible, but
Congeals into what it reveals, one vast
Oceanic drop of experience.

vii

The little that you now know is nowhere.
You're still a befuddled plumb bob, neither
Here nor there, still swaying between trust and
Suspicion. You will never find your height,
Your depth, your level best, only the fierce
Routine of interruption and counter-
Interruption, of then and now, of now
And then, of the long stretch and the short stay
In moments that punctuate the grammar
Of your existence. Do not expect the
Moment to refute its privilege, its
Sad sojourn – rich and strange – of sovereignty.
Do not scorn your bond with the scar you are:
What's not excepted ... must be accepted.

viii

A piece of you is here and now. All the
Rest of you is nowhere. You can never
Be all you are at any moment, but
Only a mutilated cell, a shard,
A fragment, torn from the organ music
Of eternity. Yet you yearn, you mourn,
As if everything and everywhere could
Let nowhere become now here in the taut
Imbalance of your ever present now,
In the imperfect tenseness of your past,
Present and future. You live where nothing's
Changed, but where everything's perpetually

Renewed, where all's forever poisoned by
Time's tawdry, toxic ingenuities.

ix

Every x-ray of unasked-for memory
Reveals the un-upholstered skeleton,
The disentangled skein of fugitive
Precursors, selves forgotten then recalled.
Like the blind rudely startled into sight,
The shock of sudden visibility
Stabs quickly without warning, revealing:
This too ... is you. One good moment of one good
Time invades your fatigue, your boredom, your
Dull round of routines with an uncalled-for
Happiness ... the happiness of being
Simply what you are ... the stubborn little
Eddy that swirls into whorls of being,
That must boldly body forth from nowhere.

x

Alas, every first person singular
   ... is always at last a plural. Thus, you
Strive to retrieve that strange race of former
Selves, those people you were that still people
Your solitude. Identity flickers,
And comedy, in a strangely tragic
Key, snickers at the unsteadiness of
Becoming and then being what you are.
Presumptions of self-knowledge are never
Probative. Yes. You are the cipher, the
Abbreviated sign of an infinite
Series ... a daisy chain of invisible
Links between persons you were, persons you
Are, and persons you still presume to be.

xi

You feared not being invited to the
Party, which you will at last choose to shun,
Yet then yearn to return, as though it were
Your very first and last visitation.

Society and solitude echo
Snobberies of your erstwhile selves. Your own
Head is the raucous assembly of snobs
You rarely meet. Yes. You've littered time with
Absurd replicas of yourself, some sad,
Some somber, some warped, some strangely happy,
But most of them near knockoffs of what you
Nearly are. Blurred copies ... early and late ...
Insist on telling you what to do. The child
That goaded the ephebe still governs you.

xii

You remember how long it's been since you
Forgot yourself. You forget when last you
Remembered what you were. You spring from a
Multitude of many sources, a mind
Of many streams, chasing many courses.
Scudding clouds of consciousness betray with
One piercing ray, one moment, one island
In the sun of the brightest day. Only
Forgetfulness of self can forgive what is
Untimely recalled. Such are the uses
And abuses of your oblivion.
Character billows, knowledge stutters. Thus,
You settle on the teacup. Consciousness,
Chasing experience, cannot catch up.

xiii

You remembered; therefore, you are. Then you
Recall yourself in an everlasting
Shock of recognition. Taking stock of
The shock, you no longer mind that the
Clock must unwind and stop, that the time that
Only seems to stand still is more alive
Than the life you presumed to be living.
Everything's given; everything's taken
Away. One moment follows another.
Haunted presences of departed acts
Give up ghosts, abandoning traces on
Eternity's welcome mat ... that tallies

Your changeless tracks. Yes. Each great vision is
Illusion in collusion with stubborn facts.

xiv

Joy jumps quivering in the air downstream,
Long gone from the forlorn pond that spawned it.
Always you're on the other side of joy.
Happiness, born posthumously, is the
Only happiness you know. Each moment
Arrives before it passes your notice,
Before you receive fully the shock of
Its passage. Such is the law of your late-
Born exaltations. Your certain slant of
Despair is steepened ... beyond compare ... by
The lasting promise of oblivion.
Before you're through, the uneven pavement
Of the past that rattles ... will rattle you.
Wherever joy was ... was always elsewhere.

xv

You acquired habits of breathing, seething
In the stew of what you could not do, of
Always bequeathing to yourself bankrupt
Legacies, re-living without living,
Of grieving without achieving what your
Life wants most to grasp but cannot cling to.
Each Eden sought gets lost in the swerving
Train of perceptions, those isolated
Edens lost but conjured up in separate
Moments of memory when the train curls back
Upon itself, winding its way around
Mount Oblivion. In convolutions
Of time's tracks, the head gets wind of the tail,
The engine gets its glimpse of the caboose.

xvi

You refuse to ride on any train that
Welcomes you as a paying passenger.
You are the legion of little men who
Litter your history, a multitude no

Man can number. Restless in your own skin,
You were enamored and hammered by sin.
The future, not eagerly sought, arrives
In the here and now ... used up, dull and
Diminished ... too soon ... already finished.
Boredom measures time in terms of what it
Envies, and envy jealously wants a
Bigger, brighter room for itself, a room
Where it might be safely elsewhere and yet
Be strangely and impossibly at home.

xvii

Habit is that heroin sans pushers
That pushes itself ever deeper toward
Dark inertia. Thus, your life becomes a
Parable of shrinking ambitions. Yes.
In the middle of desires you could not
Sate, of fires you could not bank, of tortures
You could not abate, your letter of safe
Conduct is constantly brought up to date.
Crowded to smothering by abundance
Of sensation, you reject equations
That define variables of what's deemed
Best in you, as if fame reserved no term
For suffering. Your life, though boring to you,
   ... is an adventure for everyone else.

xviii

To proustify is to convert every
Character into an explanation,
A failed experiment that always fails
Beautifully, a shipwreck of experience,
Not quite tragic, not quite comic, but that
Sails beyond cowardly definition.
Yours is a joy that astounds and confounds
All sorrow, but with each joy you come to
Know, there's always that undertow ... of woe,
That overtone ... of zero at the bone.
Yet always there's a higher stair of self-
Deception. Between the unicorn and

Sphinx is the faith that links your fate to the
Courage for continued experience.

xix

The bee who's lost all hope for the hive will
In his loneliness still strive for beauty.
The moments redeemed, instants outside of
Time, are never orphans. It's true … there are
No fatherless moments; no motherless
Tatterdemalions of time. Thus, you must
Open the other eye, the eye that sees
And seizes eternity … Each attempt
At reduction tortures the nature of
Each person into a warped disclosure,
Each experiment hoards chaos into a
Moment of clarity that reveals, at
The expense of what's forever concealed,
Those lies that tamper with what time anneals.

xx

Your life's an experiment, a trial
And a test of your level best. Through the
Peephole, you must show yourself naked
And exposed. Thus, you sniff those false scents of
Eternity, those rare, meretricious
Resurrections of wasted time that can
Only stammer what eternity must
Pronounce. Despite the baggage rejected,
You remain dejected. Again, and then
Again, you stumble on what you renounce.
Far worse than losing your way was finding
That troubling cost in what's forever lost.
There's no one single thing that's true. No. Not
One, not others, not you. It is … all … true.

xxi

Knowing all your frenzies by name, you soon
Recall them all, as if to pierce the cloud
Of unknowing between past and present,

Between self and self, between yourself and
All your equally lonely others. Each
Pilgrim's regression into obsession
Reveals futilities of possession.
But your wayward instinct still deploys its
Restlessness in unrepentant fits of
Habit. *Desire fathers suffering,* Buddhists
Say, *Desire must die*. But bliss never reaches
What suffering teaches. Desire must die. It
Will. Do not let it go before it's gone.
No ... Do not let it die before it does.

xxii

Lost times are bodies lost. Thus, your still too
Sullied flesh still searches for precursors
Lived afresh. But spiritual adultery
In every quest cannot enflesh lost lives
You yearn to re-live with zest. As Noah
Must have grieved in his ark: *the true life is
Always lived elsewhere*. It is nothing and
Nowhere. The moment's body quickens with
Traces of what's forever lost. All those
Intermittences of the heart that no
Longer hold still haunt but are dispelled at
The zone of evaporation. To be
Dead is to be different from what you are.
But all that is alive ... is eternal.

XII. THE MIDDLE OF NOWHERE

*You are not required to complete the work,
but neither are you free to desist from it.*
        — Rabbi Tarphon, *Sayings of the Fathers* —

i

Long dead, your father is ... and will always
Be ... long lost, but still you hunt for the heart
Of him, his sour odor of oak leaves in
Autumn, the nicotine of Camels, his
Brown sweat, his Right Guard, the deeper real of

Him that still you feel but cannot fathom,
The menace in the muscles of his frame,
His calloused hands that held you hard in crowds,
The shock of that terrifying temper,
His anger that would flare then explode in
Killer smiles, that thrilled, then assuaged what first
They warned and worried, the ears that waggled,
Or his eyes that crinkled as they widened
To let you in on a little secret.

ii

But the puzzling sum of him that never
Quite adds up is ... now ... nowhere, or nestles
In those memories which are also nowhere,
For if you crawled inside your skull, you would
Find no memories, no oak leaves, no Camels,
No nicotine, no Right Guard, no sweat, no
Smiles, no crinkles, no secrets, no father,
But only crumpled convolutions of
Your brain that bear no resemblance to the
Endless rain of rhapsodic perceptions.
This, you must confess, is all too poorly
Stated, yet still ... you know ... your walnut-like
Stump is an image pump from which the tree
Of life has been rudely amputated.

iii

Somewhere in the middle of nowhere, there
Still lives the moment that made you happy.
Midnight, your boyhood dog, still dogs your dreams.
Your father, you suspect, must have arranged
His arrival, a pup he plucked from the
Litter of your uncle's mutt. If your world
Does not merely happen, but will recur
And then again occur, then there's nothing
More you could prefer to recur than this
Four-footed joyfulness in fur. You ... who
Could ... yet would never dance ... had a little
Dog who danced for you. And yet ... only fools,
You feared, find happiness like a mutt, as

If joyful self-deceit should dance or strut.

iv

Neural explosions are all or nothing:
A gaggle of ganglia fires, and you
Become entangled in the snaggletooth
Briars of perceptions and deceptions.
Thus, self-deceit is the perpetual
State of temporary dishonesty,
For you cannot deceive yourself always
And forever, for you are always and
Forever at last remembering before
At first forgetting what you are, and then
Remembering, you forget again. Such is
The rhythm of illusion and hence its
Necessary intrusion into what
You pretend to fathom and think is fact.

v

Everyone and everything you come to
Know remains as elusive as the snow,
As strange as the boxer your father loved
Named Joe, as elusive as the father
Your father's friends once knew as *Satch'emo*.
Recounting legends of Joe's childhood,
Your father said: *Joe's mama started him
off with fiddle lessons. Never one to
fiddle with fiddles, Joe pretended to
attend his music lessons but hid his
boxing gloves in a violin case. Thus,
would-have-been, could-have-been violinist,
Joe Louis Barrow, becomes Joe Louis,
Heavyweight Champion of the World.*

vi

Joe Louis had leaden feet, like me, your
Father said, *he could not ... or he would not ... dance.
And yet, Joe had a punch*, your father said,
called Dead on Arrival. *Yes. He punched and*

*punched with a terrible force, and yet ... as
they say ... he was always a gentle soul ...
of course.* Always the artist, the ring was
His concert stage, and his performance, a
Recital of deadly blows. But as your
Father explained: *No black fighter in his
day could depend on an honest count: Joe's
fist had to be his referee. Joe let
others train for fame, for honor, for wealth.
But Joe always trained for the knockout punch.*

vii

His smartest opponents, your father said,
*always studied the moves Joe made before
he threw a punch. Because ... well ... because Joe
never telegraphed anything. His left
hook always seemed to come out of nowhere.
Bang. If he hit you with a shot, you could
never see it coming. You just saw the
light going off in your head, bang, like a
thunderbolt, like a flash of lightning. Bang.*
Strangely unobservable was the sheer
Physical force of each blow. The arm cocks,
Pumps, thrusts with fist on chin, but force itself
Was mist ... was grist for mystery, and yet
Never ... a visible reality.

viii

Nowhere's now here: Yes. You hear your father's
Voice that thrills, that chills, that kills, as it tells
The cruel twilight of his champion's
Last fight, and then finally on the verge of
Tears, on the threshold of trembling, he cites
The final chapter, at that funeral
Many years later when his champion
Kisses the corpse of his former rival,
That other fallen champion, the one
Who ended the Brown Bomber's career. Yes.
*Your whole life is your funeral, or so your
Father thought Joe Louis said. You'll learn and*

Relearn this truth, apply and reapply
This truth a thousand times before you're dead.

ix

Then there's that day, that day it was revealed
To you by yet another maternal
Indiscretion: *Daddy destroyed your dog ...*
With one immortal ... mortal blow, blunt and
Brutal, a full frontal shotgun blast ... up
Close and personal ...*Bang* ... into the heart of
The most loyal mammal that ever made
A young boy happy. Midnight transgressed a
Fatal boundary, darkened the wrong threshold,
Opened a forbidden door to acquire the
Bloody taste of fowl in your neighbor's coop.
The dog must die, your neighbor insisted,
But you'll never know whether your father
Coolly complied or ... at first ... resisted.

x

No matter how harsh the test, no matter
How long it took, you learned and then relearned
Whatever's important to overlook.
There's a desire that stops desire. That is
The only desire that should be stopped. There's
A belief that stops belief. That is the
Only belief that comes to grief. If it's
True that you imagine there is no truth,
Then that's the only truth that has no use.
Like punch-drunk champions, you shadowbox
But cannot keep pace with the lightning speed
Of paradox: Yet when you stopped fearing
Self-deceit, you learned that despair is the
Depraved hope that nothing really matters.

xi

You learned lessons no one learns in college,
That blood touches blood without name, without
Blame, without shame in the gem-like flame of

Your darkest knowledge, where life is always
Short and the funeral's always in session.
But discretion marries indiscretion,
And the future becomes a progression
Of further mistakes. Wisdom always plays
Second fiddle to folly, always plays
Foolish music when it fiddles with the
Wrong fiddle. Right instruments are always
Required, and right instruments are always
In short supply, which is precisely why
You rely so much on the trusted lie.

xii

Resound and then rehearse the supremest
Syllable. Each cresting wave still carries
Rhythm's rumor of the unkillable.
You may try, but you cannot remember
The act of sex that connects what's nowhere
And no one to what's someone and somewhere.
All this is the conception beyond your
Conception, a forgotten ecstasy
Embittered by the appalling fact that
All sex is at once body and spirit,
A body of spirit that blindly craves ...
That must miss its psychic bliss, a spirit
Of body that always blithely waives its
Birthright of physical satisfaction.

xiii

A rigorous net of words can capture
Within its mesh only the right-sized flesh
Of the fitting. It lets go the large and
Lets slip the small. Of what slips and goes, you
Remain unwitting ... of those large, those small
But unanimous facts of a life that
Begins but which never admits to quitting.
Yet you are always prepared to sift through
The wreckage of yet another *as if,*
As if you cannot stop what you started,
As if you must pause to examine the

Feeble cause of those depraved, those craven
Equivocations of your half-hearted,
Half-started jabs at justifying life.

xiv

Every life that begins and ends, begins
And ends in the middle of nowhere, for
Life already is where it always was,
Life, as evanescent as snow, that melts,
That fades, but always has nowhere to go,
A life ... as out of time ... as out of place,
As the gentle breeze and mighty wind of
The past you're so convinced can never last,
A life where each blow threatens with its squall,
Where wisest fiddlers play a foolish song,
Where all that strives for greatness seems so small,
A life so marred by grief, that seems so wrong
That it must breed the duty of belief ...
The belief that every blow must strike home.

NINE
PART TWO
GOD'S LATEST IMAGES

I. RUMORS OF THE ROSE

Suppose there is a plain with established paths and fields full of hedges, ditches, stones, timber, with obstacles of every kind blocking the way except along the narrow paths. Snow has fallen so that it covers everything and presents the same image in all places, so that no trace of any path can be seen. A man comes from one side of the plain and wishes to go to a dwelling on the other side. By his own efforts, by using his own power of observation and intelligence, and by taking himself as a guide, he proceeds along the straight way in the direction in which he intends to travel, leaving footprints behind him. After him comes another wishing to travel to the same dwelling, and he has only to follow the footprints left behind. Yet, although he has been shown the way which the other man was able to find for himself without guidance, by his own fault, he wanders and twists among the bramble and brier and goes where he should not. Which of these ought to be called a worthy man? I reply, he who went first. And what should the other be called? I reply, the basest of men.

– Dante, *The Convivio*, Chapter VII –

i

The ghost of an origin must trespass
The snowed-in paths. It is the image of
A dead man living ... and unforgiving.
As he makes his way through treacheries of
Snows, only rarest imaginations
Can imagine where he comes from ... and where
He goes. There are always some, the dead man
Knows, who would, if he let them, lead him by
The nose ... to skirt hazards buried now by
Centuries of fallen snows. Despite grave
Doubts, despite fears ... of what he thinks he knows,
He alone has caught the scent, he alone
Can flesh out the hint of what hitherto
Were only vaguest rumors of the rose.

ii

After your imagination masters

Your imaginings, you cannot follow
In someone else's footsteps. Thus, you say:
Follow me. Or fall away in folly.
Two testaments were one too few. There must
Perforce be another one, a third, one
That enshrined the lasting monument of
The course you cut through life, your path, your word.
Earlier than Adam, you made your madam
Mistress of eternity. Every death,
Every first life and lasting death, her death, is
Insane … inane … obscene … so you sought to
Make the insanity mean something sane,
Something everlastingly safe … serene.

iii

Your imagination, like that of your
Lessers and one better, is a restless
Splurge of demonic desire that wants most
To feel and fathom images of what
It wants, what it inspects, and then rejects.
That greater imaginer imagined
Not order, not chaos only, but a
Chaos made of many orders. Yet you
Imagined order unshakeable and
Austere, an intimidating rigor
That embraced tenderness, but tenderness
Impelled by fear. Everywhere you looked, and
Everywhere you saw your lust reflected
By the mystical awe of love and law.

iv

You compiled indecent indices of
Hell. These are the famous Dantesqueries:
The stage machinery of eternity,
The wheels, the thrills, and the grotesqueries.
But then a girl of such brief use becomes
Immortal. In abasement, you're reborn
In the smiles of a woman's tender scorn.
There's never a dearth of perceived self-worth
In this golden era of self-esteem.

Alexia's all the rage ... in an age
That won't be tempted to turn your page. But,
No, the damned do not decipher themselves.
Chasing novelties, they stay forever
What they are by repeating what they were.

V

Reading established your love before you
Sinned. Then dice throws, like startled doves, betray
Disquiet in the fate of loves. Dark eyes
Of desire double down on lust, then dance
Their dance upon the perpetual wind.
The first crisis is that she would not say:
Hello. The last crisis is whether you
Would at last let go. A life of lust that's
Only lust is hell already. Thus, you
Needed something more to keep you steady.
Along the edges of wisdom are the
Hedges of silence. Where feeling begins
To think, thinking begins to feel ... as you
Pass beyond the precipice of the real.

vi

Despite the persistent mumble of the
Humble, you had the nerve to swerve away
From scripture into fantasy. Before
Sarcasm became sacred, yes, before
Irony became every wit's ideal,
You seized the mantle of prophecy to
Create images plainer than the plain,
Fantasies more real than the really real.
Whatever cannot be perfected is
Rejected but returns unrepressed in
Visions of the obsessed. Minding your own
Advice, however nice, portends too high
A price. Thus, the path you pursue defects
From the vast paternity it reflects.

vii

The trick of every comedy is to
Make the perfectly normal seem odd. Thus,
The driving genius of your poem is the
Genealogy of girl become god.
Yours was the tender cruelty of a
Fierce routine that renders the non-routine
Obscene. No humbler tenderness could you
Bring about and bear but that tenderness
That left you quaking at your remaking
Of that everlasting love, your love, which
Was for you always an astonishing
Accident in the substance of what is,
As if those snows you traduced foretell that
Shadow which you alone could cast in hell.

viii

Oblivion's dust you no longer trust.
Each time always invents its own sublime.
Thus, you neither accept nor reject the
Standard practices of passion. Perhaps
There is a ferocity fiercer than
The alpha male, a passion beyond the
Pale, a lust you could not trust, so now you
Must disguise, a deceptively leopard-
Like purr for her, that dissembles a tale
You cannot tell, that must make her panther's
Pretty eyes a mask of contempt, a hell,
For whom orthodoxy is a spasm
In the corkscrew chasm where you'd sooner
Be banished than be vanished forever.

ix

Filaments of the real are unspindled.
Desire for damnation precedes all sin.
The preparations are eternal, yet you
Are only burned by the fire you kindled.
Your punishment is reality with
Nothing added. It is what your passion

Pursues. It is the pain that is never
Padded with consolation. It is where
All that can be added is more of the
Immortal pain that is the immortal
You. Yes. Your punishment is eternal
Self-fulfillment. Follow your bliss, and the
Heaven you sought to kiss will go amiss.
Your bliss becomes your everlasting hell.

x

When lust meets lust in the circle of your
Sin, you perceive how vice and virtue are
Close akin, how close in kind are the blind
That lead the blind, how near, how far, are the
Saved and damned, how all that's serious is
Delirious, how delirious is
The serious, how close allied are the
Brightness of a star and the hideous
Radiance of an everlasting scar.
You abandon hope to resurrect it,
You explore damnation to dissect it,
And at last ... you deflect it ... from yourself.
The unlimbered arms of goodness reach long
And wide. Those who say otherwise have lied.

xi

Lust plunges so deeply to reach what it
Wants that memory cannot retrace its steps
Without oblivion's exhaustion. Thus,
The empire of light is a bright dead blank
Where no visible imagery survives
To salute or thank the poet for the
Pain and trouble. Nothing remains that is
Plain in the main of light. What you do now
You must do for good, something not you nor
Anyone could do in the darkest wood.
Given time enough you can undo what
You did to undo yourself in time. Your
Thirst to be the first is a curse surpassed
Only by returning to things that last.

xii

Heaven and hell are not where dead people
Live, but where the already dead must go
When there is nothing left to give. At the
Center of your rainbow's gravity is
The poison of sin's depravity. Yet
There are times when the gift of gravity
Seems but a toy, when for one moment you
Recover in ghostly origins, the
Unbearable lightness of unnumbered,
Unremembered, yet immortal joy, where
Sorrow, in its deepest burrow, knows a
Joy that never grieves, where your past never
Goes, your present always stays, and where your
Future keeps arriving but never leaves.

xiii

You must become what you love. The love you
Establish and that established you is
A love that makes you tremble, and trembling
... is always here to stay for your love is
Trembling through and through, a trembling through time,
Through eternity too ... that cannot pass
Away. Spending time in eternity
Only for a while, you learn that mockery
... is the meaning of her smile, that trust in
A fallible god prescribes gall and guile,
That this is how you turn halting, trembling
Accidents of style into eternal
Substance, into whatever there may be
Of you that still wants to last forever.

xiv

Oh, yes, paradise is another mode
Of deep regret for what you lost, as if
Only delusions could nourish the facts
You established and the love that muddied
The earliest of snows with fresh-made tracks.
The best is not the best if you can say:

There's always more to come. More snow to fall.
More poetry to tantalize the crowd.
More women in eternity's courtyard
To call your name out longingly and loud.
Every desire, lewd and crude and weary,
Cannibalizes all it fathers as
It fasts. The earliest image of your
Eternity is the only one that lasts.

XV

If there's no place for what has ceased to be,
Then nothingness and nowhere make of you
Only what you see ... as if no one could
Ever follow seen into unseen, heard
Into unheard, felt into unfelt, thought
Into unthought ... or unword into word.
Nothing that is ... or that ever was ... can
Cease to be forever. The resonance
Of elsewhere settles in one place, in you,
That unmarried life you call eternity.
All joy lives from lives long gone, lives that are
From nowhere to nowhere gone. Here is the
Happiness you forget but fear, for the
Unlived lives you have not lived are lived out here.

II. PANIC AT THE PICNIC

Yet some there be that by due steps aspire
To lay their just hands on that Golden Key
That ope's the palace of Eternity:
To such my errand is, and but for such,
I would not soil these pure Ambrosial weeds
With the rank vapors of this Sin-worn mould.
But to my task.
– John Milton, *Comus* –

To make the way easier from Hell to and fro,
they pave a broad Highway or Bridge over chaos,
according to the Track that Satan first made.
– John Milton, *Paradise Lost, Book X, The Argument* –

i

Frail perfection was your head start, the lull
Before the dull but longing null ... sets in ...
In every heart. In crude catalogings
Of genius, something always surprises
And persists, but rarely ever ... resists
Plunging more deeply into what cannot
Be fathomed, or submits to one law that's
Gratefully obeyed. Nothing taxes your
Imagination like prolongations of
Peace, for happiness needs more energy
To sustain itself than to cease. Obscure
Perils in every cloud rain down like drums:
Nothing's easier to predict than the
Panic at the picnic that always comes.

ii

Long before nostalgia for Eden stings,
You will hasten into the midst of things
Where neither darkest demon nor brightest
Angel sings. You will never at last be
Through with all that Satan and his motley
Crew could do to you. Your saga begins
In the center of nowhere, a center
Without circle, a place that's not a place,
A primitive streak of desolation.
You will call this chaos. Out of chaos,
The rumors of the dawn arose, the rose
Of dawn, the breaking of chaos, and the
Making of something new and fatal out
Of dateless, fateless, bedamned disorder.

iii

With equivocal hopes for coherence
You begin with an initial dark blur,
A vague stroke of personal daring that
Lets you call the universe *Madam* or
The cosmos *Sir*. Everything that is far
Or near, that's hope or fear, even gravest

Matter, that most neutral stuff of the most
Inhumanly austere, is in your face ...
... is indubitably up close and personal.
In the glare of the common air of the
Sane everything becomes at its best and
At its worst ... inane. Life is moving, and
Motion living. All in you was moving
Matter, never vain, but unforgiving.

iv

Eternal bureaucrats believe only
What the system reports to itself is
True. And always there are reports, always
Rumors of new creations. Always there
Are upstart creatures, those whose faces, they
Say, rudely reflect features in traces
Of God. Out of God's latest images,
Pandemonium builds itself, and the
Peers of chaos begin to consult each
Other. Hope's reinforcements resolve not
To court despair by starting small, but you're
Left at large ... in charge of all ... when you claim
Your own place, when mind sets itself apart
In desolate palaces of the heart.

v

Every long poem creates a memory
Of itself, or it cannot keep going.
Every strong poet must imagine the
Unremembered, or it won't keep snowing.
Any and all protest against the dull
Tyranny of heaven is already
Contaminated by Satan's better
Arguments. Everything you read, you thought,
You knew, was obsessively re-thought ... through
And through ... by you, and though the diligent
Reader may strive, he may never reach
Where you arrive, for you arrive where you
Started, the self-charted labyrinth of your
Eternity, whose end no eye can reach.

vi

There was never any snow in Eden.
All history is your history, an endless,
Repeatable and repeated rerun
Of eternity, the sum of events,
The cosmic stanzas that always happen
All at once, the zero point, the re-set
Button, pressed to clean the chronometers
Of your precursors. In your disheveled
Innocence, there is a shock that cannot
Be absorbed without the machinations
Of a clock that cannot be stopped, but that
Never starts and that never stops ... as if
That one eternal author who wrote all
The books felt his worth most deeply in you.

vii

First touch, then sight, then motion, sound and smell,
Then taste. All sense smiles with the fragrance of
Eternity. And each smile's an image,
A wave that breaks, that cannot be rescued
From the flow that flatters and shatters it.
If truth's the only style that matters, then
Eloquent Satan leaves truth in tatters.
Life's a terrible example for one
Who lives it and gives it to others. You
First felt pain when you felt the strain of being
What you are. Apart from every other
Sense, it's touch alone that's never tasted
Sin. Yet to touch the truth of another
... is always to share the same delusion.

viii

Sacred truth is always a near-ruined thing.
The excessive joy of others is a
Tyranny that tries the patience of the
Desperate. With the future behind your
Back, you plunge into the beginning. There's
A winnowing and a sinning that is

Always thinning matter into spirit.
Matter more than spirit, for you, is much
Fatter by a far piece, but spirit is
A piece of matter of which there is no
Part, or a part for which there is no peace.
The shape you're in could be anything now.
Nothing else but you and the shape you're in
Could tell you how to live or how to sin.

ix

There is no lasting joy in the joy of
Innocence interruptus: for each joy
That would last .... must cloy ... then soon corrupt us.
Panic sets in, even before Satan
Insinuates into Eve the dream of sin.
Always in your magnificent diction
There is something akin to fiction.
No. There is no way to say it nice: The
Sex act, sans tact, is the fundamental
Fact of paradise. The garden of joy
Heavy with sweetish scents has already
Begun to cloy, when all your itchiness,
All your imagery ... goes blind ... in Eden,
When father fucked the mother of all mankind.

x

No one but you had seen it plain: On your
First attempt, before the invention of
Temptation, you failed to reach the organ
Of her fancy. In Eden, your nature
In you ... failed, for there was no thorn on which
Even a rumored rose could be impaled.
As if sin's a goad that keeps you going,
Wisdom, treasured for what it neglects, smiles
Like similes with eyes that cannot see
Bitterness in carnal acts of knowing.
All centuries, alike in most respects, keep
Shoveling the past while it keeps on snowing.
But your century ... most ... this truth will vex:
Happiness is never the fruit of sex.

xi

The way is always ready, for the first
Nakedness is a glory unperceived
And unreprieved. Thus, you continue ... to
Continue ... to compare ... small things to great,
Foul things to fair. In this peerless moment
Slumbers ... all ... all dream, all tedium, all
Nightmare, all joy. History collapses
Into eternity, into the rut
That is cut through time, the illustrious
Track through the dark abyss ...a thoroughfare
Through the untrespassed continent of sin.
Punished by the shape of sin you're in, you
Cannot seize your elusive prize without
Eyes that spurn the transparency of lies.

xii

You are taken wherever your thoughts may
Lead, and taken there, you wander through the
Labyrinth of hedges they begin to breed.
Every happiness conceals then reveals
Its own abyss, begins to envy what
It's not, begins to embrace its stuttering
Doubt and discontent ... yearns to propagate
The curse. There's an error coiled within each
Soul that makes all happiness a hell in
Waiting ... that keeps dealing and repealing
The ever shuffling deck of redemption.
For the virtuous there's no exemption.
In states of perpetual temptation,
Virtues always punish the virtuous.

xiii

Happiness, when scribbled, is never black,
But white, while sorrow slouches forth with the
Glamorous darkness of the night. You and
Your faithless progeny answered the call:
Just and right, you were made, yet free to fall.
Should you re-ignite a vain and desperate

War, seek ignoble ease and peaceful sloth,
Stay where and what you are by building a
Prosperous empire of evil, or invite
Human kind to the Devil's Party? Each
Philosophy charms misery for a
While, until life discovers anew what
It must revile. Hell always grows darker
With the frown of just one unhappy man.

xiv

Nowhere to hide, you're blinded with open
Eyes that open wise. When your eyes open,
You always remember a paradise
You never saw, recall the memory of
A bliss that's lost before the conditions
Of freezing begin to collect the frost.
Centuries before and after the thaw, you'll
Still be warming the coldest crustacean.
Never returning to what you saw, but
Enamored of awe, you call that *Law*. Stay
As you are, or stumble into change. This
... is the perpetual prelude of the
Fall, the unshakeable anxiety
Of continuing to be what you are.

xv

All sorrow, all regret, all despair, all
The noblest vices, all the vain and the
Variable algebra of pain and
Pleasure argue for something more sublime
Than what your cruelest histories malign.
Self-blame's despair, recoiling from the blame
Of others is the last infirmity
That vanity tries to tame with the shame
Of submission, as if you ... on bended
Knee ... could still be free ... to be ... forever.
That you may act apart from self-deceit
... is a task that is never quite complete.
That you do the task is certain, that you
Must do it willingly: that is freedom.

xvi

Clouds obscuring all that's seen only serve
To demean the invisible promise.
You neither abide nor disdain what is.
To dally with dark idolatries of
Expedience is to consult with the
Promiscuous crowd that stands aloof from
The wavering promise of obedience.
The blind turns toward vision, the first place, the
Last place, face to face with the unseen. One
Taste, one misstep, opens the blind eye of
Innocence, sheds the see-through aprons of
Self-deceit, seen through because you know that
Wherever you are ... whatever you do,
That ... you ... alas ... are always, always you.

xvii

Despair devises death for those who live:
Mist by night descends upon paradise.
Proceeding with the unanswerable
Guile of style, snake philosophy gets its
Start, pulls the trigger in an otherwise
Still untroubled and unglamorous heart.
The hated habitations of the past
Will in future eternities still last,
Will hold their fatal sway forever. You
Cannot teach an erring soul what only
An erring soul could teach. Thus, you must preach
As if only the out-of-reach could teach
What must be taught, as if only those who
Time cannot teach can reach what must be sought.

xviii

Each day brings back the night, each night the day.
But then you go your way ... and disobey.
There's a restless error in the soul that
Sees itself apart from nature as a
Thing unfinished, a gathering void, that fills,
That empties, but that's always replenished.

This is that hurt that hurts and then re-heals
And then reopens like the hurt of a
Wounded angel that cannot be killed but
Only annihilated. God's fiercest
Freedom is first realized in you ... when shrewd
Chaos within a larger order forms,
As when darkness looming in the spate of
Late-born light unwittingly warns the day.

xix

If the devil ... is a deity, or
The deity ... is a devil, then can
Anything you know be on the level?
There's the fear in you, always near, that you
Are among the devilish engines of God.
You yearn to reject what you brilliantly
Reflect, the image of your own dread voice,
The eloquence that argues so well for
The other choice, the dreaded voice that had
Almost persuaded thee to another end.
All the shattered pieces still falling, all
The ragged shards of truth are still calling
Your name ... as if testaments old and new
Were invisible arrows aimed at you.

xx

The palace of Eternity: Yes. You
Stormed it once or twice, reshuffling the deck
And forsaking dice. In Eden, perhaps
A solitary lime tree lingers in
Far corners of the wild where neither snake,
Nor Adam, nor Eve can be beguiled. Yes.
Underneath this tree, all's in order, all's
Sublime, and blankest verse conforms to rhyme.
Such stanzas may not kill, but still can thrill
With counterfeit thunder, as if shrewdest
Hypocrisy could disguise your blunder.
Ah, perhaps there's no dagger in the wound,
But mere delusion, a sweet recess, a
Longed-for sheath you seek but cannot possess.

xxi

Whatever's perfect is made mutable
And inscrutable. The day is large, but
The night is never small, for you never
Grasp the sublime insomnia of a
Sleepless God who always keeps his promise.
The law of falling bodies makes every
Thing fall until it seems to stop, but when
It bottoms out, it never stops but keeps
On moving ... keeps proving itself uncursed.
Thus, you imagine yourself consoling
Yourself from the higher hill of a far
Happier world. But hell is always where
You fell, where you paused to catch yourself in
The fatal act of naming your despair.

xxii

Minimal is the charm of paradise
And the alarm quite desperate, for only
Freedom's folly leads from hell and back to
Embrace a cosmos that cries: *Alack, Alack.*
Yet it is never nihilism that
Names your greatest horror but always the
Possibility of happiness that
Others might share when you're no longer there.
To be nobody and nowhere is a
Refuge neither safe nor free. There is no
Sanctuary, no cosmological
Cul-de-sac, no escape from a world that
Can take revenge on you, or that has the
Gall to push you out and to watch your back

xxiii

You are always something more, more than the
Clouded lens of erstwhile glory, something
More than besotted eyeballs full of the
Already experienced, something that
Justifies not merely the ways of God
But the way of man, one way, one man, your

Way, your man, the man you become in the
Sum of all experience, the one still
Falling, the one that catches if you can
The man you must become, that long ago
Lucifer in you, now Satan, now Adam,
Now Samson, now Jesus, striving always
For something that can please us, but cannot
Quite appease us with sublime concoctions.

xxiv

You sat on the middle tree devising
Death for those with life to live and love to
Give. Huddled next to life is the urge to
Know that wound of delirious hue that's
Hardest to hold when your heart's in plain view.
Happiness, your gift, is eternity's
Task. Yes. This time, your time, is the masque of
Many others, many fathers, many
Mothers, many daughters, many brothers.
Each wound that does not kill closes upon
Itself and is healed by self-deception.
What does not kill strengthens in self-deceit
The thrill of survival till once again
Your revival reassembles the truth.

xxv

It is the disappearances that must
Be saved. Eloquent lies you tell about
What's gone missing are ways ... broad highways to
Hell are paved. The time transfixed is alive
And is fiercely snowing, never finished,
Always replenished and overflowing.
It is the lasting promise that lives and
That gives without restraint, that harbors no
Complaint, no greed for the more that never
Fails to come. This is a happiness that
No one enjoys alone, for there is no
Warmth in icy solitudes of God, no
Joy on thrones of an unpeopled world, no
Fitness in the power that lacks a witness.

xxvi

Somewhere in time, the infernal rebel
Will rise again to stand unterrified.
Unlike yourself in your dimensions, you'll
Be shocked by the sudden view of all the
World inhabited by you, by those who
Were made in your image. Each devilish
Engine must recoil upon itself. Each
Borrowed visage betrays the counterfeit
You have the wit to commit and admit,
While art continues hypocrisy by
Other means, continues to continue
To entertain the dismal time until
Each rebel regains a freedom that will
Astonish eternity … forever.

III. YOUR OWN ARMS

I have resolved to open a new route, which has not been followed by anyone, and may prove difficult and troublesome but may also bring me some reward in the approbation of those who will kindly appreciate my efforts.
– Machiavelli, *Discourses on the First Ten Books of Titus Livius* –

This is the right way to go to heaven:
to learn the way to hell in order to escape it.
– Machiavelli, *Letter to Francesco Guicciardini, 17 May 1521* –

One thing yet remains to be done, which perhaps is of the greatest concern of all, and that is, that you, my countrymen, refute this adversary of yours yourselves, which I do not see any other means of your effecting, than by a constant endeavor to outdo all men's bad words by your own good deeds.
– John Milton, *A Defence of the English People* –

i

There are those who wear your words like a badge
Of shrewdness, those who fear to be naked,
But are nonetheless proud of their lewdness.

You forged a path never before trodden
By all those hitherto duped and sodden
By ideologies. Your honesty's
Always unforgiving, embracing the
Facts of a fate you keep reliving. You
Were a paladin of your day: Clever.
Would travel. Charged florins by the hour.
After reading you, oh yes, centuries
Of astonished scholars still discuss the
Endless mystery of why anyone at
All ... could trust anyone of us ... with power.

ii

Always, for you, there's the dark, the stark, the
Cruel, unsteady, unsullied malice of
Fortune, and the necessity that spawns
Your lust for power, your solution to
The terror of all-too-human weakness,
The fear that prolongs the life, that spurs the
Continuing error, of those ancient
Afterlives that are still alive in you.
Fortune, that god unworshipped but wisely
Feared, is what you sought to master. Yet you
Could have of your savage god all that you
Could have, and it would never be enough.
No Machiavel ever gets it right
Till fortune coincides with appetite.

iii

With lucid wit, with ruthless grit, your prose
Sustains the cynical lyricism
Of power. Yet there are hysterics in
All lyrics: there is an idiocy
In every line that confounds the genius
That produced it. The squatting gargoyle, not
Bad, not good, not guilty, the one armed with
An ironic smile of true guile, with the
Appalling neutrality of what is, the
One overlooking your shoulder, the one
Under-booking your account of what might

Be good, and overbooking your account
Of what is not, the one who left the blot,
The stain, your self-forgetting kiss of fame.

iv

Paradise is a promise that cannot
Be kept. For deities you substitute
The necessities and the wavering
Fortune of politics. Your desire to
Command others, perhaps a sin, is still
The only way that master and victim
Can ever hope to win a home in an
Otherwise wayward world. The state is not
The soul writ large; the soul is not the state
Writ small in the body of a little
Man. But he who would be big must begin small,
Or inherit or steal his largeness from
Others. Beginnings with a chance to last
Entail ruthless extinctions in the past.

v

Each morality's underpinnings are
Its beginnings in immorality.
Every society, lest it succumb
To decadence, must return to where it
Began, to the earliest terrors that
Spawned its rules. You must publicly honor
But privately forget what is taught in
Other schools. You must return to the stream
From which you spawned, if you are to avoid
The error of an imagined goodness
That could thrive without the complicity
Of evil. Evil must be your good, if
Only for a while. Evil, and also
Good, must be the instrument of your guile.

vi

Though all may be driven to speak it, men
Are strangers to peace and rarely seek it.

Your victory is another's Waterloo,
And your Waterloo, another's victory.
Only foolosophy, yes, only those
Benighted follies of philosophers,
Not mute but dumb, could believe that the world
Could ever hum with harmony. There is
Only the isolated uncontrol
Of your equally lonely others lost
In lustful heat for power. Yes. It's a thrill
To idolize the king of the hill, while
Forgetting those he had to lie to, those
He had to swindle, those he had to kill.

vii

Each opportunity awaits like an
Open fig. If you do not act quickly,
Nothing but wasted wit will come of it.
More Machiavellian than any Machiavel,
You could also do good when doing good
Was not good but necessary. There will
Come a time for cruelty well-used, or
For a mercy belied, but well-applied.
Oily ostentation in all matters
Religious or moral is the ointment
Of politics, the salve of salvation
That soothes, that enslaves, that depraves the mob,
That makes one blind to all that does not throb
With eternity of another kind.

viii

Your *virtù* is the virtue the body
Knows. Moved by the body's sole self-good, you
Saw all else as the fatuous *should* of
Unreality. There was for you no
Soul, only the spirit that bodies forth
As aggressive self-assertion, that must
Pride itself on its distinction from the
Ideally good. Virtue is the gusto
That grabs and stabs for yourself alone. Your
Virtue is vigilance on the make that

Cannot forsake the hour's demand. And yet,
Virtue cannot quite ... get ... complete command.
Fortune is always sure to drive a stake
Through the heart of every will to power.

ix

The dictatorship of conscience cannot
Be followed first to last if you are
To resurrect and renew the nobler past.
Conscience is a conspiracy against
Yourself. The dictatorship of conscience
Must be overthrown, yet still you yearn to
Rule as one alone. You must learn to be
Good and bad at will, knowing when to give,
When to lie, when to cheat, and when to kill.
Conscience, an obsolete appliance, must
Be discarded for the sake of science.
If conscience is confidence in the one
True way, then conscience, for you, is always
A confidence game that has had its day.

x

No. Nothing that is strong is clearly wrong.
Conscience always is and ought to be the
First casualty of effective politics.
Only rarest brains are deprived of that
Confusion called conscience, that last forlorn
Refuge of self-deception, that not-so-
Noble mask of naked self-interest.
But the nakedness of power unmasked makes
Power harder to grasp and harder to wield,
And would-be victims less willing to yield.
To see rulers as they are makes the ruled
Unruly. You were the author of this
Chaos. If you swallow this chaos, then
Chaos, before you're through, will swallow you.

xi

There is no invisible virtue. The

Profession of the good swerves toward the
Effective, from the unsustainable
Good man, to men who are – and always will
Be – ready to do what's necessary.
Whatever uplifts are the womanly
Gifts of the unmanly weak. All noble
Ideals are womanly retreats from what
Every man of manly virtue should seek.
In a soul unseeable, there is no
Virtue. The only thing agreeable
For you was the bodily spirit you
Could see and feel, because only the
Real can ever deal with the really real.

xii

You added colors to the chameleon.
Your crooked ways could walk no straighter path.
You always went straight to the truth of the
Unimagined thing, the one thing needful,
The power that must, if it would survive,
Always strive for more and more of itself.
You advised strong men how and when to fake
A vote ... or to cut a throat . You did not
Recommend cruelty for cruelty's sake, but
Urged it mercilessly as an option
When there was no other path toward what you
Want than its adoption. Morality
   ... is placebo for the mob, a tool ... to
Exploit the self-deceit of every fool.

xiii

The steps of a good man and the steps toward
A viable state diverge too early
And converge too late for utopia.
The void between an unattainable
Heaven and an all-too-attainable
Hell is refreshingly honest and grim,
But is always filled to the brim with the
Counter-romance of politics. Venal
Calculi of power know neither good

Nor evil, neither mercy nor cruelty:
Only victory or defeat. And victory,
Despite its wobbly feet, is always sweet.
Yet every victor who meets defeat will
Recollect the shrewdness of self-deceit.

xiv

You're always quick to offer advice to
Those who dare to be sure of paradise.
For you, there is no middle way, and yet
Lopsidedness in the lust for power
Creates a center with opposing sides.
Power, a many-splintered thing, always
Fractures into faction. Those who would seek
Glory rarely find traction in the mire
Of history. The principality stalls and
Sputters. The strongest republic goes to
Ruin. And the prize, if the prize be glory and
Distinction, like the cause from which it sprang
  ... is fleeting, and ends at last in hoary
But rarely ever honored extinction.

xv

The shock of the real is hardly shocking
To any age obsessively clocking
The velocity of change. Always there
Will be a worship of novelty. But
Every erstwhile novelty's now old hat.
There's no older story. Power surrenders
To power. Thrill to thrill. Will to will. Master
To victim, and then glory to glory.
Always scholars unfurl the welcome mat
For one bold enough to renew the shock,
The one who puts all that's believable
On the chopping block. You did not concoct
This swill but merely described it. All your
Virtuoso men have always imbibed it.

xvi

Blasphemies revealed and unrepealed make

Each unwary reader your accomplice.
One should never stoop to be a dupe, not
Even he who thrills at nostalgic dreams
Of a shining city on seven hills.
Every Machiavelli must compose his
Anti-Machiavel. All your most shocking
Maxims must be openly refuted
By the upstart desperation of that
uno solo without a soul that vies
In vain for self-control. It is never
Too late for good words to begin to breed
Good deeds, for another encomium
To a well-managed pandemonium.

xvii

Always ready to man-handle Lady
Fortune, you await the call that never
Came, condemned by virtue's only standard,
The shame of being lame, of failing to
Be as strong on the stage of politics
As the lusty, lucid song of your prose.
Fortune's fool, you die apart from the strong,
Deprived of the power you seek, and at last
You expire, lost, without losing the will
To win or sin, neither mild nor meek, with
Just an ironic grin to light a path
Through the wayward wilderness of the weak.
Such is your wit that never quits but charms
A life born and bungled in your own arms.

xviii

Always, for you, the promised land, of course,
Must be taken by lies, by fraud and force.
Everyone can smile a while before the
Game gives way, as it must, to guilt and grief.
The purity of nihilism is
Always spoiled by urgencies of belief.
Nothing's so unthinkingly clever, so
Shrewdly adept, as unsought-for results
Of promises kept. Yet pagans rough and

Atheists gruff will huff and puff that there
... is such stuff in the structure of the world.
Yes. Self-deception, first and foremost, a
Cruelty to oneself and others, is – at
Last – one of the tender mercies of God.

IV. THE MIDDLEBROW BLUES

Everything was going to be new; everything was going to be different. Everything was on trial. ... "Old Bloomsbury" ... Let us trespass at once ... Let us trespass fiercely and fearlessly and find our own way for ourselves. ... "The Leaning Tower" ... It is the figure of a man; some say, others deny, that he is man himself, the quintessence of virility, the perfect type of which all the others are imperfect adumbrations. He is a man certainly. His eyes are glazed, his eyes glare. His body is braced in an unnatural position, is tightly cased in a uniform. Upon the breast of that uniform are sewn several medals and other mystical symbols. His hand is upon a sword. ... Three Guineas *... But all I can say is that, when lapsing into that stream which people, so oddly, call consciousness, and gathering wool from the sheep that have been mentioned above, I ramble round my garden in the suburbs, middlebrow seems to me to be everywhere. ...* "Middlebrow" *... I resent the power of Percival ... Yet it is Percival I need; for it is Percival who inspires poetry. ... The looking glass whitened its pool upon the wall. The real flower was attended by a phantom flower. Yet the phantom is part of the flower, for when a bud broke free the paler flower in the glass opened a bud too. ... We saw for a moment laid out among us the body of the complete human being whom we have failed to be, but at the same time cannot forget. ...* The Waves *... Losing personality, one lost the fret, the hurry, the stir, and thus rose to her lips some exclamation of triumph over life when things came together in this peace, this rest, this eternity. ... To the Lighthouse ...One can only believe entirely, perhaps, in what one cannot see. ...* Orlando *...*
–Virginia Woolf–

Life is a pure flame, and we live by an invisible Sun within us.
...Urn Burial ...There is something in us that can be without us, and will be after us; though it is strange that it hath no history what it was before us, nor cannot tell how it entred in us. ...

– Religio Medici, *Sir Thomas Browne* –

i

You feared to feel the heat of the sun, yet
You burrowed a hole in the glowing coal
Of death's desire and made life visible.
You may call this life without illusions.
But the party's always almost over
Before it begins. Then ... somewhere around
1910 ... marks the beginning of the
End of sin ...the moment when all who are
Still accused deny their guilt ... the moment
When it was thrilling to throw a shilling
Into the Serpentine, the moment when
A little death in life could defy the
Daylight world, the lies, the chatter, all the
Prattle about things that do not matter.

ii

Somewhere around 1910, you became
Suspicious of every specious present ...
The moment when the bluebird of every
Happiness becomes an elusive pheasant.
Everything ... for one moment ... is solid,
While constantly shifting, as if life was
A miserly recipient of all
Your efforts, a miser who's forever
Re-gifting all his unwanted presents.
Greatness in any field hovers over
All the illusions that have just been killed.
But sooner or later, you'll find ... yourself
Convicted ... by what's never depicted ...
What's never contradicted ... by any mind.

iii

You're always on the brink of the present
Moment, on the brink of the real you could
Not think but feel, for when you choose to feel
You cannot think without illusions that

Unavoidably shrink from what you call
The brink. Is it better to catch or chase
The goose? Either way there are illusions
Not nailed down that are always on the loose.
This is what gets the captain's goat, habits
Of reeling that are learned by rote, this rude,
Rough law of history in the raw, that must
Denote what you surely saw: that chasing
Geese is ... of all ... one piece, well-worn paths through
Patches of perpetual illusion.

iv

Rapture that alone is real must fade, and
You are left alone to feel its loss. The
Life you lost is the cost of living, an
Inflationary spiral that cannot
Quite complete your self-deceit. But, then, when
All is out of proportion, mistaking
The chaff for the wheat, conflating the big
With the small, when the best moment of that
Great good place that's nowhere, keeps harking to
Your beck and call, you are repeatedly
Enlightened ... emancipated ... from all
You've always hated. And yet you remain
A prisoner in the thrall ... of imagined
Raptures ... that recall ... the unabated.

v

The here and the now ... is it this? Is it
Torture? Or is it bliss? Perhaps ... *this* ... you
Saw too clearly, and loved too dearly, the
Wonder you could witness but not embrace.
Each moment is a ripening egg that's
Always about to break its shell. There is
Only suspense and the interruptions
Of suspense. The passage between the two,
Itself unmoving, you forever call
Intense. Always, then, there's the eternal
Itch and the time-ridden urge to be scratched.
Out of this rude rhythm of disruption

And suspense, all those illusions that you
Extol, and hold most dear, you fear, are hatched.

vi

Once again the latest order will be
Resented; thus, plunge into the newest
Order unrepented. You're the clue ... to
Puzzles that someone else, another you,
Presumes to solve. There are many answers
But only one, the one that's always you,
Can fit the larger pattern. Solitude
... is always your undoing. Whatever
You do undoes itself in solitude.
There will be no summing up, no truth
To intrude, only another front to
Occlude the reeling past, another wave
Of feeling good ... or bad ... that recalls the
Erstwhile raptures you only dreamed you had.

vii

There is always something awful about
To happen ... and then it does. Only the
Future which ... *now* ... does not exist can
Tell you what it was. Each wave in its wake
Carries a terror beyond bearing, each
Moment's desperate vigilance of what
Life must unmake is always ... almost ... but
Never ... quite yet ... beyond caring. For you
Must care ... if awake, but only then do
You care enough ... to dare ... to fake concern.
Every organism's orgasm is
A spasm of confusion and despair.
When equivocation equivocates,
It lusts at first, then mates ... with certainty.

viii

All such moments become chilling cinders
Of a history that still inhabits you.
There is no seen without a seer, no
Seeing that fails to seize the one who sees.

Always there is an ancient heritage
Of lives not lived that have led to you. The
Dinosaurs on the evening lawn that
Were there in the dark will be there at dawn.
You must at once trespass the leaves of grass,
The greenest fingers of the earth that have
Not yet learned to touch, that do not revere,
But fear the dishonored soil, that dark and
Desecrated ground, the fossilized past,
From which everything that's green must spring.

ix

Every inhuman universe is so
Vast a void, you yearn, then learn, to fill it
With overpopulations of intense
Sensations, with copulations that must
Increase the surplus populations of
Discontent. But all who would be alone
In one moment are ineluctably
Thrown together with other moments. There's
No moment standing still in which you will
Not thrill at the touch of other moments.
In Eden, it begins and ends with sin,
With father, mother, and child disunion,
With family traumas that mar and make you
What you are … one who resists communion.

x

Every manly man wants to be someone,
Get somewhere, conquer … lest he be conquered.
You always saw the present moment as
Rest without conquest. But in conquest there
… is never any rest. Yet there's something
In you, you must fear, that's always impressed
By the uncommon infinity of
The common, something that embarrasses
And then harasses masculinity,
Something akin to sympathy and tea,
That you cannot shake off … with a nervous
Laugh or a long, pretended cough, something

Desperate that wants to conquer every *Me*
In *You* ... and the *You* that's in every *Me*.

xi

The perfect man, the fascist, gets where he's
Going before he starts. The imperfect
Man, the unmanly man, the better man's
The man who does not go at all, the man
Who does not stand and fight, who prefers flight
To being right, who toys with death to shun
The invisible sun of perfect men.
Some say, some deny, that such talk is a
Bald-faced lie, that to drown is an act of
Perfect submission. Some say, some deny,
It's the perfect, snobsnubber grouse in you,
Not the spouse ... who always voiced her aitches ...
Some say, some deny, it's the perfect man
In you, who killed the angel in the 'Ouse.

xii

Forget not ... the perils of Paulina:
Eternity's news is mortal to one
Who would win renown, to one who's seen the
Eternal Mrs. Brown, to one who has
The courage that looks down ... looks down and sees
What death is doing ... as if every life
Were all about illusions you're eschewing,
While always undoing, renewing and
Then screwing them all to one sticking place.
Now here and ... then ... *nowhere*, death, for you, is
The future of every illusion, the
Death that breaks every life in two, the death
That divides the life of others, and then the
Death of others that divides you too.

xiii

All your mounting moments do not make a
Visible monument of moments, but
Always lurch into another specious

Present, another saddled perch on the
Pale rider, another moment, a hinge
Between two invisibilities, from
Which others can be remembered, can be
Imagined, and then vicariously
Explored, enjoyed or deplored. At any
Given moment, all but this dubious
Perch, almost all of ... what you are ... will be
Invisible. Body will fail, mind will
Fail, and then after that, there will be one
Last faithless flail at the seesawing sea.

xiv

No one can ever slake the thirst for the
Memory of the first in every series.
Half awake, half asleep, in between, the
Waves will break, for in the middle of each
Moment is the specious present that must
Always break into death and life, into
Past and future. All that arrives must pass
Before it gets where it's going. Always,
The greatest ecstasy is recalling
What never came when you waited where you
Thought it was and where you thought it happened.
There's rapture. There's ecstasy ... the looking
Glass shame of happiness, not lost, not had,
That's unrecalled, but bravely imagined.

xv

Your strongest urge was to loiter on the
Trembling verge ... just shy ... of revelation.
You could not, would not, look as happy, as
You thought you ought to feel, or even feel
As happy as you tried to look. But on
The edge of the reel, you see the face of
One beastly but alive, the one you feel, but
Cannot still or kill. You're alive, you are
Dead, and then you're alive again. You're dead,
You're alive, and then you're dead again.
Yes. This must be how your eternity

Looks and sounds: ebb and flow, the endlessly
Irresistible urge to stay ... and the
Always irrepressible need to go.

xvi

Hidden in blindsight, what you see without
Any awareness is neither foulness
Nor fairness, neither large nor small, but the
Substance of the only thing that is. A
Bird out of hand, but not beheld, is no
Bird, and a word not understood is no
Word. You are the one who holds, the one who
Understands. If you do not hold, there is
No bird, no word, no world, no you. All this,
You may say, is plain delusion, but this,
This honest self-confusion, allows that
Profusion of the real you may doubt but
Always feel. Toward death from conception, this
... is the miracle of self-deception.

xvii

Like a phantom flower you emerge in a
Splurge of meaning ... always there and teeming
With every possibility of change.
If the self's an illusion, then ... you ... as
The final court of appeal, are then ... of all
Things ... the thing most real. The self is not an
Inconsequential ghost but the very thing
That can gain or lose the most. To divide
Illusion from the real or the really
Real is to confuse the issue and to
Queer the deal. As the sea ebbs and flows, your
Worries may wane or mount, but the oyster
In the bursting shell of experience
Can always count on telling what must count.

xviii

There is a fountainhead in your head that
Never goes to bed, a nor'easter in

Your mind that keeps on snowing … yes, even,
When there was for you no longer any
Cause to keep on going. But whether it's
Artifice or artifact, the soul that's
Enfolded in the flesh cannot fail to
Extract itself from flesh and exact a
Meaning. Once this happens, you've already
Arrived at nowhere. From nowhere to now
Here, you're here … and as though chaos were a
Verity, you must emerge into the
Clearing to reach the clear … that brazenly
Self-confused clarity called consciousness.

xix

Consciousness creeps or careens like a train
That has no need of riders. When the world's
Too much with you, you fled into moments.
When the moment's too much with you, you fled
Into the world. The closet closest to the
The skin and skein of flesh and mind is the
One you cannot help but find when you want
It least, and the banquet you cannot reach
When you want to feast. The fugitive in
The closet, the cloistered virtue, when at
Last let out, stumbles on consolations
Of self-doubt … will find … when blindsight is no
Longer blind that looking *inside in* looks
A lot like looking on the *outside out*.

xx

All this is quite disconcerting … the way
That time keeps flirting … with eternity.
You cannot quite … cremate … the last remains
Of religious hope. Incineration
Fails. Death does not disinfect the living;
The contamination continues. Thus,
You may kill all the imbeciles but the
Idiot questioner is here to stay.
The long struggle of elimination
Continues unabated, so even

Honesty's overrated … and must give
Way, as the last philosopher gave way,
The one who had the final say, the one
Who died by doctoring himself away.

xxi

Loneliness is the well into which you
Fell, the lasting illusion you could not
Dispel. Each specious present offers up
The illusion of eternity … when
The crowd of selves that is yourself and your
Equally lonely others congregate
In the cave of solitude, the timeless,
Placeless time and place, when the woman in
Each man who thinks through fathers and the man
In every woman who thinks through mothers
Meet … face to face … and should at last … embrace.
But in the midst of the privileged moment,
The life of the party dies. And there's no
One left alive to tell you what is wise.

xxii

Harried by the middlebrow blues, you can't
Abide the shock of eternity's news.
Percivals, the poetry of each good
Moment, are never enough. Piercing the
Valleys of vast extremes, you fall so low
You must get high again on other dreams.
But a little bit of theory is a
Dangerous thing, and a lot is lethal
To the farthest side of itself, the facts
It presumes to fathom. Every attempt
At explanation does not explain but
Blurs the hammer blow with scurrying snow.
Yes. There's perhaps a frump, with a widow's
Hump, who still loves the life you could not know.

xxiii

What you want most from others, from yourself,
… is the illusion of a dancing world.

What you gave others were illusions that
Were more terribly real than tender.
Golden moments in a golden bowl do
Not of their own accord make up a whole.
Overdressed for rehearsals of dispersal,
Each ort that's out of sort is a piece of
You that will never comport with wisdom.
Not gone, but to be anti-gone: Yes, it
Requires more than a sunlight-splattered whim
To refute the grim empiricism
Of him who kicked the stone, who thus rejects
The paternity of eternity.

xxiv

Extremes meet at the opposite side of the
Circle from the point that was thought to be
The middle of a line whose actual
Arc is far too slight to ever notice.
And you, alas, are the center of this
Circle, the center of perceiving and
The perceived, of grieving and the aggrieved,
Of relieving and the unrelieved. Each
Moment of imagined ecstasy forms
A ring of conscious stones with eyes that stare
Back at each other, astonished at what
They must encircle. The darkness in
This cave of solitude has issues of
Itself that will never be published.

XXV

Only if you renounce the privileges
Of now could you ever overcome the
Chauvinism of the present moment.
This is the will to struggle, the would-be
Conquest, in every desperate urge for rest.
There's a garment and an undergarment
Underlying all the arguments of
Ideologies that fear the naked.
Go-betweens, fluttering in the middle
Of the great unseens, must gather themselves

From time to time to think on what it means.
Yes, even the most elite of the most
Effete must finally allow: Oh yes,
Everyone, one and all, is middlebrow ... now.
Post-Dedication:
With undying admiration for Virginia and with gratitude
for the small, but important service performed by Robert.

V. WHY ANTIGONE WEPT

Antigone: Follow, follow me this way with your
unseeing footsteps, father, where I will lead you. (183-184)
        – Sophocles, *Oedipus at Colonus* –

Antigone: I know that I am pleasing them I should please most.
Ismene: Perhaps. But you're in love with the impossible.
Antigone: Then when I've used up all my strength, I'll be through.
Ismene: You should not hunt for the impossible at all. (89-92)
        – Sophocles, *Antigone* –

i

Emblematical, you always thought you
Were, of something not quite beyond yourself.
Yours was the darkling rumor that spreads in
Secret to wed in mourning the Lord of
The Dark Lake. But when rumor augurs death,
Savage fantasy may deliver fact.
To feel the real is to feel as all the
Other players feel. All else is passion
Sans the middling ration of common sense.
You summon the inadequacy of all,
For no one's equal to your solitude.
No admiration, no scorn can match the
Rage and ravaging nobility of
Your most ungenerous self-delusion.

ii

You were born and bred in opposition,
A non-Theban in Thebes, a desolate

Girl, bravely alone among the ephebes.
Your business was to define the spot of
Blindness and unkindness in your father's
Heart. Harbored within is the wilderness
That will not be tamed, the depths of a guilt
That will not be named. But subtlety will
Always seek escape from catastrophe.
You seek in vain the safety of elsewhere,
But could put no distance between yourself
And your own pain. Yet you would, if you could,
Transport yourself out of that vast despair
Of despair that cannot compare with joy.

iii

Every time they use slime for mortar, you
Reach for another clever device, a
Teleporter to beam you out, and yet
No art, no technology will ever
Escape the rigor of the argument
In you that will not be clinched. There is no
Last word on desire. Thus, you must content
Yourself with your yearning to aspire, for
The patience you need but cannot acquire
Will never require an ending. All that
You are, all you were, all you will be, is
Forever tending toward what never ends,
As if you could become in your longest home
A monument of unresilient stone.

iv

Your father, who fathered the fierceness in
You, lived a life that was born outworn, a
Life forsaken, already lost, when born.
If your father could not complete the work,
Then the task belongs to you, for no one
Else will do, but you. From first to last, you
Could invest no trust in what turns to dust.
When the life you've already lost becomes
The cost of living at all, then there will
Be much forgetfulness to recall. There

Are those who walk the line; there are those
Who cross it. You pierced that great barrier
Reef of sorrow where all that's once safely
Forgotten is relentlessly remembered.

v

Your tragedy is the depiction of
Affliction without consolation or
Conviction, for kinship eats its own kind.
Only that family that forgets itself
Can foster happy children. And yet a
Family cursed with memory cannot forget
Itself. To live together ... and to love
Together in harmony and peace is
A promise that cannot be kept. Is this
Why, you, Antigone, wept? You promise
What cannot be kept, and this promise is
Both necessary and impossible.
You wound forgetfulness when you express
What your integrity could not repress.

vi

Your surest stronghold, the home, is shaken.
All that's familiar has been forsaken.
In the wake of war, you could find no peace,
For the blood of the dishonored dead that
Bled in battle now bleeds in you, who must
Trespass the fraud of the familiar, the
Fraud that calls for peace when there is no peace.
Caught red-handed, you stand unterrifed
In fatal acts of illicit honor.
However hard, it's easier to boast
Of what you know than what you've left undone.
Yet hardly knowing what you hardly know,
Admirers revere what you hardly know
Less than the hardest fate you would not shun.

vii

You were too much, too little, and far too

Brittle to be molded by habit, by
Compromise or calculation into
The daily routine of any hearth and
Home. The perils of domesticity
Were for you more perilous than death, for
You feared the one and braved the other. There's
A greater insanity than wanting
Death. There is that wanting that waits for the
Impossible rival that never comes,
That refuses, when it refuses joy,
To traffic with the merely possible.
Your fatal choice arises from nowhere,
As if what was impossible ... now is.

viii

Palaces of patriarchy threaten
To crumble. They already have, but you
Still stumble in puzzlement over their
Left-over platitudes that still survive
Without the beatitudes of belief.
There will come a time ... it is always now ...
When not much of the truth can still remain,
But there will always be much to learn, much
To gain from the burdensome heft of falsehood.
Yours was the clash of possible voices,
Impossible choices, not right or right,
Not wrong or wrong, but point and counterpoint
Of a remorseless song sung always at
The threshold you might not have crossed but did.

ix

Your path to death is a path that only
One of a kind would ever try to take.
No one else will go with you, for you are
Precisely this: the one who no one's with.
Anyone who is one of a kind is
Perpetually un-akin, unkind and
Blind to others. An anomaly that
Constantly repeats itself becomes as
Rigorous as a rule that everyone

Else but you should follow. Is this why you
Find the logic of the rule so hollow?
There are some, who say, you promiscuously
Obey, for you're the one with no other
Way ... but to make or forsake the promise.

x

Lost reverence of the dead weighs heavily
On the head of him who's lost it. The flame
Of sacrifice sputters and smokes and the
Author of your necessity then chokes
And stutters over his cruel undoings.
Death always signifies the loss of the
Unlived life, the knife that divides all that
Might have been from what now must always be.
Yet the essence of your splendor is that
Everyone yearns most to believe you're free.
When idle cant meets the uncanny,
That's called philosophy. When death impends,
All such wisdom is a convention
That only a tactless fool would mention.

xi

There's a blight that will never let you be.
To become what you are, you must repeat
Yourself. To be at home, you must return
Again and again to your beginning.
But whatever might be home is always
A long way from whatever you call joy.
Yet when joy departs without return, then
At last, you learn, you are at home no longer.
Nothing's more terrible than beginning.
When it's over, nothing that is ... can last
So long and seem so wrong as what once was.
The joy you freely lost is both the source
And cost of your deathless beauty, for you
Did as you saw fit ... you did your duty.

xii

Just before dawn, beyond the gates, you would

Conspire with your kin to save your kind. But
You're the kind to which no one is akin.
You insist that no one share your sorrow.
Yours is the splendor that illuminates
And blinds, that obsesses when it reminds
The seeker of what he seeks but never
Finds, a splendor so demanding that it
Can survive only beyond the ken of
Common understanding. The uncanny,
The unshrewd, in you, is that unwitting
Cleverness that guards what you traduce. You're
That furrow never plowed by others that
Never succumbs to those you still seduce.

xiii

In the heat of greed for a chilling deed,
You spoke silences whereof no one should
Speak. Your crime must be trumpeted. It must
Disturb quietudes no one breaks but you.
You undergo the worst, but you thirst for
Nothing more than what's already happened,
For you're born enduring what you will be.
No temptation of consolation can
Muffle the hideous roar of what you
And your kindred have always heard before.
Your life rumbles with echoes of itself.
A vicious circle makes your life complete.
Every terrible lucidity is
Always buried alive in self-conceit.

xiv

You are the vexing angel of all who
Profess prudence, but not-so-secretly
Detest it. Thus, you disrupt the calm of
Common understanding. Whoever
Would be sane will always owe a measure
Of madness to the madman or to those
Who entomb you in a vault of stone, to
Those who become no more than nobody.
Your earliest fear foreshadowed your loss

Of nerve. Yet in the solitude of the
Cave, you pause in tears but never swerve from
The petrifying pain that bares your fears.
You should die in the cavern unexposed.
Do not reopen what the casket closed.

XV

And yet, your eternity's still alive:
It's fiercely dwelling ... in what your anger
And agony keep retelling, while time's
A torrent that keeps on raining, keeps on
Straining, keeps on going, keeps on snowing,
That keeps on throwing everyone off the
Scent of its perpetual pollution.
Nobody whispers in Chinese whispers
What you keep yelling. Yet you weep, you weep
For you, for what you did and did not do.
There is always another way to end
The play. It didn't have to be this way.
But, alas, poetry has no defense
Against the objections of common sense.

VI. THE BOOK OF EXPECTATION

With all my soul have I desired thee in the night; yea, with my spirit within me I will seek thee early: for when thy judgments are in the earth, the inhabitants of the world will learn righteousness.
– Isaiah. 27:9 –

*Thine heart shall meditate terror. Where is the scribe?
Where is the receiver? Where is he that counted the towers?*
– Isaiah. 33:18 –

*Not one, not two, not three, there is an infinity of Isaiahs, but out of this multitude without number, there will always be the one,
the one and only one Isaiah who reaches and teaches you.*
– An unpublished poet –

i

Out of the book of expectation comes
Forth the fervent hunger for fulfillment.
There's a touch of terror in every love
That tramples wisdom, for one already
Ruined can bring ... at best ... his smoldering
Ruins to another. You expect a
Curse. You receive a blessing. In all
The ironies of life you become quite versed.
In all its evils, you have been well-nursed.
The tribe of pseudo-Isaiahs ever
Larger grows, but when infinity's reached,
There's only the one you know, the one who
Knows, the one who knows that you always know
But never believe what you truly are.

ii

The spirit stammered, offering only frail
Murmurings of itself, until it found
Its full-throated voice in you. From the realm
Of the trivial to the sublime is
The shortest step from the darkest day of
The petty and the small, to the day of
The Lord, the brightest day of all in all.
You could not cry. You could not keep silent.
Between scream and silence is the ruling
Love that has not quite lost its lasting hate
For whatever it is that you become.
To return or go: always your m.o.
   ... is to be appalled at the demonic
Instability of the status quo.

iii

There is ruin before restoration.
This truth, trite and true by definition,
Marks the condition you always forget.
From cradle to the grave, the string of your
Disappointments, some still unmet, will be
Obsessively spoken but unbroken.
You search for signs and wonders. Then, you lurch
To and fro, wallowing in your blunders.

Whenever the standard-bearer faints, there
Will be a profusion of fresh complaints.
All that is good goes away backward: the
Head is sick, the heart is faint, and history's
So heavy with accumulated groans
There's hardly a corner for your complaint.

iv

The stupefaction of sin is the Slough
Of Despond, when the self forgets itself
And can't respond, when the insomniac
Conscience is fast asleep, when it forgets
The promise it cannot keep, when even
Your highest calling falls fast and deep in
The arms of disarming idolatries.
You must begin as a prophet, you must
Begin by shattering all indifference.
The scandal of particularity
   ... is the shock of each solitude that would
Embrace the universe, that must face in
Final disgrace what it cannot embrace.
What is ... cannot pretend ... it never was.

v

Great forsaking in the midst of the land
Never turns out the way you planned. Magpie's
Pawn, you're what's picked up. Bottomless unrest,
Life makes of you a bungled nest of odds
And ends, an open maw without measure.
Each new abyss loses its glamour. Brave
Genius, calling evil good, tomorrow
Will always refuse what today you choose.
Now there's no longer any pleasure
In the treasure of darkness. Thus, you go
To bed with your gods and wake up sated,
Rising again to pretend to love what
You've always hated. You must burn before
You learn how satisfaction is overrated.

vi

Recall solitudes you've already tried:
You know, or so, you say, you know, what's known
Most surely is what's deep inside. Yet no
Matter how you've lied and tried, you return
To what self-deception can never hide.
Earlier than wrath, earlier than love,
Earlier than mercy, the self you seek
... is your loneliest other in the time
Before your living time began, before
The evening and the mourning that was
The first day. But every earliness is
An earliness that's still born too late to
Receive its blessing, an earliness that
You must share with every lonely other.

vii

You suffer in confidence or the lack
Of it. Barefoot and naked, you walk and
Squawk in vain that you lack the eloquence
To talk like a prophet, as if you could
Undo the doubt of all the doubters and
Bring them back to belief. You're the one who
Suffers, who might yet serve yourself and those
Lonely others, who might yet swerve ... from the
Abomination of desolation.
Ruin and restoration yield no relief:
The search for salvation is the search for
Motiveless benignity, an Eden
Freed from the need and greed for self-deceit.
The seed in every stump sprouts this belief.

viii

A deceit's never smooth enough until
Sleek and slick as a fish it leaps out of
Its element to surprise you with its
Rainbow glints. In its vanishing wake, in
Its titillating hints, you and your world
Which desperately want to be deceived, wink,

As they always do, at dishonesty.
You want most of all to fall in love with
Your own past, lest the first time you betray
Your solitude should be your last. Yet your
Lies are as wise as the prophet of sin
You try but fail to suppress, for just when
You think it's gone, there will arise in you
The remnant of the wise you must express.

ix

In the beginning is the bang, a bang
So big, so loud ... that makes the witness
Himself seem as small and as silent
As the loneliest man in every crowd.
God, first and last, is the iconoclast,
The original idol smasher. Yes.
Idolatry is forgetfulness of
What counts, what mounts and mounts, even as you
Fail, as you always do, to keep accounts.
Every image of the human is an
Imitation, a cherished idol with
All its limitation. And every
Image of God is an imitation
Of eternity's endless struggle with ... infinity.

x

Let it be the terror or the thrill, but
There's something alive in you that despair
Cannot swallow and that time cannot kill.
You may return, if you will, to every
Now, every nook, every cranny of your
Life, and what you restore you may ruin,
And what you ruin you may restore. The
Remnant that's smoldering deep within is
Both the enemy and the friend of sin.
It's threat and promise, promise and threat.
The fire that is your strength from first to last
Will not be quenched. Every remnant is a
Promise and a threat of the returning pain,
The regret ... that you haven't met with yet.

xi

All the ages are living creatures: when
You fall asleep in time, you slumber in
The belly of a beast. The watchman is
Nothing if not awake, for the sleeper
Needs awaking. Startled at the ruins
Of his own making and forsaking, he
Stands and stares before the wreckage, before
The miracle of *once upon a time*.
The infinite reaches the end of its
Tether when all your energy has been
Accosted and exhausted by the
Merciless weather of eternity.
Whether you succeed or whether you fail,
Once again the snake must swallow its tail.

xii

Meaning that tumbles, high to low, like the
Proverbial ball of snow, cumulates
The freight of dross and frost, becoming too
Heavy to lift, too hard to throw. Meaning
In exile wanders for a long or a
Little while, then returns unrepressed like
The blessing of a curse … expressing the
Significance of suffering as the
Suffering of significance. Belated,
Delayed, deferred, you'll at last arrive at
The unrecurred. In the virginity
Of that unrepressed moment, in early
Mournings of the unabashedly new,
You'll learn to believe what you always knew.

xiii

Eternity never stops because it
Never starts. It is what *Is* always is.
No matter what you believe, forever
You're what you are … without reprieve. And yet
Tautologies, near and dear, cannot soothe
The dreadful competency of a soul

You can't be sure of, a soul that despite
The promise of everlasting love, still
Sweats the solemn sweat of Gethsemane,
The sweat of blood and tears, of belief in
Grief. You never stop but always pause to
Feel the effect that's lost in another
Cause. You are established by your belief,
And yet every belief will come to grief.

xiv

There is a sacred insomnia that
Never sleeps, but that keeps what the sleeper
Never keeps: the promise of fulfillment.
Continuation is confirmation,
Conjecture or refutation. And all
Confirmation or refutation is
Conjecture dully perceived. Yes. In the
Wings, all remains conjecture in disguise,
Awaiting the fate of final lies. But
Every false rumor may be a servant
Suffering for the truth. Arts of redaction
Cannot erase but only deface the
Trace of the truth in the palimpsest that
Obscures your history ... of eternity.

xv

Everyday's any day and always is.
For whenever you summon the power,
Apocalypse arrives in every hour.
What's unknown is what's yours, what's hers, what's his.
Until the promise comes alive in you,
You must always accept, not ask: what gives?
This alone's the moment you own that lives.
There is no wisdom bottled. There is no
River of imagination dammed. There
   ... is a truth that can only be fought for,
And a forgiveness that cannot be shammed.
Thus, await in haste the day of the Lord
When every soul will feel its worth: this and
This alone is the meaning of the earth.

VII. THE LAST CONVICTION

He remembered now having stretched out his arms to that ocean of light and blue and wept. He was tormented by the idea that he was separated from all that. What was this feast, this endless festival, to which he had so long felt himself drawn, ever since his childhood, without ever being able to participate in it? ... Every being has a path and knows it; he comes and goes singing; but he, he alone knows nothing and understands nothing, neither men nor the voices of nature, for he is everywhere a stranger and an outcast.
— Fyodor Dostoevksy, The Idiot —

Snow is falling today, almost wet snow, yellow, dirty. It was snowing yesterday, too, and the other day. I think it is because of the wet snow that I remembered the incident which gives me no rest now ...
— Fyodor Dostoevsky, The Underground Man —

The hardest thing in life is not to lie, and not to believe your own lie.
— Fyodor Dostoevsky, The Demons —

i

Should your time, should any time, unaided
And degraded, withstand one more prophet
Of eternity? After prophecy,
There will be no rest for the weary, not
In dream, not in fact, and not in theory.
For every enigma there is always
An explanation that will entice but
Not suffice. Nothing's more dreary than a
Promising theory that perpetually
Quivers with what it never delivers.
The gospel of self-realization is
The imperative to become someone
Or something else. And yet there is always
Something amiss in following one's bliss.

ii

Your desire beggars that of others. No

Desire is stronger than your desire. No
Passion is so strong or could last so long
As your passion. No ration's cheaper than
The cheapest ration of those who lack the
Immensity of your intensity.
Greatness of desire gives permission for
Your mission of ruthless self-fulfillment.
If everything is permissible, then
Conscience is easily dismissible.
Yet if conscience were easy to kill, there
Would be no lacerations of self-will.
That others suffer more is not quite fair.
You too deserve your fair share of despair.

iii

You lived a long and happy life, and yet
You were deeply wrong about yourself and
Your life. Would you, if you could, extinguish
The delusion in this happy creature?
Perhaps in another verse you'll tell us
What is worse: an id that has tasted all
It wanted and wasted, or an id that
Has never tasted what it wants yet taunts.
If you have no need of consolation,
Then you're unworthy of consolation.
And if you are so unworthy, then of
What last great sins are you still capable?
When all you are has been exhausted, you
Will still be accosted by what remains.

iv

The inner light is the glint that's always
The hint of life at its peak, the moment
Before the expected rifle shot, that
Impends but never ends, that's final but
That keeps recurring. Always you abide
Just this side of a paradise that is
Almost possible. Your epileptic
Fit is your only glimpse of it. This god
Of gilded time is your momentary

God, the god of every moment, of all
Your equally lonely moments, as if
You drank the ocean, but did not drown in
It ... as if your poetry were all the
Gobbledygook it took to make a book.

v

Every being is beleaguered by what
Passes by. The promise of the moment
That's always broken is the makeshift dam
Of an instant in the flow of time that
Explodes and succumbs to what must follow.
As the crisis grows near, you fear the smear
On the verge of your urge to act: guilty,
You are, all and none, and one and all, so
Guilty that almost none but you would flee
From every accusation. Each gamble's
A preamble to the constitution
Of your guilt: to stay, to go, or to go,
To stay, to decide or not, or to act
Before desire petrifies into fact.

vi

Whatever demands you become something
Else is not in you. You leave home when you
Accept the false promise of something not
Yourself, when you succumb to the lure of
Lost eternity. The false promise of
Autonomy trades the possible for
The impossible, sells short what is for
What you cannot be. Ideals must shatter;
They do. Idols must topple; they do. Gods
Must die; they do. The only issue that
Remains is whether there is any time,
Any path, any room left for you. The
Only residue that's left ... before, now,
Hereafter ... is the residue that's you.

vii

The promise you fear is true for others

Can never be true for you. That others
Share this fear, that the promise may be true
For you, is a fear you fear to share, a
Fear that intensifies with lies that can
Put no end to suffering. The promise of
Everlasting bliss is what for you and
Others must be put at risk. Every fear
Fears most to be found out. That the gates of
Paradise are blocked would be bearable
If others should believe what you ... and they
Too ... always knew. Fear is universal,
Scandal's specific, and run-of-the-mill
Deceit's the usual order of things.

viii

Vainly, you scramble to resurrect the
Original impression of yourself,
Which is the subject of your repression.
In rare moments, forged by the fierce routine
Of false extremes, hastened by habits, and
Hoodwinked by dreams, you stumble upon your
Final obsession, your most reluctant
Confession: you serve as the minion of
Someone else's forgotten opinion.
That original impression, so says
Your confession, is merely a copy
Of what you imagined someone else, your
Champion, your nemesis, your idol,
Had tried to be ... but could never become.

ix

To be possessed is to be obsessed with
An impossible other, another
Who, like you, is obsessed with another
Impossible self. But to possess what
Obsesses you portends disappointment,
For the fundamental transformation
You avidly sought must come to naught. What
Was sought was metamorphosis; what is
Found is restoration of an order

You seek to reshape but cannot escape.
To imitate or not to imitate
What you love and what you hate thus blurs your
Desire that must arrive too late to let
You love or let you hate without motive.

x

Before your confession you never reach
A vivid impression of what you are,
Of your ownmost self, an idiot, a
Buffoon in earnest, who relentlessly
Stokes the furnace of metaphysical
Desire. Nothing could be more obscene than
This furious routine. All envy, all
Resentment, all your corrupted desire
 ... is this: you want to become someone else,
Yet somehow impossibly be yourself.
Your character, carried to logical
Extremes, always embodies an ideal
That refutes itself. Whatever's sauce for
The goose is good for the propaganda.

xi

Whatever you come to know is always
a propos of the wettest snow, as if
All you knew, you thought, you felt, had asked but
Refused to answer why, had already
Begun to melt whilst in vain you vie to
Accumulate ... to amount to something.
The more you suffer the more you learn how
Solitude's invaded at every turn.
There is nothing less private, nothing less
Closed than the closet of the self. It is
Not cracked; it is more than ajar; it's wide
Open to everyone and everything.
Yes. The solitude on which you suppose
You sit is always the throne of others.

xii

Between what's real and what's really real lies

The fantastic that can become plastic
Enough to embrace anything. History's
As vaporous as every object or
Obstacle of desire, for each desire
Misses its mark at moments of sought-for
Fulfillment, naked and stark, of its dark
Romantic hopes. Here the definition
Of romance rhymes with the desire that pants
... as such ... for the more and more of every
Much. These tawdry rites of failed devotions,
You'll dismiss ... at moments of would-be bliss
With false rumors of newborn lies. In hell,
Fresh paint begins to peel before it dries.

xiii

Nothing's harder than being happy, for
Just when you think you've slipped beyond desire,
What remains is the burnt-out district of
Your erstwhile self. The metaphysical
Ghost of your lost desire still wants to want
But murmurs all-too-vaguely, as if to
Tease the desire you lost with desires of
Others. You will attract others as one
Who holds a secret that he cherishes
But will not share. As that strange attractor
Of befuddled others, you'll in turn be
Duped by those you dupe, as though this troop of
Befuddled admirers has at last seen
In you what you never see in yourself.

xiv

Explanation of the last conviction
Sets the first stage in the next depiction
Of despair. Resumptions of assumptions
Of eternity, to which you repair,
Are always there on the ever higher
Stair of a justified skepticism
That knows no end. You must change your life, says
Every exalted moment. Yet again,
As always, you continue as before,

Becoming first and last what you abhor.
But the hedgerow country of history
Allows no running score. Alas, every
Benediction's a fiction about the
Imagined benefits of affliction.

XV

To count each moment as if it's the last
Worships the causality of the past.
To greet each moment as if it's the first
Rejects all the remembrances of thirst.
Remembering yourself at your best and worst
Forgets the muddled middle that's always
About to burst into eternity.
Every history of self-mastery is
Disaster and mystery ... for when you
See your lies reflected in another's
Eyes, you do not think of yourself as wise.
One good moment of one good time is not
The life or death of you. No one waltzes
Away with wisdom from the dance: the dance ... goes on.

VIII. THE FINAL YOU

Yet we must know in order not to know. The supreme lesson of human consciousness is to learn how not to know. ... each individual has his own Holy Ghost ... Fantasia of the Unconscious *... The goal is to know how not-to-know. ...* Studies in Classic American Literature *... There is only one thing a man really wants to do all his life and that is to find his way to his God, his morning star, and be alone there. ...* The Plumed Serpent *... First and last, man is alone: born alone and dies alone, lives while he lives most of his time alone and in his deepest self never ceases to be alone. ...* "Deeper Than Love" *... We torture ourselves getting somewhere, and when we get there it is nowhere, for there is nowhere to get to. ...* The Apocalypse *... "So there is a final you".... "Still", he said, "I should like to go with you nowhere. It would be rather wandering just to nowhere. That's the place to get to – nowhere. One wants to wander away from the world's somewheres into our own nowhere."* Women in Love

– D.H. Lawrence –

Here's lookin' at you, kid, and Holy Ghost.
  – A prize-winning poet, "Ecce Halo" –

i

There is something rotten in the state of
Loneliness, as if the mystery in you,
You loved, was in love with you, as if you could
Make your world anew ... then marry it,
As if there's one critique of all that's bleak,
As if the rainbow's ark could carry it,
As if intensity of life alone
Could ferry it to the other shore, where
Every *I do* bids *Adieu* to suffering.
Alas, your universe is a monad,
A register in one cell, a great gaunt
Gonad of yearning. And each monad, though
Brightly burning, is a mirror of what
You're always only partly conscious of.

ii

Each monad, though rippling with vibrations
Of everything, is incapable of
Complete enlightenment. Thus, whatever
Passes for reality is the still
Unrefuted, undiluted remains
Of your exhausted imagination.
It takes a great imaginer to make
Cosmic vagueness seem strikingly exact.
But imagination is that crippled
Blessing genius that may see, yet not seize,
What portends, that must confuse expanse with
The expense of each experience, that
Cannot separate freedom's ends from the
Fantasy it forever blends with fact.

iii

Few, if any, came quicker to the quick
Of things. Your life's the volcanic lava,

The scalded blood of quickened mountains; it
Flowed into fountains of prose that bubbled,
Then troubled you into beauty. For you,
Life lived at maximum intensity
   ... is the only duty. Yet you feared that
You too were a middling soul, for middling
Souls are wedged between two oblivions,
Hedged between every thirst and fast, between
Sex and snow, between first and last, between
A place to come to and no place to go.
The question's not: *Are you more or less?* But
Always: *Are you equal to what you know?*

iv

Nothing makes you quite so queasy as snake
Oil nostrums of sleazy, all-too-easy
Immortalities. Malingering in
This abyss is a state too uneasy
To populate with happy citizens.
You stumble, mumble and scumble: then you
Pause to bumble into idolatrous
Consolation. You want to believe that
Time's a phantom, a trick of the eye that
Expiates your gravest offenses. But
Time's the instrument of eternity:
You quicken into what you think, what you
Do, and feel. Time's the way eternity
Turns the holy ghost into what is real.

v

You were so vexed by mysticisms of
Sex that now everything depends on the
Crisis of coition, on the extreme
Unction of bodily function, as if
The act of sex were redemption and not a
Mode of exemption from happiness. Sex
In bed, in the heart, or in the head: All
Sex that's lewd, that's shrewd, naturally yearns to
Be screwed to that great good place of rumored
Satisfaction, a place that is retried

And occupied, while occupiers have
Repeatedly lied about what's been tried.
For you, sex is nowhere, and never now
Here, a rapture that's far gone or foregone.

vi

Consummatum est: Orgasm is your
Perpetual image of ecstasy.
When it's finished, there's silence in heaven
For just half an hour, barely long enough
To revivify your readiness for
Brisk rehearsals of further ecstasy.
Transfiguration in the numinous ghost
Names the coming change that troubles you most.
The promised land beneath your feet is but
A fragile sheet of imaginary
Geology. And nothing you know now
Could refute without apology the
Dourest scientology of sauerkraut
Philosophy or fraud's psychology.

vii

Revelation rebels against hedgerows
Of history. Its frustration flutters toward
Foreclosure, the fate that feels like freedom,
But that's a promise of escape, never
To nowhere but to somewhere. But when you're
Somewhere, there's always still some place to go,
A destiny that's postponed, a fate not
Now but then, a life that's not a life but
An afterlife. You lived as though life could
Reach its peak and stay there, as though you
Could leapfrog the clockwork kingdom, as though
You alone, *sans* others, could teach a creed
As bleak, as meretriciously chic, as
The final critique of pure ecstasy.

viii

There is a nakedness beneath the skin

Of blood and sinew; only the skin can
Hold it in. There's nakedness beneath the
Leaf; even the deepest grief of belief
Can't hide your sin. Nakedness negates a
Nakedness that isn't there. Nakedness
For you, an achievement, not a fact, an
Autistic rapture of the itching eye,
A delusion of tact you cannot share,
Resides in the deepest reservoir of
Despair, the nexus between the cortex
And solar plexus, that might sex us or
Unsex us, but that invariably
Infects us with the lie of solitude.

ix

The mother lode of agony is still
Un-mined, and the hard core of aloneness
Hides a stubborn ore with no clear center,
But with many veins of likely breakage.
The solitary novelist always
Imagines himself untouchably wise.
But when the intoxication of his
Last loneliness sobers up, he learns in
Surprise that only an unimagined
Person can disrupt the benighted and
Besotted solitude of well-wrought lies.
Alas, at last, thou shalt acknowledge this
Wonder. Then there shall be nothing left to
Plunder but the unlived lives of others.

x

A rainbow is an ethereal bridge
From nowhere to now here, from one nowhere
To another. If mind could manhandle
This rainbow, then you could lay your hands on
Joy. If you could trace the trajectory
Of its arc from first to last, then your gods
Need not be dark nor your promises coy.
You were no wronger than any other
Would-be eternity-monger. For when

The uselessness of any goal is reached,
Then you can only go willingly or
Unwillingly to nowhere. Yet to go
Nowhere unwillingly is mere defeat.
But to go willingly: that is freedom.

xi

Look beyond the regalia of genes and
Genitalia: *No one, but the final*
You, is ever gonna know what life's been
Trying to tell ya'. Gods, light and dark, are
Gone, there is only the godless dark, the
Final, naked bark of oblivion.
Death's shipwreck sorts the cargo out: out of
The vastness of its hold come vilest dross
And furious gold, more than finest psalms
Of touch have told. No verse is vial enough
To hold your essence, or to capture your
Blind, unknowing will that keeps bestowing.
To know how not to know is not to know
Nothing but to be someone worth knowing.

xii

Waters of oblivion body forth,
Flow fiercely in rivers of forgotten
Life. Here, fleeting memories die with no time
To sigh for the jilted bride of Buddha.
There's no deeper discipline than the rain,
Though its many variations are the
Perpetual strain of undisciplined
Water. There's no deeper destiny than
The blood, though its lust may at last yield up
The betrayal of all that's good. And there's
No greater health than the health that closes
The darkness up and pours all your cruelty
And all your tenderness into the cup
Of your contagious hunger for more life.

xiii

You sought to say about eternity

Something new as if something new about
Eternity could be said by you that
Could never be said by any other.
Eternity rebels at every scheme.
Only time, all your time, and between first
And last, the middle, reveals its lasting
Theme, that discombobulating riddle
When moral panic in the moralist
Greets unknown others in the final you.
Solitude's the trembling emblem tattered,
That mattered till the mourning star's last groan.
When the monad's solitude has shattered,
The errant midnight will assist your moan.

xiv

There is a house not made with hands, a house
Not sought, not planned. This house, the house of the
Holy ghost, this is the house that matters
Most, the house shot – through and through – with all the
Cruelty … the tenderness … the otherness
That's lodged in the final you. If there were
No space, you'd not be here but everywhere.
If there were no time, you'd not be now or
Then, but everywhen. Of you, there'd be no
Beginning, no end. Thus, if someone asks
Where nowhere is, say: It's neither here nor
There, but it's foul and fulsome like despair,
Or as warm, as bright, as forever fair,
As kittens asleep on a sunlit chair.

IX. ON REMBRANDT: THE OTHER SIDE OF YOU

i

The plumb line cuts the painting in two. There's
The one who claims to be the artist; and …
There's the one always claiming to be you.
The soul in its countenance stutters, harbors

That muffled protest that mutters: are you
More or less than this monument of flesh?
Muscles, firm or flaccid, were artifacts
That make exact what they extract from pain.
You paint yourself placid, laughing, grim. Are
You really the successor to him, the
One who becomes, who became what you are,
The one with the promising glamour of
A beard just beginning to grow, the one
With the grizzled stubble that smacks of snow?

ii

Envy launches originality,
Your intrusion into the archives of
Self-delusion, an origin first feigned,
And then attained, when the imitation's
Veneer has cracked. Your painting begins not
As a blank but as an afterimage
Of the re-imagined, not a copy
But a painting over, an obsessive
Repossession of something already
Encountered, dearly purchased and possessed.
Your obsession is the repossession
Of life's intensity in the quiet
Moment, the shock of the lacquered sublime
That bodies forth from the mediocre.

iii

Folding infinity in a thimble,
You make eternity tremble with the
Fierce urgency of a life that's lived, that's
Living, and that still wants more. But neither
Happiness nor truth can be organized
Into a single moment. Thus, you paint
The way a person gets born, the way your
Life stays before it goes and goes before
It stays. There are just so many ways ... of
Becoming a person, and you paint them
All in one portrait, condensed into a
Grin, neither sly nor grim, but that chuckles

At the infinity toward which you strain
And the wry banalities you disdain.

iv

The promise is always the promise of
More experience. But any road that
Leads the way from home can lead you back, toward
That vision of spurious eyes … eyes that
Spy the paths that led you there, that led you
Back, that greet warily those paths that still
Might lead you on. Life breeds hedges that hem
You in. Thus, you hunker down into the
Labyrinth of your sin. Your mask becomes a
Role, your role a task, your task a soul, the
One sure mortar that binds the mortal to
What you still ask of immortality.
This, your art insists, is the one meaning
That persists in your murky universe.

v

Death inhabits each portrait, inhabits
You, for you're the timepiece who knows you must
One day stop, whose final moment in the
Series makes brute fact of all your erstwhile
Theories about what you thought you might have
Been but now – fatally and forever – are.
Death is already there at the first, there
At the very beginning of thirst, an
Incipient step on the road to your
Demise, a germ that bears its fruit in the
Body of your life, a life unfoolish,
Unwise … that must at last unwind … the coil
Of bitter truth and cherished lies … that blind
Those eyes in you that seek a deeper justice.

vi

Faith, the wit once said, is believing in
What you know ain't so, yet believing's still
Believing when nothing you know still stands,

When life, retouched by art, continues to
Show what you face, confess, but never prove
You know: that the day's demands are neither
In nor out of your most capable hands.
There is you and the other side of you,
Not the reflection but one who reflects,
Not the seen but the seer, not the one
Fulfilled, but the one neither stilled nor thrilled
By the time you've killed, the one on the edge,
Of here or there, the one that is always
The riddle in the middle of nowhere.

vii

Of myriad ways in the maze, there's just
One footpath for you to the common home.
The Bible's your one true book, your one true
Bible, where the promise of transcendence
Found its only means of survival in
The continuing mystery that's you.
The self-portrait of each moment, by time
Annealed, by rhyme congealed, is the history
Of your eternity, that is never
Still but that keeps on moving, keeps proving
The remorseless necessity of a
Law unique to you, a law that in the
End can produce the only possible
Answer to the misbegotten question: Who?

viii

Each step's not one step, not the first step, not
The last, but the long and arduous path
That led you here and to where you keep on
Moving. Each stance is not one stance but is
The reflected glance of a lifelong fate,
That's too late to love, too early to hate.
You paint the outward to look inside and
What's seen inside, you do not hide. Neither
Do you whisper, neither do you shout what it's
About. You merely make it visible.
For good or ill, your still life's never still,
Never bows to conditions of freezing.

Even as your portraits stand still, they're still
Coming through to the other side of you.

ix

Religion at the end of its tether
Still wants to grab the rope that's out of reach.
Dogmas of erstwhile comfort bark at what
You no longer recognize. Absence of
What consoled intensifies the greed for
Justification, for glory hoards of
Dogma or storyboards of illustrated
Bibles. Life, good or bad, grabs for what can
Not be had, as if life could radiate
Beyond itself and reach what could teach it
How to live. What life establishes is
Never the life it wants, for what it wants
… is more life. But life's that eternity
In motion that never gets established.

x

Each moment in the middle between first
And last reaches for the numinous light
It thinks must last. This then is your way of
Life, of unorthodox devotion to
Eternity in motion. Each moment
Promises to define what you are, and
Among those promises you reject or
Accept, this is the only promise kept.
That you're responsible for each moment
– and that each moment is responsible
For all you are – is the peril of great
Price, a gift impossible to accept,
A gift, exquisitely, damnably odd,
As if the other side of you is God.

xi

In vain, you sought the weather vane, your one
True north, your promised path to that lonesome
Dove that roosts on the roof of your world. But

The business of being alive is an
Enterprise that can't quite cover its cost.
Somewhere amid the hustle and bustle
Of life's transactions, your tidy little
Capital gets lost. Each self-portrait's a
Puzzle that points to its own solution,
But that never gets there, as if from the
Sweep of time there arises a swirling
Eddy, a life made ready to receive
And give what's too heady, too unsteady
To believe. This is what it means to live.

xii

There's a light that lives in darkness, a light
That gives what each one lives without remorse.
With a little bit of light, you thought you
Could see it plain and make it right. This is
The legend of light. With each act of will,
You'll turn your fantasies into something
Real. This is the legend of will. In good
Faith, each deed that's done undoes the knot of
Grief. This is the legend of belief. When
At last you're wise, you'll learn to revise the
Formulas of strife. This is the legend
Of the wise. Corruption in any guise
Thinks of itself as wise, as right. This is
The legend of legends: Good night. Good night.

X. THE LAST MOHICAN

Man springs out of nothing, crosses time and forever disappears in the bosom of God; he is seen but for a moment, wandering on the verge of two abysses, and there he is lost. ... Have all ages been like ours and have men always dwelt, as in our day, where nothing is connected? ... Do you notice on all sides beliefs are giving way to arguments and feelings to calculations? If amid this universal collapse you do not succeed in linking the idea of rights to self-interest, which provides the only stable point in the human heart, what other means will be left you to govern the world, if not fear? ... Equality is the expression of envy. It means in the heart of every Republican: "No one

shall be better off than I am," and while this is preferred to good government, good government is impossible.
    – Alexis de Tocqueville, *Democracy in America* –

Since you are here, Monsieur de Tocqueville, I want to hear you talk a little about America.
    – King Louis-Philippe to Alexis de Tocqueville –

You do not know and will never know who the remnant are, nor what they are doing, or will do. Two things you do know, and no more: First, that they exist; second, that they will find you.
    – Albert J. Nock, "Isaiah's Job" –

i

In the blur of upheaval, you search for
The retrieval of the upended, for
The *status quo ante* upon which your
Lonely others once depended. Perhaps,
If past and future could be wed, you could
Restore lost nobilities of the dead.
But between the forward and the backward
Abyss, your only stability is
Your dread over the instability
That persists. You outlived your country but
Abided what followed it with gravest
Doubt. Your country cannibalized its heart.
Though mightily you tried, you could not ride
The wave of history that hollowed it out.

ii

The heart of the old order contains the
Germ of the new. And it's the start of
A troubled heart. Pursuing your fate, you
Play a part that seems, alas, so badly
Joined with all the other parts. And yet your
Interior malaise also has a
Crucial part it plays. There's larceny in
Your heart that loads the dice of politics.
The soul of the state is a beast. The state
Of the soul … a demon. Thus, your better

Angel keeps returning to its starting
Place. Politics of soul and state reflects
The age-old dictum: Your angel returns
To its demon ... and your beast to victim.

iii

Democracy marks the age when change no
Longer happens but is manufactured.
Your fantasies of a past restored clash
With knowledge of its perpetual loss.
This awareness sees loss at the heart of
All that purports to be progress. Each step
Closer to equality pulls the dear
And near farther and farther apart. What
Once connected is rejected, and you're
Dejected about its loss. Counterfeit
Equality dissolves the glue of the
Noble civilization that's lost. Now
Everything flies apart at a pace too
Fast and furious to assess its cost.

iv

To be equal with another is to
Become someone that you're not. No theory
Can erase this metaphysical blot.
Thus, equality is the fantasy
Of misguided imitation: that you,
Though different, could achieve the sameness of
Another. The lust for equality,
Envy's relentless craving to enjoy
The success of the other without his
Failures, chases the false security
That presumes no one should be happier
Or luckier than you, as if you could
Claim the serenity of another's
Solitude *sans* the anguish of his risk.

v

With the ballot or with the gun, freedom's

Easily lost before it's hardly won.
There is always the danger that freedom
Will perish and perish forever. It
Would not matter so much without this risk.
That all are morally equal, you must
Agree, but that all must be equally
Moral is the beginning of what it
Means to be unfree. Morally equal,
You have the right to fail or succeed. That
All must be equally moral means the
Outcome of your freedom is guaranteed.
When all outcomes are perforce made equal,
Despotism is always the sequel.

vi

In the long run, democracy without
Liberty and law slowly devastates
What it develops and confounds what it
Founds. Counterfeit equality, carried
To extremes, dashes hopes and razes dreams,
And freedom pushed beyond limits negates
The conditions that make it possible.
Democracy will live on in name long
After history has signed its epitaph.
Democracy in name, though surpassed in
Fact, mimics values it makes no longer
Viable. Thus, *Freedom*'s a worship word,
But you're no longer free, and whoever
Has the bummest rap is the most p.c.

vii

A poorly fledged democracy conspires
With the lust for equality to yield
The opposite of the liberty which
Spawns it. Liberty under law gives birth
To the individual who pawns it
For the promise of false security.
Democracy is a providential fact.
The sole stability in the human
Heart is self-interest, which is never the

End but merely the start of liberty.
The self only serves itself when it loves
What it does and does what it should. Only
Self-interest that's wisely understood can
Lay a lasting foundation of the good.

viii

You keep dwelling on the next election,
As if a minor inflection in the
Voting population could avert the
Fate of your country. In your heart, you
Fear that all is lost, that you, your family,
Your neighbors, your fellow citizens are
Lost, that America is lost because
You have lost America and yourself.
Freedom cannot be saved by blubbering
Patriotism. Nostalgia for the
Nobility that's lost is always an
Obstacle to the next step you must take
Toward the renewal of freedom. Freedom's
A fight that can be lost but never won.

ix

Ideology is myth made literal.
A world of ease, of comfort, of peace is
Easily within reach if only you
Could follow what the ideologues teach.
You shiver with the fierce urgency of
Now, with naïve dreams of utopias
You cannot deliver, as if you could
Change what remains eternal, as if the
Latest ideology tells you how,
As if you could master the disaster
That even now is about to happen.
Utopia is no place to be you.
Dystopia is always here to stay.
A free man would have it no other way.

x

Are you individual or tribe? Are

You more, or are you less than the sum of
Tribalisms you imbibe? You work for
What you have. You always have. You must earn
What you acquire. This is what the trouble
Of being born should always require. All
Other nostrums are the utterances
Of a liar, of the self-anointed,
Who profess to tell you how to live. No.
There are no experts in living. There are
Only experts in giving bad reasons
For reliving the same mistakes in a
Different guise. There are only those who make
Promising what lacks promise and call that ... wise.

xi

There's a finite set of tropes in use by
The dopers and the dopes. The lust for false
Certitude that replaces joy seems like
Pleasure until it abandons you to
Inconsolable pain. Despair yields dogma,
Belief's on the margins, and doubt's central to
Every experiment in self-deceit.
Consolation fades, substance dissipates,
Boredom persists, but nothing resists the
Irruption of eternity in the
Banality of the world. Without the
Love of the good, happiness can never
Happen. And happiness that loves the good
Springs from self-interest rarely understood.

xii

Yet outside the dominion of public
Opinion, you search again and again
For yourself ... you search for America
In the forests of your fate and freedom.
You rediscover what those who founded
It discovered first, for good or ill, that
You, an individual, must carry
The blessing and the burden of free will.
From last to first, the remnant of freedom

At your worst remains a lasting beacon.
This declaration is perpetual
And profound: you have not seen the last of
What the first American found. You have
Not seen the last of the last Mohican.

XI. THE MISER'S JAR

Zeus anointed me with none of that sweet liquor
from his miser's jar, once the illusions
and the dream of childhood died. The happiest day
of life is first to fly.
— Giacomo Leopardi, "Sappho's Last Song" –

It seems absurd but it is precisely true, that since all reality is naught, illusions are in this world, the only true and substantial things. ... The most solid pleasure in this life is the vain pleasure of illusions. ...The horror and fear that a man has of nothingness on the one hand, and eternity on the other hand, is manifested everywhere, and that "never again" can never be said without a certain reaction. ... Two truths that men will never believe: one, that they know nothing, the other, that they are nothing. Add the third that is closely linked to the second: that they have nothing to hope for after death.
— Giacomo Leopardi, *Zibaldone* –

The ultimate illusion
that I thought was eternal died. It died.
— Giacomo Leopardi, "To Himself" –

i

It happened before; it happened again.
But no one left alive can believe your
Report, for those who condescend to live
Distrust your words. But the moon fell last night.
It fell. And the moon that fell made a mess
In the middle of your meadow. From where
It fell in the night sky, there's a smoldering
Absence that tells you it's no longer there.
You will always remember where it was,
But now you must deal with where it is. You

Must live with this muddle of lunacy ...
Now ... here ... in the middle of your meadow
Where it's made a mess at the very heart
Of what you're not so pleased to call your life.

ii

Desire grimly clings to the dark curtain
Of your direst thoughts. Brittle it becomes
Through use and abuse, then collapses all
At once, shattering into strange fragments
Of lost eternity, jagged mirrors
Of your long goodbye. There's a fanatic
In each farewell that would, if it could, delve
Deeply into pain and find its hidden
Paradise. Yet all that's human flickers:
Like flame that's fickle, it gutters, stutters,
Does not quite go out before it does, but
Must always doubt, for it remains loyal
Neither to its first task of warmth and light
Nor to its final task of going out.

iii

Your world ... just born ... is dying again and
You're trying anew to keep it safe or
To let it go. Shall you love or hate one
Life or many? Or is time too ripe, too
Fat, to embrace the latest skinny on
Immortality? Shall you be first or
Last to make the ancient myths come true? Are
You strong enough to accept what oldest,
Wisest illusions can't renew? Worn-out
Illusions revive. Vagueness comes back so
Clearly that you yearn ever more dearly
For the vague, for the perpetual egg
Of rebirth, for familiar novelties
That rediscover what your life is worth.

iv

No frail illusion could alleviate

Your allergy to others and yourself.
Some are born to live; some, like you, are born
Already dying. Untimely, you spared
No time for happiness, for a mortar
That builds with better bricks than mud and blood.
You could not evade the fate you felt, that
You must go farther than the faithlessness
Of your forefathers. Thus, what life offers,
You cannot take, and what life denies, you
Cannot forsake. Human reality's
A put-up job, a counterfeit, a fake,
A cryptogram of illusions, a jar
Of marmalade, you neither break nor shake.

v

Infinity says: *Not now, but always
More*. Eternity says: *Now is enough*.
You could not rest content with pleasure, with
One or none, for you want the fountain of
Pleasure to run undone forever. The
Image of this never-ending fountain,
Of relentless thirst, spurs the fatal lust
That lets you imagine the best while you
Endure the worst. The illusion that you
Are happy, or that your happiness is
Perhaps possible is the lure that leads
You on and keeps you going. All the while,
You yearn to forget, while always knowing
That only nothingness can quench your thirst.

vi

With or without your Gilgamesh, you will
See afresh the logic of everything.
There is no innocent eye. Thus, as you
Wend the winding stair, the beholder's share
In the miser's jar is already there.
Never quite shorn of consolations you
Scorn, you rediscover the dubious
Dignity of being born to despair.
It's happened before but nothing that's new

Compares to you ... to the mimetic gel
Of your desire, to the eternal lure,
The broken promise of being alive
That made you sure that your despair is a
Disease that only nothingness could cure.

vii

Amid the infinite sprawl of stars, a
Shard of wayward matter begins to crawl
And the universe that ripens into
Consciousness summons its voice and tells its
Story. What is the universe doing?
It never doubts it's something until it
Begins to think and speak. Thus, your sense of
Nothingness is an artifact of thought,
Of speech. And what does the universe seek?
It seeks an image, a word, an ism,
A belief, or a redeeming grief that
Would never let it regret the end of
Boredom or shun the dubious fable
Of glory that's sought but that comes to naught.

viii

The will to truth is always overwhelmed
By the infinitasia of pain and
Pleasure. On earth as it is in heaven,
There is a perpetual conflict of
Infinity versus eternity,
A war between the insufficient and
The relentless. There is no hedge against
The insufficient as long as desire
Persists. There is no defense against
The relentless as long as time exists.
Fate makes a talent of self-deceit, a
Shipwreck as sweet as a holiday from
Caring, a defeat because time loses
Its bearing in a sea of indifference.

ix

You never dreamed that a life of pleasure

Could have hedges so rough it makes you bleed,
That life could be so hard to take, or so
Easy for imagination to make
Into a lasting parable of pain.
Ashamed of your regret, you will look back
Unconsoled, by gifts you left unopened,
Unexplained, unenjoyed, and unextolled.
Illusion dies, imagination wanes,
And you, with time to kill, begin to feel
What's really real. The last illusion dies
The death of illusion, imagines it
Sublime, imagines it real ...because it
... is what imagination says it is.

x

There's no limit to imagination's
Freedom, but there is a limit to its
Afterlife, its pain, the void between the
Dream and what life unimagined cannot
Attain. Infinity ... eternity
Are both illusions, extreme substitutes
For the indefinite, for the vague. Yet
You fight for life on their battlefield. The
Difference, therefore, between your destiny
And self-deception is negligible.
Yet your equivocation strives to be
Decisive. You wield your philosophic
Broom that would sweep away all pleasure, yet
Still you try in vain to polish the pain.

xi

First to fly, the dove of the happiest
Day cannot learn to die in peace, for the
Latest anguish makes earliest joy as
Blah as the blight of boredom. Then there's her
Song, her voice, that's eternal, or it's not,
But the possible fact that it doesn't
Persist or exist can never resist
Your urge to stay with her forever. Your
Moment of illusory bliss defies

The throng of universal pain, as if
Your heart were not a clot of flesh, but a
Knot of beliefs and griefs, as if her voice,
A slender, ageless finger, could touch your
Heart and last as long as forever lasts.

xii

Times are worsening in all their courses.
Toward oblivion you ride with noisy
Desperation on exhausted horses.
Yet there's a faith in futility that –
For ill or worse – uses up the curse,
That cannot heal what time must kill, that
Can never set aright the crooked and
Perverse, but that can in one rare moment
Seize the light it saw, and then, in awe ... of
One splendid burst, revivify the life
You lost in your desolate universe.
There was a smile on the lips of despair.
You saw it there. The laughter of one lark
Suffices to shed pale light on all that's dark.

XII. FIFTEEN MINUTES OF FAMINE

When we are disappointed by some pleasure which we have been expecting and which finally comes, the reason for the disappointment is because we are expecting the future. As soon as it is there, it is present. We want the future to be there without ceasing to be future. This is an absurdity for which eternity alone is the cure.

To explain suffering is to console it; therefore, it must not be explained.

Every being cries out silently to be read differently.

The presence of illusions that we have abandoned, but which are still present in the mind is perhaps the criterion of the truth.

I also am other than I imagine myself to be. To know this is forgiveness.

Who is able to flatter himself that he will read correctly?
– Simone Weil, *Gravity and Grace* –

i

Divinity divides infinity
In two. One end is God; the other's you.
Some things there are that never happened, but
That always are: such is the end of your
Eternity, the immortal scar at
The beginning of time, the time before
Your living time began, the time of all
In all. There was no outside because all
That was ... was inside itself, before the
Sacrifice that laid the foundation of
Your world, when God withdraws, when in the wake
Of that withdrawal, all that's left is his
Lost, abandoned kingdom. Yes. The cost of
The universe is the absence of God.

ii

You're in the way of the God you worship.
You seek to remove the impediment.
Your vocation's the evacuation
Of yourself. Thus, you must render unto
God what your God hath wrought to make it naught.
The rhetoric of nothingness and the
Regimen of self-annihilation
Persist as your metaphor of what the
Self must always lack. The great divide is
An infinite gap. God crosses it first.
Obedience is the track that follows
Him back. Thus, you hunger to be free from
Hunger, but nothing in all creation's
Older or younger than your urge to be.

iii

The Martian in you, the troll, belittles
Every goal. Each fetish for fulfillment
  ... is obsession for a false paradise.
In the quarter hour of eternity's
Ordeal, there will be fifteen minutes of
Famine for everyone, time enough to
Feel and to examine the endlessness
Of the void. When no food nourishes, when
Exhaustion overtakes everything, when
All's used up, there will be fifteen minutes
Of famine, an infinite hunger in
The soul that has refused to cry: *Enough*.
Here you touch with the blind man's stick the point
Where God, despite his absence, still exists.

iv

There is a void that waits in the wake of
Physical and spiritual exhaustion.
When the ore's played out, there is only the
Absence of what was. What was ... was what you
Imagined, the roles, the goals, the motives,
The pastimes, that you invented and which
Prevented your perception of absence.
This absence is the white noise, the silence
That screams, the sacred insomnia of
That darkest of darkest nights when the soul
Sees through itself to the nothing that founds
And confounds it. This is the terrible
Lucidity of insomnia, of
God who knows neither sleep nor distraction.

v

Goodness here below smacks of the false, the
Counterfeit. It promises but cannot
Deliver more than a shiver of doubt
That time is more than the tracks you've made, more
Than the games you have played, more than the plans
You've laid. Nothing here below is final:

Everything wearies you and wears out, and
In moments of doubt when you lucidly
Discern this truth, you soon succumb to the
Perpetual shout of lies that make you
Forget your doubt. Or you may deceive with
Truth itself. This is the cynicism
That's as near ... as far ... as anyone could
Possibly be from impossible truth.

vi

There are as yet varieties of pain
That have not been named. But when pain assumes
Its maximum limit, more than you can
Sustain, fatigue falters, weariness wears
Itself out, exhaustion exceeds itself
And then becomes as perpetual as
Rituals of relief from grief: To face
This for the first time, for the last time, for
The first as if it is the last, for the
Last as if it is the first, is to know
The history of eternity not as
Another book on a crowded shelf but
As the unfolding of your withering,
Ever dithering, everlasting self.

vii

The miser's misery is that he saves
Without savoring his guarded treasure.
He saves with the hope of future pleasure.
But the habit of having, of getting
And keeping, becomes the condition of
Continuing what keeps creeping toward
Oblivion. His treasure is the hoard
Of the unfulfilled, the merciless sum
Of all the time he's killed. Here the miser's
Money is merely a metaphor for
Every species of idolatry that
Falters before what it never alters:
That every miser must forever live
With what he's always wanted, always willed.

viii

Time is the trap door that's sprung in the floor
Of eternity. It's the escape hatch
Of your distractions and the substitute
For all that matters, or it's the snare that
Leaves the lies in tatters, the cunning lure
That can prepare you for eternity.
Neither fire nor ice is the way to go
To hell or to arrive in paradise.
Nothing in your life ever disposes
Of the friction of strife and the rumors
Of roses. This is the book of life that
Opens, then poses, what never closes.
There's no way to be without resentment.
Eternity never knows contentment.

ix

Each sin is a flight from nothingness, from
The perpetual perishing of the
Present moment. There is always folly
In remembrance and hope whenever they
Exceed the scope of the present moment.
To remember and to hope are always
Temptations to exalt your worth. In the
Perpetual perishing of present
Moments, what you will be and used to be
Have far less significance than a flea.
Each sin, each crime, each moment of wasted
Time is a flight from whatever fails to
Rhyme with your history of eternity.
Eternity names what you want to last.

x

All that sheer attention can know is now,
And now is perpetually perishing.
Without reward you must embrace the void, and
Acceptance confers no badge of honor.
Imagination, which manufactures
Merit badges for imaginers, must
Be stultified, encouraged to attend

To what it wants to hide, must forfeit its
Investment in the futility of
All the projects and fantasies it's tried.
Goodness can only start in the very
Heart of attention, when every hollow
Purpose is held in suspension. Don't just
Do something. Stand there. Stand at attention.

xi

Yes. You despised illusion's intrusion
Into the real. You reviled the romance
Of imagination, but embraced the
Sacred emptiness that it cannot help
But fill. To imagine is to react
To fact with fantasy, yet fantasies
Before you're through become fact by being
Part of you. Illusions are ghosting for
A bitterness that cannot be borne, and
Consolations falsify, while blindly
Fingerposting this bitter truth. All that's
Depravity falls with the force of its
Gravity. Grace is the exception that
Exalts the rule of exceptional truth.

xii

Desire, your stock and trade, is the substance
Of which you're made. Desire that cannot be
Stopped or started can only be charted
By its journey through time. Each fulfillment,
Each disappointment, nails down a piece of
You, a fantasy that becomes a fact.
And tracks you've left in time are full of facts.
A God who would gobble you up is not
The God who was tempted to resist the
Cup of suffering, not the one who resists
That temptation to do what only he
Could do: let you be you. There's only one
Path toward being damned or saved. To walk it,
All your rights to extinction must be waived.

xiii

Your self's a warrior of the will, and it's
Armed with an arsenal of lies. The *I*
The lie, in each idol, cannot abide
The bridle of obedience, for when
It pretends to kneel it worships itself.
Thus, as if to absolve yourself of the
Purely personal, you want a landscape
Austere, pristine, one that is already
Clear, already clean of every trace of
You. Everything has sacrificed part of
Itself to make you something. But the gift
That's freely given must be returned. You
Must yield up all for which you've yearned. All you
Yearn for, all that you've learned must be returned.

xiv

To accept the void, you say, is still to
Suffer but you are happy. This is the
Happiness that sees itself for what it
Always is, while still it suffers. You smile
With only the slightest trace of guile. Yet
There are no cornerless ontologies.
In eternity, there is always a
Dirty, cobwebbed corner that has not quite
Been cleansed of the purely personal. That
You or anyone could be cleansed of the
Purely personal is, for you, the last
And noblest attempt at consolation.
Practicing eternity to the hilt
Cannot relieve the guilt that you are you.

xv

You were possessed, or so you confessed, by
The fullness of the godhead bodily.
Fantasy or not, this confession is
A fundamental fact about you. You
Are born outside the source that gave you birth.
Thus, to exist is to be sent forth in

Exile. The first sacrifice sends you forth
In separation. The last sacrifice
Brings you back again in preparation
For eternity. The last continues
To do what the first intends because the
Practice of eternity never ends.
To endure suffering without nightmare, you
Become in patience what you cannot bear.

xvi

Conditions of freezing collect their frost,
For eternity is precisely this:
That nothing's lost. Not the consequences
You choose to own, not those you would dethrone.
Not even the cost of the universe
 ... is lost. Stripped naked, dead and bare: even
Then a remnant of the self is there. The
Remnant's the mote in consolation's throat,
The part you cannot play by rote, a voice
That's always just about to sing despite
The everlasting sting of creation.
You are different from what you imagine
Yourself to be. This ... the unwitnessed grace
Of self-forgetfulness ... God sheds on thee.

xvii

Tempters insist: think not of the polar
Bear. But you do, you can't resist. Tempters
Insist: think not of eternity, just
Live, exist. But you do, you take the risk
That life's a mare's nest of illusions that
Dims a destiny you've almost missed, but
Can't resist. Such is the uncreated
You, the remnant unknown by you, unknown
By God, your one free gift, the one gift that
Leaves behind the logic of the gift it
Has exceeded, the gift of your essence,
Your freedom, which God without knowing it
Has always needed. ... The liberty of
The essential is the harshest freedom.

— NINE —
PART THREE
A DRASTIC MISTAKE

I. THE ETERNITY RECKONER

I know not who put me into the world, nor what the world is, nor what I myself am. I am in terrible ignorance of everything. I know not what my body is, nor my senses, nor my soul, not even that part of me which thinks what I say, which reflects on all and on itself, and knows itself no more than the rest. I see those frightful spaces of the universe which surround me, and I find myself tied to one corner of this vast expanse, without knowing why I am put in this place rather than another, nor why this short time which is given me to live is assigned to me at this point rather than at another of the whole eternity which was before me or which shall come after me. I see nothing but infinities on all sides, which surround me as an atom, and as a shadow which endures only for an instant and returns no more. All I know is that I must die, but what I know least is this very death which I cannot escape.

– Pascal, circa 1642 –

The last thing one settles in writing a book is what one should put in first. ... Nothing is more important to man than his state: nothing more fearful than eternity. ... For after all, what is man in nature? A nothing compared to the infinite, a whole compared to the nothing, a middle point between all and nothing, infinitely remote from an understanding of the extremes; the end of things and their principles are unattainably hidden from him in impenetrable secrecy. ...

What else can he do but perceive some semblance of the middle of things, eternally hopeless of knowing either their principles or their end. ... How could a part possibly know the whole? ... Jesus will be in agony until the end of the world. We must not sleep during that time.

– Pascal, *Pensées* –

i

All would-be human certitude shipwrecks
On the tangled reef of the infinite.
You are what you are, the eternity
Reckoner. You make your bet. You lie in it.
For life's a gamble, an experiment,

A wager made in the muddle between
Infinite extremes of all or nothing.
The last in every book is settled first.
The first in every book is settled last.
But principles, first and last, you fear, are
Not distinct, not clear. Nothing distinct or
Clear is more important than even your
Vaguest fear of eternity. For your
Terror of eternity never ends.

ii

The strategy of your apology
Mirrors the tragedy of your life: What
Shall it be? The lady ... or the tiger?
Misery ... or joy. Nothingness ... or God?
Freedom from time, or from eternity?
Murdered slowly by crustacean wisdom,
You seek to save God from oblivion.
No reason, no science, no bauble, no
Drug, no philosophy, no pleasure can
Cure your misery. In the looking glass
Gaze, each metamorphosis of self must
Measure the vanity of its treasure.
Each self-betrayal does not diminish
But amplifies the hiddenness of God.

iii

Self-gratification yields to fear of
Future denials. Thus, the moral of
Pleasure is the future of unpleasure,
The gnawing and quickening belief in
The clear and present danger of future
Grief. What you need the most you fear the most.
What you fear the most you need the most. And
You fear God as you fear your snow-blind self.
Self-deception is that allergy to
Truth that forgets it fears what it avoids.
But there's a time when truth will have its say
In the blinding light of the clearest day.
This truth, you haven't met with yet, comes when

You no longer recall what to forget.

iv

To God, you'll always be you and never
I, never the idols you decry. Thus,
At first, everyone's nothing to you, but
Between first and last, the river of your
Ruin runs so fast, so deep, it must sweep
Away the freight of your past to make of
You nothing to no one. Between anguish
And ecstasy are mediocrities
In every way you experience the
Everyday. You could not stand to touch or
Be touched ... as if nothing touching nothing
Cancels out the nothingness and only
Then leaves something lasting, something real that
You lacked the courage to admit or feel.

v

Not you, not the universe, not any
Of its lesser parts, standing alone and
Untouched, is intelligible. Thus, the
Whole *qua* whole, the part *qua* part, the cosmos
qua cosmos, and you *qua* you mean nothing
By themselves. Neither you nor the cosmos
Knows self-justification. You are cast
Adrift in the abyss with no pillars of
Wisdom or unwisdom to buck you up.
Nothing's ever so large as the largeness
Of the night, so much so that in each phase
Of self-enlightenment there's a shortage
Of illumination. The sense you seek
Lies not in yourself but in another.

vi

Just one more enticing distraction is
Always enough to numb the nerve of truth.
Diversions tranquilize despair but do
Not dissolve it. They make you unsteady,

Unready, unsure ... of any lasting cure.
Despair is unconscious boredom on the
Run, the pain that accelerates when you're
Having fun. Such is the cruelty of self
To self, the unpardonable sin, the fact
That heaven can never be imagined
Without boredom, but only believed in.
The damned need not stay damned forever, but
They shall forever be deprived of the
Good they did not desire when it arrived.

vii

After every path has been trod, the last
Resort is always God. The unknown gets
Personal. The embodiment of the
Mystery is the last chapter in the
History of your relentless despair.
Thus, there'll be those who insist on making
A cozy nest in the common abyss.
But desperate midnight hours in the garden
Cannot soften your hardening heart, for when
You sleep you miss the essential moment.
You're the would-be winner of souls, whose fates
Already decided, cannot be changed.
Predestination of the heart is how
You get where you're going before you start.

viii

You'll find salvation in the moment when
You become someone for everyone, and
Everyone becomes someone for you. Thus,
The meaning of your poem's another
Poem, and of your life ... another life.
First and last, you and your lonely others
Are events in each other's drama, the
Comic relief in the perpetual
Tragedy and the remorseless trauma
Of continuing to be what you are.
History's the pattern of eternity,
Of your predestined heart, of your freedom

To become and to surpass what you are
For yourself and for others ... forever.

II. WHERE YOU LIVE
We are always successful when our sole aim is to do good.
— Jean-Jacques Rousseau, *Emile* —

No doubt God is eternal, but can my mind grasp the idea of eternity? Why should I cheat myself with meaningless words?
— Jean-Jacques Rousseau, *Emile* —

What if there is a state where the soul can find a position solid enough to allow it to remain there entirely and gather together its whole being without needing to recall the past or encroach upon the future, where time is nothing to it, where the present lasts forever, albeit imperceptibly and giving no sign of its passing, with no other feeling of deprivation or enjoyment, pleasure or pain, desire or fear than simply that of our existence, a feeling that completely fills our soul; as long as this state lasts, the person who is in it can call himself happy, not with an imperfect, poor and relative happiness, such as one finds in the pleasures of life, but with a sufficient, perfect and full happiness, which leaves in the soul no void needing to be filled.
— Jean-Jacques Rousseau, *Reveries of the Solitary Walker* —

For me there has never been an intermediary between everything and nothing.
— Jean-Jacques Rousseau, *Confessions* —

i

Always you're occupied by one affair:
Your own. You begin from a single point:
Yourself. And when you feel yourself, you feel
As if that single point is everywhere.
The self is born in imagination,
In deceit. Your blurred memories of what
Has been imagined and what has happened
Cull fantasy from fact as chaff from wheat.
You feel yourself feel what conscience cannot
Help but kill, as if joy and sorrow once

Bespoken have already been battered,
And then broken by speech, as if your lapsed
Propensity for specious intensity
Remembers rare summits you could not reach.

ii

Exquisitely sensitive to your own
Sensitivity, you were enamored
Of proclivities for the natural:
When to be ashamed of anything was
The only shame; when mood becomes master;
When conscience becomes emotion, and your
All-too-beautiful soul a practice of
Constant self-devotion; when, with one great
Original whack, you make barriers
Of civilization buckle and crack;
When your conduct was blameworthy, but your
Heart was pure; when you, forgetting how fraud
Invariably gilds the fact, were so
Ruthlessly sure of your sincerity.

iii

Rummaging your unconscious, you unearth
Another excuse for bad behavior.
No child, you advised, should ever have his
Way. For neither you nor anyone else
Could be yourself without contradiction.
You were an exception from all, a point
Of comparison for everyone else.
Yes. You fancied yourself a source of the
Sacred who would disdain but not escape
The profane. You worshipped the destiny
Of exceptions, of which your life, for you,
Was the chief exemplar. Rigorously,
Therefore, you assign to others duties
That you would not and could not execute.

iv

Out of unbroken unanimity,

You knocked three times on the wall of silence
And no one listened, no one answered. But
When nature is silent, the will still speaks
And shrieks its most unnatural torments.
Those with the most power see the least. Those
With the most hunger miss the feast. There is
Unfailingly in each false profession
Of honesty a crude calculus of
Belated spontaneity. Thus, you
Never proved a reliable witness
To your own good will, for unanimous
Consent is in truth a fiction born of
Desperate hopes. There are only exceptions.

v

Always you preferred oblivion to
The reputations of ordinary
Men. Your value, you thought, was visible
Only in the opinion of others.
Only their admiration could save your
Reputation and your image. Thus, your
Image was at stake in every social
Gathering, in every conversation.
But you chose to forego the risk. If you
Could not have it all, you wanted nothing.
For you, the loss of paradise is the
Absence of heart-to-heart transparency,
The failure to share your solitude with
Others ... in certainty and conviction.

vi

The onset of corruption is a chain
Reaction. One sin links to another
And then another until the necklace
Of nagging necessity drags you down.
After the scorn of equally lonely
Others, after the last judgment, there is
The remaining hiddenness of God, and
The possibility of a promise
Fulfilled face to face. Thus, to justify

Yourself you speak to no one but yourself
And to God, who does not declare himself.
There is no obstacle, no veil, no shroud
Between yourself and God, for you're the one
Who broached the truth without interruption.

vii

Accuser and accused, alone in the midst
Of everyone, you're the understander
And the confused. Thus, you elude what you
Select and select what still eludes your
Grasp. You remain disabused of nothing
You've refused. You awake to the moral
World, as one guilty, as one already
Tangled in consequences of your flaws.
The more self ... the denser the mask. The less
Self ... the tenser the task of becoming
Something rather than nothing. Sanctified
By misery, the self, always elusive,
Remains an itch that cannot be scratched, a
Drastic mistake that wants to last forever.

viii

That all should emerge or vanish from the
Middle is inconceivable to the
Logic of extremes. Thus, whatever may
Happen between your birth and your death is
Always a dangerous supplement to
The dream of eternity. Each dream is
Touched by the trace of terror. Each present
Moment between before and after can
Never quite establish itself before
It drowns in the rush of time. Each time that
Dreams of an endless now rediscovers
The ancient nightmare: whoever begs to
Differ, whoever decides or defers,
Makes a difference that lasts forever.

ix

The spirit that folds back upon itself
Defects from the happy state of nature.
If you would achieve self-reliance, you'll
Be allowed to sidestep no obstacle,
Escape no incidence of suffering,
And evade no unnatural torments.
Your love for others was so great, you said,
You could not abide their presence. Neither
Could you abide nor understand your own.
You could never endure the pleasure or
Enjoy the pressure of being just what
You are – yourself – in the present moment.
You thirst for more than life can give. *You live
Not where you love and love not where you live.*

III. HUNGER TO BE

For the true heaven is everywhere, even in that very place where thou goest and standest.
— Jacob Boehme, *Aurora* —

Every life is a clear gleam and mirror and appears like the flash of a terrible aspect. But if this flash catch the light, it is transformed into gentleness and drops the terror, for then the terror unites itself to the light. And thus light shines from the terrible flash, for the flash is the light's essence; it is its fire. ... What we make of ourselves, that we are; what we awaken in ourselves, that is moving in us.
— Jacob Boehme, *Six Theosophic Points* —

The one to whom time is like eternity, and eternity like time, is free from all suffering.
— Jacob Boehme —

i

Your will is but a wisp in the well of
Nothingness. Out of chaos kindled is
The shimmering fire, the white starlight that
Betrays the darkness, the seething void that

Begins to fill itself with something, the
Bottomless ability to be that
Spawns your restless universe of desire.
At the heart of nothingness is your will.
Everything begins with almost nothing,
With the wisp of will, with the desire to
Be that sets eternity in motion.
As nothingness, as God, as primordial
Will, your eternity is free, free from
Everything except your hunger to be.

ii

You saw the backward dark abyss in the
Heart of divinity, as if its core
Were your core, as if there could ever be
A ground floor to infinity, as if
You do not want what God wants, as if you
Do not love what God loves, as if you do
Not hate what God hates, as if you do not
Think what God thinks, as if you do not feel
What God feels, but you do, for everything
That is there in God is there in you. In
The eternal image that makes you ... you.
In astonishment, you think how odd: when
You behold the despairing nothingness
At the heart of yourself, you stare at God.

iii

You're always overshadowed by what you
Want, for corrupt desire awakens the
Vanity of the visible world. Your
Will yearns to seek and seize the anguish of
Its ineluctable desire. And the
Pain revealed and intensified yearns for
Freedom from pain, yearns for an escape from
Its agony. There's no other way to
Rescue the risk of freedom from despair,
To weave the fabric of revelation.
You cannot sidestep hell to live a joy
That only your suffering can unveil.

Such is the trial of every soul who
Undergoes the trouble of being born.

iv

Each character has its own star and each
Star its character, which descends into
The created world. Blind striving is the
Dark abyss at the heart of God, at the
Heart of every star. If God would behold
Himself, he must body forth from nothing
Into something, and from something into
Everything. But when nothingness bodies
Forth into something, it encounters a
Strife that cannot be borne. Thus, it begins
To crave redemption. It yearns to catch the
First light of its origin. It craves what
Eternity's sunrise first enraptured.
It craves the ransom of starlight captured.

v

You start where God starts with the desperate
Nothing, with the dark abyss, the raging
Bottomlessness at the base of everything,
For each hungering soul who begins his
Life anew must do what God must do to
Be born. He must imagine another.
Only imagination can restore
Your lost image, your one true face, the one
Held hostage by the hell of your making
And forsaking. The image of yourself,
Like the image of God, is always an
Image of another, the one you yearn
To touch. If you do not touch another,
There is no stirring of eternity.

vi

From everything: nothing; and from nothing:
Everything. Yes. All that is brings forth its
Other. Attraction yields to resistance,

And the struggle of the two brings forth the
Vortex, the fiery wheel of anguish. In
Anguish, you yearn for deliverance, for
Freedom. Then a terror in eternity,
A tremor, strikes like lightning, but with a
Fire that illuminates, that surprises
Eternity with the mysterious
Sound and haunting resonance of heaven.
What resounds below echoes from above.
Whoever would be freed from suffering is
Delivered by the lightning flash of love.

IV. AT THE SPOT

What, however, the age needs in the deepest sense can be said fully and completely by one single word: it needs ... eternity.
— Soren Kierkegaard, *The Individual* —

To become oneself is precisely a movement at the spot. To become is a movement from the spot, but to become oneself is a movement at the spot. ... Eternity asks of thee and of every individual among these million millions only one question, whether thou has lived in despair or not, whether thou wast in despair in such a way that thou didst not know thou wast in despair, or in such a way that thou didst carry this sickness in thine inward parts as thy gnawing secret, carry it under thy heart as the fruit of a sinful love, or in such a way that thou, a horror to others, didst rave in despair.
— Soren Kierkegaard, *The Sickness Unto Death* —

Properly understood, every man who faithfully desires a relation to God and to live in his sight has only one task: always to be joyful.

—Soren Kierkegaard, *The Journals* —

For God is himself really the pure like for like, the pure rendition of how you yourself are.

— Soren Kierkegaard, *Works of Love* —

Purity of heart is willing one thing: this thing willed is total

devotion to God.
— Robyn Graves Winder, *Works of Love: A Study ...* —

i

To exist in time is to become a
Citizen of eternity, but this
Citizenship is possible only
If it is impossible, for you must
Believe what you cannot believe. You must
Believe what's impossible to believe.
You must believe that eternity has
A history, that eternity dwells in
Time, that the moments that inhabit you
Inhabit eternity, that just one
Moment can justify eternity,
That eternity can justify one
Moment, or every possible moment.
You must believe this myth about yourself.

ii

Always you and your lonely others share
The cruel and crowded labyrinth of despair.
And the untruth of the crowd, always loud,
Always proud, becomes the shroud that conceals
Your shallowness and your self-deception.
Though apart from the herd, in loneliness,
You must face a crowd of moments in your
Life you cannot abide and must deride.
These are moments in your eternity
When midnight cries its desolate music.
Eternity whispers to your conscience: you
Must become conscious of yourself, of your
Myth, of the constant possibility
And uncertainty of self-deception.

iii

You must become a myth about yourself.
Something that is *both/and,* but *neither/nor.*
Something that mindless flux cannot conceive.

Something in the middle of *either/or*.
Something that fear and fraud cannot deceive.
Something that believes but cannot believe.
Something that's neither doubt nor certitude.
Something self-deception cannot relieve.
Something pain and pleasure cannot delude.
Something that wants, that fears what fools dream of.
Something that insists on you being you.
Something that longs for eternity's love,
Something without which nothing counts … nothing's true.
You must become a myth about yourself.

iv

You were an eternity too old for the
One you loved. But you lacked the courage to
Become what you understood, to embrace
The love of your life and proclaim it good.
Your life, finished before it began, was
Lived as the life of one already dead.
Your every now nattered of nothingness,
And every moment of your life always
Folded and then doubled back on itself.
You were thus permitted to imagine
What you could neither attain nor embrace.
The pure immediacy of presence,
Of joy, could only be imagined, could
Only be endured as your fantasy.

v

Despair's the difference between solitude
And a loneliness grown enamored of
Itself, between becoming sober and
A drunkenness that insists on nickel
And diming your eternal destiny.
That clever fellow is still a fool who
Hides from himself his own self-deception,
Who lets himself have no inkling of how
Inconsolable his life has become.
In heaven, there's no habit, but what more
Can be said of habit's cunning, but that …

Unbroken ... it ensures your life keeps on
Running ... away from yourself. In hell, the
Clock always indicates: ... eternity.

vi

You are the perpetual villain of
The vapid, the one who saw clearly that
Eternity does not stand still but is
Infinitely more rapid than time. Yes.
Everything always happens so fast in
Eternity it takes no time at all.
But your eternity, which does not and
Cannot exist, nonetheless comes alive,
Fully quickens in the fullness of time.
Eternity, therefore, finds its place in
The nothingness that's you, in the coldest,
Cruelest, and shakiest ground of being.
The prospect of eternity puts you
On the spot ... and at the spot ... where you live.

vii

The more you add or subtract from God the
More God stays the same. Infinity is
God's logic, and eternity is God's
Code. To become a self, you must dig deep
And deeper into the same abode. You
Must add to yourself more and more of the
Same, but a sameness always leavened by
The novelty of each new moment. For
Each new moment is always another
Opportunity to choose or not choose,
Your ownmost self. Eternity is the
Novelty that never dulls, that never
Lulls, that never pulls you back, but pushes
You forward to what you forever are.

viii

You must acquire the myth in order to
Repeat the myth, and you must repeat the

Myth again and again in order to
Achieve the constancy of faith, in order
To preserve the myth that you are ... and will
Continue to be ... as long as you are
Free to choose yourself. There is no other
Way to fight the flux, no other way to
Forego the disgrace of vacillating
Self-assertion and self-erasure. The
Myth that you are is more real than any
Fact you could possibly imagine. Yes.
All that is eternal is alive, and
As long as you're alive, you're eternal.

ix

The endless prattle of philosophy,
Science and theology, deserts of
The heart, is the salacious eloquence
Of self-deception. Abandon hope, all
Ye who justify yourselves in such words.
After all the idols crumble, there is
The unmistakable rumble of the
Absolute. When the strategies of self-
Justification fail, you stand at the
Crossroads of now and forever, alone,
Naked, and frail, before God, in one stark
Cell of infinitely many mansions,
A cell molded into eternity
By your fair share of anguish and despair.

x

In despair, eternity's splayed out like
A squashed frog, hideous and blind. Only
The leprous hand of dawn can teach you this
... is kind. The myth about you, that you
Meet your eternity in person, is
An eternal fact about you, a myth
That makes the false false and the true true, a
Myth that makes all that's old quite suddenly,
Everlastingly new. Yet you fear, you
Tremble, for you want to remember what

Can be remembered forever, because
Whatever you say and do to others
Will be said, will be done to you, and then
Infinitely repeated ... forever.

xi

By the dragon, you pass toward the father
Of souls, for suffering is how the father
Speaks to those individuals who choose
Belief in the impossible, in joy.
The great riddle of eternity is
Solved by what lies in the middle between
First and last. It is solved by your life and
How you live it and give it to others.
To become eternal is to become
Oneself before another, before God.
Neither God nor you achieve the joy of
Good alone. The pure heart, bound first and last
To the living God, wills but one thing, wills
What God wills, wills joy, wills eternity.

V. YOUR BOLD APOCALYPSE

I wouldn't give two cents for life if there were not something infinite, something deep, something real.

One may have a blazing hearth in one's soul, and yet no one comes to sit by it. Passersby see only a wisp of smoke rising from the chimney and continue on their way.
– Vincent Van Gogh –

i

What you dreaded most was insomnia.
You feared that day might prove as complacent
As the soporific crowd. You feared the
Waking nightmare consciousness that foretells
The shallowness of the ordinary.
Thus, you sought to shine your brightest light on
The mundane, to seek what is sacred in
What is most profane. At first, you admire,

Then desert from the common scheme of things.
So you tried, but could not shrink from suffering
And the unintended wealth it brings. Yes.
Dismissed again and then again for your
Excessive zeal, you felt—with maximum
Intensity—the impact of the real.

ii

First drunk on religion, then drunk on drink,
You saw too clearly, too intensely to
Use your time to think. For you, vividness
Was a vow of value beyond what is
Merely visible. How much love, how much
Passion, how much useless energy do
You require to admire the ordinary?
To be human is to pretend to be
Infinite. But what can your pretended
Infinity make of the mediocre?
You gambled recklessly, but neither lost
Nor won. Such is the moral luck of one
Who risks all and wins nothing, or one who
Hazards nothing and squanders everything.

iii

You could not cast a cold eye and call that
Objectivity. Thus, you paint as if
To name the guileless nativity, the
Newborn marvel of your hard-won feeling.
Each dawning emotion that protests its
Innocence is always delivered more
Than a little bit guilty into the
Wayward world, like an antiquated sin
That now enjoys your bold apocalypse.
You painted the invisible halo,
The aura of essence unseen but there.
With convulsions of color and care, you
Point toward the hidden hemisphere of
Life. Every path that leads nowhere leads there.

iv

In despair your world is ugly, and you
—far uglier than your world—could never
Abide your hidden beauty, your solemn
Worth. You did not shrink from Gethsemane,
But you neither saw it through nor pictured
Salvation in desolate olive groves.
There's crookedness in the path that leads from
Lark to crow, in learning how despair gets
Tarted up by the presence of absinthe
In your cup. After molting time, there comes
Something large and lasting out of many
Small beginnings. You were nobody once
And somebody too, the somebody who
Bodies forth from the deepest part of you.

v

Across the naked breast of sky, the large
Few stars of a larger night conjure up
An image of consolation. Even
That truth that is akin to terror is
A calling and a consolation. Of
Such is that constellation of stars that
Winks at the unwisdom of your sorrow,
Those troubling stars, beyond your reach, those stars
That say nothing to you, those stars that spin
In vortices of turbulence, those stars
That mimic the human will that vies in
Vain, those stars that offer only their vow
Of silence. If you do not speak now, their
Silence will go on and on ... forever.

VI. PERPETUAL MOURNING'S AFTERGLOW

No will, no representation, no world.

To desire immortality for the individual is really the same as wanting to perpetuate an error forever; for at bottom every in-

dividuality is really only a special error, a false step, something it would be better should not be, in fact something from which it is the real purpose of life to bring us back.

But beyond all this, death is the great opportunity no longer to be I.
– Arthur Schopenhauer –

The World as Will and Representation –
That the world has only a physical and not a moral significance is a fundamental error.

For a man of correct insight among those who are duped and deluded resembles one whose watch is right while all the clocks in the town give the wrong time. He alone knows the correct time, but of what use is it to him? The whole world is guided by the clocks that show the wrong time; even those are so guided who know that his watch alone states the correct time.
– Arthur Schopenhauer, *Parerga and Paralipomena* –

i

The will, the innermost core of what you
Are, knows no birth, no death, no last, no first,
No creation, no destruction, yet it
Persists with the perpetuation of
Its thirst, a thirst that is now, nowhere, and
Forever. It is a thirst that cannot
Be quenched. Out of life's grave difficulties,
You sought with clarity to impart this
Single thought. What you are at core is an
Act of will that has no after, no before.
The character you chose is what you chose
Before your living time began. This is
The choice that happens so fast that it takes
An eternity ... or no time at all.

ii

The hands of every clock point always and
Only to now. Every past, present and
Future ... that happens ... happens now. There is

No time without a now, and whenever
There's a time, the time is always now. All
You will – all that is, was, and will be – is
Happening now. For now is the only
Time in which anything could possibly
Happen. Now is the only time that could
Ever possibly be. All the rest can
Only be ... everlasting perjury.
The now, which is always and forever
Present, can neither stop nor begin; it
Continues to continue without end.

iii

Before the first eye opens, the world is
Neither open nor closed, for there is no
World, no visible manifestation
Of your will in motion. Before the first
Eye opens, there's no before, no after,
No time, no beginning, no end, for all
Your beginnings begin and end in time.
You start from what you yourself first put forth
Before your mind, from the first image you
Imagined, from the very first fact of
Consciousness. You are what you embody,
And what you embody is your will made
Visible. Therefore, your body is what
It wants and the image of what it wants.

iv

That it's better for you to be than not
... is the surest sense of self-deception.
The illusion of sexual pleasure
Lures you into life, and the illusion
That death should be feared then keeps you living.
A false step and a guilty lust are just
The beginning of mistrust. What is most
Sublime and sacred marries a tawdry
Lie, and steals from that falsehood the lion's
Share of its strength. For you, this pious fraud
Was the indelible monogram of

The moral world and its fatal meaning.
You must become what you are: will, what your
Life cannot wither and time cannot kill.

v

You and your world are will and image through
And through, and beyond your world and image,
There is nothing, nothing you could dream of,
Nothing you could possibly do. And yet
All the visible world is as vain, as
Empty, as pointless, and as beautiful
As a magic lantern show. Whatever
There is that makes it go is alien
To what you imagine, infinitely
Stranger than anything you claim to know.
There's no future, no past, only this gift
Of presence from nowhere, where you vanish
Into eternity, where you become
The inner, true, and indestructible you.

vi

You are not in time, but time is in you.
Thus, time is an eternity drawn and
Quartered, an image nestled in your brain.
There is no death, for your essence, your will,
Never dies, but you experience the
Death — that is no death — as the last dream, but
The last dream is still a dream, for nothing
Outside the dream can be seen or felt, for
Eternity is what you cannot feel,
And cannot see: *That* ... you can only be.
You cannot fall out of being. If you
Could ever not be, you would not be now.
Yet you're never what you are quite yet, and
You're never quite yet what you really are.

vii

Time is what's been sown in the knower and
The known, an image of what you lack an

Image for, of eternity, of what
Fools alone deplore, of a timeless time
That has no place and a placeless place that
Has no time, a place with no after, no
Before, where everybody who becomes
Somebody becomes everybody once
More, a neither where nor when, without the
Slightest trace of time or sin, a placeless
Time where the face of everything and of
Everyone you know, is the evening
Shadow of a haunting rhyme, and the joy
Of perpetual mourning's afterglow.

VII. THE PATHLESS PATH

Man's last and highest parting occurs when, for God's sake, he takes leave of god. ... The eye by which I see God is the same eye by which God sees me. My eye and God's eye are one and the same – one in seeing, one in knowing, and one in loving.
– Meister Eckhart, *Sermon 23: "Distinctions Are Lost In God"* –

Likewise that there is a certain castle in the soul, which I have called at times the guardian of the soul or the spark.
– Meister Eckhart, *The Defense* –

i

You walk as God walks in the circuit of
Heaven. You talk as God talks with whispers
Of the word. You chalk as God chalks the image
That cannot be seen. You stalk as God stalks
The voice that cannot be heard. You saw the
Soul's orbit revolve inside the transit
Of eternity, from that ocean of
Emptiness that overflows into God,
Into persons, into spirit, into
You, into the substance and matter of
Your world, and then back again into that
Blissful oblivion, that startling joy
Of an emptiness that's far too full, and
Yet far too unfinished to comprehend.

ii

Countless are the streams, countless are the dreams
That flow through the well of eternity.
This is the well that teems with abundance.
This is the cup that runneth over with
That desire that's beyond desire, with that
Love that's beyond the love that overflows
The rim of eternity. This is the
Beginning of time. There's no greater good
Than God, but the greatest good surpasses
Itself, for God transcends himself in his
Goodness. God is that infinity of
Infinities become beautiful, good,
And true, the one in eternity, who
Takes his stand on the other side of you.

iii

All that sweats, that grunts, that despises, has
Roots that touch the eternity from whence
All your sweating and grunting arises.
In the wilderness of your soul, you must
Create a place where God can arrive, and
Thrive, and shed his grace. When the naysayers
Natter, as they always do, that all's in
Vain, that all that lives is rotten, in the
Face of the harshest disdain, you perforce
Must remember what you've nearly always
Forgotten, you must recall and rejoice
In the varieties of rain, you must
Remember what love, despite the ruin
Of the world, has endlessly begotten.

iv

God reveals himself in three ways: as I,
As you, and as everlasting other.
You are the shadow on the wall, and you
Are the eternity of what casts it.
No eternity, no shadow, no wall,
Only the everlasting call, and the

Ceaseless longing to be, to become that
Species of belonging that's loved, yet free.
There are abject evils in your life: your
Lust, your sin, your sense of futility,
And its perpetual stench. But on the
Other side of futility and sin,
There is, in the deepest part of you, the
Spark that nothingness cannot touch or quench.

V

There is exodus from the throng of things,
And there is return to God, and there is
The perpetual deepening of what
You have always and already been. All
That departs from this deepening is sin.
There is in you the stubborn thing you are
That defies qualification, the one
Who perceives yourself and God in the eyes
Of eternity. As you, the spark, rose
Fierce and blue and true in the eyes of God,
God rose fierce and blue and true in the eyes
Of you, and at last you both became one
Bright remorseless flame, for those eyes of yours
And those eyes of God are one and the same.

vi

The you that is free is the you that is
Beyond yourself, the you that has released
Its grip on your own desire, the you that
Must let slip the noose of your false self-love.
No matter how deep the despair, and no
Matter how deep the fear, the kingdom of
God is always near, nearer to you than
You are to that self you must abandon.
And the better part of you, the spark that
Exceeds mere goodness is the spark that sees
Through despair and fear, that sees through all the
Goods and all the desperate rivenness
Of earth, the spark that sees clear through all you
Are to know what your life on earth is worth.

vii

That you must will to live is not your sin,
But that you do not will to give yourself
An end that matters, that you cannot yield
The self that endlessly chatters of what
It wants and needs to excuse itself, that
You cannot yield the self that trembles and
Shatters the gleaming castle in your soul.
The pain of every divided heart brings
Ruin, brings shocking desolation to
The self's own desperate, misguided kingdom.
To depart from god for God's sake is to
Depart from all the idols the mind could
Make. You must embrace the nothingness at
Your core that makes you more and more ... like God.

viii

The why is never the way to God, for
To love God is a way that is no way,
A why that is no why, a where that is
Nowhere, a when that is no when. You must
Break through the throng of things to go into
The ground that has no ground, the time that has
No when, the place that has no where. You must
Know – and go into – your uncreated
Share of eternity. Abandon place;
Abandon time; avoid the trace of each
And every image. Go forth on the narrow
Path without a way, where there will be no
More scrimmage with fact, only the trackless
Track in the desert of your solitude.

ix

God is the negation of negation,
The splendid defiance that nullifies
Nothing, the ultimate dispensation
That transforms all that is empty into
Fullness, all that is impoverished into
Abundance, that accepts futility

And exceeds it, that embraces the word
And the love that breeds it, that turns every
Despair that's devoid of purpose into
An exorbitant whylessness that stands
Beyond the greed for self-justification.
Your way to God's a path unmarked, untrod.
Hide, if you will, this wisdom in your heart;
Then walk the pathless path that leads to God.

VIII. HOW IT IS

All men must die, and no man can escape.
We turn and turn in the same atmosphere
In which no new delight is ever shaped
To grace our living; what we do not have
Seems better than everything else in all the world,
But should we get it, we want something else.
Our gaping thirst for life is never quenched.
We have to know what luck next year will bring,
What accident, what end. But life prolonged
Subtracts not even one second from the term
Of death's continuance. We lack the strength
To abbreviate that eternity. ...
The gods were paid no worship—no one thought
Their presence worth a straw—the state of grief
Had altered all proportion. Funeral rites,
Interments, which these pious people held
In all traditional reverence became
Quite out of fashion; everyone in grief
Buried his own in whatever way he could
Amid the general panic. Sudden need
And poverty persuaded men to use
Horrible makeshifts; howling they would place
Their dead on pyres prepared for other men,
Apply the torches, maim and bleed and brawl
To keep the corpses from abandonment.
   – Lucretius, *De Rerum Natura*, from Book III and Book VI –

i

The eternal rain of matter falls down
Through an infinite void that has no top,

No bottom, no middle, and no purpose.
The slightest swerve of first beginnings takes
Place nowhere and nowhen, for that's how the
Way things are can begin but never end.
There's matter, and there's void, and there is their
Commingling in time that congeals into
The tingling of whatever senses, and
Whatever feels. Thereby created is
The wound that life engenders but never
Heals. Just or unjust – grudgingly – you come
To trust this cruel desert. All you're left to
Manage is the magnitude of the hurt.

ii

The originality that touches
The origin of your soul dissolves the
Mask of obscurity and makes known the
Pillars of your now and your forever.
Few tillers of the human soil have been
So clever. Few singers of another's
Wisdom have had the strength to dissever
Lust for life from that death in life that can
Only trust the futility of lust.
From logic to lyric, from lyric to
Logic, and back again to epic cure.
No longer could you stay, as once you were,
Stone blind – you discern, the obscene, the fat,
The all-corrupting love of human kind.

iii

Out of the futility of lust and
Love, your wisdom, as any authentic
Wisdom, derives its confidence, and its
Consolation. Wanting what you do not
Have, and having what you do not want is
Your recipe for endless thirst. Thus, you
Lift the veil of soul-making to reveal
How your despair is built on the firmest
Foundation, for the ebb of pleasure and
The flow of pain is always about to

Burst into fatal knowledge of what your
Life can and cannot attain. Nature barks
Its bitter truths. All those sweetest drops of
Life condense into cold anxiety.

iv

Useless, your gods fell through the cracks of the
Universe. In those blessed gaps between
The myriad worlds, they live their useless
Lives, beautiful and happy, eating and
Drinking, speaking Greek and never thinking
The slightest thought about humanity.
Your formula, then, is plain: Banish your
Passion, then banish pain, as you've banished
Your useless gods, to serenity, to
Indifference. Then strive, admonish others,
To mimic that dispassion, for caring
Causes pain; not caring releases it.
Meditate, then, on the impotence of
Gods, for if gods don't count, then how could you?

v

Again and again, you must confess. You're
The architect of your distress. And yes.
You stand in the middle of your mess. But
To be equal to the gods you must get
Out of your own way. You must sidestep care
And enjoy the sublime indifference of
Being you. To counteract misery,
You prescribe the useless life of a self-
Sufficient god. Yet you keep on thinking
How it's terribly odd to be a sum
Of atoms that cannot … does not matter.
To ensconce yourself in rock hard coolness,
As if divine dispassion were a throne,
Underrates the consciousness of a stone.

vi

You can never stand in the middle of

Infinity, and if you could, there'd be
No way to stay where you purport to stand.
The value of the void is that it makes
Motion possible. It cannot offer
Rest, only never-ending passage through
Eternity. There is no bottom to
Your universe, no roof. The notion that
There is, is an imaginary spoof
Of desperately misguided religion.
Merciless, you expose to ruin the
Sacred truths. Only a fierce, relentless
Logic can corner and kill the blight of
Religiosity in human will.

vii

You fight the losing battle of beating
Back yourself. Divided against yourself
And your doctrine, your intensity, your
Passion betrays your call for serenity.
It's fair to fear some malice in one who
Honeys the rim of the poisoned chalice.
You cannot drink it down without a frown.
That nothing matters but matter is your
Axiom. All else for you is merely
Superstitious chatter. Such are the hard
Won certitudes of what you claim to know.
But to overrate the certainty of
Cognition is to suffer self-deceit
More supple, more sleek than superstition.

viii

Alive, you've lost the knack for living; grown
Weak, you no longer summon the strength to
Recall what you've abandoned; distraught, you
Lack the power to abbreviate the
Looming eternity of your own death.
You will in life lament what you have not
Lost and cannot lose, as if you could stand
As mourner, as pall bearer at your own
Burial. But you cannot imagine

Your absence because imagination
Requires your presence, your eternity.
Death has no volume of experience.
Yet you fear the death that can never touch
You. You fear to touch what you cannot touch.

ix

There is a panic in the plague that is
Each day, in the horrible makeshifts that
Let you make your way through the night, and through
The day, that let you bury your dread in
The muffled anguish of your distraction.
All your attempts at serenity end,
But your life is a dread that never ends.
You cannot evade the shudders of the
Sublime in you. What fascinates and fastens
Fates together is your fear, your trembling.
There is a dominant atom of grief.
It is the first beginning of belief.
From first beginnings to lasting ends, you
Arrive where all your pain and pleasure tends.

x

When all the worth's leaked out of the riddled
Jar of life, before you've touched and tasted
The utmost of what it offers, before
You've ever had enough, you'll come to know
Before you've died, that hell is merely that
Horrid stuff you've lived and tried already.
You'll know that eternity, not death, is
Absolute, for the absolute knows no
Rest, no peace, only tension. It sets the
Deep-set boundary mark between the nothing
You are not, and can never be, and the
Something you forever are. It's the first
Beginning and lasting end of devotion.
It is your eternity in motion.

xi

If how it is were not duplicitous

And accursed, you could say all that is worth
The saying in one tidy little verse.
But you see only change, only motion,
Life, and the only life you ever see
... is the living blur of eternity.
To live your life between what you love and
What you hate is to remain forever
In that middling state between eternal
Life and all you vie to accept ... abjure.
You cannot purge the urge for religion.
Again, again, you strive, and endlessly,
You try. Of this, more than all else, you're sure:
You'd die and die again to be alive.

IX. YOUR SACRED WAY

For every soul has its inmost sphere, whose being is its life. But this primeval life is hidden not only from other spirits but from the soul itself ... This brings us to the second reason why a man's inmost being is hidden from him. As has been said, here the soul is truly at home. But, strange though it may sound, it is normally not at home. There are but few souls that live in and from their inmost being; and even fewer that are constantly living in and from it.
　　　－ Edith Stein, *The Science of the Cross* －

The divine light that is kindled in the soul is the light that has come into the darkness, the miracle of the Holy Night. If we have it in us, we understand what is meant when men speak about it. For others, everything that can be said of it is an incomprehensible stammering. ... Just as the first man and woman became estranged from God, though they had been his children, so every one of us is always balancing on the edge of the knife between nothingness and the fullness of the divine life.
　　　－ Edith Stein, *The Mystery of Christmas* －

i

You were an eleventh child born on the
Day of atonement, with a destiny
Deepened down to roots by the need for home.
Your life was one long continuous prayer

For truth: before God was through with you, all
You were, was absolutely true. What you
Were at core was what you were before, that
Unfolded itself ever after. Truth
Saturates all you are ... all you desire.
In the middle of potency and act,
There is the everlasting fact of your
Becoming what you are. To find your home,
To go there and to stay: This was the deep
And the narrow strait of your sacred way.

ii

As a perpetual beginner, you
Sought the first beginning for beginners.
You are conceived, you're born, you are. That you
Are you is a fact you know more dearly
Than all else. You know you are. You know the
Relentless fact that you are you. But what
You are, you almost always forget; you're
The *now* between *no longer* and *not yet*.
Just as one dimensionless point must be
Invisibly nested in the teeming
Infinity of infinite lines, so
Must your moment, your ever-present now,
Be indivisibly nested in the
Infinite matrix of eternity.

iii

Every idol must give you what you have
Already: It gives you despair. It gives
You death. The solitude that clamors and
Despises dissembles yet enamors
Itself of trust in its many guises.
You could not escape the terror. You could
Not escape your death nor the despair that
Forms the very foundation of your faith.
There is a sense of being beyond care.
It's to be found in your personal share
Of the eternity sought by every
Joy and shunned by each and every despair.

The deeper your despair the nearer you
Are to your fair share of eternity.

iv

There is no Christmas without the Cross, and
No Cross without Christmas. Thus, despite the
Argument of your agony, God will
At last outwit your stubborn resistance
To the impossible experience
Of undeserved, yet everlasting joy.
The first beginning of the first Being
   ... is a burgeoning plenitude. What lasts
   ... is endless abundance of more and more
Into which nothingness cannot intrude.
Yet you're balanced on the edge of a knife.
This is the innermost sphere of what's real.
It's there and there alone that you feel the
Touch that gives the taste of eternal life.

v

The moment your unbelief collapsed is
When first and forever you listened so
Profoundly to the life of another.
No persons. No community. And no
Community. No persons. You are made
Of others, and others are made of you.
You're an eddy in the stream of others,
And others eddies in the stream of you.
To listen deeply to the voices of
Other persons is to hear God himself
Speak with love in the voices of others.
Go find a lonely, rugged spot for prayer,
Then kneeling in adoration there, let
Speak the God who speaks what He speaks through you.

vi

Despite your fear, you do not feel alone.
Despite your pride, you do not think alone.
Despite your zeal, you do not wait alone.

Despite your verve, you do not seek alone.
Despite your will, you do not find alone.
Despite your lust, you do not love alone.
Despite your care, you do not live alone.
Despite your dread, you do not die alone.
As you grow in grace, it no longer seems
So odd how the joy you share with others
And yourself is the joy you share with God.
Despite your dread of death, there's tenderness
In the dark infinity of the night.
You go there unalone. You go with God.

vii

From others, as from yourself, you demand
The impossible. But, as you strive, there
Will, with passion, prayer and patience, arrive
The unjustified grace of God. Out of
Sorrow, out of pain, arrives infinite
Gain, your ability to envision,
And to act upon the truth you attain.
You must always listen first before you
Pray, for when you listen with surety
Of surrender, knowing no other way,
The quietest whisper of God's wisdom will
Have its say, and – summoned – your judgment knows
There can be no better day to seek God's
Way than doing what must be done today.

viii

To become a person is to endure
The affliction of self-inflicted change.
To be a person is to be free for
Now, forever, and for eternity.
All that's alive is unfinished. All that's
Dead can be replenished by the light that
Illumines your night of desolation.
Let this be your lasting prayer forever.
Fight the good fight. Let there be no shadow
Of darkness in your light. Let there be no
Lasting triumph of sorrow in your night.

What you are in your eternity is
The unfinished matter of your life that
Never ends but continues to matter.

X. KEEP COUNTERFEITING ETERNITY

To be me is to reach toward being God. Or, if you prefer, man fundamentally is the desire to be God.
– Jean-Paul Sartre, *Being and Nothingness* –

There is no good father. That's the rule. Don't lay the blame on men but on the bond of paternity which is rotten. ... One writes for one's neighbors or for God. I decided to write for God for the purpose of saving my neighbors.
– Jean-Paul Sartre, *The Words* –

So this is hell. I'd never have believed it.
– Jean-Paul Sartre, *No Exit* –

We make it happen, we're middlemen, we don't judge them, we don't ask for anything in return, not even for them to be good republicans. We're available to everyone equally. Isn't that what you always wanted to be in the end: the means by which others could be free?
– Jean-Paul Sartre, *The Last Chance* –

I sink into the snow up to my knees; if I pick some up with my hands, it turns to liquid in my fingers; it runs off; there is nothing left of it. The in-itself is transformed into nothingness. My dream of appropriating the snow vanishes at the same moment. Moreover, I do not know what to do with the snow which I have just come to see close at hand.
– Jean-Paul Sartre, *Being and Nothingness* –

i

The father, who is always guilty, is
The one who is absent, the one who has
Recused himself from your life, from your own

Happiness, from his own existence. He
Will not and could not exist, even with
Your insistence. There has been and there will
Continue to be ardent pronouncements
Of many deaths: the death of God, of man,
Of truth, of beauty, of goodness. These brusque
Obituaries are distractions from
Your guilt, from your responsibility
For what you are and cannot help but be.
In the end, you swerve, you lose the nerve to
Abandon yourself to God without reserve.

ii

There's an idiot in every family,
And it is you. Everything that happens
To you, that will happen, that's already
Happened, has already happened in your
Childhood. Each child's always the apprentice
Of a desperate adulthood. Your childhood,
Like every childhood, nurtures the waiting
Future, which betrays it. If nothingness
   ... is the truth, then truth is the progeny
Of a troubled youth, of God's little orphan,
For whom the resonance of absence is
The sole presence behind it, the rainbow
Gleam of your original dream that flees
You forever as you try to find it.

iii

You're the sorcerer for yourself each time
You find yourself the source of what you are.
You would – if only you could – become your
Own beginning. This is the dream that kept
You sinning and spinning the impossible
Truth. You dispensed with God, for you would not
Be captured by his gaze. You would not be
Seen by one who cannot be shuttered, who
Never sleeps, who's always here to stay, who
Never goes away, whose universe is
So alive, so free, yet so uncluttered

With justifiable consolation.
The rhetoric of authenticity
Cannot exonerate your desperate guilt.

iv

When you envision cause, you imagine
The place where imagination must pause.
You imagine presence marked by absence.
In despair, you populate this absence
With substitutions, with those convulsions
That first desire and then strive to replace
Your nervously awaited orgasm.
For the painter, there's presence that defies
The brush. For the thinker, there's moment that
Survives the rush ... of thought. This then is the
Eternity you sought ... but lost, the thing
That makes you live, that marks your absence with
The tattered flag of desire, that gives your
Nothingness local habitation and name.

v

There is only boredom that waits for you
Beyond being what you want to become.
No one can die for you. No one can try
For you. No one can think for you. No one
Can feel for you. No one can be bored for
You. No one but you directs the drama
Behind the boredom. In complacency,
You languish; you learn to equivocate,
To mask your anguish. You make your anguish
Into a new mode of perception, a
Pseudo-sense of touch that tells you what it's
Like to know so little and hurt so much.
Yes. You crave relief, but without belief,
Without the pettiness of human grief.

vi

There's no bottom to consciousness, no top.
Nothing you can think of can make it stop.

When consciousness begins to disrupt your
Eternity, you crave self-deception.
But self-deceit is self-defeating: its
Evasion of truth is always fleeting;
It's forever retreating from your lies
To the truth that cannot sustain itself.
Every you that is alive must flicker,
Before self-deception can cast its spell.
Consciousness returns, and then you snicker:
You try to be yourself but fail. Thus, in
Vain, you quiver and deliver yourself
Into the nothingness of a new you.

vii

Your life is a wave always breaking, a
Moment that's never quite established, that's
Forsaking what it was, is, and will be.
You want to justify your madness by
Sharing it with others. You invade their
Perfect moments, because hell is other
Persons ... and you too. Would-be madeleines
Crumble like neglected trust. Everyone
Who goes there goes bust. No one survives the
Leper's kiss without contamination.
Those who lose their sense of perfection lose
The same illusions, and to lose the same
Illusions is to share the same solitude,
To share the same madness, and the same hell.

viii

You begin by saying you choose what you
Do. You conclude by questioning whether
Anyone can justifiably say
I did it. You found the source of human
Responsibility, then you *hid it*
... in history ... in befuddled dialectics.
Nothing's more bleak than another critique
Of history; nothing's more bleak than shopworn
Causality that must speak its antique
Meaning. There's really very little you

Know. And what you know deeply you cannot
Say. The wealth of truth and the poverty
Of perception transforms would-be wise men
Into taciturn anthropologists.

ix

You must dare to desire or die. You must
Hunger to be … to become. Each moment
You live is one more chance to lose your way.
Your life and the history you inhabit
Are cut from the same cloth. When they move in
Complicity, they're chasing the same moth.
You assumed a false but prudent air of
Bitter despair, a glamorous and crowd-
Pleasing mood you could not avoid without
The risk of seeming rude. Thus, you exchange
Fake authenticity for a series of
New impostures that cannot save your life.
The gap between authenticity and
Artifice is always negligible.

x

What do you want? Everything. What do you
Settle for? Nothingness. Do you carry
The day, or does the day carry you? You
Throw away the answers before you're through.
You outlived yourself. You always did. You
Always do. Then, you died without a view.
What you become will be you forever.
This then is your eternity, not a
Monument of inert marble, but a
Movement that never loses its suspense.
You're a promise, a vow that can always
Be remade, broken or fulfilled. In your
Eternity, you will be forever
Tried and convicted by the time you've killed.

xi

Your anguish is your fear of not finding

Yourself at the appointment you made with
Yourself. Always you're elsewhere, nowhere and
Now here. You're in anguish in order to
Flee it. You're in bad faith in order to
Be it. You exist at a distance from
Yourself. The self you would be disappears
As you become yourself. Thus, your life leads
You to elsewhere, to nowhere and now here.
The beginning and the end of being
In nothingness is a promise, a vow.
You are a promise; you are a vow. You're
The summoning of an eternity
That is always here and now ... and nowhere.

xii

The most valuable part of yourself is
What you imagine, and eternity,
For you, is imagined, the tender fruit
Of your desperately misguided desire.
No one will ever know where the snow must
Go. You will never know what to do with
The perpetually vanishing you,
With the truth that becomes and emerges
From the scarcity, the greed, and splurges
Of human strife, from the praxis that can
Always tax us with unwanted outcomes.
What becomes of the snow is the you, you
Do not know. There's never a triumph more
Sweet than the miracle of self-deceit.

xiii

Goodness is the ghost that haunts despair. Yes.
You're the nothingness that goodness haunts, that
In deceit still flaunts the futility
That taunts your leading motive, your will to
Risk all your labors to save yourself and
Your equally lonely neighbors. Every
Ecstasy must fail. Every grasp must stall.
Every rise of self-deceit must call forth
Your idolized desideratum, God.

But between making history and making
Good, there's the middleman who promised what
He did and did what he could. Forget all
Those deceitful lures. To enable the
Freedom of others is to enable yours.

xiv

The dreaded ghost of a God long dead still
Haunts human kind and inhabits your head.
You cannot outwit what you counterfeit.
Thus, keep counterfeiting eternity.
Keep clinging to the rotten, to what you
Imagine could ever be forgotten.
Each vague remnant of the authentic you
Will be found, then lost again and again
Before you're through. But you're never through. You're
Never finished. You keep on flickering.
You keep on bickering with yourself, while
The nothingness you are is replenished
With more nothingness, with the useless urge
To go on counterfeiting what you are.

XI. ARC OF PROMISE

It is through the condition of being hostage that there can be in this world pity, compassion, pardon, and proximity – even the little there is, even the simple "After you, sir."
 – Emmanuel Levinas, *Otherwise than Being:*
 Or Beyond Essence –

To be for a time that would be without me, for a time after my time, over and beyond the famous 'being for death', is not an ordinary thought which is extrapolating my own duration; it is the passage to the time of the Other. Should what makes such a passage possible be called eternity?
 – Emmanuel Levinas, "Meaning and Sense" –

Are we entering a moment of history in which the good must be loved without promises? May we not be on the eve of a new form of faith, a faith without triumph, as if the only irrefutable value were saintliness, a time when the only right to a reward

would be not to expect one?
The first and last manifestation of God would be to be without promises.
  – Emmanuel Levinas, *Alterity and Transcendence* –

But infinite time is also the putting back into question of the truth it promises. The dream of a happy eternity, which subsists in man along with his happiness, is not a simple aberration. Truth requires both an infinite time and a time it will be able to seal, a completed time. The completion of time is not death, but messianic time, where the perpetual is converted into eternal. Messianic triumph is the pure triumph; it is secured against the revenge of evil whose return infinite time does not prohibit. Is this eternity a new structure of time, or an extreme vigilance of the messianic consciousness?
  – Emmanuel Levinas, *Totality and Infinity* –

To know God is to know what must be done.
  – Emmanuel Levinas, *Difficult Freedom* –

i

You would rather be someone and somewhere
Else. But you are here and now and nowhere.
Your true life is always absent but you
Live it nowhere, now here and forever.
You would be nothing if you were not a
Contradiction, an unsaying of the
Word, a word you've longed for, but cannot shake
Off, a word you've barely heard, as if you're
A melody you hardly remember,
An ancient song that yearns to unlimber
Your character and undo your wrong. You're
Free, it's said, to be what you are, but there
Are limits to being free: if you are
What you are, you're not what you ought to be.

ii

The conch shell roar of surging emptiness
Has no after, no before, only waves
Of silence that keep pounding the shore with

Their anonymous roar of unmeaning.
Do not be seduced by what you've reduced
To yourself. Apart from you, apart from
Everything, there is never nothingness
But always more, the infinity of
The Other who aims his shocking claim at
You. You begin with the anonymous
Night, and you end with endlessness, with what's
Wholly other, with what keeps going on,
Keeps eluding your grasp, yet which intrudes
Itself into your now unsettled life.

iii

Sincerity's your unbetrayable
Reply to the Other who insists that
You must not murder, that you must not lie,
For to lie is to murder the truth, and
To murder is to lie, to deny by
Holding in cruel reserve the truth you
Lack the nerve to embrace: the infinite
Worth of the Other's face. Thus, you're tempted
To lean on the lie, the transparent fig
Leaf that reveals what it pretends to hide.
Eternity, the time of the Other,
   ... is the moment when truth must start. It is
The beginning of the only thirst that
Lasts in the hunger of the human heart.

iv

Time is how you greet what is stranger than
Yourself, how you're no longer seduced by
The consoling fraud of the familiar.
Biting through your being to the bone is
The revelation that you're not alone.
The shock of the Other breaks through the ice
Of your isolation, your solitude.
Before your living time began, before
You become you, you're responsible for
The Other. From nowhere ... nowhen, beckons
The revelation you neither evade

Nor spin to your advantage. Before there's
Time to kill, guilt is how you happen, how
You suffer what you are without appeal.

v

Your sin, your guilt, is your belief that you
Could be or become your own foundation.
You keep adding yourself and Others up,
As if to overfill that already
Overflowing cup you cannot contain.
You proceed, heaping hollowness upon
Hollowness, until your ego gets the
Cramps in your empty suit of armor. Yes.
Each person is always a dangerous
Supplement to eternity, for each
Person fails toward time, each person fails toward
The Other, each person fails toward the good,
Each person harbors within ... its remnant
Of the dreaded and the beheaded God.

vi

Out of the vastness of the void erupts
A face that can displace but not erase
The constant threat of anonymity.
There is what there is; there is the silence
That rumbles. There is the silence that is
Neither nothingness nor being. There is
The silence that dreams of freeing itself
From eternity. You must abandon
There is when you hear eternity's silent
Thunder, when the point's not to understand
But to stand under the authority
Of the Other, of that shredded God who
Dares to live, who thrives and still survives in
The heart of one who hastens toward the good.

vii

You become what you become, and you stay
What you are ... in accord with the promise.

To become what you become, you stay what
You are, as if you retrieve from afar
The lost, blinding light of a long dead star.
Remember ... you. Remember ... me. This is the
Motion of your eternity, of the
Promise that must be kept, of the promise
That must be remembered to be kept, that
Must be kept to be remembered, that must
Be remembered if you are to dwell in
Eternity ... with Others ... and with God.
When the messiah comes, your face shall weep
For all those promises you did not keep.

viii

You are neither nothingness nor being.
You are otherwise than either. You are
Otherwise than something, otherwise than
Nothing. You are here and now and nowhere.
You are the trace and the trembling fragment
Of the eternity you cannot help
But lose, yet still promise to remember.
This is the only promise that you have
To keep, a promise that is always far
Too steep to be kept, for even if you
Should give your all, it always stands too tall;
It rises far too steep for you to keep.
Eternity, therefore, never rests, for
Everyone dies with his work unfinished.

ix

The time without promises promises
A promise of another kind, betrays
The promise that's too steep to keep, betrays
Eternity, the trace of nowhere and
Now here, not an archetype on Plato's
Shelf, but the passage from self to Other,
From Other to self. This, then, is the arc
Of promise, the shimmering bridge from now
Here to nowhere ... from nowhere to now here.
You live this promising lack of promise

In the image of God, in the trace of
God's passing by, in the echoes of his
Eternity, with no reward, no fear,
With no consolation of knowing why.

x

After you, sir, the same will never be
The same again, yet your infinity's
Nonetheless still blind to eternity
Of another order, another kind.
Your time is never less real than what you
Feel in the face of the Other, but the
Infinity of otherness always points
To eternity, to that goodness, that
Bounty, that blessing without boundaries,
Where destiny is doing what you should,
Where every action in time finds traction
In eternity, in what's nowhere, now
Here and forever, in the unsung, all-
Too-uncommon glory of doing good.

xi

The time that never rests relentlessly
Attests to eternity. The sugar
That melts, that disappears in time, is the
Sweetness of eternity announcing
Itself, the sweetness that can never fade
Forever, because the sugar always
Begins to melt and be felt again. Your
Eternity never fails to rhyme with
Melting time, for the life you learn with is
Never the life that learns how to stay dead
Forever. Eternity, never time's
Mask, is an achievement, a task, and your
Time is the path taken by the task that
Leads nowhere and now here forever.

xii

No joy that's true can undo the power of

Law. No solitude can be so coy as
To reject the ultimacy of joy.
You search for the lasting mood that's beyond
Your middling state, a way of being in
Which you're no longer tempted to hate what
You become or become what you hate. You
Keep returning eternally to the
Same. For this, you've only yourself to blame.
The sobriety of a starless night,
The exalted disaster of your own
Forsaking, is futile unless it leads
Beyond itself, beyond being and time
To the goodness in you that's awaking.

xiii

You keep returning to the same mistake,
As though duped, as though you could free yourself
From the specter of eternity with
The counterfeit death of a bankrupt God.
To revivify that certain God, to
Make eternity visible, is to
Make and remake yourself with promises
You try, but fail to keep. It is to make
Yourself, your history, your eternity,
Indivisible with the good, through the
Unwitnessed trial of doing what you should.
Eternity must be freed from those who
Would be free of it. Eternity must
Be freed for those with the strength to love it.

xiv

Out of the darkness, there will come the light.
Eternity, what you lack an image
For, the trace of a lost perfection you
Cannot attain or master, is your last
Cruel light's blind angel calling in this time
Of your disaster. Do not fail the light.
Do not buckle beneath the burden. Do
Not bow to woe. Do not justify as
If to worship sins you're now confessing.

Do not in your haste neglect the taste of
Eternity. Do not fail to taste what
You must not waste. Do not waste the blessing.
Be bold. The true life that's always elsewhere
  ... is ready to hand but hardest to hold.

XII. WONDER NEVER ENDS

God contradicts Himself with His world, His eternity with time. This self-contradiction is the Creation. All doubts concerning God's will are correct if He – had not created the world. For then He would be alone with Himself, alone with His eternity, alone with his ubiquity, or otherwise expressed (and this is only apparently the opposite): alone with his Nowhere and No Place. (For eternity is nowhere, and everywhere is no place.)
  – Franz Rosenzweig, "The Science of God" –

In ethics, everything is uncertain. Everything, after all, can be moral, but nothing is moral with certainty. ... Eternity is a future, which without ceasing to be future, is nonetheless present. Eternity is a Today which is, however, conscious of being more than Today. ... Life, and all life, must first become wholly temporal, wholly alive, before it can become eternal life. In short, eternity must be accelerated. It must be always capable of already coming 'today'. Only thereby is it eternity. ... Eternity is just this: that time no longer has a right to a place between the present moment and consummation and that the whole future is to be grasped today. ... Eternity is after all just this: that everything is at every point and at every moment. ... To walk humbly with thy God – nothing more is demanded than a wholly present trust. But trust is a big word.
  – Franz Rosenzweig, *The Star of Redemption* –

Yet the soul does have a place, though it is no 'there' to which our finger could point, but an 'in-between.' The soul moves or it can move between two poles: delusion and truth, world and service, masks and the face.
  – Franz Rosenzweig, *Ninety-two Poems and*
       Hymns of Yehuda Halevi –

i

All you are begins in the middle of
The All, begins in the middle between
Your long lost beginning and your unfound
End. As your life awakens, you never
Quite plumb your limit. With faux certainty,
You worship false gods that first condemn it,
Then hedge it in. To diversion and to
Perversion you succumb, to idols that
Make you numb to life beyond distractions,
To idols, the instruments of your sin,
To those previews of coming attractions
That never come, to idols that give the
Lie to the liability of the
Love you once imagined could never die.

ii

Something happened in 1923
That was the beginning of the end of
Your eternity. The love that founded
You, confounded you, when it died, and the
Promise once spoken, now broken, made a
Mockery of your word, as if you lied,
As if only you and your beloved
Had ever tried to keep a promise that
Would not abide. But Rose of Jericho,
You come to life, no matter how severe
Seemed the certitude of your death. Deathless
Remnant, your star-like flower, revives and
Thrives, and then anew you burn as you take
Your turn in the firmament of heaven.

iii

How can the imagined be more real than
The stubbornly unimagined? There is
Confusion, disorder in how you feel,
As if to summon fantasy beckons
The real. That you loved a woman is a
Fact no less exact than the fact that she

Loved you back. This love once so deeply real
  ... is a love that's lost, that you no longer
Feel. Was this love fantasy, or fact that
Failed, a hope that quailed, a utopia
Enjoyed, awaited, but too heavily
Freighted for everyday life to sustain,
Or was what you once so deeply felt a
Sign ... of what loss of love cannot malign?

iv

To be wise, so the cynic says, is to
Know that all love dies. To be wise, so the
Cynic says, is to know that all love lies.
The promise kept is the miracle that
Makes the fantasy real. Nothing could be
More empirical than the miracle
That lets you feel the depth of a love that
Never dies, that never lies, that shocks the
Desperate cynic with wonder and surprise.
Miracle's the sign of a promise kept.
When you experience this miracle,
You experience the God that matters.
You experience the love that shatters
All your obsession with self-possession.

v

Here, now and everywhere the ground begins
To shift. As you come alive, you accept
Your uncertainty as a gift. But the
Loss of your confidence that leads to grief
Undermines the possibility of
Belief. And yet your disbelief is a
Risk that must be run. The eternity
You seek, whether false, whether true, is the
Burning obsession behind all you do.
You seek what will last. You find what you sought
  ... is already past, already beyond
What can claim the right of presence. As you
Keep drifting, the eternity you thought
True, keeps shifting slyly away from you.

vi

Your dream of completion, of perfection,
Of ending, is your act of defending
Yourself against the infection called hope,
Against the promise you make but forsake,
And yet everything you think, you feel, you
Say, you do, always follows in its wake.
The demon driving you that defies all
Explaining is the only part of you
That has no trouble remaining ... alive.
And what remains, the remainder of the
Unexplained, the restless reminder of
The promise unattained, is the twisting
Screw of moral friction that makes you you.
Such are the consequences of a screw.

vii

Jealously, you guard your eternity
As the only one that's true, the only
One bearing witness, the only one bearing
Fruit from the tree of life. But redemption
That's only a promise only whets your
Thirst, and redemption that's already here
Cannot sustain itself. Thus, where you are
Becomes the way, and the way ends where you
Are already. Neither nowhere nor now
Here can keep you steady. Only the call
To love can ever make you ready to
Live as though first were last and last were first,
To live as though any moment you were
About to burst into eternity.

viii

Expectation of your end at every
Moment beckons your eternity. That
The last can think the first and that the first
Can feel the last is the history of your
Thirst without longing for the future or
The past. It's the history of your worst

Which still struggles to redeem the dreaded
And accursed. The kingdom in your midst that
Arrives today is your future that is
Already happening here and now and
Forever. Do not be grim. Do not be
Snide. Be unironically exact. Your
Eternity's not your fantasy, not
Your slyest self-delusion. It's a fact.

ix

Whatever *now is* can never *not be*.
This, then, is the minimum view of your
Eternity. You seek the appointed
Time, and the appointed time is nowhere,
Now, and forever. The now you would cling
To ... is no longer here. And the nowhere
You'd escape to ... is here and now. Is this,
Then, finally ... how ... your moment becomes
Eternity: by echoing what is
Nowhere, yet what's here and now ... forever?
All that's deep contradicts itself. All that's
Deep echoes promises you cannot keep.
All that's deep echoes nowhere and now here,
Your world ... to come, your world ... already here.

x

The eternity that's just as much now
Here as nowhere is never clear, yet your
Hope is how you live your future now as
The tension between nowhere and now here,
The moment of suspense, in which what you
Desire or fear, what you want or taunt, could
Feel as real as what could last forever.
To be redeemed, for you, is to expect
A nowhere that is now here, and a now
Here that is nowhere. It's a miracle
Not yet happening but just about to
Happen; it is a promise not fulfilled;
But about to be; it is the splendor
Of that suspense you call eternity.

xi

To be is to become what you are; to
Be is to be a fire that always turns
Toward the eternity that burns in you.
Yes. You are the fire this time, the first time,
The last time, the next time. Becoming is
Being on fire. To be and to bear your
Name is to become. To become is to
Be aflame with meaning, to be word and
Fire. In deepest despair, not even your
Greatest folly can prepare you to be
On fire. In truth, it's no use. Not even
Cynicism can make you fire-proof, for
All life is passage to eternity.
When the now seems like forever, it is.

xii

The star at the end of the way means what
It means, only if the perfection it
Embodies lives this very day, this day
Of days, when you come alive, now, once and
Forever, on this day, your longest day.
What keeps living alive is giving what
You've been given, reliving what you've been
Forgiven, in ways that welcome others,
In ways promising, but unsure, like that
Stranger awaiting the warmth of your hearth
On the coldest night in January.
There's no exemption from redemption. To
Save yourself, all others must be saved. That's
How the road to forever must be paved.

xiii

Prophecy unlimited: Imagine
The world to come where every act of will
Must speak, where every act of will becomes
A voice, where every voice, as an act of
Will, utters what it must feel and cannot
Repeal, where you must reveal the mystery

That was you, but that you can no longer
Conceal. This is the nightmare of troubled
Grace. This is the nightmare of the very
Face of God that shines his naked light through
You and your equally lonely others.
This is the blunder of a world without
Wonder, a world unfree. This lie is the
Mask of truth that smothers eternity.

xiv

You hear what Others say, but never hear
What Others hear you say. The former is
Revelation. The latter is mystery,
The lure of trust, which yearns for honesty
About the desperate hazard of its lust,
And the threat of trust. Each eternity,
It sees, as false eternity, as one
More species of self-deception. No feast,
No fast, can mask this past, can forget how
The history of your trust goes bust with no
Exception in the void between truth and
Self-deception, where each promise you make,
You must break, where to love is thus to risk
The mistake that puts all you are at stake.

xv

The Other asks: Where are you? You answer:
Nowhere and now here. It's a miracle
You're anywhere at all, but nothing can
Remain the same after the call of your
Name. Yes. Everywhere and nowhere are
Overwhelmed by the miracle of now
Here. Lost in nowhere, you're born now here, and
Long to be as strong as death, as fresh as
The breath of Eden, as green as the word
You've always heard, the word that repeats with
No exclusion an *unto eternity*
That's no delusion. You come as close as
You come to kingdom come when you honor
With awe the flaw in the law of your love.

xvi

Your life's the delicate imbalance of
Would-be knots, the cat's cradle of promise
And fulfillment, of nowhere and now here,
The shivering swerve of suspense that lets
Everything that's in the moment, but you,
Become perpetually new, that lets
You see the light in which the light is seen,
The light before and beyond creation,
The light before your living time began,
The light before any spark could hope to
Span the abyss between promises you
Keep and do not keep. Yet there beyond the
Deep, you see what a face must mean before
The raging lie could demean the human.

xvii

The mystery of love is the miracle
Of shared blunder. You experience the
Mistake of promises made to a heart
You cannot break. This miracle within
You, within the heart of the one you love,
Within the sway of wonder, is wonder
With authority you don't understand
But stand under. You're what you cannot fail
To be: expert on matters concerning
You, expert in giving excuses for
All that you've tried to be and failed to do.
More than you care to admit you step forth
Without a trace of wit, you blunder, as
You step forth into the heart of wonder.

xviii

There's an eternity that's final, that's
Ever new. This is the eternity
That's here and now for you, that's readied for
The final, but still unfinished you. Your
Task is to accept the grace to shed ... the
Mask of what in you is relentlessly

Dead. Nowhere but now here, where you see a
Face so true, could you embrace the task of
Giving what's forever alive in you,
Where you will no longer be admonished
By the aggressively unastonished,
Where the truth in you keeps striving where the
Goodness of giving tends, and your future
Keeps arriving where wonder never ends.

— NINE —
PART FOUR
THE COMMON DAY

I. WHOLE DAMN SCHMEAR

In isolated moments we all know that we have deliberately complicated the arrangements of our lives only in order to evade our real task.
– Friedrich Nietzsche, *Untimely Meditations* –

The breeding of an animal that can promise – is not this just that very paradox of a task which nature has set for itself in regards to man? Is not this the very problem of man? ... I am what I am: how could I get away from myself? And, verily – I am sick of myself. ... Everyone who has ever built anywhere a "new heaven" first found the power thereto in his own hell ...
– Friedrich Nietzsche, *The Genealogy of Morals* –

A soul which knows that it is loved, but does not itself love, betrays its sediment: its dregs come up.
– Friedrich Nietzsche, *Beyond Good and Evil* –

I shall show them the rainbow and all the steps to the overman. ... What was silent in the father speaks in the son; and often I found the son the unveiled secret of the father. ... This is my way; where is yours? — thus, I answered those who asked me 'the way.' For <u>the</u> way – that does not exist.
– Friedrich Nietzsche, *Thus Spoke Zarathustra* –

i

You were trapped in an accident of your
Own making, in the makeshift wreckage you
Have the gall to call yourself, the self you
Keep revisiting and forsaking as
Strange, as stranger than you know, as strange as
The alien self of your unmaking.
The bliss you miss blesses you with danger,
With the fateful risk of sanctifying,
Or sacrificing joy. You are what you
Exalt. Nothing's stranger. Yet you desert
Yourself with the dodge of darker wisdom,
Wisdom you reach by default, wisdom that
You wallow in and can't shake off, that you
Cherish in solitude, while others scoff.

ii

Your loneliness beyond bearing you bore
Quite well, as if solitude were both your
Heaven and your self-manufactured hell.
You were most of all an example, an
Exception, one who shrewdly, ruthlessly
Fought and lost and won the battle against
Self-deception. Though martyred to madness,
You had, you thought, a genius for hygiene,
When your genius was for narcotics, for
Whatever puts your will to power to sleep.
With every possible method and cure,
You doctor yourself until you're sure of
The fate you could not cure. You lapse into
The hypnosis of self-diagnosis.

iii

You enjoyed the privilege of having the
Right father, an incomparable father,
Almost unknown to you, who died at the
Stroke of midnight to the din of brawling
Dogs, a father whose way, whose legacy
Of wisdom, founded and confounded you.
A father whose gift to you, the gift of
Eternity, you misconstrue, but which
Hounded and hounded you, until at last
You propounded it anew. *Father,* for
You, is that very word that beckons you
Toward eternity, toward perfection. As
The son, the secret of your father, you
Prove your loyalty by your defection.

iv

You rise in distinction as the epoch
You could not cure approaches extinction.
Victim and vanquisher of your epoch,
You're the latest, greatest murderer of
God. There's no standpoint on which you stand, no
Bar to pry your secret loose, no knowing

How ... your life congeals into its now. There's
No decisive caesura, no time to
Pause, no cause for time to depart from its
Cause. There is no harbor, safe and serene,
That you could not demean with justified
Cynicism. There's at last no lasting
Defense against your God, or against you,
God's lonely assassin and lawless prince.

v

You no longer mind that there's no longer
Any *behind* behind the soul, any
Orchestrating wizard behind the mind.
You caused and killed your God according to
Your needs. You sought to grasp ungraspable
Eternity with the self-deception
Upon which it everlastingly feeds.
The beyond in self-deception is the
Vision of a bond that can't be broken,
A promise that can be spoken again
And again without the remotest threat
Of confirmation or refutation.
For you, the wisest now lack the wit to
Sustain this self-deceiving counterfeit.

vi

Your wisdom shifts as it sifts through the sieve
Of contempt, before you can make your last
Desperate attempt to negate what you hate.
In you, the concept of the good man goes
To seed. What follows is merely the man
Who knows how both to blather and to bleed.
Yet you're always quite pragmatic about
The stimulus of the enigmatic,
For each attempt to master history
Only serves to prolong the mystery.
If you can ask and try to answer why,
You undergo the greatest need to lie.
Honesty must take its breath: you cannot
Win the truth by beating the lies to death.

vii

The soul only knows what the body knows.
And your body's the mechanical clock
That creates the first and then the lasting
Shock of your bodiless eternity,
For the soul that is no soul, for the soul
That has no goal, for the soul that plays one
Role, for the soul that is merely the urge
To keep going on and on forever.
Never knowing who you are ... you ... your most
Cherished ideal, undermines itself. Your
Strictest rule provokes disobedience.
Your highest value takes itself in vain.
And your exhausted life wonders what mere
Continuance could ever let it gain.

viii

The barking dogmas at midnight dare not
Declare that they only lead the way to
Desolation and despair. Why on earth
Are you here on earth? What on earth could your
Life be worth? Why are you here, and not there?
Why now, and not then? Why now here, and not
Nowhere? Eternity mongering is
How you deal with the path you did not take,
With the thirst you could not slake, with the sins
You could not shake, with all those promises
You make and then forsake. From hereafter
To here and now, and from nowhere to now
Here, you'll seek new myths to stanch your fear. This
  ... is the light of the common day, my dear.

ix

You traced the thread from the ideal to the
One who needs it, from the value to the
One who breeds it to keep breathing. You scoffed
At the goodness of the good man as though
His unwitting spirit of revenge bleeds
Him of all goodness. You took sides against

Yourself, struggling harder and harder, till
Nothing that's good could still survive in the
Understocked larder of uncommon sense.
The death of God is a revelation
And an absolution. It's your tempting
Solution to those who would deny their guilt.
Your glamorous subversion of the good
Does not accomplish what you thought it would.

X

Your lucidity's the clear-sightedness
To which your ecstasy clings as it sings
And stings of bitter truth. To love life is
To love error, to live the terror of
A truth that cannot be disentangled
From deceit. Thus, take your medicine, and
Take it sweet. Pull down, in self-deceit, the
Curtain on what is certain, on all those
Demons of sin within that you cannot
Appease. Joy deceives what it cannot please.
Thus, not even joy puts your will to lie
To sleep, for what guides you in its wake is
The cowardice that denies what it knows,
And that wants what it wants, but must forsake.

xi

Again, you return to revelations
Of your eternal return. Once again,
You unlearn what you learn, to learn once more
What you unlearn. No one else can take your
Turn, for you are the unquenchable fire
This time, next time, now and forever. As
Long as you live, you yearn to burn, for you're
The fire that cannot cease to yearn without
Forsaking your return to what you are.
What you are at core is what you've always
Been before, this burning, yearning, endless
Returning, this humming fear that never
Stops becoming, that never stops strumming
The rainbow between nowhere and now here.

xii

When the guttering lamp of the world goes
Out, what happens, happens in darkness, in
Terror. That you matter so little and
Chatter so much lets you lean in sin and
Error on the crutch of what you cannot touch.
Absurdest, tritest dogmas keep pleading:
Just try us! Try us! No. There's nothing more
Pious than your philosophic bias.
The most foolish thoughts that can be believed
Wait in this desolate eternity
For those they would deceive to be deceived.
When overcoming's over, never fear,
It's never over, for the whole damn schmear,
Keeps starting over, in darkness, right here.

xiii

Ditto, ditto, dearest Kiddo, early
Returns always foreshadow the late, and
The blackest widow that bites her mate can
Never avenge histories of the fate you've
Learned to hate, nor hallow those tedious
Hijinks … that bewilder Oedipus and
Discombobulate the Sphinx. Life's lewd lace
Of lies, laid down as the maze of events,
Conspires to kill, but never prevents your
Return to the thrill that resents your will
To render it still, as if you could pull
Rank with Alexander, with Caesar, as
If eternity were a female god,
As if you – and you alone – could please her.

xiv

The pigtail of long lost care dangles there,
Limp and dull, in the labyrinth of your skull,
Your crooked cauldron of despair; and there,
A good, fat, honest mediocrity
Simmers in your debilitating stew.
Morality, as once you thought you knew,

Serves up that common brew for others; but
Never for you, only for the lowing
Herd, for those who've never heard the word, for
Those who've not in the least been spurred by the
Splendor of your intensity, your word.
Spite, lust and envy grow spiritual,
And resentment remains as scriptural
As the preemption of your redemption.

XV

After another buffoon gets taken
Seriously, you begin to sing quite
Deliriously of eternity,
As if to salvage a tenuous Yes
Out of the infinite mess you confess
Was a hitherto all-too-certain No.
With your precursors, you come to know, there's
No end to endless snow. Thus, again you
Go on a binge against the spirit of
Revenge. You pawed and pawed at each pious
Fraud to snatch error from the tenacious
Claws of one monstrous cause, as if you could
Bid all that's promising to pause before
The prophetic gauze of eternity.

xvi

You warned against the way of others. Let
Others be warned against the way of you:
You heard the rumor that God is dead and
Had to repeat it. You fought your lasting
Obsession but could not defeat it. You
Attack sacred convictions to master
The disaster that's within called sin. And
Yet, when your apple of delight is cored,
You rest your hope in what you once deplored.
Despite your lucidity and all it
Knows, you're still defined by what you oppose.
That your life has meaning is not your choice.
Each soul, lest its dregs come up, must take its
Sup from another's voice, another's cup.

xvii

Every now's an apocalypse, bold, cold,
Monstrous. And yet: do not pet this monster,
Lest you become the monster's pet. Trumpets
Of Jericho are blaring ... blasting. Oh,
Yes. You become what you are ... here and now,
But do not forget to bet on what is
Lasting. The apocalypse happening
Now is all there is to tell you how to
Live, how to give dangerously what you
Would not live to give in vain. There is no
Lasting joy without this lasting pain. Out
Of your restless sleep, awake, awake, for
Now is the appointed time to keep those
Promises you must not break or forsake.

xviii

Will to power is will to remember
Your word, to remember what you'd become.
Coming to be is a foretaste of your
Promise to yourself and others, your first
Omen of eternity, that points the
Way to perfection, to your destiny,
Your home. No matter what it prefers, the
Recurrence recurs. Passage passes through
Passage, motion into motion, heaving
Ocean into heaving ocean, endless
Joy and pain into life's devotion to
Itself, a devotion that insists on
Eternity in motion ... the here and
Now that's nowhere, and the nowhere ... now here.

xix

Always, your subject was eternity:
How life passes, rises, falls, and calls for
Eternity, for the passion to last.
And this urge, an urge you cannot resist,
Makes you forever insist on something
Rather than nothing. This condition you

Cannot overcome is the condition
That keeps overcoming overcoming.
Eternity ... your ever-present chance
For beginning anew, is your constant
Maladjustment – above all else – to you,
To what you are, and to what must be, to
What is forever now but nowhere. It's
Your quenchless thirst for the impossible.

II. RUMORS OF REGRET

So I do not want to forget this further scar, very unfit to produce in public: irresolution, a most harmful failing in negotiating world affairs. I do not know which side to take in doubtful enterprises. ... I can easily maintain an opinion but not choose one.
— Michel de Montaigne, "Of Presumption" –

If my mind could gain a firm footing, I would not make essays, I would make decisions; but it is always in apprenticeship and on trial. ... There is no one who, if he listens to himself, does not discover in himself a pattern all his own, a ruling pattern, which struggles against education and against the tempest of passions which oppose it. ... If I had to live over again, I would live as I have lived. ... God must touch our hearts.
— Michel de Montaigne, "Of Repentance" –

The greatest thing in the world is to know how to belong to oneself. ... Remember the man who, when asked why he took so much pains in an art which could come to the knowledge of so few people, replied: 'Few are enough for me, one is enough for me, none at all is enough for me.' He spoke truly: you and one companion are an adequate theater for each other, or for yourself. Let the people be one to you, and let one be a whole people to you.
— Michel de Montaigne, "Of Solitude" –

i

Involuntary certitude is your
Certainty of returning again and
Again to your uncertainty. Such is

The trauma of your drama. Confidence
Rises, act after act. But then you pull
The curtain on what's certain, exposing
Trauma with faithless fact. You're the reed that's
Shaken, the trembling truth, the truth shaker
That would prove yourself forsaken, of truth
You imagined unmistaken, truth you
Presume that's too unreal for you to feel.
That all you know seems too familiar, too
Strange ... to be true ... rallies your readiness
For the unsteadiness in all you do.

ii

Despite all your ego lust, despite your
Desperate thirst, you were neither the first nor
The worst to say: Me, first! Neither wife, nor
Daughter, nor friend, nor protégé, nor you,
Could rescue you from the hazards of your
Solitude, from dreaded desolation.
Yours was a life not fully written, not
Fully read, not fully led, a vessel
Into which the cruelty and tenderness of
The world had bled its bitter blisses, its
Hits, its misses, its blessings, its curses,
Its full measure of poison and pleasure,
All the maddening mystery you treasure but
Never distill into prose and verses.

iii

There's that certain slant in you, that bias
In time, that unmistakable scar where
Eternity's arrow stabs through and through
Your deepest marrow. Always there remains
In you this wound of irresolution
In all you do and would not do. Thus, you
Have not lived the life you've lived but the
Life of someone else, of one who stumbled
Into being, someone you did not want
To be, as if you shirked the prophet in
You that's still unborn. Yet never do you

Forget that you are you, that your dread of
Indecision ... that makes you what you are ...
Bequeaths to you your everlasting scar.

iv

Each attempt to sketch and catch your self is
Another evasion, yet another
Futilitarian chase in a game
Of hot pursuit, a game you cannot and
Do not want to win, a gruesome pursuit
That cannot help but bear its bitter fruit.
You sought in solitude a citadel,
Where wisdom that would unwind itself with
Unsurety, in peace, might dwell, as though,
Alas, in solitude, you could amass
The wherewithal, not to seek the wayward
Truth, but to seize the light that makes Montaigne
Montaigne, an unpremeditated light
You might, alas, attain, but not sustain.

v

You vacillate on the vertiginous
Edge of a vicious, vain and vapid world.
You step aside from what you say even
As you say it. You unpray what you
Would pray even as you pray it. Your wits
Tardy, your imagination weak, you
Could never remember what you struggled
To say before you speak, before in turn
You learn how bleak it is to be unique.
Thus, always you forget your promise to
The one unborn in you, to the one who's
Below and above your ken, the one who's
Nowhere and nowhen, the one who tells you
How to live, how to give, and how to sin.

vi

You were born. You died. In between was all
That you promised, you kept, you broke, you tried.

All that you see in yourself, you see in
Others. All that you see in others, you
See in yourself. In all you wrote, there is
The foreshadowing of the familiar
Note your equally lonely others have
Already promised, already written.
The more you keep returning to yourself,
The closer you get to one you haven't
Met with yet, and the nearer you get, the
Queerer seems your strangely familiar, all-
Too-dubious bet that you could ever
Reach yourself without rumors of regret.

vii

Your self-portrait is vividly vague like
An anonymous egg about to hatch,
A self-portrait, uncertain, confused, and
Unsteady and yet still ready for change,
Ready for the bleakness of uniqueness.
You were monster and miracle before
The fact, yet to be exact, already
You were too empirical to remain
Yourself, for to experience is to
Undergo change, and change is how the strange
Chooses to derange all that's familiar.
Eternity never wasted your time
So much as when you thought it could never
Rhyme with motion and metamorphosis.

viii

If happiness had heard your name, would it
Rush like mad to find you? If truth could stay
The same, would its clarity still blind you?
After a long life, you retire again
Unsolaced by the lie or the liar.
Retired, you are nonetheless still wired for
Worry. You try to slow your step, to calm
Your stride, but you cannot help but scurry.
For the quantum of your dread is constant.
In defiance of all the wisdom you've

Acquired, you can never help but hurry to
Yet another worry, another woe,
Yet another familiar stranger you
Can never help but meet, and greet and know.

ix

Epicurean, Stoic, Skeptic, you
Cleansed every dogma, every doctrine,
With your ironic anti-septic. You
Made no promise unless you kept it, yet
You made so few there was very little
At all you committed yourself to do.
You yourself, the experiment, are the
Latest try-out, the oddest out-take, the
Readiest ratification of what
You take to be real. But your life is a
Shimmer, a ceaseless shaking, a glimmer,
Perpetually aquiver with what it
Promises to deliver but which stays
Forever a promise in the making.

x

You come to yourself as one who comes to
The point of a promontory, just one
Footfall away from fate, just one small step
That's never too late to drown in the void.
To die properly, you must now unlearn
Foolosophy. Of all it taught you, you
Must now think *not*, for life never fails to
Tell you how to die on this very spot.
Forget what you learn, stay uncommitted.
Only then are you properly fitted
To take your turn at happiness. You may
Become wise at your own expense. Against
Vagaries of self-deception, the risk
Of uncertain truth is your sole defense.

xi

You're what you said. You're what you keep saying.

You're prayers you pray, prayers you keep unpraying.
Each avowed belief that's divided from
What you do is already a lie from
Yourself to you, another broken oath,
A violation of your trust in truth.
Your wisdom is the uneasy balance
Between life's cost and what you've never quite
Lost, between the consequences of here
And now and the promises of nowhere.
Love without fiction, you saw, is merely
Friction of flesh against flesh, but change with
Conviction, if it's lived afresh, must never
Fail to merge and mesh with eternity.

xii

Century follows century, yet your
Self-portrait still greets its crowd of lonely
Others, still ventures to surmise what your
Silence says of truth's surprise, still speaks to
The loneliest crowd, which, though unhumble
And unproud, resembles you as you still
Resemble the resembled. At this late
Date, how quaint for you to find the entire
Estate of humankind still enthimbled
In your mind, a mind that knows the silence
Of the self unborn, that spurns resentment
And surpasses scorn. You know you cannot
Know the restless truth. You can only risk it
As you live it and give it to others.

xiii

There's nothing more empirical than your
Readiness for the miracle of the
Everyday. There's monster and miracle
In every empirical fact, for each
Miracle is the lens wherein you see
How the ordinary always transcends
The ordinary, how the familiar
Hides the strange and the strange the familiar.
There is chaos in the canon and good

Odor in cannibals. There's your savage
Longing for belonging to yourself. But
To grasp yourself you cannot grasp what you
Are, but only what you promise, what you
Presume to be ... now, nowhere and forever.

xiv

Eternity's not joy, not sorrow; its
Your life in motion, life you borrow, as
You live it and give it in devotion
To yourself, to your lonely others, to
Your damnably distant, relentlessly
Persistent and insistent God, the one
Who touches you with the only piece of
Humanity you ever knew, the one
Who knows the prophet unborn in you, the
One who tells you: Do now what you failed to
Do. Know yourself; accept yourself; know it;
Show it now; share yourself without delay.
Do not fail to share yourself with the one
You love in the light of the common day.

III. STATE OF GRACE

Inquisitor: *Do you believe that you are in a state of grace?*
Joan: *If I am not, may God put me there; if I am, may God keep me there. I would be the most miserable person in the world if I knew that I was not in God's grace.*
– Joan of Arc at trial –

i

Your piercing eyes could never disguise your
Destiny. Confident, yet still unproud,
You burned with the radiant splendor of
An angel culled and kidnapped from a cloud.
Your armor, brilliant, your standard aloft
And bravely flying, your sword, miraculous,
Upheld and gleaming. Nothing could stop you
From always seeming to be what you are,
The impossible, a warrior goddess,

Fierce, implacable, gentle, kind. No lie
They might try could blind them to your beauty.
No force they might try could unhorse you from
Your duty. But then, at last, you wept as
You kept the promise that could not be kept.

ii

The arc of your brief life begins and ends
At noon, when fierce white light pierced the light of
The common day. And this bright light cast its
Shadow over the common light of day,
As if to say: *This day you begin to*
Live and die. You begin to live and die
This very day. Your light comes no other
Way, but in the name of the voice. Your voice
Speaks no other way, but in the name of
The light beyond the light, the voice beyond
Your voice, beyond the conscience that guides your
Choice. This is the voice and the light that does
Not shun what must be done, what's right, that yields
A destiny you cannot flee or fight.

iii

What happens in you is the parable
Of will, of a fable that's overcome
As you're overcome by overhearing
What you have never asked to hear, while your
Continuing fear of not doing what
You're asked, turns either to the lie or to
Trusting a conscience you cannot deny.
You asked the King for an army; he gave
It. You fight for your country; you save it.
Those who'd murder your voices, would also
Murder you; and this, they do. Thus, to act
On the truth of the voices is to risk
Your life; and this you did, for you found that
Sobering truth within that you could not kid.

iv

No one, you knew, could be excused from the
Promises they must keep. No one could be
Rescued from fire, from human agony.
Thus, your voices were not alibis for
Ecstasy, for rapture, but ordeals of
Calling, of a mission made manifest.
Only those who have never been assigned
This test could pause in puzzlement to ask:
But is it necessary, this task? This,
You never ask. The voice, the moment of
Transformation in you, is the moment
You knew what you unmistakably knew:
That boldly forth you must go and boldly
Do without reluctance what you must do.

v

All your visions, all your voices, point to
The impossible: they point to you. To
Accomplish the impossible you must
Become as impossible as one who
Listens to the voices of God, to all
Those voices, all those choices in you that
Begin to churn, begin to burn, begin
To turn you without restraint into a saint.
Dangerous was your virgin desire, a
Desire to make desire impossible.
Dangerous was your inner fire, as if
Your fire could make their fire impossible.
But all your desire must conspire with fire
To reach what mere desire could not acquire.

vi

A leaf torn from pages of your history
Fell to earth and cut the cynic's heart in
Twain. Thence you remain the only balm that
Could ever mollify his pain. Martyr,
Mystic, mascot, witch, liar, lunatic,
Feminist, bitch, fool, prophet, heretic
Or saint, no one can tell you which, without
The taint of self-justification. This,

The legend of lies, toys with motives and
Wrestles with whys. This is the legend of
Fables, that flees from faith, and that turns the
Tables. But this, Joan, is not the legend
Of you. For you're that rarest of legends,
Joan. You're the legend that's forever true.

vii

When your voices arise in the guise of
Of God's messengers, you'll know what your brain's
Confusion cleverly contrived: how the
Cauliflower folds inside your skull grow
Dull, when deprived of all your usual
Suspects, your registry of fears. Then your
Parietal lobes go dark, and frontal
And temporal lobes, in a burst of too
Much spark, lose their shaky hold on time, on
Self, on tears. The difference engine on the
Blink then comes to think it's one in all, all
In one. Your brain takes a tumble, and the
Self you do not know stubs its tawdry toe
On infinity ... or divinity.

viii

Do your voices come with the grace of God
Like rain? Are they episodes of an all-
Too-muddled brain? Every age worships in
Confusion its own shameless profusion
Of lies. But was your life the truth or self-
Delusion in saintly guise? Truth is a
Summit few can climb no matter how many
Promises, no matter how many tries.
In vain, you search for the strain within the
Brain that could ever tell you what is wise.
The uncertainty of God's grace is the
Impossibility of meeting God
Face to face, the impossibility
You'll never rue the fact that you are you.

There's not anything you wouldn't do to
Shun the face that faces that you are you.
You might even choose to become yourself.
This face, your face, is a place in the heart,
A place that could not exist until you
Exist and no longer resist the task of
Becoming you. This face, your face, is one
More door to paradise, a door only
You could enter. When voices that you did
Not seek begin to speak, chaos finds its
Center, its sobering God. There, beyond
The back of the beyond, you confront no
Front but the haunting trace of your true face.
This is how you live in a state of grace.

IV. ROAR OF SILENCE

You ... think everyone is a mythomaniac?
         – Andre Malraux, *Man's Fate* –

'And then, the fundamental fact is that there's no such thing as a grown-up person.'
         – Andre Malraux, *Anti-Memoirs* –

There are no great people. There never have been. Never!
         – Andre Malraux, *The Walnut Trees of Altenburg* –

We know that to ourselves each of us is like a monster out of a nightmare.
         – Andre Malraux, *The Voices of Silence* –

We always hear our own voices through our throats, and those of others through our ears. If one were suddenly to hear the voice of another through one's own throat, one would be terrified. I had written that each of us hears the sound of his life through his throat, and that of others through his ears, except in fraternity and love. The book was called La Condition humaine.
         – Andre Malraux, *Lazarus* –

... the Eternal in its death throes was not replaced by any sorry

substitute, until an adversary worthy of it had been discovered, a new Eternal. What was up against it was the only enemy of the Eternal which the human mind could find to cope with it, and that enemy was – History. ...

Solitude, viceregent of Eternity, vanquishes men's dreams no less than armies, and men have known this ever since they came into being and realized that they must die.
    – Andre Malraux, *The Voices of Silence* –

Eternity's in a bad way.
    – Andre Malraux, *The Walnut Trees of Altenburg* –

i

You were there when that great barrier reef
Of eternity broke, when out of the
Gaping rift ... thus spoke ... the voices of your
Silence. To your desperate thirst, they spoke at
First in a language you could not hear. They
Spoke in the vernacular of your fear.
And while you did your worst, they did their best
To burst those impervious walls that hem
You in, your citadel, where direst dread,
Like a thief, rummages your self-made hell.
Disbelief chases belief, and belief
Chases disbelief. Such is the history of
Your grief, for nothing can relieve the
Spasmodic enigma of your suffering.

ii

The clash of ignorant armies, the roar
Of silence on the darkling plain, summon
An intensity that you no other
Wise attain. Every metamorphosis
Becomes an act, a force, that suffers the
Humiliation of a destiny
Designed by yourself, of course, by all you
Did ... by all you did not do. But before
The monstrous voice breaks through, hurry, please, and
Bore us by rehearsing yet another

Sanctimonious chorus. Yes. Oh, yes.
All those demons that belong to you are
Alive and well, in hell, and taking notes. You
Hear the discordant murmurs in their throats.

iii

After the joys, after the pains, after
The losses, after the gains, what is there
That still remains that can give a lasting
Meaning to your furious solitude?
What's fundamental keeps recurring, while
The quiet rage of futility sleeps,
Preferring the consolation of self-
Deception to remorseless misery.
Everything that begins and ends, begins
Again, and ends, like every plot that tends
To repeat, complete, and defeat itself.
Sincerity's in ruins, honesty's
In retreat, and nothing that survives can
Compete with the glamor of self-deceit.

iv

The perpetual return of noon and
Midnight repeats the voicelessness you fear.
But the one long folly that is your past
Cannot summon a different future and
Make it last. Folly begets folly. No
Matter what you say you prefer, all that's
Wanted and unwanted in your past and your
Future will again and again recur.
All those beloveds that you beget, the
Children of your belief, are relics of
Regret that can never forget your grief.
The smile of spent desire's corrupted guile's
Still there. The faintest rictus, you think, will
Convict us, of irony and despair.

v

You always arrive too late to save your

Infancy from its fate. And returning
Too soon, you mistake the troubled midnight
For the lucidity of noon. Always
You would, if you could, be a child reborn.
Yes. You would, if you could, be shorn of the
Wearisome mask that you've always worn. As
You approach this rediscovered childhood,
You grow older, bolder, colder. In each
One of destiny's darlings, you see the
Little man, the one who could never grow
Up, the one who could, if he would, do all
He could, except show up and thus manage
In vain the mundane on Monday morning.

vi

There's nothing humane about the human
Condition. All would be utterly true,
Thus hellish, if you could scorn the liar's
Instinct to fabricate and embellish.
What you are is appallingly clear. You're
What you most fervently fear. You're the last
Thing you want your lonely others to think
You are. That you're what they all suspect is
The last thing that you want them to detect.
The myth you choose, that's you, is that restless
Distraction that allows you to live and
Give yourself in vain, minus the lucid
Vision of futility, minus the
Constant accentuation of your pain.

vii

From your image of yourself, you erase
What you cannot face; you invent a myth
As if you could replace the myth you can
Neither abandon nor control. This is
How you convince yourself you have no soul.
The key to soul is the quality of
Anguish. That isolated monad of
Loneliness, in which you languish beyond
Control, is how you know you have a soul.

If you had no soul, your loneliness is
A fate you'd never fear, you'd never know.
Your life's your soul, if you do not fail it,
A life that cribs an answer to its quiz.
Only your pain can tell you what it is.

viii

You reach the threshold of revelation
But never traverse it. You tremble on
The verge of truth, but you never bless it,
Never curse it. The door remains ajar
In perpetuity, in a state of
Limbo, of questions that yield no answer,
But eternal ambiguity. You
Could not confess. You could not admit one
Whit of truth about yourself. You fill in
All the gaps with fiction, with the glamor
Of sonorous diction. You're eloquent
Midas, spreading fantasy with your touch.
All you claim you are, is born out of bluff,
Like trickster goatlings in *Billy Goats Gruff*.

ix

Of the thousand voices you hear, you hear
And fear most of all your very own. That's
Why you fear so much to be alone, why
You never quite hear the voice that keeps you
Quaking in loneliness and fear, why you
Never complete the choice you keep making,
Why you never keep the promise you keep
Forsaking. The debt you owe yourself and
Others mounts and mounts. But the history of
Eternity never waits to settle
Your accounts. You never expect what you
Detect in the spectacle of suffering.
Your anguish that never ends always tends
All-too-anxiously toward the absolute.

x

In your throat you hear the other's voice, and

It is yours. You break the roaring silence,
As if your broken solitude ensures
That silence now will shout about what the
Audible leaves out. You'd make the world your
Own and master it. You'd conquer the world
And plaster it with your image. The first
Rule of conquest is: exaggerate the
Strength of your forces. This you do. But that
World you would conquer is no more lucid
Than you, which you would, but cannot, conquer.
Any makeshift absolute, you shrewdly
Refute. But the nightmare voice within, the
One that resists all conquest, leaves you mute.

xi

There is the absurd, and your reaction
To it, and there's the third: there is God, the
Dreaded certitude of judgment that drives
Your escapist dreams of the absurd. Each
Reaction's a task, each task's a mask, an
Evasion that lets you answer with a
Lie what you're afraid to ask: Isn't the
Absurd, the last best mask of the absurd,
A betrayal, a detour from the dread
Of judgment, that fears not the absence of
God, but the absence of the absurd? The
Action you advise for the wise, minus
The absolute, loses its traction in
The logic of life you cannot refute.

xii

No lie you tell can ever quite quell the
Spell of nothingness. Yet shadows of your
Ideals will blur, then again recur till
Once again you believe what you prefer.
You will be religious or nothing at
All, for when nothingness is no longer
Prestigious, then you will learn to live like
You'll live forever with what can never
Dissever you from your happiest truth.

Thus, you welcome into your decrepit
Temple, the gods of the defeated, the
Cheated and depleted, of those who, drained
Of all passion, strive in vain to enjoy
The miser's ration of eternity.

xiii

No charlatan is perfect, who cannot
Brazenly adore his fate, who cannot
Perfectly simulate the authentic.
Yet without loving it, you keep living
It, your fate, one man's fate, your fate, because
No other fate will do at this late date.
Metamorphosis is will in motion.
Apollo becomes Buddha, and Buddha
Apollo. Vaunted values under siege
Go hollow and follow noblesse oblige
Into the dustbin with eternity,
An eternity you would, if you could,
Secure by loving your fate, by lurid
Exaltation of rank complacency.

xiv

Of those demon voices in your throat, take
Note. These, the sources of what you wrote, these
Echoes of your lasting scar, summon your
Fears of what you would not be, but are. You
Never believe what you tell yourself till
You hear your words in another's throat, your
Voice in hers, and hers in yours. This life now,
One of a thousand tours, that one in a
Thousand thousand, endures the communion
Of a shared solitude, that's forever
Entangled her life with yours. You never
Fail to hear her voice, the voice that never
Fails. No. You never fail to seek the voice
That never fails to speak your lasting choice.

XV

Your soul lost cogency, but not its life,
For life goes on without persuasion. On
Eternity, you no longer stake your
Claim. Eternity stakes its claim on you.
You are alive in every past, every
Future. Neither the living nor the dead
Can justify your mourning. In their own
Eternity, they keep living, they keep
Dying, as you keep failing despite all
Your trying to understand how what you
Are, is something you never cease to be.
The eternity you know you crave is
Only replenished if you, in your pain,
Remain what you've always been: ... unfinished.

V. BLIND MAN SINGING

The soul, wounded and impregnated, possesses deep within itself, a device which permits it to solidify time into eternity. It is the pearl, it is this realization of the essence, it is this Necessity, it is this epitome between our fingers of every possession that serves as a gate, the Apocalypse tells us, to the Heavenly Jerusalem. It does not sparkle or burn; it touches; a fresh life-giving caress for the eye, the skin, and the soul. We have contact with it. ... The humble mollusk is dead, but what is made within itself without seeing it, that incomparable being it has given, that continues to live.
– Paul Claudel, *The Eye Listens* –

And mortal? For me there is no more death.
Every being as the work
Of Eternity is also its expression.
Eternity is here and the things of the moment happen within it.
– Paul Claudel, "The Spirit and Water" –

Lala. I am the promise that cannot be kept and in that very fact resides my charm. I am the tenderness of that which is with the regret of that which is not. I am truth with the face of error and he who loves me is not concerned with dividing the one from the other. He who hears me is cured of repose forever and of the

thought that he has found it.
– Paul Claudel, The City –

It is a great blessing for man to have had the opportunity to try his strength against eternity.
– Paul Claudel interrogee L'Apocalypse –

i

You and your troubled universe are born
Together, knowing each other, vying
In vain to establish yourselves. Always
Your sole establishment is this endless
Trial of your failed establishment, of
That dire experiment that you botched, of
That game of grownup children, that sidewalk
Contest in which eternity hopscotched
From one moment to the next. You would, if
You could, arrange for something sensible
And defensible in your text, something
Less mysterious, less delirious
Than your crabbed desire that always balks, then
Defects in the face of satisfaction.

ii

You were once so young, so free, so full of
Hope, so ambitious, then your life began,
And all that ended. Desire, a species
Of despair, you saw, is meretricious.
Thus, you face the fate toward which you've tended.
In time, you'll learn to endure your time. But
Now the world that's always about to end
Has already ended. That you're happy
You try to deny. Yes. Happiness for
You is a tedious lie, a promise
That is always broken, that you cannot
Renew. No matter what you choose to do,
Always, in the middle of the rainbow,
You are you: you're the one who's painted blue.

iii

In the madhouse mirror, you keep posing
Again and again in front of yourself.
You're a tornado congealed, a storm that
Could not be stilled, a promise unfulfilled.
You and your truth point to one end which is
Always present, to the jubilance of
That instant that never ends and never
Begins, to that joy that cohabits with
All your lustful terrors and quisling sins.
When at last you know that all is lost, you
Pause at the narcissism of the lost
Cause. No. There are no longer any sins,
Only symptoms, only signs of what your
Lust for joy no longer trusts but maligns.

iv

Vespers had its way with you on Christmas
Day. In your starkest instant, your heart was
Touched. You believed you received, undeceived,
The joy that's now so near it no longer
Seems so distant. Everything always called
You elsewhere. Yet you're never far from what
You promise yourself you'll be but never
Are. You're never far from the joy that jumps
Too high downstream to catch, that leaps too far
To fetch. The nearer to the mountain you
Are, the smaller you seem, the closer to
The fountain you come, the thirstier you
Are for joy, the more desperate you become
To live in truth the melody you hum.

v

You're the cipher full of promise, for you're
Just beginning to be what you are, just
Beginning to babble of your absence,
Just beginning to sense the faintest hint
Of what you must become. You remain – no
Matter how vain – a promise unfulfilled.

And if you still believe the promise, you
Never believe what everyone knows. You
Never dispose of your lust for repose.
You never cease believing that dreary
Theory of final rest for the weary.
You never cease questing for certainty's
Consoling sound. You never cease hoping
Serenity's just about to be found.

vi

Your dissatisfaction persists, lost as
It always is, in the philosophic
Mists of failed explanation. Yet again
And again, your cryptic life never fails
To sustain what the latest wisdom fails
To explain. Like an addled, bedraggled
Pup, you wait for the summoning and the
Summing up. What's happening resembles
Most a lie. No expert alive or dead
Can advise you how to greet with grace the
Fatal obstinacy of Why. Oh, no.
Not even the longest-armed poet or
Philosopher hugs it all in just one
Try. Yet they all pretend they do; they lie.

vii

When somewhere sours, you seek a nowhere that
Promises a happiness that tries in
Vain to hoard and honor what it devours.
The city is in ruins; it always is.
Your impossible role, if you accept
It, is to make it whole. Yet no mighty
Struggle can ever build it back the way
It was, for it never was the way it
Was, for the way it was existed as
An illusion that persisted in the
Weary dream of those already tired of
The perpetual quest for happiness,
For promises kept, for music deeper,
Darker, than solitude's silent partner.

viii

Every true poem is a registry
Of hallucinations, a testament
Of failures to touch what is really real.
A poem upsets the universe then makes
It darker, deeper. When it's as dark, as
Deep, as darkness, as deepness gets, that poem's
The keeper, the poem without regrets.
Your gift is to speak the unspoken, to
Offer a promise that's always broken.
With words, you cannot reach what only your
Eternity can teach. No. Each promised
Noon's always another troubled midnight.
You're the satisfier, not the satisfied.
All those who promise otherwise have lied.

ix

In each utopian dream, you detect
The frailty of the seam that unravels
The tattered arras of the dream. Wiser
Than you, you confess, is that advisor
Who makes a lasting meaning of this mess.
Blind repression is the family way, and
Despite the highest price of the latest
Advice, repression is the only way
To be a family, the only way to
Love and learn through pain but not deceive it,
The only way – not to pantomime peace –
But to deserve it and to achieve it,
The only way to live with the promise
That's always broken, yet still believe it.

x

For you, her body was a scoundrel in
Complicity with itself, a body
That tempts itself to want, to conspire for
What can never satisfy its desire.
If she would stay, then you must go, for what
She wants is infinite, more than you could

Ever proffer, ever dream of. What you
Want, alas, is another episode,
A clue, another bit of evidence,
Another fact to prove ... to you ... her love.
Desire without limit trades frauds of the
Familiar for lures of the strange. Oh, yes.
The surest path to what's always worst is
To confuse what lasts with your thirst ... for change.

xi

You shudder at the soul that shudders at
What's within. This, the enemy of your
Joy, is your latest and your greatest sin.
As rare, as common, as the light of day,
The will of God must have its say, and then
Repression exacts its dreadful price. You
Cannot have all you want in paradise.
This gift your irrepressibility
Gives back to you. It gives you back your guilt.
The voice that murmurs within makes use of
Thee. The murmur within forgives but does
Not forget your sin, the forbidden love
Of a woman who saved what remains of
You, your invisible remains: your soul.

xii

You cannot see, but you hear the blind man
Singing. You know he hears the words you speak,
Even as his music keeps on ringing
And stinging in your ears. You know he's the
Soul you seek, because, though he sings like a
Ghost in the middle of nowhere, you know
He's here, he's now, he's there, you know because
The sound of his soul in yours resonates
With care, and care, alas, that's the only
Treasure two lost souls can share. Only if
You sin can you share his darkness. Only
If you love can you share his light. Glimpse, if
You will, the joy in his blinding stare. Glimpse,
Then share ... his lasting promise of despair.

xiii

Sorrow has no loopholes, joy no exits,
And eternity no heirs. You cannot
Inherit another's joy, another's
Sorrow, another's eternity. Not
Even that geometric poem of
Genius is capable of bestowing
What God alone keeps proving, keeps showing
With bloodied conviction. Reality
   ... is more imaginative than fiction.
God's most inventive depiction, that he
Should make all you do, all you say, seem fake,
Like fiction, a wind-up toy, unleashes
The voice within you gaining speed, that blurts
The vapid sound of your desperate greed ... for joy.

xiv

Each season, as even the surliest
Cynic knows, the earth repeats the crocus,
The iris and the rose. Yet redness is
Never the property of a rose, for
What it cannot absorb, what it never
Becomes, it shows, and then it glows with the
Radiance of what it's not. Thus, of the
Red ... red rose, please speak no more, for you live
Through the midnight of abomination,
And the snow that falls like absolution
Prophesies puzzles as its solution.
Your task is to replicate enigmas,
Not to do any good, but to add to
The sum of what is never understood.

xv

There is an hour absolute in which the
History of your eternity bears fruit.
Each hymn to eternity tries but fails
To refute the humiliation of
Your paternity. You cannot respond
To your son's lament. You cannot live the

Life of your son and tell him what it meant.
You cannot help but let your tenderness
Be overtaken by what's forsaken.
The heart hath its secrets it cannot tell.
To say all you think you think you know are
Lies inquisitors make you tell in hell.
Damned lies are shrewd, but the truth's more clever.
Not even the damned stay damned forever.

VI. THE GREAT UNWINDER

To act freely is to recover possession of oneself, and to get back to pure duration.
– Henri Bergson, Time and Free Will –

All the molds crack.
– Henri Bergson, Creative Evolution –

The gradual relaxing of the spring, that makes the phonograph turn, unwinds the melody inscribed on the cylinder: if the melody which is played be the effect, and the relaxing of the spring the cause, we must say that the cause acts by unwinding.
– Henri Bergson, Creative Evolution –

[From the pure repetition that is matter] ... toward a duration which stretches, tightens, and becomes more and more intensified: at the limit would be eternity. This time, not only conceptual eternity, which is the eternity of death, but an eternity of life. It would be a living and consequently still moving eternity, where our own duration would find itself like the vibrations in light, and which would be the concretion of all duration as materiality is its dispersion.
– Henri Bergson, Creative Mind –

Strictly speaking, I am not certain that the question 'where' can have a meaning when we ask it of something different from a body.
– Henri Bergson, Mind Energy –

i

Stretched taut between now and nowhere, you fail

To command those elusive facts that would
Let you overcome your misery and then
Relax. Your life, forever in suspense,
Forever in the making, is always
One fragment of an unfinished story.
Duration's poem, your perpetual
Saga, is your transition from nowhere
To now here, and from now here to nowhere.
The cosmos is its history, and so are you.
Neither it nor you can avoid the fate
Of becoming new, an evolution
From never-same to always other, an
Endless passage that never stops at you.

ii

Just listen to the demon within who
Whispers the word *impossible:* the world
You see, you hear, you taste, you feel, is not
What you've been told it is by those who claim
That they alone can know what's really real.
The present passes before it begins;
It ends before it starts. Each moment, each
Putative state, leaves too early and then
Arrives too late to be anything but
One more stretch of perpetual change. When
You imagine that the torrent stops when
It doesn't stop, when it cannot stop, that's
What you mistakenly call a state, an
Imagined, impossible state of rest.

iii

You flow without measure and without gauge,
Without the ability to pause at
Anything that could justly be called a
Stop or stage. Thus, unfasten the cocoon,
Waken the chrysalis of eternity,
And you'll discover a time that flows, that
Flutters, as your eloquence stumbles and
Stutters at your best attempt to explain
What does not change but that contains all change,

An eternity that does not unfold
From one stillness to the next, that never
Becomes what it is, but that always shifts
With the radiant splendor of its gifts,
That forever billows forth from nowhere.

iv

In the depths of duration, there is that
Incessant humming, that clue that you and
Your universe are never satisfied,
But always arriving, always coming,
The clue that says too much is never too
Much, the clue, whose hue, the light of common
Day, is the way your eternity has
Its say in the universe. This inner
Light, this inward absolute, this is the
Eternity you cannot refute or
Compute. In this light, all that is now, all
That is after, all that's before, is one
Great fact you may abhor or adore, but
That you'll forever lack the image for.

v

You could, if you would, remember moments
Of your life, the points where memory matters
More and more, and all the habits you come
To deplore turn green with envy for the
Emotion that fostered them. Another
Genealogy of morality,
Of religion, strives to recover the
Slightest smidgeon of life long left behind.
When meaning matters, it reveals to life
The emotion that spawned it, the spur that
Left its scar, that nudged you forward to what
You are, to whatever your mystic lusts
Connive. All mysticism will contrive
To bring you back where memory comes alive.

vi

All the moments of your life are inside

One another. Each moment carries the
Burden of the past and the promise of
Future. You are what you are forever,
One motion, one long unbroken moment.
Eternity's your inexpressible
Self, first and last, but a middling, riddling
Self emerges to obscure what's first, what's
Last, a self of many moments that gives
Its chronicle, that tells its story. But
Your eternity's without chronicle,
Without story. The self that lets itself
Live, unspoken and unbroken, is the
Self that lives and gives in wordless glory.

vii

You must choose between two you's, between the
You that endures and the you that counterfeits
You, between the you that dwells in time and
The one that's your static emblem, between
The finished you and the you that always
Keeps becoming, the you who's never through.
Only rarely do you see the you who's
Never through. Only rarely, then, are you
Free to be who you are in all you do.
Nothing is rarer or more exact than
The freest act. In all other moments,
You're the automaton. Only in your
One long moment, unbroken, unspoken,
Are you alive and free for eternity.

viii

Your life is lived as a great unwinding
Of the real. Nothing you think, or say, or
Do, or feel can ever keep it still. Your
Unwinding remembers what it unwinds,
And the burgeoning past invariably
Binds itself to whatever the present
Seeks and finds. Yes. Your duration, the great
Unwinder, that never ceases, never
Pauses, that's how eternity relaxes

Itself into effects from causes. Thus,
The time that you're told is real is never
What you know you feel. And yet, how funny,
How strange, that your eternity in the
End becomes that small money you call change.

ix

All memory that comes alive comes from
Nowhere to now here, to your present, your
Promise to the past that the future will
Keep its meaning, the belief that freedom
Will foregather all its gleanings and make of
This chaos, of this disparate stuff, a self,
Yourself, your world, your shelter against your
Pain's revenge that remains impearled in the
Eternity of your troubled world. No.
Nothing's far away, not past, not future,
For what's nowhere is now here forever.
The you you are but cannot always be,
This is the you you are when you'd be free,
The you you are in your eternity.

x

Little by little, you let your freedom
Go, you piddle it away, as if your
Cherished habit, your obscene routine, your
Blind automatism, could ever let
You stay what you are, as if you never
Become what you really are, your endless
Becoming, your persistent humming of
This eternity, which you reject and
Never detect when you remain unfree.
Eternity, if it could ever be
Imagined, would be the moving image of
The free. It would be what you're always free
To be whenever you're free. It would be
Your moving image of infinite life.

xi

The joy you say you reach through anguish can
Only tell you how to impeach your joy,
Can only tell you how to betray your
Desperate enthusiasm for joy,
A joy that enjoys the agility
Of fragility, of moving too fast
For you or anyone else to dwell on,
Of being so ruthlessly shy in its
Speech that it offers nothing for you to
Lie about, nothing for you to tell on.
Joy does not reach far enough if it stops
At joy. To reach the good, your joy must stop
Where it should: at action, creation, love.
Be wise: desire that desire that never dies.

xii

Desire, lying deepest within your heart,
Desire beyond all desiring, desire
That's the very heart of you, desire that
Irrepressibly presses on, never
Quailing, never tiring in the sacred
Imperative to keep desiring, this
Desire, the desire you mistake for joy,
Faces without illusion the teeming
Profusion of eternity, the lure
Of desire that wants, not knowing why, but
That never knows how to die. Pray, then, that
God lets time, lets eternity conspire
To deepen in you this fire of desire
That knows no other fire but your desire.

VII. WHAT SUFFERING'S ALLOWED

None ever went about to break logic, but in the end logic broke him.
— John McTaggart Ellis McTaggart, *Studies in Hegelian Cosmology* –

It seems to me that one-empirically-known characteristic which cannot really belong to anything that exists is the characteristic of Time.
  – John McTaggart Ellis McTaggart, *An Ontological Idealism* –

What is the concrete and material content of such a life as this? What does it come to? I believe it means one thing and one thing only – love.
  – John McTaggart Ellis McTaggart, *The Further Determinations of the Absolute* –

Of the nature of that good we know something. We know that it is a timeless and endless state of love – love so direct, so intimate, and so powerful that even the deepest mystic rapture gives us but the slightest foretaste of its perfection. We know that we shall know nothing but our beloved, and those they love, and ourselves as loving them, and that only in this shall we seek and find satisfaction.
  – John McTaggart Ellis McTaggart, *The Nature of Existence* –

i

You walked with a prepossessing shuffle,
As if you feared the jolt from behind of
A wayward kick. Yet, you knew how to nail
Down an argument and make it stick. And
Stick it did. You saw through the rush of life
That blurs eternity. You proved how time
Tells one long lie to kid what's always hid.
You loved to imbibe and to consume and
Rejected every bribe by David Hume
To believe that there is no self, no soul.
Yet when your logic's rigor takes its toll,
There is in your world, for God, no room. All
But love, you thought, may be delusion. Thus,
Love, for you, is truth without confusion.

ii

You recite the ABC's of time and
Eternity, of series misperceived,
And of that timeless series that's always

Sure and that's undeceived for evermore.
Rigorous logic, you apply, to what
You already believe, and you found it
Valid, sound. And yet how could you dare do
Anything else but posit and propound
Your version of eternity? For you,
Time only masks the greater miracle,
How everyone forgets the emperor's
Missing clothes, how logic itself for you
At long last turns empirical, and how
Seduction leads deduction by the nose.

iii

Misperception's so vast that all you know
You recast, so what's future's not future,
What's present is not present, what's past is
Not past. Thus, the time you think you're living,
That you misperceive, you reconceive as
An error that you no longer believe.
The last stage in the perception of what's
Real is the state of love, a love that never
Begins, never ends, and that knows no wheres, no
Whens, a love stronger than death, a love strong
Enough, but perhaps not quite, in this too
Common light, to make you friends with despair,
With suffering, with evil, with everyday
Boredom that suffocates eternity.

iv

Either you exist or not. You cannot
Nearly be. No. Nothing and no one can
Almost but not quite be. Either you are,
Or you are not. And if you are, you must
Be a citizen of eternity.
What you are, you are. You cannot define
It, explain it, or ever restrain it
From continuing to be forever.
Thus, everything enjoys eternity,
And eternity enjoys everything.
Whatever is, is relentlessly what

It is forever, a society of
Timeless persons gradually perceiving
Each other as one vast unbroken whole.

v

Falling in love at first sight renews a
Thirst that's always right, but that's never first.
Love for cause is branded with the mark of
Incompleteness. Those who love each other
Belong together from first to last. Such
Love could never be future, could never
Be past. Such love is either eternal,
Or it's nothing at all. You love little;
Indeed, you love not at all, if you do
Not love first and last and forever. When
Love is so replete that it's about to
Burst, you've reached at last what's never first. You
Live the past that's never past. You relive
The haunted history of your quenchless thirst.

vi

At the last stage of the real, you'll feel how
Time no longer masks the imperative,
To love. You will love everyone you have
Ever encountered, those you've hated, those
You've scorned, those you've merely disliked, those you've
Underrated, those you've barely noticed,
And those beneath contempt. Thus, from your love,
No one you've ever met will be exempt.
And those that you've loved so well in this life
You'll love all the more for eternity.
Love, when time's no more, when time no longer
Makes you sleep its sleep, then love, that river
Of marvels unimpeded, flows endless,
Wide, and deep in a life at last completed.

vii

Love is the timeless expression of your
Meretricious, though still misunderstood

Immortality. There's no value that's
Higher; there's no truth that's deeper than the
Reality of love. Thus, love is no
Steppingstone to the good; it is the good
Itself. To love and to be loved is not
Just a principle, not just a pillar
Of the universe: it *is* the universe.
Knowledge and will perfected produce love
And only love. In every moment made
Perfect, that moment's made of joy, a joy
So much in love with itself it wants to
Stay what it is forever ... and it does.

viii

You saw deeply into that destiny
Upon which your dearest hopes depended.
You die old, but you're born forever young
With ashes still dissolving on your tongue.
You wait in vain for the description of
The real to be complete. Time alas must
Greet what you'd establish with defeat, for
Nothing in time can ever be complete.
Yet time's illusion is always trembling
On the verge of eternity, as if
Diurnal error, burning off its fog,
Could glimpse beyond the precipice of sheer
Confusion to see what it must be like
To discern life plain without delusion.

ix

There's no time, no space, no matter, only
Souls, the timeless continuers of all
That ever is. Can you complete yourself?
Eternity alone answers this quiz.
The eternity of your love is your
Assurance that no desire goes untried
Or unsatisfied. You yourself and your
Equally lonely others, entangled
In reciprocal perceptions, are the
Truth of this love that can never die. But

Experience, contaminated with
The unreality of time, never
Tells you why or how to feel. Nothing that's
Supremely real is delivered piecemeal.

x

Unhappiness can only feel what your
Suffering's allowed to steal from happiness.
As you become more acquainted with the
Absolute's latest determinations,
The world you know as unendurable,
Could never be so bad, for to think of
Cruelty in the world at all would be
To appall that feeling had in *Saul,* that
You are so intensely in love with the
World that all the world is love, that this world,
Which is love itself, is in love with you.
Happiness can only feel what suffering's
Allowed to steal from your unhappiness.
What your suffering's allowed to steal is love.

xi

You're an event in the life of others,
And others events in the life of you.
Your entangled perceptions reflect the
Infinity of an endless series
Whose end no one can reach, for neither you
Nor any other could ever end, but
Only forever tend to know and love
Each other. There's, for you, in death no rest,
But the revivifying breath of further
Labor. In death, there's no oblivion,
Only love that remembers what it knows.
This is the secret wisdom of your life:
When the other makes his call, then you must
Listen, and you must answer. That is all.

VIII. THE BRAGGING RIGHTS
– Snippets from Ralph Waldo Emerson –

I believe in Eternity.
>   – from *History* –

'Tis remarkable that our faith in ecstasy consists with total inexperience of it.
>   – from *Worship* –

The only thing grief has taught me, is to know how shallow it is.
>   – from *Experience* –

But I took notice and chiefly remember that the best thing which the cave had to offer was illusion. … There is illusion that shall deceive even the elect.
>   – from *Illusions* –

Other world! There is no other world. God is one and omnipresent; here or nowhere is the whole fact.
>   – from *The Ethics of Sovereignty* –

There is for every man a statement possible of that truth he is most unwilling to receive, – a statement possible, so broad and so pungent that he cannot get away from it,
but must either bend to it or die of it.
>   – from *Eloquence* –

i

You carry your unimproved infancy
Into the grizzled man. Day by day, you
Grow reliant on the desperate need to
Be defiant, to make the large the law
Of the little. For you, the giant is
The little man within each little man.
This is the riddle you must unriddle
If you can. Yes. In every genius, there's
Surprise, the bluff of an imp that blinds the
Eyes, that teases with replies to all your
Whys, that spies what can never surprise you
With its size, for when little's large, and the
Large is small, you can say with confidence
In macropsia that you've seen it all.

ii

You are alarmed by the dullness of the
Common day. The endless depth of one brief
Moment supersedes the tedium you
Detest. Each moment that's most intense, the
One you think that's best, is the acid test
For all the rest. Each drab moment is the
Image of eternities you never
Summon, but that summon you. You would, if
You could, arise and stay away from yet
Another hypocritic day. But there
Are no privileged moments. There are only
Moments that you are not equal to. Thus,
Imagine eternity's a moment,
However small, that's still too large for you.

iii

When the little man within you speaks what
He speaks, and summons what you must renew,
You stage the drama of you obeying
You. You stand again trembling on the verge
Of yet another mistake. This moment,
Even now's the moment you must forsake,
As if the only vice is the vapid
Imitation of limitation. You
Listen to you, for the sacerdotal
Yawp, the congratulatory cry, that's heard
Without converting itself into a
Believable word. Each time you cry, you
Hear it. You find yourself in the very
Heart of day, but you never get near it.

iv

The new forgets the old. It always does.
No mood that persists can tell you now what
Was ... once was. There's nobility in nomads
Going nowhere, for you're never so good
As when you become no good at knowing
Where you're going. From chaos, you emerged,

Cheated and depleted, as if God had
Short-changed you, but had on so many of
Your lonely others splurged. From fate's stingy
Chalice, there poured just one short ration for
You. Thus, pile up the pulsations, if you
Will. Go for broke till the artery's burst.
Nothing you experience can ever
Quench your lasting thirst for eternity.

v

Your sense of autonomy is always
The economy of one, of one God,
One self, your self, your God, entwined, enshrined,
And snugly, smugly confined within each
Other. You refuse to mourn as if the
Past hadn't happened, as if you'd never
Been born. Against all history, then, is your
Sense of eternity, the onliness
Of your inviolable loneliness. To
Trust yourself is to live and give yourself
Dangerously. No other can ever
Intrude into this cloistered solitude.
You live from onliness to onliness.
There is no other. There is only you.

vi

To trust in your aloneness is a threat
To the sanity and sobriety
Of your world, for self-trust is akin to
The mad-hattery of self-flattery,
As if your life's a derisory spoof,
As if your life's the one exception that
Rules the proof of everything and nothing.
There is that crux in every wise man's life
When self-trust goes bust, and then a strange new
Lust, which loses any sense of trust, is
The sole desire that assists the fallen
Giants of self-reliance with wisdom.
This lust for truth, disguised, denied, suggests
How those who would console you must have lied.

vii

You continue to live your life as if
There's not the slightest hint of the ancient
Discontent. Each worm in the apple of
Eden gnaws and betrays the promise it
Overawes with the sadness of nature's
Laws. All your dreams fall short, for performance
Can never comport with dream, with promise.
Your impulse to reach for what's gone missing
Betrays how your body's exceeded by
The soul. But the serpent in paradise
Keeps hissing: You will be as gods. As gods.
Serpentine persuasion thereby raises
The odds, that you'll swerve and then succumb as
You must to the disaster that's self-trust.

viii

You heard the prophet you seek when you heard
Yourself in solitude begin to speak
For the first time. Give yourself to yourself.
Become your master, and every path to
Eternity will be shorter, faster.
Seize the masters, grab what you can get. Do
Not in the least bit fret about what you've
Taken and forsaken. What you've stolen
You must not regret to call your very
Own. There's a longer logic that has no
Language, that enjoys no speech to teach you
What you already know. All your teachers,
All their lessons, contradict each other.
And yet, you must accept them one and all.

ix

You worship the god within, that god in
You, who would eliminate sin. And yet,
Always and already buried within,
Like the broken promise of that ancient
Sin, there's an unresolved residuum,
A piece of you that cannot perish, a

Nearly forgotten remnant that still you
Cherish, despite all your equivocal
Allegiance to what's sane, inane and mundane.
The recalcitrant residuum in
You is more than you and less; and yes, its
Accusation against the pattern of
Your life, you would not curse, but bless, if you
Had the courage of your better wisdom.

x

One day you're a genius, next day a dunce.
You'd be relieved if this only happened
Once. But it happens every other day.
All philosophy begins with blunder.
It would have you know what only a life
That's unlived could know. Above all else, it
Would have you conform, to think of hard-won
Wisdom as something cozy, something warm
That the wise so blithely inhabit. Yes.
Somewhere in his magician's hat the shrewd
Philosopher finds this charming rabbit.
All these frolic makeshifts of self-deceit
Will never cease their sleight-of-hand till their
Work's complete. And it never ... never ... is.

xi

You would perforce make consciousness conscience,
As if your grandest perception were not
Liable to rankest self-deception.
You would, if you could, declare that all is
Illusion, for then all would be truthless,
Toothless, and you yourself invincibly
Ruthless before all there is that matters.
But with a multitude of hurts, the fangs
Of truth flay and betray your just deserts.
Each intuition that would save you can
Confuse you, deprave you. Yes. Self-deceit's
Your blustery palace of frolicking
Snow, that blind and blinkered solitude you
Dwell within, vaguely sense, but never know.

xii

You would, if you could, exhume your grief from
The tomb of experience. On the death
Of your darling child, you could not grieve. You
Harbored that self-cruelty, that false belief
That your pain could never measure up, could
Never earn the bragging rights of grief, for
Nothing sayable or doable is
Adequate to your loss. And yet the loss
Smothers all meaning. No failed grief in its
Aftermath can tell its testament. No
Elegy can escape the torment of
Falling short of what it tries to honor.
You could not touch the heart of grief to find
Relief from the shallowness of suffering

xiii

You're at a loss with loss, with a loss you
Cannot face and fathom. A death that leaves
You hollow means you no longer follow
Your faith in solitude, in ecstasy,
In joy. You would, if you could, refuse your
Own refusal, for your philosophy
Of joy's defeated by the death of your
Little boy. You grieve over lack of grief,
And the death of that little man, darling
Of your heart, finds no home in even the
Remotest part of your moral universe.
And yet, when genius beckons, you answer
Its call. You say what must be said without
The slightest concern for the dead at all.

xiv

You live your life but little. You play it
Coy amid deserts of wasted time where
Few occasions have the courage to rhyme
With joy. Your grief leaves you numb but never
Mute. You speak of your pain that no one dares
Refute. Yet you grieve not that you cannot

Grieve, but that you cannot grieve enough, as if
Trauma is a melodrama that does
Not live up to its reputation, as
If the bereft must exaggerate the
Magnitude of grief to reinforce lewd
Belief in their craven self-importance.
You grieve that grief can fail to teach, that it
Points to the pinnacle you cannot reach.

XV

Carrion eaters bring not death, but seek
It, find it, speak it, and on it feed, as
Though driven by a need that cannot be
Sated, as though doomed to carry on with
The life they've always hated. With surprise,
You're disappointed you're not ennobled,
That you're never made wise, by the death of
Others. You're shocked that death never answers
Why, but mercilessly drains you dry of
The will to try. Yet you still refuse to
Die. In the death of that darling little
Man, the grief you dangerously give is
Never enough to justify the all-
Too-embarrassing fact that you still live.

xvi

The name of the game is to take the blame
For being almost the same as everyone
Else. Near tautology names your difference,
Defames self-similar contradictions.
Each time you pray you traverse the distance
From one solitude to another. It
Takes a trip to elsewhere to extract a
Meaning from the whole fact. You can never
Make a profession of faith, for your faith,
If you have one, must make a profession
Of you. You should never live your life in
Worship of the dead. Yet you violate
This wisdom with what you chose. You could not
Help but reopen what the casket closed.

xvii

If you love others, you never quite know
Why till fifteen minutes before they die.
Not crippled by the death of those you lost,
You never feel you paid the proper cost.
Belatedness remains your fate because
You are born too late for the earliest
Possible luster of mourning. You play
Second fiddle to the other's riddle.
You're never as real as you yearn to feel.
Even in your deepest solitude, where
You let no past intrude, you're unsettled
By the other's mood, by what solitude
Cannot smother. History never breaks in
Two with you, but always with another.

xviii

In solemn stupor on the stair, you find
Yourself in dull despair, already there
On your way from nowhere to nowhere. You're
The controvertible man, too little
To be large, too large to be too little,
Too little solution, too much riddle.
No bottom, no top. Long ago you should
Have ceased all trying, but no one had the
Heart to tell you: Stop. For you, it's a sin
To do less than bless the universal
Yes. And yet, each heart holds what the other
Unsettles. Your solitude would shun this
Obscenity, or bleep it. Yet this is
The only heart you have, if you can keep it

xix

You will never know what to do with a
Breathtakingly blue October day. Yes.
There is that morality in autumn,
That prophecy at noon. It says, if you
Must live your life, you must do it soon. No.
It's never too late to be party to

Your fate. In accents of the Holy Ghost
You whispered: What you love, shall you love it
Most, or shall you resent what you represent?
You looked straight into the face of her soul
And saw your fate exact; then, without the
Slightest bit of tact, you stated boldly:
You stand alone, with her, for one lone fact,
You stand for the fact of eternity.

XX

Your trembling hand reshuffles elements
Of your universe in accord with your
Cardinal love. Thus, you ride the seesaw of
Karmic law, the ceaseless undulation;
The ebb and flow; the in, the out; sunshine
And snow; the whisper, the shout; the lover
And the lout; the yes, the no. Yes. River
Retreats to its origin, soul searches
Out its source, body yearns for spirit, and
Lover looks long and longingly into
The beloved's eyes, and says: *Of course*. Yes.
The transparent eye, another pious
Lie, is ... the keyhole ... through which the other
Sees the mud at the bottom of your soul.

xxi

The day of days, your feast, will be that time
You'll enjoy the least. And you'll be tempted
To call that ecstasy. In the shadow
Of rapture lost, conditions of freezing
Begin to collect the frost and assess
The exacting cost of self-betrayal.
God always loads his dice. He lets you want
What you think you want, then calls that paradise.
Blessed or cursed, to dance with the daemon means
You can never dance or die alone. You're
Always covered by the Cherub, guarded
By that angel of midnight, all-too-wise,
The one who knows you'd pay too high a price
If she let you return to paradise.

xxii

Forget yourself to remember others;
In remembering others, remember you.
Remember that heart within, you never
Knew, the one who obeys not you, but the
Heart who harbors still its unending praise,
The one who never goes, who always stays,
The one who never forgets to pray for
The uncommon light of the common day.
Heart of your heart, she lights your wayward way;
She lights your path to the light of common
Day. Yes. Hope comes back on the day she learned
To pray. You must be another's before
You can be your own. Your self-reliance
Can never be reached by yourself alone.

xxiii

Eternity, they say, stands still, yet proves
That it moves. That it moves and would stand still
 ... is part and particle of its thrill, the thrill
That you will be what you will, a would-be
Stillness in motion forever. Gospels
Of each moment speak not of now here, but
Nowhere. Joy you seek is found like spring in
Bleak midwinter. To meet what you await,
You exit before you enter; you swerve
Too early to reach your exalted state.
And yet, this familiar news in heaven
Will still surprise the wise with happy tears.
When you hear the angel singing, you'll know
That's eternity ringing in your ears.

IX. YOUR LIFE TAKEN
*Every bird has its decoy, and every man is
led and misled in a way peculiar to himself.*
  – Goethe, Poetry and Truth –

*The human condition is so highly charged with joy and sorrow
that one cannot calculate what two spouses owe each other.*

It is an infinite debt that can only be paid in eternity.
— Goethe, Elective Affinities —

Take my life in one big chunk,
Precisely as I lead it;
Others may sleep off their drunk,
Mine's on paper – read it.
— Goethe, Take My Life —

i

Yours was the history of a soul that lost
Itself, that spent, that cost itself far more
Than you could repay, a soul that again
And again lost its narrow way in those
Hedgerows of desire that led from nowhere
To now here, a soul in heedless sorrow,
In needless fear, that endured its bleary
Days through the warp and woof of time's cruel
Maze. Without the slightest doubt, you knew from
The start how it all turns out. Though playing
To the hilt your life of many parts, you
Knew in your heart of hearts, you could never
Recapture what you lost, that your life could
Never pay you for the trouble it cost.

ii

The life you had you almost lost before
You had it. But from your most difficult
Labor, you came out alive. Always, your
Greatest joy was your joy of yourself. All
You wanted came with ease, and when you were
Most yourself, there was no one you could not
Please. Yes. You're the deepest dilettante who
Ever lived, and the most versatile, most
Accomplished amateur. You drew despair,
But did not admire it. You dissected
The body of sadness, but you did not
Hire it to bolster your own self-worth. You
Acknowledged the unacknowledged misery
Of the world, and – yes – they called that genius.

iii

You abandon all moral striving for
Petty or grandiose conniving. You
Would, if you could, beard and best the devil,
But the devil, who's almost always in
Disguise, is he whose greatest talent is to
Distract and to trivialize. Oh, yes.
Anyone who purports to be wise is
The victim of his lure, his surprise, the
Benighted darling, the damnable dupe
Of unadmitted lies. Give yourself not
The doubt of any benefit, but the
Benefit of self-doubt, for that alone's
How truth comes out. Your certainty's only
Complete when it's at home with self-deceit.

iv

Your critics, among themselves, in vain, still
Fight to live and relive your life, as if
Only they, not you, knew how to live it
Right. But with unyielding vigor and vim,
Your genius was never to pretend that
You – or anyone else – were one of them.
You could never have been more natural.
You did not think ideas. You saw them. You
Did not worship idols. You thaw them. You
Lust for knowledge, for power, for the body
And soul of your lonely others. And yet,
As your conspiracy of lust succeeds,
Shrewdly, it betrays self-trust and breeds the
Impatience of humiliating love.

v

You live in the has-been-hood of a life
You pretend was once so very good. You
Think of yourself, as if you had a life
You never really had. For the life, you
Act as if you had, is a fiction that
Allowed you latitude to simulate

Conviction. The life you seek, the life you
Vie in vain to spy out of the corner
Of your eye, is the life that acts. This life,
Your conviction about a fiction, is
The friction of your will clashing with the
Facts and consequences of your acts. This
Life, your life, your magic lantern show, is
The benign illusion that makes you go.

vi

You were the master of derisory
Tact and abiding fact. That you and that
Anyone else might be alike is a
Fate you hate and could not take. For you, there's
No creed, no prayer, for all you touch and that
Touches you is contaminated by
The uncommon air, by the all-too-rare
Unalikeness of self-assured genius.
The older you grow, you come to know with
Surety the impurity of snow.
If anyone could have saved you, it could
Only have been yourself. Yes. Wherever
You go, your footfalls on snow map the march
You stole on every other lonely soul.

vii

In the middle of your mind, there's a spot
That is always blind. This spot, where vapor
Condenses into dew, is the spot where
You imagine the unimagined that
Imagines you. Yes. Bios is bias,
And with its eros, logos tries to put
The cross on the 't' of your first truths and
The dot on the 'i' of your last lies. Thus,
Whenever you fall in love, you're never
More sure about truth's cure, about the lure
Of the lie and the lie of the lure. Though
Life is vain, life is futile, as perhaps
You know, there's no one, who chooses to live,
Who lives out his life, as if that were so.

viii

The unsententious tedium of your
Life was punctuated by laughter and
By all the women you lusted after.
You would, if you could, suck all the good from
The breast of their wisdom, but wisdom, for
You, was a quest that gives no lasting rest.
To zigzag from unrest to unrest: oh
Yes, that is your quest. And, yes, each new test
You approach with diminishing zest. Thus,
You wear each new task like a mask lest your
Fantasy see through itself and recognize
Its own agony. And yet, one long, one
Tender caress could clear the mess and still
On the darkest days brighten your distress.

ix

There is that bliss of the present moment
You feign to kiss but miss. On its very
Verge, before it's even reached, your joy, thus
Preemptively impeached, already starts
To groan and moan frustration's remorseless
Tone. With restlessness, you begin in sin
That knows no best, no worst, no rest, only
That thirst that does not end. Exhausted, you
Arrive at the unbribable, which, though
Not describable, has the patience to
Wait without wisdom, but in troubled love
For what's lost the will to strive or connive.
Those who serve below and rule above are
Startled by this terror of human love.

x

You keep playing possum with Mr. and
Mrs. Microcosm. As if each part
Could blossom into a whole, and each whole
Could fructify in each part. Yet you could
Not fill the hole in your famished heart, as
If you'd sate hunger with more hunger, as

If you'd fill the void with still more void. Yes.
You'll find, you think, in some golden tree a
Version of a better thee, one with a
Religious lust you can't distrust, a lust
Uncouther than that of Martin Luther,
As though this were your better self, the self
You were afraid you betrayed when you laid
With the Helen of Troy in every maid.

xi

The boredom of whoredom gives way to the
Lust for innocence and trust. And when the
Latest trust goes bust, you will return to
The demon orgy. If you would strive, then
Stray. If you would be drunk, be drunk. If you
Would have sex, have sex. But then, yes, boredom
Connects the logic of orgiastic
Sex with futility. Drink then, if you
Will, swill, from the bottle that has no end
Into the belly that has no bottom.
Nothing you try will ever satisfy.
Forever you're damned by your distraction.
And your dissatisfaction's the prelude
To self-betrayal and petrifaction.

xii

You feared your death and the death of others.
This fear you learned when you visited the
Mothers. You would, if you could, preserve the
Best of your westering, yet the lust that
Violates your trust keeps festering. And
The wound it continues to corrupt is
You. Each try nullifies the goal it sought.
All striving again and again returns
To naught. Your restless will's betrayed by what
You're afraid of losing. Your ego, that's
Otherwise immune to bruising, keeps choosing
Not to face its death, a fear that reflects
All your lost opportunities for sex.
In death, every triumph turns fiasco.

xiii

Resistless, the lure of her body, her
Spirit, is so violent, that you follow
It, you fear it. And yet you would, if you
Could, embrace it, get near it, without shame
That she did not the least bit feel the same.
Your skull, a conch shell roaring, disrupts the
Silence that you keep imploring to speak.
Then all you hear is its endless shriek when
She said: *no*. You have now no other life,
But the desolate one that lets her go.
In the face of what's unwise, there's even
Yet, you surmise, one last kiss beyond the
Last. Before ego melts away, this last
Imagined kiss will have the final say.

xiv

In each *despite*, there's always a whiff of
Even if. You love her despite your age.
You love her as that notorious sage
Who can't shake off the unwisdom of his
Erotic rage. You love her, even if
Your heart's the only part that still grows stiff,
A heart that still hardens at the thought of
Losing her, of being taunted by not
Having what you've never had but wanted.
You lost your trust in the lust that betrays.
You cannot brave the face of death; you swerve.
In one fell swoop, you close the loop of self-
Deception. Yes. You lack the nerve to live
And to forgive yourself without reserve.

xv

There is patient malice in each farewell
That promises heaven but gives you hell.
Recovering, passion returns, and now once
Again so much alive, you forget what
Failing passion learns. If only you'd love
Again, then your joy could go home to stay.

Your life taken, shaken to the core, fears
To say you cannot love her anymore.
Change renders all fidelities obsolete.
Thus, you're deaf to what finality has
To say, for when life teaches its desperate
Lessons, you go on holiday. And when, at
Last, your transcendence of guilt's complete,
You'll be immersed neck-deep in self-deceit.

xvi

From envied others, you sought to steal an
Ecstasy you could fake but never feel.
You acquired the sought-after rank, and soon
Afterwards, you knew how much it stank. All
You'd ever be must reek of what you seek.
All you are must continue until you
Forswear yourself in a different venue.
To and fro, you go. You're back again from
Despair to rapture. Again and again,
You're back again in a cycle that leaves
Unnoticed what history cannot capture.
In every life, there's a law that leads to
Pain, that opens a vein that bleeds what it
Needs, and what it needs is: eternity.

xvii

Eternity has no kernel, no core.
It is the relentless trust in a lust
That yearns for evermore. No. It is not
She. It is not thee. It is what you would
See, but do not see. It is nowhere and
Now here. It is everything and nothing
All at once. It is the genius in you
And the dunce. Your time, your own good time, is
Your parable for an eternity
You feel but cannot fathom, the daily
Consulted bible of the tawdry and
The indescribable. Yes. Your time, your
Best time, is the bible that betrays your
Integrity with what's still bribable.

xviii

Each life, your life, every life, continues
To speculate on the affinity
Between eternity and infinity,
On the maddening marriage of enough
And never enough, on the tragic clash
Between possible and impossible.
You could simulate this tragedy, but
You could not live it. Yes. You could receive
Unmerited love, but you could not give
It. Eternity's the proverbial
Coin of marriage. Face it. Embrace it. Then
Trust your lust. You must. That's the only way
Infinity would ever let you pay
A debt you can forgive but not unlive.

xix

Eternity, that sublime emotion,
Subtends the universe. Eternity's
Your heart's desire, your everlasting aim.
Lastingness is how love in the passing
Moment makes its claim. In all desire, you
Experience this desire. This is the
Fire you yearn to feel. This is the fire you
Know is real. Only those who yearn, know, as
You do, how to burn. Eternity, at
Its most sublime, is love surpassing love
And leaving it behind. You will not ask
For stars. You will not ask for rain. You will
Not think of love or what you hope to gain.
And the silence of your questioning shouts … an exaltation.

X. SOUL IN MOTION

What is this lack of anxiety they speak of anyway?
– Cicero, On Friendship –

The ears of mankind are filled with this music all the time. But they have become completely deaf to its melody; no other human faculty has become so atrophied as this. … The beginning

of all movement, then, comes from that which has set itself in motion: which can neither be born nor die. ... Since, therefore, it is plain that this self-moving principle is eternal, the same must evidently apply to the human soul.
          – Cicero, *The Dream of Scipio* –

Nothing is stable it if can't be trusted.
          – Cicero, *On Friendship* –

i

Your birth was easy, your delivery quick.
You knew how to gild the lily and make
Even the roughest patch of words seem slick.
Yet you could never shake the tremors of
First night nerves, for you fear before each speech
That your bravado seems to promise a
Peak you cannot reach. For you, courage was
Always an imaginary point toward
Which you strive, but from which the coward swerves.
No others could praise you quite so well as
You might have praised yourself. And so, when the
Opportunity arose for self-praise,
You could not help but try it in the hope
That others would hear it and might buy it.

ii

For you, Rome was forever your home, a
City eternal, and – yes – you watched, as
A child, how eternity begins to
Dismantle itself. Yes. You lament how
All said good night to honor, principle,
Sincerity, how they make corruption
An eternal verity and call that Rome.
Your philosophic career showed how much
In demand was the second-hand. You were,
It seemed, all too often another's man,
Seldom your own. From no man to new man,
Your life was one relentless, remorseless
Plan for the acquisition of power.
Oh, yes, all you are points to politics.

iii

There was in your life crisis but never
Consolation. Every philosophy
You studied offered up clues that taught it,
But, though you sought it, you never bought it.
While still a lad at Athens, you made your
Acquaintance with the mysteries. Yes, there,
Away from home, away from Rome, you were
Ushered unto the very threshold of
Eternity, but this was a threshold
You could not cross. Thereafter, your life's the
Fable of what you tried to find, but lost.
You searched long and hard for life's fateful clue,
But the lamp that lit the way for others
Shone with a light that never shone on you.

iv

All too quickly the golden moments of
Your youth pass by. You let them go. You don't
Know why. Theirs is a music you now no
Longer hear, a music that's everywhere,
Now, and here, but that's crowded out by the
Roaring cataract of fear. The course that
Led you there, to the music you could, if
You would, still hear, is a course no longer
Clear. There's now no means to measure the span
Between you and that long lost treasure. Like
A senile pirate, you dream of the gold,
But forget where it's buried. Yet you yearn
For the music, for those moments when you
Lost your way as you dithered and worried.

v

You fear pain, and you fear its absence, death.
And you fear what life, the perpetual
Presence of fear, makes clear. Yes. You fear your
Loneliness. You fear your grief. You fear your
Betrayal of false belief. And the lust
That drives you, you fear that too. You fear that

Your lust might stop. You fear that it might go
On. You fear every ending is always
Tending toward another dawn. You would,
If you could, escape to frivolity,
And sometimes, when you do, you fear that too.
If happiness is the absence of fear,
Then happiness must be death. Yes. You hear
It beckon as you draw your final breath.

vi

These are the hazards in moral life: that
You may do good, and yet receive unto
Yourself great evil; that you'll hope, yet be
Handed despair; that you may in earnest
Strive, yet court and win disaster; that you
May trust, and yet be betrayed; that you may
Love, yet be despised; that you may be asked
For courage, yet live afraid, surprised; that
You'll brandish your integrity, yet yield
To corruption; that you may hanker for
Constancy, yet always face disruption;
That you may promise, yet willingly break
It; that you may be granted the gift of
Eternity, then freely forsake it.

vii

You always loved your life too well to love
Philosophy too much. But you would, and
Did, wend your way from eternity to
Politics, as if, you sometimes supposed,
Politics is the definitive way
To eternity. Philosophy, in
The end, your refuge, your rescuer, left
You to fend for yourself on the skewer
Of politics. No, beneath the sword of
Damocles, there's no ease amidst ease, no
Pleasure amidst pleasure. Whoever would
Be happy is in error about the
Abundance of terror. And, yes, terror
… is the ultimate tool of politics.

viii

You labored long on the lost work of self-
Consolation. On your unflagging quest
For the bravest and the best, you never
Paused to rest. And yet you failed the test, for
You were punished by your own character.
To be in solitude is not to be
Still but to be a soul in motion, to
Wrestle with yourself in the company
Of conscience. To be thus idle is to
Throw away the bridle of business and
Break free. Such motion is the motion of
Eternity. Beware of what you think
And what you do, lest your solitude call
Its cargo too costly to carry you.

ix

As a skeptic, you saw it as a point
Of honor to make no commitment, to
Make no promise about the nature of
Truth. Thus, you tempered your wisdom with a
Little cunning. You knew your heart. Only
A lie could keep it running. Oh, yes. The
Solution to the problem of desire is
Not to dissolve it, but to tempt and to
Involve it in more desire, as if you
Could lecture yourself in solitude, as
If you'd accept your admonition and
Then not only receive it, but believe
It. But like your great detractor, you could
Montaigne opinion, but not maintain one.

x

You dream your Pythagorean dream. You
Dream the dream to remind yourself of what
You already know, that you imagine
The fable, but that you're never able
To live your life as though it were so. Your
Vision of eternity melts in the

Roman sun like a monument of snow.
There's love, but no lovers. There's friendship, but
No friends. Oh, lovers, there is no love. Oh,
Friends, there is no friend. Oh, eternity,
There is, alas, only politics. Where
There is no love, no friendship, you promise
There will be. No one, least of all you, could
Ever trust us with your sense of justice.

xi

Of your bravery, you were sore afraid, a
Bravery you feared would erupt at the most
Inopportune moments. Yet your fear, which
Never paused, could not defeat your courage.
When Rome was lost, when home was lost, when faith
Was lost, you begged for mercy, yet bravely
Died and paid in grief the final cost of
Disbelief. You believe in God because
You perceive yourself in motion. This should
Be the origin of devotion. Yet
This is the origin of your grief, that
You would but cannot accept this belief.
The betrayal of your fear is how your
Eternity in motion is made clear.

xii

One more oppressive blow reopens all
Your scars. Then you no longer care about
The intelligence of stars. Your life's a
Continuing accident in the history
Of eternity. The philosophy
You could not buy makes a promise that it
Cannot lie: that you'll be happy if you
Obey its laws, that you will be guarded
Against the hazards of your moral flaws.
But philosophy and life never work
Together as you thought they would. He who
Would be good need not be happy. He who
Would be happy need not be good. And it's
Better to be good than to be happy.

xiii

The day that you discovered Cicero
Everything changed. Yes. Anyone who writes
The history of eternity must
Be deranged. Any genius touched by God
Would think it odd that God too touched you. Yes.
They'll kill all the lawyers before they're through.
And you fear, of course, that they'll start with you.
The soul, you said, echoing others, is
A god, yet it's a god who could not, in
Even your deepest grief, earn your belief.
Yes. The dream that is the mirror of your
Life and your life that is the mirror of
Your dreams waver between two destinies,
Two extremes, between nowhere and now here.

xiv

In every here and now is the promise
Of nowhere, and in every nowhere, there
Awaits the now that is not yet here. Thus,
I love you is a promise of what does
Not yet exist; it is a trust upon
Which you have no reason to insist, the
Trust that, despite its hazards, your promise
will persist until what it promises
  ... is the justice that can at last exist.
To live and love in hope is not to lie.
God promised the May fly just one day to
Live, to work, to play, to die. But let the
May fly die, and in his day, he will try
All the melodies of eternity.

XI. WHAT RAPTURE'S LIKE

It is a bad stage manager who gives his actors parts they're unable to play. ...There is no such thing as happy music. ... No one ever understands the grief or joy of another. ... Anyone who loves music can never be quite unhappy. ... I want you for always ... days, years, eternities.
– Franz Schubert –

i

Oh, yes, of course, you fear your joy. Nothing
Could ever let you forget how all the
Moments of your time annoy. And, yes, you
Would, if you could, summon from each of them,
A distraction, a salvific decoy.
No. There is never any now that you
Face full on. Before you're ready for it,
It's gone. If ever you'd find it, you'd crouch
Behind it and watch it happen without
You, watch it as you nudge it, misjudge it,
Condemn it, and then blind it of all self-
Awareness. Happiness, indeed, you are
Perhaps sometimes allowed, but you lose all
Notice of it in the crowd of happenings.

ii

If you hear in music no movement, you
Hear no music. If in eternity
You feel no motion, then eternity's
A chord in reserve that you hold but do
Not play, a standing note for which you lack
The nerve to say: keep going, keep moving,
Keep proving you're never dead but always,
Always alive. And yet you hunger for
That mythic day when you could steal all the
Stillness in motion, and make it stay. But
Eternity is that chord that only
You can play. If you don't will it, then you
Don't feel it. If you don't feel it moving,
Then you don't feel it proving you're alive.

iii

Somewhere in you, hammer on anvil keeps
Striking. With each blow, expectation keeps
Spiking, keeps building its readiness for
Another blow. This striking, this hope, this
Fear, that keeps on spiking, is the only
Steadiness you know. And yet, rarely do

You believe this though, for your melody
Begins and ends, and in the middle, with
The time it spends, it proves it moves, as it
Tends toward the solution of the riddle
That ends what it begins. Such nonsense, you
Suspect, covers a multitude of sins.
And yet, this is how everything that could
Ever mean anything begins and ends.

iv

Oh, yes. The history of every type is
The eternity of its tokens, and
The eternity of a token is
The history of its type. Yes. Each moment's
Ripe for the promise of yet another
Tempting archetype, for there's nothing that
Eternity could ever mean other
Than eternity. You never mean more
Than what you are, for what you are is the
Avatar of an everlasting scar.
Your eternity points to what cannot
Be reached or breached. Yet eternity's not
Ineffable: it's expressed and obsessed
With all the ways your life is cursed or blessed.

v

Ineffability is token that
Has no type and type that has no token.
The ineffable's never what cannot
Be spoken, but what's spoken endlessly
And never exhausted. It's the promise
That someone, perhaps you, will continue
To speak in a way that makes the old seem
New. Your ineffable joy occurs when
Your will meets its irrepressible thrill,
Meets the wonder that makes eternity
Stand still, meets that blundering time when you
Must in defiance of the stillness still
Blunder on. Oh, yes. This, your elusive
Joy, is the rapture no word can capture.

vi

Music organizes what's nowhere as
If it's eternally now here. This is
The joy you come to fear, the rapture you
Await from afar, like a distant star,
That's temptingly near, but that's never here.
Your music is that prepared surprise, that
Programmable rapture that taunts your life
With longing for what you cannot capture.
Your music shows you what rapture's like. The
Pain in your heart, you appease, if you let
The music play, if you let it tease with
Foretastes of joys you never seize, if you
Let yourself be persona non grata
In one long fifteen-minute sonata.

vii

Nothingness is the cause of everything,
For out of solitary nothingness,
The first urge, echoes with the music of
Itself and begins to experience
Its thirst for the first time. Yes. This is how
Experience starts in the hollowness
Of human hearts, when you see yourself for
The first time as strange, and eternity
Changes into note after note, when song
After song is sung in throat after throat.
You no longer forget what you regret.
You no longer regret what you forget.
You're oblivious to oblivions
Of happiness. Yes. Oh, yes. That's rapture.

viii

There's a worm coiled in the middle of now,
For nothing now tells you how to handle
Your exile from nowhere to here and now.
Your music makes your mark. You left it stark.
You made it clear. There is in the middle
Of the most orderly day a nagging

Fear. Your everlasting May must have its
Longest day, then everything goes somber
And sober like the end of October.
From cradle song to dirge, you were always
On the verge of revelation, of joy.
Nothing ever tells you how to get the
Most of what's happening now. Only the
Aftermath, that's too late, can tell you how.

ix

Your trigger's the poetry of others,
And your music's your loaded gun. Yes. You
Understood how eternity worked. You
Saw how to pull its trigger, to make it
Run. The muffled moonlight cannot pierce your
Loneliest, darkest room, cannot refute
The argument of gloom that arms itself
With the charm of another alarming
Arpeggio, that makes plain the tremors
Of your soul, that desolate cell where ferns
Of ice decorate the crowded panes. Yes.
All joys depart before they arrive. You
Learn these lessons of defeat, yet still you
Strive. This is what it means to be alive.

x

Life, modulated by comfort and fear,
Rarely makes it clear how little there is
To gain from seeing everything as plain
As it really is. Before the corpus
Of joy takes shape, you coyly orchestrate
Its escape. Whatever would stay, you let
It go. On your winter's journey, your long
Hard slog to nowhere, to no one who's now
Here, you sing in the barren snow. There's much
To say before you're finished, before the
Emptiness you've left behind, by someone
Else, is refreshed and replenished, before
Despair, before wisdom winks, while music
Does all it can to lullaby the sphinx.

xi

All your music conspires to subvert the
Condition of poetry, that it might
Insinuate and inspire in ways that
Would not the least bit aspire to meaning.
Music does not live but simulates life.
And what you've only presumed to live has
Simulated and stimulated you.
Your music preserves traces of graces,
That were born, that died in you. Before you're
Through, to everyone's surprise, you become
The person that no one who ever knew
You ever knew. Yes. In hymns of joy, all
Things are new. But, alas, when the music's
Over, it's over, and you return to you.

xii

Each moment in the middle sets a tone,
An answer to the riddle, that springs from
The first, last and loneliest moment of
Your life. After you, last musicians do
Their worst to invent that thirst for which there's
No tonic, to tease the agony of
Desire, as if to satisfy it, while
Denying it's desirable. Exhaustion,
The end of the post-hormonal age, points
To post-tonal rage that reiterates
The song that would unvex itself, if it
Could unsex and unperplex itself with
One last ploy. But your music means nothing
At all till it connects itself with joy

xiii

There's energy in the world, a swooping
Thrill, wind so wild, you wonder how someone,
Like you, so meek, so mild, survives. But self-
Disgust can still be tender to itself
When it thinks it must. Your heart is darkened
By the brightest day. The sky's so blue, so

Serene, that it's altogether obscene
For you to be this way. Thus, peep inside
Your heart, find what's been there from the start, find
What you want is something that can never
Happen, for, alas, happiness only
Happens when what never happens, happens.
And yet, when it does, eternity makes
You forget all you think you thought it was.

xiv

There's no music that's not already a
Song. If you can't imagine the words, then
You must have gotten the music wrong. The
Clarinet in middle C warbles one
Note, one word, for thee that's one brief jot in
The tangled knot of eternity. The
Last leaf dangles, falls, mangles your clinging
Hope. All hope, so say the wise, is foolish
As wind. All consolation is sop for
Those who've sinned and now are capable of
Nothing less than anything. Your hope, like
Withered shreds, shivers then in the wind at
What it dreads. And it dreads not death but the
Bragging lack of what could justify it.

xv

You continue to insist on the bliss
You resist and resist the bliss you want
But miss. You know this pattern's quite perverse.
And yet you live your life to make it worse.
The moment before the joy you capture
Reveals the secret, forestalls the rapture.
The idyll's an idol that you smashed, the
Quivering trout that splashed before it crashed. Go
Then, go mad, add to the adoration
Of the golden calf your unwholesome half
Of a wit that can only commit to
One more brazen idolatry after
Another. The idyll that returns is
That ghost you love the most: eternity.

xvi

If the snow could speak, perhaps it would shriek
Another somnolent curse. All the
Promises you promised to keep are now
Buried in miles of sleep. If you could bear
To listen to it, you'd open your ears,
Ignore your fears, and mumble another
Idiotic question. What are the odds
That those who suspect there is no God will
Not in the least bit blink when they begin
To think of themselves as gods? Without the
Slightest pause, you hazard a guess: You say,
Quite good, because you can never really
Trust yourself to do what you know you should.
Nothing but lust commands your lasting trust.

xvii

Devotion, right and true, is the quest for
Joy that begins with you. Alone to the
Alone, you go solo with solitude.
You imagine joy you never find in
You. When you break the code, you see how all
That is, is an ode to joy, that music,
Your hymn to now, is joy you do not fear,
Joy that does not cloy, joy with the grace called
Home, joy where all your contradictions meet
To defeat despair with solitude as
Consolation. That you exist at all is
Surprise; it's to endure the aftermath
Of blunder, but to exist with music:
That is to live in a state of wonder.

xviii

Every valediction is a fiction till
You meet your contradiction. And every
Hello's already a goodbye waiting
To tell its long, loud, and lasting lie. The
Organ grinder grinds on and on. Yes. The
Hurdy-gurdy man turns into music

What you cannot handle, what you cannot
Own. He turns out a tune as you sing your
Song. He moves, as if he proves in the dark
That there's no right, no wrong, no candle, no
Plan. Without regret, he risks this lasting
Bet: he asks you to sing the best you can.
That there's no God you think you can't forgive,
Yet with your song you steal the thrill to live.

XII. ETERNITY AND ITS DISCONTENTS

If the Soul halted anywhere, then, the Kosmos, too, would halt; but the Soul encompasses all, and so the Kosmos moves, seeking everything. Yet never to attain? On the contrary, this very motion is its eternal attainment. ... What, then, does Eternity really mean to those who describe it as something different from Time? ...We are in agony for a true expression; we are talking of the untellable. ... But we ourselves, what are we? ... Really there is nothing that is truly ours that we can lose. Whatever seems to have been lost and divided from us, in this changing world, is There, where all things are filled full of life, and, we may say, boiling with life. ... This is the life of gods and of the god-like and blessed among men, liberation from the alien that besets us here, a life taking no pleasure in the things of the earth, the passing of the solitary to the solitary.
– Plotinus, *The Enneads* –

Try to bring back the god in you to the God in all.
– Plotinus on his deathbed –

i

You are always happiest when you are
Least aware. Oh, yes. You were happy once,
But whenever you were, you just weren't there.
Between eternity and time, there's the
Middleman. There's you. In the middle of
The drama, you crave that nirvana that
Still has room for you, that bliss you never

Want to miss, that rapture that would capture
All you'd save of what's still you, what's never
Old, but always new. You would, if you could,
Be one with the One and still be you. But
There's a riot in your disquiet, a
Violent order that leaves you lost on the
Border between time and eternity.

ii

Time is how you imagine somewhere the
Eternity that's nowhere, yet now here.
Time is promise and threat, relief, regret,
All those strangers you haven't met with yet,
All those moments you would live and forgive
But can't forget. From unchangingness, change
Must emerge. Nothingness, with money in its
Pocket, wants to splurge. It's always far too
Bored to buy what it can afford. Time that
Was not yet time chose to aim for something
More than presence. From this stirring comes the
Blurring of eternity, beginning
Time that never ends, that fritters itself
Away, while never saving what it spends.

iii

At the end of a life you unwisely
Spend, there will come one final warning: Yes.
Eternity impends, and upon it
Everything depends. Beware. Take warning.
No one ever hides from what abides. There's
The abiding God and the abiding
You. But what abides, what endures, abides
And endures because the abiding, the
Enduring, touches you. You resemble
God, God resembles you, yet you're unlike
That God in all you think, you feel, you do.
This familiar strangeness of God inspires
Your desperate need. In eternity, there's
No relief in God from your endless greed … to be.

iv

Simplicity is the soul of soul. Thus,
If you are aware of yourself, then the
Self you are is one too many. All things
Considered, one and only one self is
More than plenty. Self-consciousness happens
When what you are becomes its own double.
This is just the beginning of trouble,
From very first simplicity to the
Complexity of what's last. Yes. Even
The lowliest Byzantine clerk in the
Cosmic bureaucracy knows the empire
Of the self's too vast, that it's undone by
Complications, by sophistries of schools,
By the false ideology of fools.

v

You choose the body you resemble. The
Horror of this, once taken in, is more
Than enough to make the stalwart tremble.
Once you did what now you suffer. Thus, you
Cannot swerve from the fate you deserve. You're
Entitled only to the fate you've won.
You become what you've done. You've done what you
Become. Before free will, you paused till you
Saw how nothing's uncaused, not stars, not atoms,
Not you. You inspect the wreck of every
Cause and each effect. In the dance of life,
There's just one tune; and the moment of your
Decision is always noon. Salvation's
Always how you make the most of every now.

vi

Continuity of becoming is
Illusion, for all that becomes is the
Motion of eternity, is the One,
Where all that happens, happens at once, where
All that moves, moves at once, where all that proves
Anything proves at once all you didn't

Know you knew, proves once and forever that
You are you. The life you live in truth's not
Here, but there, a place that's not a place, that's
Always now, nowhere and beyond compare.
Nothing here can satisfy because it's
Never lived out here but lived out there, where
The life you live burns so fierce, so keen, there's
Nothing beyond itself that it could mean.

vii

Causality links existence with non-
Existence, and your past and present with
Future. Yes. Causality is the way
Eternity thinks. The identity
Of each now, of each event, each how, each
You, is its history, its persistence from
Then to now to you, and your history is
Eternity's time-like satire of itself.
It winks. Thus, you'll have not this, not that, but
Everything all at once. Yes. All you are
Will be what you are, unbroken in a
Single token that remains unspoken.
All events anywhere and anywhen
Continue to be what they've always been.

viii

In eternity, there's no *will be,* no
Was. All that can exist already does.
Gradually, against your will, you reveal
What you try in vain to conceal. Thus, like
It or not, the counterfeit gives way to
The real, and your better wisdom for a
Moment removes the blot and takes a peek
At eternity's endless hide and seek.
Little by little, moment by moment,
You approach the nub of the riddle where
The man in the middle delivers the
Answer part by part. Such is the mystery
Of the human heart. You change into the
Unchangeable. You become what you are.

ix

Whatever is ... is what it is because
It lives. The stars are the sky's testament,
The cosmic sprawl that lets you know there is
Nothing and no one so small that it's not
Altogether essential to the All.
Thus, star, atom, you, all breathe together.
There is a soul in each, and there's nothing
In the universe beyond its reach. Yes.
All touches all, and you touch everything.
Withdraw into yourself and look, and you
Will find eternity an open book.
There's a wakefulness in you, a life you're
Born to become, to be, this wakefulness, this
Life, that is your share of eternity.

x

You want to be alive in the presence
Of what you long for. Any less is to
Confess your discontent, to live a life you
Resent, to mourn the life you've spent, rather
Than live the one for which you're meant. Desire's
Your search for what's gone missing, your lust to
Assert your will till you've had your fill of what
You want. Life is motion. Stillness is death.
Nothing alive can suppress eternity's
Breath. It lives, it breathes, it never dies. It
Moves as it always tries to rest. It moves
As it proves it cannot help but strive. It
Moves as it proves that it never dies, that
It cannot lose the zest to be alive.

xi

This life, this unchangeable you, both now
Here and nowhere, nonetheless moves and proves
That it moves. You cannot change into what
You're not, but always and only into
What you are. You can only keep changing
Into yourself. Your every motion is

A wave, a ripple, a disturbance in
The ocean of what you are, and the life
You think you are, the experience you
Think you're having, is the warped reflection
Of the everlasting scar you are but
Would deny; it is thus the defection,
The ever persistent lie, that defies
With its disguise what's true, what's good, what's wise.

xii

The life of eternity's too near, too
Far, to notice, for you lack the wit to
See your world is counterfeit. Time begins
When eternity begins to differ
From itself. Outside time, outside space, the
Spirit moves, and life, its visible face,
The face you see, the face you think you knew,
That's only the image of what's really
True. There's nostalgia for lost presence. God
Watches your back and wants you back. Heaven,
The joy you are without exception, surrounds
And confounds the life of the common day.
You are this joy you never see or say.
You are this joy you cannot ask to stay.

xiii

The deeper your longing, the farther you've
Fallen, and the way you fell paves the path
That leads you back. Now here yearns for nowhere
And nowhere for now here. Here conspires with
There, and there with here. Yes. Let's be clear, the
Eternity you crave begins right here.
The other life, the true life, you cannot
Reach unless your life begins to teach it
Here. The lure of nowhere for now here and
Now here for nowhere is the motive for
Motion, for your life, for the motion of
Eternity, for God's motion, for your
Motion, for the motion and devotion
Of all your equally lonely others.

xiv

You keep dying to live, not die. You keep
Trying to give yourself a reason to
Live, not lie. Go home. Go stay. Go try to
Make eternity this common day. The
Path of love is wider than expected.
No one walks it alone. The One without
A second, who would stand alone, finds that
Solitude's another's throne. Thus, pray love's
Push will come to shove, that the alone greets
The alone with prayers, not of loneliness,
But love. You depart. You return. On the
Trip back home, you bring with you what you learn.
What you give you get, and what you get you
Give. Yes. This is how you are meant to live.

xv

Time is the life of which eternity
　… is the paradigm, but eternity
　… is the life with no paradigm. This no-
Paradigm life is the life that is you,
The life that's now, nowhere and forever.
You depart to return. You return to
Depart. This is the plot logic of the
Human heart. Thus, all returns to all. No
Shortcuts allowed. There must be cost, there must
Be anguish, there must be trauma. In the
Midst of the drama, it's always your turn,
For yours is the religion of return.
And each return – without relent – repents
Of eternity and its discontents.

xvi

Eternity is all the life there is, the
Remembrance of a once forgotten joy.
It is a life unwavering, a whole
Unbroken, an infinity that knows
No distinction, beginningless, endless
Motion, that finds its only rest in its

Devotion to all that is. In time the
Unwavered wavers, the unbroken breaks,
And distinction after distinction finds
Extinction as it forgets all the life it
Forsakes. The time you need, the time you heed,
Lets you know what eternity is, lets
You know the risk, the stakes. Eternity
   ... is how your life keeps the promise it breaks.

— NINE —
PART FIVE
MIRACLE OF SELF-REFERENCE

I. ON SELF-DECEPTION'S CRUTCH

By my little point I mean — what shall I call it? — the particular thing I've written my books most for. Isn't there for every writer a particular thing of that sort, the thing that most makes him apply himself, the thing without the effort to achieve which he wouldn't write at all, the very passion of his passion, the part of the business in which, for him, the flame of art burns most intensely? Well, it's that!
– *The Figure in the Carpet* –

The port from which I set out was, I think, that of the essential loneliness of my life – and it seems to be the port also, in sooth to which my course again finally directs itself!
– Letter to Morton Fullerton, *1900* –

I don't want to die – I won't, I won't, oh, let me live; oh, save me.
– *The Notebooks* –

What is it that saves you?
– *The Beast in the Jungle* –

What I want you to say is that you will save me.
– *The Spoils of Poynton* –

I'm afraid there are moments in life when even Schubert has nothing to say to us. We must admit, however, that they are our worst.
– *The Portrait of a Lady* –

I have the curious sense that I'm not the bewildering puzzle to all of you that you are to me.
– *Days before his death* –

– Henry James –

i

Amid the riddle of life, you sought for
Someone to care, someone bold, someone brave,

Someone who'd dare to intrude into your
Troubled solitude. But what never was,
Will never be, and now is not ... forever.
It takes more than reverie to remove
Your self-addicted blot of loneliness.
It takes more than fantasy to appease
The desperate if-onliness of a
Life unlived. If you had a second chance,
And second chance is delusion, then you'd
Ask for another task, for another
Confusion to mask your pain, another
Consolation that claims your loss is gain.

ii

It was appalling and galling that you
Became so serious about yourself.
Then you realized your ambition was a
Spasm of unintended sarcasm.
Thus, now you'll be surrounded by, and soon
Surrendered to, your cynicisms. When
Grievance has lost its charm, your resentment
No longer keeps you warm. Once more into
The breach, and again you learn what only
Self-deceit can teach. Into the lukewarm
Mush of a passion spent, that is where your
Courage went. Yes. Everyone resembles
Everyone else because everyone is
Smeared by the misery of existence.

iii

You found your futility again in
1910. Your nightmare, quiet and bland, was
The uneasy certainty of someone
Who always wanted to, but never takes
A stand. It's the realization you now
Recall that you've never really lived at
All. Nothing happened and keeps happening.
The fate you await, already occurred,
Recurs and reoccurs. Life's a trial.
Death's a hung jury, and you make of your

Time a useless fury. At last, you face
All the risks you took you never thought you
Took, all the experience you condense
Into one anguished look in the book of life.

iv

Your dread never stops knocking, never stops
Cocking its loaded pistol. Eternity
Will never please, unless without it you
Are ill at ease. This is why you suffer.
With your last breath, with violence, with pain,
You will step once more toward eternity's
Narrow door. In despair, you yearn for more
And more. You try for the ceiling, and you
Hit the floor. You're so scrupulous about
Your scruples your explanations become
Obsolete before you finish making
Them. You're so ruthless about promises
That you're already breaking them before
You finish making and forsaking them.

v

Consciousness is that receptacle filled
With the spectacle of life. Wherever
It goes, consciousness, for you, was obliged to
Know what it knows, and what it knows exists,
And what it doesn't know insists there's still
Something yet to know. What you didn't quite
Know or admit were places consciousness
Can't go that will not in the least submit
To the ravages of human wit. Your
Own-most self is always two: one false, one
True; one that dreams of joy it cannot share,
One that lives its joy, always unaware.
The beast springs when you expect it least, for
Your life's the famine you mistook for feast.

vi

Though you feel that you're real, there's nothing to
Justify that feeling. The groundlessness

Of your existence keeps you reeling. Each
Step you take turns reality on its
Head. You cannot escape the damnable
Shape of this destiny until you're dead.
Between now here and nowhere, there is this
Tension, tension that's not the suspension,
But the very essence of what you are.
To think of yourself as defiantly
Alone presumes that you can own what you
Cannot own, that you can own yourself. And
Yet, there is nothing and no one you can
Ever own, not even your own-most self.

vii

Knowing nothing, you knew everything, and
Knowing everything, you knew nothing. Yes.
You were familiar and unfamiliar
With the remorseless emptiness of the
Universe and all its useless stuffing.
What would stay, goes. What would go, stays. What would
Play, works. What would work, plays. What would obey,
Strays. What would stray, obeys. And yet to be
Exact is to follow the moral law
As if it were a fact, and fact as if
It were the moral law. Each breath you breathe
Must extract morality from a fact.
No, your life is not a philosophic
Quiz, for the *Ought* always already *Is*.

viii

You knew too little about too much and
Too much about too little to bootstrap
Your stubborn riddle into wisdom. Those
Vaguenesses in your father's religion,
You disavowed, were precisely those you
Unwittingly allowed to sway your vision.
Every great explainer conceals the grump,
The hidden complainer. The world, for him,
 ... is much too dim. The trick is to make it
Plainer. But, for you, it's never the least

Bit defensible to revel in the
Ostensible. A tawdry clarity
Corrupts what's meretriciously pure. Thus,
You're sure to make the obvious obscure.

ix

To save yourself and others, you didn't
Know where to start, so you begin with the
Artificial salvation that is art.
In the midst of everyone's misbehavior,
You still imagine one of your lonely
Others will be your savior. And, yes, you
Imagine that you could be one of theirs.
Want what you want, and you never get it.
Get what you want, and you regret it. Nothing
Can appease pangs of self-betrayal, the
Disease that never lets you do what you
Please. It's a grave misfortune when other
People are let loose on your happiness.
You would much rather be let loose on theirs.

x

Yes. You promised to understand but failed.
Before truth, your clarity quailed and fled
Into enigma, into fear that you'll
Never be now here but always nowhere.
You would melt into the very moment
Were it not for your ice-cold fear to be,
Not nowhere, but here. You wanted to want,
To want more wants, but your morality
Was a series of taunts at what your life
Never gets but wants. The turning of one
Last screw haunts everything you do. You know
The bottom line, but neglect it. Salvation's
Dialectic's far too eclectic: it
Would, if it could, save anyone, but you.

xi

Your life, your prose, a long period still
Longer prolonged, found it quite difficult

Putting meaning into the sentence where
It belonged. Thus, your later sentence found
No length, no meaning proper to itself.
Your mystery thickens as lucidity
Glows from clear to blinding bright. Nothing can
Attenuate your subtlety or snatch
The smallest day from your larger night. All
Your enigmas, you kept ready to hand
In plainest sight. Each ghost, an unconscious
Shadow of your intent, can haunt each line
You wrote without telling you what it meant.
Happiness is spoiled by explanation.

xii

In eternity, you'll meditate on
Your sentence, the sentence you'll execute
In time, the time that's your last and only
Chance at repentance. After death, there is
Never any time to inspect erstwhile
Passions you now neglect. You'll grieve that your
Joy has the shrewdness to deprave what it
Cannot save, that it would deceive even
The elect. You think you live. But you see
How that's a lie: Yes. You only know how
To die. Fall in love, if you will, with your
Failure to live. Marry it, and if you're
Lucky, then your better angels will let
You carry it into eternity.

xiii

The paradise that's Paris lives in your
Mind. It's nowhere in the world for you to
Find. The reality of any place
Imagined discredits your travel to
It. Now that you're there, it's best not to care,
To hunker down, and just get through it. You
Do your best to try ... to live in accord
With the decorous lie. But you're too much
In love with illusion's liability
To let it be challenged as untrue by

Anyone or anything but you. Yet
This is what you do. You call it fiction,
Truth's sly depiction that must demolish
What desperate illusion seeks to polish.

xiv

You were there on the scene when usefulness
Became useless, when just being intense
Was the only thing that made any sense.
You never quite know. No. You never quite
Feel what turns your wheel, what makes you go. The
Self-deception you continually
Refine provides more and more unmeaning
Ore for you to mine. Upon reflection
You find that each character you invent
Constitutes in you a little event,
A little piece of your befuddled mind.
You'll always, as it were, be what you were.
Yes. It's a rule. You perceive how a fool,
Gradually undeceived, remains a fool.

xv

The secret in the tattered arras will
Conceal itself but never spare us of
Truth, that home where scandal is, where what you
Thought passé returns in force to have its
Day, the day uncommon and compelling
That's too embarrassing for the telling.
There's no overt story of evil in
All its glory. There's the easy made hard,
And the difficult made hard to regret.
You want to see everything, and you do.
Yet you could not grasp that vision that ends
With the ambiguity of you. To
See too clearly is to see too much. Thus,
You slouch toward truth on self-deception's crutch.

xvi

There's always something, and then there's nothing.

Like a water-starved desert wayfarer,
What you need you lack, and what you lack you
See but cannot seize. The meaning of your
Life, your consolation, is the mirage
That's designed to please but that can never
Appease the worst of your lasting thirst. Yes.
You suppose what only a fool thinks he
Knows, as if your chosen philosophy
Were adequate to each emergency,
As if your life amounts to more than a
Spasm of stardust and protoplasm.
When life no longer savors what it gleans,
You'll seek eternity by any means.

xvii

To wait is your portion. And, in meeting
Yourself, being late: that is your fate. If
Your life could be finished before you start,
There would be no need for the human heart.
You let yourself be vague in the hope that
Life would happen to you, that you would hatch
Just like an egg from accident into
Purpose. You sought the mercy of muddle
In the midst of dangerous clarity.
You choose lies you trust, lies that protect you
From the rarity of seeing all-too-
Clearly, with far too little charity,
The unopened gift. Yes. The gift unshared,
That's the gift that is spared eternity.

xviii

You remain unimpressed by the return
Of the repressed, by the secret that is
Not sex but a joy unhad, uncherished.
You had a glimpse of it more than once, but
It ran its course, and it quickly perished.
In this world you learn the meaning of the
Lie. In the next, you learn to apply the
Lessons of that lie, the lie of deepest
Dye, the lie that never lets you tell the

Truth, no matter how hard you try. No, dear.
Everything, you fear, can never be clear,
For you, a little piece of everything,
Stir up the middle and bemuddle it.
Yes. Life keeps gumming up the summing up.

xix

You yielded to the succor of self-love,
To self-deception, to the means whereby
The serpent tempts the clueless dove into
Deeper justice, deeper wisdom, deeper love.
There is, for you, no image that captures
You. Yet you mistake yourself for your own
Self-portrait. Thus, flee yourself. Meet what you
Reject. Flee yourself, and you meet what you
Never expect or detect. That it is
Yourself you fear made everything at once
So clear, so deep, that you knew in your heart
That never, by yourself alone, was there
Any promise you'd keep. In the tideless
Deep, you're that promise only God may keep.

xx

Self-love's in flight from something or other,
From self, from father, from God, from every
Equally lonely brother. Vanity
Points to moral sense when it's undone by
Its own expense. Finally, it will cost too
Much to love yourself. And this love depletes
What you think it completes. Yet, no one knows
Completion without this bewildering
Species of depletion. Love's the lifeline
That's tossed from solitude to solitude.
Yes. The noblest lust, for you, for all your
Lonely others, dares to reach what only
Love could ever teach. The highest branch of
Solitude is the one that reaches others.

xxi

Your best philosophy was a tone, the
Faintest tingling in the bone, a fragrance
Of unvanishing fears, a brutal chill
On naked skin, a ringing in the ears,
An error not unakin to mortal
Sin, a lingering trace of vain disgrace that's
Still unlost in the wake of wasted tears.
You were never more sure of salvation's
Necessary detour. Thus, you strayed from
That source from which everyone and all takes
Its course. In time you take your turn, and the
Lesson you learn is your means of return.
Forgive yourself for your failure to live,
And you'll learn to give what you could not give.

xxii

To meet in person is to meet mask to
Mask. There is perhaps no more desperate task.
Yet you expect of this meeting more than
It can give. That's why you never cease
To ask yourself to live when always there's
One word heedful: to give all you can give.
If you could be what you like, if you could
Do what you like, if you could think what you
Like, if you could feel what you like, then you
Would perhaps know what it's like to like, but
You would not be free. It's not too late to
Live, not too late to be free, not too late
To give the gift you now must freely give,
To live the gift you must give dangerously.

xxiii

In death, your vagueness will have had its day.
Thereafter, fate will no longer pay an
Annuity for ambiguity.
The one thing needful is to desire God's
Will. This will, and this will alone, is yours.
That's the be-all and end-all of all

Your tours. All that is not this will is the
Baggage that emerges from the petty
Urges that limp astray from the flickering
Light of your common day. That this will is
Yours alone means there's nothing else you could
Call your own, not even your own-most self.
This will in you is a force so clear, so
Vast, it's only choice is to last … forever.

II. ONE MORE LIFE

With history as a mirror, I try, by whatever means I can, to improve my life and to model it by the standard of all that's best in those whose lives I write. As a result, I feel as though I converse and live with them. By means of history, I receive each one of them in turn, welcome and entertain them as guests, consider their stature and their qualities, and select from their actions what's most authoritative and best so that I may know them as I know myself. Is there a greater joy than this? Is there a better way to improve one's character?
  – Plutarch, *Parallel Lives (Timoleon)* –

God is the brave man's hope, and not the coward's excuse.
 – Plutarch, *Moralia (Of Superstition or Indiscreet Devotion)* –

i

Out of many gods, one hope, one God, one
Prayer that was still a rumor in the air
When the oracles all fell silent. There
Are, you believe, demons in the soul that
Tease you there with illusions of control.
Myth goes where philosophy could never
Follow. Eternity fills what time could
Never hollow. The mythic veil conceals
More than it could tell. In the universe,
There's life; there's motion; there's generation;
There's corruption; there's history waiting for
The interruption that's eternity.
Yes. You lost the grace of your true face when
You lost the vision of eternity.

ii

Anything once known could be known again.
Anything once thrown could be thrown again
Into the discombobulating world.
Against all odds, you're a man of many gods,
Whose language, if they could speak, would, of course,
Be Greek. But now logic's austerity
Has become too chic to let existence
Have a meaning or let deepest desire
Catch what it must seek. With infinity,
Enigma reached its peak. No first, no last,
Only the everlasting riddle of
A muddled middle. No bottom, no top,
No law that would let you yell for help and
Challenge the restless universe to stop.

iii

You'll eavesdrop in your house and hear whispers
Of your own walls. You will hear the lisping
Truth that stutters as it mutters and calls
Your name. And you will not avert your ear
When the closet demands its secrecy.
Before the sacred mystery you tremble
At the awful auspices of death, at
The mystic ritual that compared the
Spiritual with the spiritual. When you
Return from the festival, you revere
But no longer recall the rapture. You
Reach into thinnest air for ecstatic
Speech. But what you capture is the rankest
Despair of your inarticulate screech.

iv

Are your heroes offspring of gods or their
Precursors? Are they echoes of gods or
Vain rehearsers of what's been imagined?
The announcement's shocking: *Great Pan is dead.*
That's when the panic begins to spread. The
Death of God's an event that causes what

It would – but can't – prevent. There's need beyond
Morality in the sober deed that
Sustains all the while your stubborn guile and
Greed for eternity. When gods begin to
Bleed, gods begin to need eternity.
With eternity, there is no long, no
Short; there is only the chance to fulfill
Your mission, or, by stumbling, to abort.

v

You were there at the beginning of the
Lust for self-trust, there on the ground floor, when
Belief sneaks out the door, and everything
Else goes bust. Knowledge is so frail it's not
Surprising that everything you know must fail.
Erotic solemnities you perform are
Never enough to keep you warm. Nothing's
More demanding than misunderstanding,
As if *nothing in excess* was a maxim
Recommending a superfluity
Of nothingness. Logic's sharpest claws pause
To lacerate your own laws. Thus, you find
In common conceptions, in the muddled
Mind, the most rarefied self-deceptions.

vi

You sought a logic, that's not cold, but hot,
One that points the way to what is worthy
And what is not, one that rummages each
Failure and each success for clues that might
Snatch a telltale moral from the mess. Thus,
You study one more life, for you would, if
You could, suck all the good out of every
Life. All the life you want but cannot feel,
Shamelessly, you contrive to steal from your
Equally lonely others. In every
Portrait, you distill what you steal. Yes. You
Reveal the signs of soul. You betray in
Each biography visible strands of
What you strive to master but can't control.

vii

To know that you know nothing is not to
Worship nothingness but to overcome the
Threat of futility with a promise
And still to know the threat remains. Do not
Be a victim of what you know. Do not
Weep to break the promise you cannot keep.
You are what you are, born of earth and star.
The soul out of its soul-bubble bursts into
Variegated thirsts of the embodied.
Your promise is born of the madness that
You will be what you become and become
What you are, the vision that your life's at
One with the trajectory of your star.
Any change in you changes all that is.

viii

You begin by imagining what a
Person is. A heap of bone and flesh is
Not quite blind to soul and mind. Yes. It must
Reckon with what has begun to beckon.
Your life is buried in this bone, this flesh,
This, the ethereal, material
Mesh of spirit. Flesh-stuff is star-stuff is
Sun-stuff is mind-stuff is soul-stuff is the
Everlasting flame without you, and then
Within you, there's the same everlasting
Flame. If you fail to justify your name,
You have only yourself to blame for such
A crime. From the first to the last of time,
You and you alone are the fire next time.

ix

You are but a drop in the ocean, and
The ocean is but a drop in you. Yes.
Each biography recapitulates
The universe, just as the universe
Abbreviates itself in one person.
The life of the universe is never

Through till it does what universes do,
Till it begins and ends with you. You are
The essence of world unfurled in one life.
Even the wisest who believe in the
Impersonality of the cosmos
Are unwittingly the ambassadors
Of evil. Yes. God is the promise of
A face that evil threatens to erase.

x

There is always a promise of order
In a time of dread. That's why you would, if
You could, communicate with the dead. At
The end of the road, there's no turning back.
There you'll find the eternity you lack.
You will see God face to face in a place
That is no place. In eternity, you
Will be what now you cannot see. You will
See what now you cannot be. You would not
Be somebody when being nobody
Would do. Yet the somebodies you portray,
You knew far better than those somebodies
Could say. Now you do what you must do. You
Make but break the promise of being you.

xi

Your coercive parallels abandon
History to find where character dwells. It
Dwells in eternity. What you can, you
Give, and you never cease giving the gift,
The shining example of happy living,
Of how for you the practical always
Traffics so happily with religious
Awe. Wherever your biographies might
Go, you always proved you're wise without the
Gaudiness of appearing so. Truth is
Your greatest good, the forgetfulness of
Forgetfulness only God may give. Yes.
Truth's the splendor of eternity, of
The simple thing that is that makes you live.

xii

E for enigma, e for eddy, e
For eternity, e for *thou art* and
Thou art not, yes, e for what you'd be but
Cannot be. The letter on an antique
Stone betrays how you give away what you
Need to own, how God hands you your life on
Loan. The world's created in time so that
Eternity could begin and end in
Every moment, so that eternity
Could enrapture each moment, so that each
Occasion could recapture eternity,
Eternity that never nullifies time,
But makes time deeper, deeper, deeper, makes
Time the instrument of the promise keeper.

xiii

You write your life with the life of others.
Each life has the look of recognition,
Of novelty too familiar to seem
New, the look of originality
So sure, you know in your heart, you could go
No other way, that this, and that only
This, must be the only way that you could
Ever be you, that this is the way that
You must live when you live your life in the
Brightest ray of the common day. And yet,
Every life is always a choice and a
Chance to change or confirm your character.
Down eternity's endless road, there is
Always someone else waiting to be you.

xiv

God gave you one more life to live: you do
What you must do. *God gave you one more life
To live*: you try to live it true. *God gave
You one more life to live:* you try to say
It plain. *God gave you one more life to live:*
You keep what can't remain. *God gave you one*

More life to live: you learn all you should know.
God gave you one more life to live: you should
Not let it go. *God gave you one more life
To live*: you know you're never through. *God gave
You one more life to live:* you know not what
To do. *God gave you one more life to live:*
You throw away your plan. *God gave you one
More life to live:* you do it all again.

III. EDEN'S BACK DOOR

If the unattainable feeds on my innards, and the eternal builds its eternity out of me, then what still stands between the divine and me?
 – Hugo von Hofmannsthal, *Moments in Greece (The Statues)* –

What do you imagine Nirvana would be like?
 – Hugo von Hofmannsthal, *An Impossible Man* –

Where is your self to be found? Always in the deepest enchantment that you have experienced.
 – Hugo von Hofmannsthal, *Book of Friends* –

i

There is no one in the dark standing at
Your door. The hour is late, and no one still
Alive knows how to wait there anymore.
With each tragedy you rehearse, the news,
It always seems, gets worse and worse. You would,
If you could, buy a little touch of human
Kindness, but nothing in your purse can pay
The cost. Nothing in your heart can remind
Us of what used to be, now that it's lost.
The journey from where you were to where you're
Going is like that from summer days to
Deep Decembers that keep on snowing. All
Your history taunts with what you want but miss.
Why should your bliss dream a darkness like this?

ii

You were, they say, not quite bleak enough to
Be unique, but you were certainly strange.
You shunned that part of you at the heart of
You that stayed the same in every change. You
Were, they say, a man apart, yet you sought
A home in the loneliness of every
Lonely other's heart. Life, for you, a force
Too great to berate or underrate, was
Grasped by you, not piecemeal, but entire, as
Something whole, absolute, not a makeshift
Contrivance, not a clever connivance
Of chewing gum and baling wire, but with
Logic so austere it refutes what's dear.
No. You're never thrown clear of what you fear.

iii

Each ego earns the dubious honor
Of one moment. Each ego now lost is
The relic of an aborted skirmish,
A failed attempt to crowd and conquer time.
These, if you please, are egos of yester
Year you no longer love, no longer fear.
They're echoes of nows no longer here but
Nowhere. You're aware only of what you've
Moved beyond. Only nowhere knows what's now,
What's here. In life's great net, you catch what you
Can't forget, and what you can't forget is
The vanishing promise, the lasting threat.
History melts your monuments of snow. Now,
You're the nobody nobody can know.

iv

History is how your valuables get passed
On. It's how you spend your petty cash, how
You discard your unwanted trash, how you
Buy what keeps arriving with what's already
Gone. Sooner or later, there'll come that day
When accumulations of history melt

Away. This day, which could be any day,
Was the day you slipped beyond the shoulders
Of your rut, the day your fraying cord of
Consciousness, pulled taut, was cut. The rumored
Morality, now nought, can be dissembled,
But never reassembled. It's lost. There
Are those who would rebuild what history's killed,
But no one's rich enough to pay that cost.

v

You thwart yourself in what you seek. And you
Foreswear yourself in what you speak. Rather
Than face the sternest judgment, you'll plead the
Alibi of ambiguous words, that
Every indictment is yet another
Cruel incitement about the dubious
Impossibility of anything
Meaning anything. Truthlessness warrants
Ruthlessness. It incites it, recites it,
And before it's through, it invites it to
Be part of everything you say and do.
Thus, sing your happy apocalyptic
Song. Please, O please, do whatever you please,
For nothing you could ever do is wrong.

vi

You're all self-love, all urge, all lust, all the
Relentless splurge of mystery and mistrust.
You're part-time evader, part-time facer,
And full-time disgracer of the truth. Thus,
You lack the stamina to exist on
A permanent full-time basis with what's
True. Yes. You looked for the liar in the
Mirror once, but immediately you
Knew that if the reflection were true, it
Could, of course, be anyone else but you.
You never thought of your appearance as
Something true enough to be part of you.
No. Your appearance is how you leave on
Others the scar of what they think you are.

vii

Your dream could have been your destiny if
Only you'd made it seem more real. You sell
To the highest bidder. You auction the
Virginity of your identity
To the slyest kidder. Dreamer, gamester,
Pallid enactor of the forever
Invalid, you were the master but played
The servant. You were your future's favorite
Forecaster, but at every chance you had
For a moment's joy, you're unobservant.
Your flight from yourself was useless, futile.
Alas, you are the one you're always with.
Never could you flee from what you'll always
Be. Any other theory's just a myth.

viii

You learn now how little you can recoup
From daring to dodge the fate of the dupe.
You keep on deceiving yourself because
You must. Lying is the only way you'll
Ever keep trying, the only way you
Can sustain the instinctive trust to go
On living, despite always going bust
In everything you tried. When anything
In your life really counts, philosophy
Wisely dismounts and lets your instincts ride.
Whenever you would tell the truth you have
Always, always lied. As self-deceiver
Deceived, you receive your due. Yes. You are
A nomad in the desert of the true.

ix

Here's the news, little girls, little boys. You
Live out life with parables, with playthings,
With toys. And stories you tell yourself are
So much noise, for by now you've abandoned
The poise that lets you say in simplicity
Anything about anything. If you'd

Capture the rapture, you should, if you could,
Feel what you ought to feel. Then you'd become
As real as you know you should. You fumble
For revelation. You come up empty-
Handed, for nothing meets the test that you've
Demanded. Yes. You grasp for the hem of
Destinies too great to cling to. You punt.
Your spear now blunt is no longer fit to hunt.

X

You will always take time to coddle the
Frail homunculus in the bottle. But
Somewhere along the way, you lost the thrill
That you still have a self you could fulfill.
Yes. You fear that you'll be heir to a will
That can no longer will, a thrill that can
Never again enjoy itself as thrill.
The self, your lost self, is a metaphor,
A specialized tool, customized to hide
The variegated ways you play the fool.
Eden's back door won't open anymore.
Your karma takes a curious turn. It
Swerves. Then, suddenly you know, nirvana's
That nothingness for which you lack the nerves.

xi

Your death's the life you left behind, the joys
You endured but paid no mind. When death comes
To have its say, it says: you're always the
Spectator, but never the hero in
The play. The cycle keeps revealing the
Emptiness; the snake, swallowing its tail,
Leaves only a void to tell it once was
Hungry. That all is vanity is an
Inanity you should forget. Amid all
The lies of life, death's the first thing that must
Ring true. It says: You're the fool, fool enough
To imagine you're never through. Without
Death, you would never be admonished or
Astonished at the miracle of being you.

xii

There is life, there is death, and there is the
Bright cold day that betrays your breath. There's the
Chilling fog that precedes your speech. There's that
Mysterium tremendum coiled in you,
That the beggar in you cannot beseech.
A child sequestered, secluded, you dream
What you cannot shake. You take the first step
In the long trek of the self-deluded.
You become a character in your own
Fairy tale, asking yourself to reveal
More than you could tell. To this fairy tale
You would, but cannot, say farewell. Yes. You
Lurch toward hell when your deepest enchantment
Becomes what you are most afraid to tell.

xiii

You're the child of early self-hate and late
Lament, of the love that could never have
Meant what you hoped it meant. Thus, you hide your
Torment. You blur your longing. You dull your
Zeal, until you only dream about what
You're no longer allowed to feel. You're one
Without category, whose shallowness
Conceals your age's allegory. Yes.
Every consolation is a boast that
Somehow, some day, you'll get what you want the
Most. Your scattered self will gather itself
In ecstasy. You'll be ripped from home and
Returned to it. The moment you lose your
Soul is your last best chance to renew it.

xiv

You were there on the scene at the heist of
The latest Zeitgeist, the day the scandal
Broke, the day everyone discovered that
Every lasting value on every shelf
Was fraudulent, mispriced. All the words you
Want to use are dead, the relics of the

Already said that have already lied and
Died in someone else's head. These words, though
Dead, you used to live the life you led. They
Got you through it. Now you welcome death, for
You despise the life that led you to it.
Long after life, after you've abandoned
Any plan, life's blind angel asks if you're
A man who's just ... or just ... one lonely man.

XV

Society most maligns the man with
No designs. Those who lack all motive can
Never be reduced to the worst thing that
Can be said about them. Yet those who want
Most to be alive can still be seduced
By what remains dead about them. You were
Childish, mature, simple, complex, one who
Avows undying loyalty, and then
Defects. Your deepest doubt voids the value
Of all your favorite words. Then there follows
That disgust with your self-trust, with all those
Unattainables, with what haunts and taunts,
With the presence of unremainables.
It is a law: the best in you is awe.

xvi

By violating every norm, you prove
That the greatest violence is to conform,
To feel the cold, disconsolate death in
The very heart of your own life and then
To pretend that your frigid life's still warm.
You lived like a manikin, empty, vain,
With little to want, with nothing to gain.
You sought to climb inside your manikin
Skin and take a stand, yet there's nothing left
In you to stand that you could stand, except
Cruelty to yourself, and that cruelty is
How you ask yourself to meet your one true
Task. The very last thing you want to do,
That's what your cruelest task will ask of you.

xvii

Your art's an armor, your poetry, a
Pledge of innocence on the edge between
What's true and the innermost heart of you.
The way you live your life could not compare
With your cherished apothegms of despair.
Yet each axiom of art you'll anoint
With another exclamation point. Yes.
Art is more life-like than life, and life more
Art-like than art. Such is the destiny
Of the human heart whose most desperate part
Plays art like life, and life like art, an art
That should neither resent nor represent
Life, but, remaining resolute, offer
A prayer of consent to the absolute.

xviii

Something terrible's about to happen,
And you – in the heart of it – are part of
It. Though you come from where you'd go, you know
In your heart you've never really been there
Though. Thus, you sniff the concept; you touch the
Whisper; you taste the vision; your words grow
Crisper as you utter them in absent-
Minded praise. On the verge of revelation,
You stand ready to anoint what you fear
Will disappoint, what will deepen, what will
Darken your desperation, and then amaze.
You stand without shadow. You stand at noon.
Eternity is about to happen.
Whatever will happen will happen soon.

IV. SHOW HIM HOW

After experience had taught me that all the things which regularly occur in ordinary life are empty and futile, ... I resolved at last to try to find out whether there was anything which could be the true good, capable of communicating itself, and which could affect the mind, all others being rejected – whether there was something which, once found and acquired, would continuously give the greatest joy to eternity.

– Spinoza, *On the Improvement of the Understanding* –

But notwithstanding, we feel and know by experience that we are eternal.
 – Spinoza, *The Ethics, Part V. Proposition XXIII. Scholium.* –

i

The universe is large and you're so small:
How's it possible you matter at all?
But largeness itself, minus you, never
Begins to matter, if no one's there to
Unsettle its silences with chatter.
You've always been taunted by the cost of
What you wanted, yet all that's unwanted
Costs something too. Thus, it seems that the cost
Of the universe is the presence of
You, a condition vexing the sanity
Of the sane. Yes. Great poetry is what
You might have said if you were not inane.
You verge on the border of psychosis.
Your diagnosis is self-hypnosis.

ii

If God's uncertain, futility pulls
Down the curtain on all that is. In the
Body alone, you thought you'd find a home
For the human. But the true life for you,
The life of mind, remains blind to what it
Wants but cannot find. Nothing, not you, not
God, not the universe can be other
Than it is. That you are at all makes you
Essential. Yet you're just one player on
The stage of metaphysical showbiz,
Just one pretender to the splendor of
The true with the dodgy potential to
Be you. Thus, you learn to love what you love
The most ... to expel the ghost ... of despair.

iii

From faith, from tribe, from tradition, you stood
Apart. Eternal thorn in the flesh of
Your ancestry, you wormed your way into
The blood of the universe. And through the
Circulation of its lymph and logic,
You reached, or so you thought, its beating heart.
In you, your reason was never purer,
Never surer of its noble art. And,
Yes, you courted rejection. You welcomed
Banishment. You fell in love with exile.
Alas, not one last withering whit did
You care that whatever there is that's there,
That whatever's there, toward which you'd dare to
Grin, is most of all akin to bear shit.

iv

You wait with the cockeyed visage of a
Clown, as if, not you, but eternity
Itself has broken down. Thus, you wanted
A theory, a reliable lens, to
Focus on the consequences of your
Sins. The frozen empire within, that is
You, the target of persistent snowfall,
Cannot ignore its nothingness without
Reaping its due and giving up its all.
You can never quite disguise your descent
From an all-too-human bad intent. Thus,
You dream of a life remote from how it's
Spent. Yes. Towards your dream of untroubled self-
Esteem, that is where your innocence went.

v

To be you is the essence of being
You. That there's pollution, that there's taboo,
Means you could only be you. You become
What you are without consent, but freedom
Makes you conspire with what life, without your
Asking, has handed you, what life, when it

Stopped masking the truth, demanded that you
Do. Death's face awakens those who'd evade
It. It threatens those who'd succeed with the
Lie, those who've never quite made it to the
Truth. You sing your song with eternity's
Breath. But your music means nothing if it
Can't redeem the time, if it cannot make
A molehill out of the mountain of death.

vi

Dread names the agony, the tension. You
Become what you are, yet you would, if you
Could, escape it. Yet your reluctance, your
Acceptance, will seize your future and shape it
Into what you never wanted to be.
You would, if you could, limit your sin to
Only one part of yourself, but your heart
Which is the part that does the sinning, is
A part too much a part of all you are
To forestall mistakes of re-beginning.
Yes, the self you're forsaking keeps making
You and remaking what you are. In the
End, you'll be tempted to exalt what you
Again and again become by default.

vii

You're handed a life. Then, you pursue it.
Only the fact that you are you can get
You through it. And yet, why be so attached
To yourself? There is no reason; there is
Only the fact that self-denial, for
You, is treason. Thus, your unshakeable
Commitment is to yourself. You're defined by
What you want, and you want to be and to
Continue to be … in your eternity.
Salvation only serves when it unnerves
The wisdom of the self. Being you is
Paradox: Even when you abandon
The self and no longer bless it. Then, you
Nonetheless confess the self: you stress it.

viii

The truth for you shows itself, knows itself,
Proves itself with implacable certainty.
Ideas, my dear, that are clear and certain,
For you, pull down the curtain on fear and
Falsehood. For you, the skeptic is not a
Doubter but a fool. This would-be finder-
Outer still belongs in nursery school. Yet
You undervalue the plague of being
Vague, how self-doubt can render the clear and
Distinct extinct. With unintended tact,
You betray how value transforms the essence
Of a fact. If all your definitions
Are taken as exact, then value too
Must be as necessary as a fact.

ix

You are what you strive to be, striving and
Conniving. This is the remorseless law
Of your genius for surviving. And yes.
Eternity happens when you take time to
Be you. Benedictus becomes Baruch,
Baruch Benedictus. Self-identity
(Becoming you) is that virtue or that
Vice for which eternity alone can
Convict us. To be finite means that you,
Try as hard as you might, never quite get
Anything right. The universe is God
Through and through. Yet, no one else can do for
You what you alone can do. There's no more
Pressing fact than the fact that you are you.

x

Above all else you were sure to become a
Clandestine saboteur. You subvert the
Common way of perceiving the common
Day. You believed in the embodied God.
Ruah, nashamah and nefesh, along
With the scriptures, point to the flesh that is

His world and the world that is his flesh. The
Salvation which by most is neglected
Lies on that path you alone detected.
Whatever happens, happens because it
Must. There's no greater cause in which to put
Your trust. There's but one substance, solitary
And real. And you can only know it well
When you are in command of what you feel.

xi

There's only one individual, and
It's not you. Yet throughout all that is, God
Resonates as he impersonates you
And all your equally lonely others.
Counterfeit desire for happiness cheats
You of it. You must learn to live with God's
Lack of love for you. You must learn to love
It. The individual you assume you
Are is miraculous misconception.
Conatus, for you, names your desire to cheat,
But offers no receipt for self-deceit.
No. There is, for you, no person first and
Last. Thus, if you would ever become the
You you are, you had better do it fast.

xii

Whatever there is, is God through and through.
Such is the nature of the atom, the
Apple, the dove, the cratered moon, and you.
At the pith of every concept is a
Myth, a visual of the receding
Residual of the fugitive you
Try to grasp but cannot hold. The mystic,
Not you, glorifies this elusiveness,
This emptiness, this poverty and pretends
It's gold. The mystic leaves you in the cold
With nothing to believe in, nothing to
Grasp, nothing to hold. The same is never
The same as you thought it was. Whatever
The same embraces, the other undoes.

xiii

Your substance, your truth, had a standard all
Its own, which let you know what it's like to
Be absolutely certain and alone.
Oh, yes. The body, more than the soul, wants
Eternity. It needs it. In every
Omen, in every portent, it reads it.
And in every experience, dull
Or extreme, it bleeds it, in the name of
Your suffering. The eternity of
The transitory feeds on what it bleeds
In ravishing lust for lasting glory.
You would forsake every lonely other,
To know joy that knows no other story.
But there is no joy without another.

xiv

By reason, you reach what reason cannot
Beseech. The prophet can see what he can't
Imagine, what he does not know. But for you,
Knowing needs no proof. You can't imagine
Your God, but you could think it. All else is
Satire, a malevolent spoof of the
Really real, as if God were a phantom,
And you could wink it out of existence.
To imagine is to delimit, to
Seize the light of divinity and to
Dim it. You'd know rather than imagine.
And yet, without your knowing, perhaps you
Imagined what you know. Thus, your logic's
Brightest day gets buried in scurrying snow.

xv

You must not wait but demand of knowledge
The demandable for the world you know is
Utterly understandable. Gnostics
Keep practicing puzzling acrostics of
Being, chasing the truth, forgetting the
Good they're always fleeing. There's no alphabet

That would let their bet be a wager they
Cannot regret. The winds of doctrine are
Too brisk to take that risk. For you, your truth's
Too true to be good, but that the good is
Never understood makes it no less good.
For belief in grief, there's always room. A
Trace of what doubt would sweep away always
Swings back again on the straw of its broom.

xvi

Realist or nihilist, you enter
The gates of nowhere, the mind, in order
There to feel your striving and to find what
Cannot be found now here. There you'll seek an
Adequate idea to mollify your fear.
The placeless place, nowhere, is the haven
You seek, where you find the eternity
Of your mind, an eternity that is
Nowhere and nowhen. You will become and
Welcome the oblivion that conjures
A joy you teach but never reach. Yes. Your
History of eternity, your striving
And conniving, is the promise you make
That must forsake the joy of surviving.

xvii

Eternity is the power that deepens time,
That makes the otherwise vapid rhyme with
What's most important, what's most discordant.
Every time you tell the truth you lie a
Little. Every time you take a step you
Die a little. It's natural to be led
By a desire that's blind. It's natural for
The mind to will the truth it seeks to find.
You find a way to revere what you fear.
And this reverence you will hold most dear.
You are that urge to make now here nowhere
And nowhere now here. Yes. You'd be a piece
Of the whole damn schmear you revere but fear.
Your peace is knowing you're a piece of God.

xviii

For you, it was not the least bit odd to
Start not with creatures, not with matter, but
With eternity in motion, with God.
There is for eternity no first, no
Last, only a relentless thirst that can
Never be recast as vacuous time.
If you'd be wise, you shrewdly surmise, then
You'd see yourself through eternity's eyes.
Whatever is most dear: that is what you
Want most to persevere. Your will to live,
To preserve yourself, is evidence of
Your eternity. Yes. Every moment's
Fleeting stretch is time meeting and greeting
God's lasting sketch of your eternity.

xix

In the mind of God, you are as you are,
An immortal scar of what you are that
Lasts forever. As one never-ending
Tone, that's to know yourself as you are in
Spirit, in flesh, in bone. Your history's a
Timeless series, minus the myths, minus
The fables, minus the theories, minus
All the ironies that turn the tables.
Ask not of this moment: *forever stay.*
Ask not of this moment: *return again*
This very day. Ask this moment, you care
Not how, to steepen and to deepen this
Moment now, to steepen and to deepen
This moment now, nowhere, and forever.

xx

You thought through the alpha and omega
Of nature to ferret out its laws, with
Logic as your sacrament and love as
Your never quite forgotten cause. The love
Of God's a one-way street. You must love with
No promise that God could return the love

For which you yearn. But like a glutton, you
Glut on God, and your intoxication,
Forecasting hangover, never lets you
Pause to find in yourself this final cause:
Yes. You're how God sends a reminder to
Himself. He cannot, you say, love you here
And now. But in the eternity of
This moment, your task is to show him how.

V. ONE OUNCE OF ONCE
Tell me what you want and I'll tell you who you are.
  – Anton Chekhov, "A Boring Story" –

Masha: *Still, is there a meaning?*
Tuzenbach*: A meaning ... Now the snow is falling. What meaning?* [Pause]
  – Anton Chekhov, *The Three Sisters* –

The only thing that dies in a man is what is subject to the five senses. Everything that lies beyond those senses – and is most likely immense, unimaginable, sublime – continues to exist.
  – Anton Chekhov, *Notebooks* –

i

In your vanity, you think of yourself
As clever, as if your storied life could
Make of you a prophecy forever.
What you can't have now you might have had, but
Don't. And yes, you repeat the pattern of
Getting what you don't want. You're in a bad
Way on a very bad day, and you want
To get away in the worst possible
Way. In you, the demon destroyer keeps
Scrounging in vain for a new employer.
The life you want, but cannot have, would be
Even better, if you could be a more
Strenuous forgetter of the one you
Have. You're a stranger to the life you want.

ii

You would, if you could, be Hamlet, without
His sullen soliloquies. But you'd have
No defense against being that intense.
You disguise the embarrassing absence
Of a cause in your life for trauma, by
Living out this fraud of your life, as if
It were a drama, a story worthy
Of having been experienced and told.
But on that topic you're never quite sold.
You've reached what's impossible when you no
Longer recognize the impossible
When you see it. When you arrive now here,
You know it's impossible to see the
Impossible, you can only be it.

iii

Your life, you always thought, was a rough draft
Of what you'd finish later, as if your
Dream of yourself was more real, more complete,
Than this moment of solace and deceit
When you try to lord it over worries
And woes you wrestle with but can't defeat.
In despair, in simulated bliss, you'll
Insist on seeing what doesn't exist.
Boredom is how you see yourself when you
See yourself as you really are, a bit
Of lukewarm ash dropped haphazardly on
A floor it lacks the heat to char. Any
Other way of seeing is looking and
Talking past your constant state of being.

iv

Tarara-boom-de-ay. Yes. Today's your
Washing day. And you'll do this every day.
Today is every day. Years of laundry
And of yet another baby makes you
Think that – yes, just maybe – you should have been,
Should have become someone or something else.

Your heart aches for what you could plainly see
But overlook. Yes, in the banal, you
Overlook all that matters as if what
Matters, because it is banal, matters
Not at all. The hour's too late to divide
Humanity into small and great. There
Are only the small, some of whom are just
A wee bit tall, and those who are merely small.

v

Every day in every way you're alarmed
By the dullness of the common day. Yes.
You would, if you could, make yourself master
Of the rolling, runaway disaster
That you are not so pleased to call your life.
There's a horror in the ordinary
That is never dispelled by becoming
Grand. There is a boredom in being you
That is never quelled by the demand to
Overcome the despair of being bland.
To unlock the grand piano of your
Heart. That is the art of doing your part.
Each honest man winces; he does his best
And worst and faces the consequences.

vi

Ninety-nine percent of human evil
Springs from boredom. And yes, all the other
Varieties of murder, of whoredom,
Sooner or later lead back to boredom.
You shilly. You shally. You dream. You scheme.
You pretend to be more than you are, that
You really are what you try so hard to
Be ... or seem. Thus, to thrive, you connive to
Persuade yourself that through the tedium
Of suffering you still survive, that, no, you're
Not really dead at all, but still alive.
To everyone's surprise, including your
Own, you find yourself desperately alone,
Yet madly in love with living badly.

vii

You most sought a life brilliant, beautiful,
Daring, caring, brave and full, but when you
Examined your means to this end, you knew
That what you sought was just plain bull. Oh, yes.
The blood you have is far too thin ever
To have sustained the drama of what you
Might have been. There is no way to make this
Insight stay. What you need is a hammer
Striking each hour to disturb the glamor
Of the life you might have led but didn't,
As if to make all your eloquence an
Embittered stammer. That's how it sounds when
The grand piano only gets played to
The groaning sound of sausage being made.

viii

Your fear of everything found its sole
Comfort in nothing. Thus, you do what you
Do and then don't do what you don't out of
Boredom, out of emptiness, out of want
That can only be nourished by the pain
Of the remorselessly vain and mundane.
Your ecstasy and inspiration will
Be diagnosed and dosed with pain's bitter
Medicine. To find the cure, you drink of
Wormwood until you're sure there's no joy, no
Ecstasy, no way you'd wring fear from rags
Of the mediocre to render you
Stylishly austere. Now, you no longer
Care: Each somewhere that goes nowhere goes there.

ix

Your misery is dull, null, another
Name for nothingness, for suffocating
Despair, that tightens its grip as you gasp
For air. As you keep gasping, your voice keeps
Rasping its muted song. Everything you've
Done with your life is wrong. And yes, even

For you, the tragedy must stop somewhere,
So you declare: the despair stops there. It
Stops right here, at the point where you pretend
To overcome your fear. That's comedy
As you declare it. All your plays are meant
To share it. You saw how tears and laughter,
Like sister and brother, for each must burn,
But are bound by law to spurn, each other.

X

You keep paving the way for more paving,
As if the future, much more so than the
Present, will be something worth saving. In
The future, you'll discover at last that
The only use of the future is to
Remember the past. Utility is
The self-deception of futility;
It's the false belief that a function will
Let you live your life without compunction.
There was, in you, a grand piano that
Was waiting to be played. You played it. There
Was a point about pointlessness that was
Waiting to be made. You made it. There was
Joy that made you afraid. You evade it.

xi

You made a shocking discovery that the
Forward thrust of your life leaves utterly
Overturned everything you thought you learned.
You wanted truth but then you settled for
Exalting illusion. Each gooseberry
Gives up its goodness grudgingly. Truth, as
It unravels, betrays its clarity
Smudgingly. All that once was so clear, so
Distinct, is now extinct. No. There is no
Discernible basis to believe, though
Still you're driven to do it. There's nothing
Of value over which to grieve, and yet
You crave consolation, as if you could
Trust your lust for life to get you through it.

xii

Shallow people have the deepest needs. Yes.
Their sheer complacency hides their hunger,
And then disguises their bottomless greeds.
If you could know what you want and get it,
You would remember what you are and not
Forget it. But you do. Even when you
Get what you think you want, you regret it.
For you, life is a perpetual quiz.
Its essay question is: Do you know what
Suffering is? Even more, do you know what
Suffering's for? God answers not with what you
Want but with what you need. You're tempted to
Predict God's answer, but don't. As God sees
It, what you need is never what you want.

xiii

For you, details accumulate into
A mood that cries: *alack, alack*. Yes. The
Time of your life keeps happening behind
Your back. You never quite notice what you're
Like, save for those moments when you forget
Not merely your survivor's guile, but your
Obsession for a life you deem worthwhile.
The habit of craven self-importance
Feigns and falsifies your life. Yet you'll keep
Dreaming of going elsewhere though, but to
The Cossacks, to Moscow, you'll never go.
Struggling to connive, you strive to be glib.
Thrown out on the stage to live, you barely
Pause before you ad lib another fib.

xiv

You need to lie. To speak it, you try. You
Succeed. You satisfy your need. And your
Soul – that would be beautiful when it's not –
  ... is full of guile. You can fool all the fools
For quite a while, but in your heart you're sure
You're as vile as the common crocodile.

History begins with the fretter who fears
Someone's better. Like everyone, you'd like
To become someone else, even if it's
Only yourself made better. That's how time
Gets started, keeps moving, how every now
Scorns itself and wants to keep proving to
Itself it's another now. Time is the
Way eternity tells each moment how.

XV

Each would-be sigma yields to enigma,
An explanation that becomes a self-
Deviating sum that never adds up.
To dream of your eternity, that's the
Problem, you see. You try to be what you
Cannot be, and you try to see what you
Cannot see. Yes. You would make of now here
Nowhere and nowhere now here. And yes. This,
And anything else you'd do, you'd do to
Justify yourself and disguise your fear.
You would, if you could, reduce everyone's
Lies to just one size. Thank God. There's mercy
In the diversity of our lies. Yes.
It's wise that no one's lies are the same size.

xvi

In your drabbest interior, there still
Survives the myth that you're superior.
And yet, you never know how to spend your
Time, when you've been told that your life and all
You claim to love are being bought and sold.
In your solitude, you would if you could,
Nitpick the pattern of if-onliness
To find the picnic in the panic of
Your loneliness. You would ex post facto
Trim your dog-eared life with an x-acto.
And yes, you, who imagined so many
Characters, have lived the lives of others,
But not your own. You have, you might say, lived
A crowded life, but lived it all alone.

xvii

You exposed the plain to the main of light,
To the common day. That was your genius.
Not winged, dinged, cornered, entitled, you had
To be what you were ... unbridled. For you,
There'd be no wing in the museum, no
Corner in the school, no title other
Than that of a very gifted fool. You
Were eternity's no-see-um. No one
Noticed what you're doing till your bite had
Left its sting, its itch, its mark. While others
Merely suppose, you're the one who knows a
Rose is still a rose, even in the dark.
And you keep telling it straight to the end,
That truth, like you, may break but cannot bend.

xviii

Miracles of self-deception promise
What they never deliver, yet each is
An undeniable giver of God's
Cruel grace. Without eternity, no time's
Worth living. Nothing's important enough
To do. No gift's worth giving. Nothing's as
True as two time two. Your joy's an orchard
Lost till just before it's about to go,
Till just before it dies with the lies that
It lives in eternity, till just before
You betray the filth below by peeling
Back the snow. And yet, if the promisers,
Who promise to love you, should ever come
To take your life, then you should let it go.

xix

Just beyond thought and extension, beyond
Body and mind, there's an infinity
Of senses that you never know, never
Find, in this life you lead that's lame and blind.
When you die, you lose not all your senses
But only five. All your other senses

Remain alive. Despite incomprehension,
What's there is there in its strange dimension.
Life is there, moving and proving itself,
Even as the best of it by you is
Undetected. With infinite mercy,
Your life, unnoticed, becomes perfected.
Your life is given once and only once.
But just one ounce of once is everything.

VI. THE UNSUREST TOURIST

It is necessary to say and to think What Is is, for it is possible for it to be, but it is not possible for nothing to be. ... To be and to mean are the same. ... One way is left to speak of, namely, that What Is is. Along this way are many signs: that What Is is unborn and undying, unique, unmoved, complete; it never was nor will be, since it is now, altogether one, continuing.
– Parmenides, *On Nature* –

i

You were among the first to look beyond
Facts and follow their troubled tracks toward truth.
Everything depends on the meaning of
What is is. To be is to be something,
Anything, and to be something is to
Be what you are forever. Anything
That is ... cannot *not be*. That is your bold
Assertion of eternity. First and
Last, you know what is, is. All else drinks in
The sham pain of a life that's lost its fizz.
Once you say what is, you can no longer
Say what was or will be. What is, is what
It is. Because it is, it can never
Not be. Hence you conclude: eternity.

ii

From clutches of deceit, your precursors
Retrieve these hidden truths: *All is water;*
All is fire; all is air; all is number;
All is infinite, and all is in all,
In all you call the lumber of what is.

For you, all's true, all's one, all is here and
Nowhere else, and all that can be done is
Already done because nothing could ever
Become more than what it is already.
Light and night in the cosmic mixing bowl
Are stirred until everything that there is
Begins to resemble what you preferred.
No logic can excuse logic from its
Offense against the claims of common sense.

iii

You are you. You're not only what you are,
But it's impossible for you to be
Or do anything other than be you.
It's impossible for you not to be.
You're the evidence for eternity.
All that is, is one, which neither begins
Nor ends nor moves, but only proves again
And again that the one is one is one ...
Forever. And, yes, the one is unique,
Complete, replete, full of all that could fill
It or will it. This tautology that's
Trivial, inane, is your link with the
Will to remain the same, with your desire
To plumb the deepening of being you.

iv

Being asks the questions; then becoming
Replies with what never satisfies, but
With what time and time again still tries to
Tell the truth while telling no lies. For you,
Learning the lies is the key to wisdom.
For those who presume to be wise, being
And becoming can never measure the
Size of what you are, as if to grasp the
Large or small, as if to fetch or catch the
Roundness of a ball, that dreadful sphere, your
Image of the vividly unclear that
Most of all mirrors the universe that
Mirrors you. Yes. The only way there's room

For you is for you to be all there is.

V

No now can ever leap from now to now,
For the now only knows how to be what
It is and stay there now forever. If
What's just been said is true, there's no one so
Clever who could tell you how you'd ever
Have time to say what's just been said just now,
Not ever. If you're right about the claims
You make, you couldn't make them. If you're sure
About promises you make, you couldn't
Break them. Yet you do. This paradox is
The perplexity that makes you you. Thus,
Understanding's nothing. Your dilemma's
Standing under what's not understood. You'll
Never think or mean what you thought you could.

vi

You fathered a logic that refuted
Itself at birth, for nothing could ever
Be born, nothing could ever be new on
The face of earth. In your life and times, it
Was too early and perhaps too late for
Consciousness to clash, as it did, with its
Paradoxical fate. You begin to
Think against what you feel and feel against
What you think. Logic, just getting started,
Stared itself down in the mirror but did
Not blink. In your thought, there was no time to
Think, no thought that could be thought. Yet, even
For you, the impossibility that
Anything could be new was something new.

vii

You cannot fathom the futility
Of being the one that's immutable,
Immovable and unimprovable,
Of being the one and only one that

You could call your own, of being caught in
The thrall of the roundness of it all, caught
There in the careless despair of going
Nowhere, unmoving, indivisible,
Everlasting and alone. If so, you'll
Never summon the will to believe what
You know. You'll never feel that you're real. You'll
Defer to illusions you prefer. And
The history, you claim can never start, must
Begin with your unoriginal heart.

viii

You sought the thought that would not wander. You
Sought beyond the beyond and found that there's
Nothing beyonder. There's nothing beyond
The sphere of thought that you could ponder. You
Were, so you thought, the last line of defense
Against the nonsense of common sense. Thus,
For you, nothing means anything unless
There is one, but the one and only one,
You insist must exist, is what all of
Your experience must resist. All those
Who resist the one are those, you insist,
Who know nothing, as if nothing's something
Someone could know, as if thought that wanders
Leads you only where no one wants to go.

ix

You've already lost five of your senses
When you begin to question the logic
Of tenses. Do you need eternity? Do
You even want it? Would you rather keep
Turning into someone or something else?
Would you rather not just endure the wear
And tear of change, but brazenly flaunt it?
The one you never are and cannot be,
The promise you would keep but cannot keep,
You nonetheless still covet. And, yes, the
Time you think you never have, you need, not
To grasp eternity, but to love it.

Because you're you, you're never true. You're the
Promise you want to keep, but never do.

x

Whatever is, is and can never not
Be. On the face of eternity, there
Would be an indelible blot, if you
Could say there could be a time, any time,
When you could say *it is,* is ever, *not*.
What is, is now, nowhere and forever.
There is no nowhere. There is not even
Any right to say *no*. There is no *no*,
For in your heart, all says *yes* to what must
Stay what it is forever, and never go.
When 'now' becomes now, it no longer quotes
Itself, no longer votes itself into
Office. It remains unelected. All
That resembles change goes undetected.

xi

The truth your goddess tells is so awry
It seems less like truth and more like a lie.
And when she tells her lies, the seeming and
Teeming of frauds seem more like truth than truth.
The one is the same. And the same is one
And the same forever. Any way you
See it, it remains the same forever.
There never was, never is, never will
Be any other. There never was any
Was. There never will be any *will be*.
There wasn't one today. There's only now,
You say. What's real can't be seen, but only
Deduced, as if you mastered a logic
That confuses the victim it seduced.

xii

You answer night with light to know what *must*
Be must be like. *Must be* must be much like
You, who are more than a bit confused about

Who you are and what you ought to do. There's
No unshaken heart, untrembling. There's no
Certitude sans dissembling. You're not a
Confident traveler, but the unsurest
Tourist of here and now. Yes. You want to
Go home and stay there forever, but all
Your experience never tells you how.
It's the uncertainty of what you think
You want that keeps everything humming the
Indefatigable, incompatible
Marriage of your being and becoming.

xiii

Your heart was pure enough, sure enough, to
Will one thing, the one and only one, the
Now that can only be now, because to
Be other than now: that's just something now
Never does because it never knows how.
You bring with you your spirited lust for
Something you could trust, and this passion you
Could never fashion into something real.
Thus, your living self ironically winks
At the sphinx it thinks but cannot feel. When
The loneliness of one stares back at you,
And your equally lonely others, it
Blinks. It says: *You're the ones who merely live.
I am the one who is, who means, who thinks.*

xiv

Eternity's your strong suit; some scholars
Say you invented it. Prophecy says
Yours was the wrong fruit, not good, and that you
Prevented it from being understood.
You begin to think what eternity
Might be. But the concept you invented
You prevented from being understood,
As if only the intelligible
Could ever prove itself eligible
For eternity, as if eternity
Could only be something that's understood.

Yes. Only now do you feel the thrill that
Eternity moves, even when it's still.
Understand this now, or you never will.

VII. THE BENT STICK

Eternity is a child at play, moving pieces in a game. ... Dogs bark at those they do not recognize. ... It is hard to fight your heart's desire. Whatever you wish to get, you purchase at the cost of soul. ... Awaiting you when you die are things you neither expect nor imagine. ... Wisdom knows what steers all things through all things. ... So deep is the soul, you could never find its depth, even if you travel every road. ... You step and do not step into the same river; you are and are not. ... Changing, it rests. ... The way up and the way down are one and the same.
– Heraclitus –

i

With Heraclitus, there's no symphony
Of opinion to unite us. There is
No vice you could splice into virtue to
Reconcile us all to all that strives to
Spite us. There's no thread that lets us enter
Your maze and leads us through to you. History
Hands you down as Humpty-Dumpty king of
The jagged shard, a bit of wit too hard to
Reconstruct or counterfeit. Each fragment
Of you hints at harmonies you suspect
It should reflect but that you can't detect.
So, this Heraclitus will not be mine,
Not theirs, but yours. Consider him just one
More stop in the history of all your tours.

ii

You're the first Greek, not so meek, that he could
Not point to soul, to depths in you deeper
Than you know or speak. For the soul, there's no
Limit, nothing that can dampen it or
Dim it. The deeper you go, the deeper
It gets. The farther you go, the more it
Remembers, and the more it forgets. Where

You dive, there soul will be. No matter how
Deep you dive, there's no depth where the soul does
Not still gasp to stay alive. Your depth has
Something you want to know, something to speak.
But the truth you seek dwells too deep. To get
There, you must dive so deep that you perforce
Must surrender all you'd prefer to keep.

iii

You don't understand how your world is planned,
How it lays upon you its strange demand.
Those, who know not what you say already
Before you say it, are, you say, not ready
To hear it. Those, whose hubris is here to
Stay when they hear the truth, are too brazen
To fear it. No matter how much they boast
About how far they go, they never get
Near it. What's truth is so near it's what you
Fear to see or hear. Distractions are ways
The distracted keep going, keep staying.
Those sleepwalking, keep talking, keep squawking,
Keep saying nothing, keep balking rather
Than talking about something worth saying.

iv

You go in search of yourself. You come back
Empty-handed. You flinched as you followed
The promptings your heart demanded. You dodge
Who you are by becoming what you're not.
This is the story arc of your never-
Ending plot. It's impossible to deny
Your heart's desire. That's going too far. What
You want, you buy with the cost of what you
Are. Horizons within are beheld that
Can't be held, but they let you know that, no
Matter how far you go, it's too far to
Go, as if the self you lost, that's hidden,
 ... is forbidden for you to know. Yet still
You try in vain to know what you can't know.

v

Truth comes to the door of your heart and knocks,
Saying: there, in you, beyond this door, lies
The core of what you are, lies paradox.
Cosmos at its heart is contradiction.
Cosmos at core is never-ending war.
What you are, in the balance, is strife and
Only strife: that's the essence of your life.
Oh, yes. The way of paradox puts the
Impossible in a box and then says
Understand it. But the certainty you
Clamor for is too uncertain to demand
It. You're a lion. You're not a lion.
You are the lion's share of each. You are
The lesson only paradox can teach.

vi

Every day in almost every way you're
Oblivious to the light of common day.
When asleep, there's none to shake you, none to
Wake you, none to let you know it's snowing.
Yet in wakefulness, you try to catch what
You chase, to abandon what you gain, and
Then you chase, try to catch yourself, and then
Abandon it again. Unlike mounting
Snow, all about yourself you claim to know
Never accumulates, yet still it snows.
Self-deception thrives in the best and the
Bleakest weather. Your forecast will at last
Ordain your past. Thus, you become what you've
Long suspected, but never detected.

vii

Self-deceit's too bitter to be other
Than sweet. In the sunshine of the spotless
Mind, it is always already snowing.
The end is already beginning at
Beginning's end. The way you want to go
... is no way to get where you're going. You

Go the way of no way. But there's no way
To get where you want to go because you're
There already. That's why it starts to snow.
The wrong end and the right end bend, meet and
Blend together. It's best not to forget
Too quick the parable of the bent stick.
Truth is unforgetfulness, the talent to
Remember what's straight in crookedest timber.

viii

The whirligig's not that big. It's too small
To be the thing that steers it all. No one
Single eddy is ever ready to
Be the reason for all that happens. The
Crux of flux is the river that flows as
It stands still, that replaces what it loses,
That clarifies what confuses, that fills
What empties, that empties what fills, that stills
What moves, that moves what stills, that refutes all
That proves that it moves and never moves. No
Stubborn little eddy's ever ready
For the thrill of standing still. And yet, you
Search for something that steadies the eddies
And readies them all for eternity.

ix

Fire's first and last the cause of all that is.
Everything that is burns and burns as it
Turns into what it's not. And everything
That's not burns and burns as it turns into
What it is. What is, is never the same
As what it's not. But each is the path to
The other, and the other to each. That's
At the heart of all the lessons you teach.
You search not just for some single source, but
For the pattern of how everything must
Run its course. The way it lives is that it
Burns. The way it burns is that it lives, as
The ever-living fire that never stops
Giving what it takes and taking what it gives.

x

Consciousness happens. It illuminates
And conceals. With one hand, it gives. With the
Other, it steals. Each step, each gain, absorbs
The cost of what it's lost and the pain of
What it wants but can't attain. Again, in
Disdain, you search for what you might sustain.
Eternity flickers, it kindles, it
Gutters, as it comes and goes in starts and
Stutters, in its passage from now here to
Nowhere, from distinction to extinction,
From winter's coming in to summer's going
Out. That's what flickering's all about. It
Never sleeps. It keeps what never stays, and
Prays for the staying of what never keeps.

xi

Nothing could dissever the logic of
Forever from its passion to be what
It can be and what it must be in you.
Only the stable is ever able
To become unstable. Difference is born
Already dreaming of identity.
Through conflict all things come to be. The back-
Bent bow, the strain between what would stay and
What would go: this is the sum of what you
Know. This is your eternity. For you,
There is this clarity in coming to
Be that never breaks free of the burden
Of what it is to be. Now with nowhere
Thus contends in a war that never ends.

xii

When the dead go quick, and the quick go dead,
You're no longer sure of the path you took
And the life you led. You turn to yourself,
Learning all you learn. You long to belong,
Yes, to burn, not in the oblivion
Of the obvious, but in a promise

So deep it's impossible to keep. You
Make the promise you make to stay awake
To what you're able to forsake. The only
Point in living is knowing precisely
What's at stake. Nothing turns out the way you
Planned. Thus, you stand under what you fail to
Understand. Joy exacts a heavy price.
There is no cut rate tour of paradise.

xiii

Nothing changes. Everything changes. You
Saw how each moment estranges itself
From one another into another.
In the moment, no one lives. There's only
The eternity that always gives what
It takes and that takes what it gives. Now here's
Never now and here, but always a child
At play, always another not-yet-now,
That's never able to tell itself how
To go or stay, a would-be now that would,
If it could, be you, a now that's always
On the way from nowhere to nowhere, that's
Always lost in what its life has cost, lost
In the changing light of the common day.

VIII. THE UNMADE MAN

If then God is always in that good state that we sometimes are, this compels our wonder; and if in a better, this compels it yet more. And God is in a better state. And life also belongs to God; for the actuality of thought is life, and God is that actuality, and God's self-dependent actuality is life most good and eternal. We say, therefore, that God is a living being, eternal, most good, so that life and duration, continuous and eternal, belong to God; for this is God.

– Aristotle, *Metaphysics* –

This would seem, too, to be each man himself, since it is the authoritative and better part of him. It would seem strange, then, if he were to choose not the life of his self but that of something else.

– Aristotle, *Nicomachean Ethics* –

i

Your philosophy begins with wonder,
Which it quickly moves to abolish, as
It strives to cleanse and starts to polish the
Common day with reasons, with common sense.
Your thought made the rounds of all the common
Nouns: *change, cause, part and whole; matter, motion,
Goodness, god and soul.* But *substance* was your
Subject and your mainstay, your long and winding
Way through common sense to the light of the
Common day. What's human starts in human
Hearts when being touches Being, when your
Seeing starts to know what it's seeing in
All its works and days. You see what you see:
The sensible changes; the stubborn stays.

ii

If you could distill all the substance of
Aristotle in a bottle, it would
Be nothing that could coddle anyone
With doctrines of science. Alas, for you,
The life you are and the life you want is
The tragedy of a botched appliance.
You choose whatever you choose for the sake
Of happiness. But the happiness you
Choose you always confuse with something
Else. Your eternity's in motion; its
Essence is act; and its destiny is
Devotion to remorseless fact, a fact
Impervious to the most ambitious
Reaches of self-contradictory tact.

iii

On the edge of the abyss, you see in
Aristotle all the perfection you're
Doomed to miss. You're not so shrewd that you could
Easily manage your disquietude.
In this querulous age, there's a passion
For time, a veritable rage, that is

Always cool to eternity, for in
Eternity, a judgment is always
Implied. Eternity says: Oh, yes. You
Dreamt you lived your life, but you lived your life
As if you long ago had died. Time is
Eternity's child at play. Each moment,
Each step it takes, is a step in the dance
You dance in the light of the common day.

iv

To understand and care for the soul, you
Must invent it, if you're to prevent it
From being unhappy. Your soul's first home
Was the midriff. And ever since, your soul's
Only seen more so of the lower torso.
Yes. Your soul's the jelly in your belly
You mold into meaning. You're too many
Things to tell in one sentence. Alas, it's
Too late to make all your crookedness straight.
But you would, if you could, beat the odds by
Neutering the gods, by making what's obscene
Seem clean, as if only one thing was all
Any word could mean. But every word has
A crookedness that no one yet has heard.

v

Your autopsy of poetry as an
Art dissected its limbs and ripped out its
Heart. Yes. The name of the game is to make
Oedipus tame, as willy-nilly, as
Low, as the next man, as if drama that's
Too clear, too austere, can't mean all that a
Text can. But it can, and always does, mean
Not less, but more. That's what makes of meaning
Such a whore. To state the truth, the whole truth,
And nothing but the truth is to complete
Yourself. To be wise is to see through this
Guise of what you think is wise. No truth that's
Complete is quite that neat. Truth's promise is the
Promiscuity of ambiguity.

vi

Out of ritualistic ecstasy,
You invent the drama that continues
The trauma by different means. There's nothing
That's ever quite so sad as to insist
On the reality of a joy you've
Never had. Deprived of ecstasy, of
Pollution, of guilt, all that's brave, all that's
Noble must wilt on the poisoned tree of
Futility, which vies at odds with your
Disappointed gods. Dionysius
Continues to tell beautiful lies that
Truth denies. When tragedy is rendered
Mundane, the cure of which you seem so sure
 ... is no longer worth your tour through the pain.

vii

Your theory of ethics made tragedy
Unnecessary, undesirable.
But tragedy, a known convict, is still
That desperate, hungry man, who needs a job,
But remains unhireable. There's desire
That knows what it wants and gets it. There is
Desire that gets what it wants and regrets it.
There is desire that haunts what it wants but
That never gets it or forgets it. Through
Self-blunder, the mind in blindness stumbles
To its own ruin. Self-deceit reconceives
What it never retrieves from truth. Your gods
No longer make you do what you must do.
Your only source of agony is you.

viii

Your mind in blindness is at home with the
Riddle of self-deceit. You live in the
World but no longer see it. You'd become
What you are but can no longer be it.
You'd purge your guilt, but your middling truth no
Longer points to what might free it. Regret,

Despising its own reason for being,
Wreaks defeat from which it would, but cannot
Retreat. This makes your unlived life complete.
Through desire you become what you are. You
Move toward what moves you and makes you you. But
The tragic flaw, you do not know, is the
Source of error and the strange defender
Against the terror of your self-blindness.

ix

To be human you must be more. You must
Be more than human. To be that self that's
True for you, you must become and be that
Self that's more than you. As you aspire, you'll
Tire of the *no-longers* and the *no-not-
Yets*. You'll weary of the *always-wrongers*
And the lure of the safest bets. To grasp
The meaning of your life, you see the point
Of it as a story or joke, as if
You could get in the maw of your mind the
Meat of it and not choke. You feel how time
Must cut its rut in you, how it carves in the
Rough-hewn canyon of your soul its lasting
Scar. This is the essence of what you are.

x

Time's not motion, but its number. It takes
A soul to tell its tale, and that tale is
The history of your soul's devotion to
What it wants. There's a promise that dogs your
History. This is the covenant of the
Unmade man, the man who knows he'll never
Quite do all he knows he should and can. Thus,
In your deepest self, there are two of you,
And they contradict each other through and
Through. There is that self you are and there's that
Self you would, if you could, become. You're the
Promise you would, but can't fulfill. You live
This paradox of human will. And that's
What makes your universe hum ... with meaning.

xi

With no care at all for the trend of the
Season, to do good is to do the right thing
In the right place at the right time in the
Right way for the right reason. But the slide
Rule of ethics runs from both ends to the
Middle. That's where extremes collide and turn
All you'd think, and feel, and do into a
Riddle. Your solution to the riddle
Of the middle is to reach toward the mean
Between what's too much and too little. That
Vagueness, of course, is another riddle.
Oblivious to hazards of the vague,
You overstate truth's ability to
Divert us from all that threatens to pervert us.

xii

Any demon god you choose will abuse
You, if you let it confuse you with what
You choose in its ever-changing light. Thus,
Follow it, if you will, with all your might.
But it takes a proper organ of sight
To see what's godly and to see it right.
To begin to think clearly and to love
What you value and love it dearly, that's
To begin to imagine God as clearly
As God can be imagined. What gives your
First push and final shove, that's your fatal
Will toward what you love. Thus, to live toward God,
To love that toward which you move, that's what your
Love must prove every time you make your move.

xiii

In your universe, everything has its
Proper place except the universe. A
Place, to be in place, is always in the
Middle of something else. The universe
Contains every place, but is no place, for
It lacks the grace of being placed in the

Middle of somewhere. The universe is,
Therefore, nowhere. Every now and here is
A little piece of nowhere. The spirit
That's love, that's nowhere, touches now and here
And makes it move. What's not matter touches
Matter, makes it move, and proves it matters.
Matter yearns for what makes it move, for the
Unmoved mover and prover of your love.

xiv

In the beginning that's every moment,
All was loneliness, and God said: let there
Be touch. Each moment is a drop in the
Ocean of promise. Each moment is a
Start in the heart that begins what never
Ends. Each moment points to perfection, to
That party of the first part in the contract
Of the human heart, to that motion of
The heart in devotion to that toward which
Everything tends. The world is becoming
More and more like God, and God more and more
Like the world. Matter moves toward spirit, toward
Nowhere, toward nothing. You must come close to
Nothingness to be touched by anything.

xv

You'll get no diploma for coming to
Out of your coma. At the end of life,
You still won't act, as if you knew that there's
Never any end to your coming to.
Yes. You would, if you could, keep coming to
Yourself. But there's no prefabricated
Version of you idling on a shelf. But
There is, in the feeling of first sensation,
Delight. There's the sublime, misbegotten,
Oft-forgotten sense that you are you. You
Touch; therefore, you are. Your foremost touch, your
Primordial scar makes you what you are, the
Inner wit that knows throughout the universe
There is life, and that you are part of it.

xvi

In your eternity, there is your time
Entire. It is the now, nowhere and the
Forever of your desire. Yes. You are
What you could and could not be. You are what
You are and must become and be. You are
The beginning, middle and end of your
Story. You are what you would, if you could,
Become in all your imagined glory.
You are the life begun, the life undone
And done, and the life completed. In your
Eternity, there are no *no-longers*
And no *not-yets*. Eternity's the time
That never forgets what it remembers and
Always remembers what it regrets.

IX. WHAT HAPPINESS IS

I find in an old diary: "I think all happiness depends on the energy to assume the mask of some other life, on a re-birth as something not one's self, something created in a moment and perpetually renewed; in playing a game like that of a child where one loses the infinite pain of self-realisation, in a grotesque or solemn painted face put on that one may hide from the terror of judgment. Perhaps all the sins and energies of the world are but the world's flight from an infinite blinding beam."
   – William Butler Yeats, *Per Amica Silentia Lunae* –

What is the explanation of it all?
What does it look like to a learned man?
Nothing in nothings whirled, or when he will,
From nowhere into nowhere nothings run.
           – William Butler Yeats, Untitled Poem, 1938 –

But if these be right
What is joy?
           – William Butler Yeats, *Vacillation* –

i

You would, if you could, become what you're most

Unlike. You'd become yourself. And yet, your
Destiny's darling, the ecstasy of
Self-fulfillment, waits in vain for its long-
Looked-forward-to instillment. Fluttering
Behind your philosophic brow is the
Image of what's always nowhere and never
Now. You or your mask might choose to ask the
Daimon for a bit of news. Ask if he
Lied about being satisfied. If he
He replies, you'll know he lies. The eddy's
Never ready to accept any truth
To make it steady. Its nature's to spin.
The lust for stillness is its only sin.

ii

All your poems were the marginalia in
The history of your genitalia, and
Your life, the counter-life you might have led,
But didn't. But what else should you do with
This futility you fumble with and
Mumble over? What, pray tell, is the boon
Of history's longest, languid afternoon?
What is the use of a star, a song, a
Psalm, a four leaf clover? The climate changed
When your moral barometers fell, and
The hollow ring of the superhuman
Began to tell all who would listen that
The age of the overman is over.
Your voice no longer knows the word: *rejoice*.

iii

Futility likes to ask, *What then?,* then
Push the reset button, and start again.
Each age reverses its precursor as
It grows perverser than what it followed.
Yet still, the remnants of goodness in the
Will, will try but fail to fill the heart its
Age has hollowed. Now you're nourished only
By the bitter pills you've swallowed. Lost in
The labyrinths that you've built, you would, if you

Could, escape the encumbrance of your guilt.
You'd mock the mockers and be done. You'd knock
Them off their rockers just for fun. What's true
You know no longer. You try, but fail to
Die. What does not kill you makes you wronger.

iv

Ecstasy begins when you imagine
A vision that is vast, but then your cramped
Imagination can't last and barely
Starts to imagine joy before it's passed.
Thus, you keep on seeing Dionysus
Dying. No. Every ecstasy that was
Once religious is no longer quite as
Prestigious as your sexual plunder.
Your poetry always alludes to its
Unsuspected nudes. Each poem describes the
Act and fact of sex or the interludes
That justify why it didn't happen.
In a void devoid of idolatries,
You're lost, with only the void to worship.

v

In the old man, you buried the all-too-
Exuberant boy. You forget that there's
Anything in life you could still enjoy.
And yet, in your old age, there will still be
Lust. There will still be rage. And you'll never
Be old enough to act your age. Oh, yes.
You'll remember eternity as a
Boy, as always the embodiment of
Your favorite toy. But now each joy begins
To cloy as your lofty dreams go flat with
Your realization of: *been there, done that*.
The poet, middle-aged, learns the lesson
Of sex. When lust touches what it cannot
Love, then whatever it touches, it wrecks.

vi

You dream of a secret self that lives what
You left unlived, for therein lay your hope
That, amid what's missing, there's something in
You that still might cope. But, no, that self you
Dreamed, but never knew you knew, was never
You. It choked when you gave it too much rope
To hope it could not doubt, as if that girl
You dreamed you loved, the pearl the oyster spit
Out, was your self-born agony, just as
Real as toothache and just as fake as what
You yearned to feel but could not take, the girl
You did not kiss and yet still miss. At death,
The silence in heaven lets loose this shout:
Yes. That's what your life should have been about.

vii

You would, if you could, become someone who
Could never be less than what God might bless,
But your worm invisible is always
Divisible into segments of now's
Own nothingness. You were there on the scene,
Never quite saying what you tried to mean,
When chaos became deliberate, when
Anarchy rose like a fog of vapid
Prose from mouths of corrupt politicians.
Your morality's miserly reward
Teases, but disappoints, like the tawdry
Handkerchief of your erstwhile lord. No. There
   ... is no mystic rune, no single tune, that
Harmonizes the phases of the moon.

viii

Your hedge is to negotiate the edge
Of a miracle that never becomes
Empirical, to expect what never
Makes the scene, to point to the messiah
Or the monster that promises to mean
What you were never able to mean, as

If meaning were not the meandering
Slither of a serpent going yon and
Hither. When you're exhausted, when all your
Life is spent, your existence continues
To continue without your consent. The
Demon inside you again and again
Will hiss his taunt: *You must always want, but*
Never get, more and more of what you want.

ix

All that's distinct becomes extinct in that
Fluttering shade, in that stalking shadow
That haunted you before your world was made.
In dreaming back, you're reliving without
Forgiving what you've done. You meet what you
Hate most about yourself but cannot shun.
You are the eddy in the stream of a
Never-ending dream. And you are never
Ready to discover if the eddy
In the stream is ever ready for you.
Your afterlife will repeat the one you've
Had and will be just as beautiful and bad.
To want another life is to welcome
Sadness at the badness of the one you've had.

x

You want most to believe in ecstasy,
In the possibility of your joy.
When your daily round goes to ground, you'll no
Longer dream of finding yourself as the
You, you might still be, at *The Lost and Found.*
The worm turns. The daimon knows the worm gets
More and more morose in the belly of
A ghost. Nothing can eclipse your impulse
For the apocalypse. You wait too long,
If you wait for your body of fate to
Accumulate in the soul whose lust it
Clips. Despite your vaunted wisdom, you keep
Wanting, and ghosts, you thought you dispelled, keep
Haunting with temptations you thought you quelled.

xi

You're exhausted by dreams that could never
Seem any more than a dream. You are old
And sore. You'll never be again what you
Were before. You long for what you lost but
No longer want it. Even if you still
Had it, now you'd no longer flaunt it, yet
You would continue to taunt it and haunt
It with the ghost of your old ambition.
What you dreamed looks back at you, saying: the
World you dreamed is now also dreaming you.
Your life has a logic it must fulfill.
This world is a promise in your keeping.
Now, at last, you must do what you've dreamed you'd
Never do. Or you must go on sleeping.

xii

Stopped by the self that's your own stumbling block,
You go to the door and knock to share with
Others the shock, that behind the door, no
One's there, but the smoldering relics of
Burnt-out despair. Only the smoke of self-
Indulgence and sacrifice lets you know
That once upon a time someone like you
Was there. You cannot surpass yourself. You're
Stuck with what you are. On every path, you
Meet yourself, returning, still learning what
You never knew you knew and didn't know
You didn't know. Nowhere you go, for there's
Nowhere to go. Your punishment's living
Out the lies you're condemned to fantasize.

xiii

To cry peace when there is no peace: that's to
Babble in a bubble. Narcissism
Always wants more and more of itself in
A different guise. And such wantonness, that's
Trouble, that's falling in love with your own
Lies. Your world, like your life, was made by you,

Was made by one you could not trust. And this
Alien maker is the paradigm
Of you, the maker and forsaker of
Damnable lust. You could never live your
Life without remainder because like a
Bill of attainder some laws are meant for
You ... to learn. You must give all you can give
Before you earn the right of no return.

xiv

Each winding stair in every tower lacks
The power to attain and sustain its
Lasting desiderated hour of joy.
The ever-widening gyre accentuates
The emptiness of desire, that of which
Eternity must never tire for that
Defines it, and all that's not eternity
Thus mines it for meaning. All your sluggish
Anxieties revive and bristle. In
Your endless nightmare, the cradle's rocking,
While the heart, that never sleeps, keeps cocking
Its pistol. Each rough beast survives its scandal.
But what the world needs least is another
Dire absurdity it has to handle.

xv

Before lying began to decay, you
Had your say. But your skepticism's the
Vacillating kind. It provides no relief
From belief for the disenchanted mind.
Missing no beat, you go on believing
In the possibility of joy. The
Heart's fanatic never quite forgets what
It's like to be ecstatic. You would, if
You could, let the facts relax and yield to
Fantasy. But you see how your bootless
Quest for self-satisfaction was your most
Ridiculous caper, how you would, if
You could, remember just one ember of
Truth to scorch enigma's wrapping paper.

xvi

You envied your precursors. That's what got
You going. You kept returning to the
Starting point, and that point you anoint with
Meaning. The point's your birth or the birth of
Anyone with ambition for self-worth.
But down there on the square, they learn life's not
Quite fair. Self-worth's that strange money that got
Passed among the crowd in the middle of
Town, but the crowd soon learned that there's never
Enough self-worth to go around. To self-
Justify, you first require a lie. But
Even the noblest lie can't mummify
What you justify. Tomorrow and the
Days after will require another lie.

xvii

In your despair, the ancestral stair leads
Backward to the orchestra that's never
There, but that has been where it has always
Been: it's always been nowhere. Oh, yes. Once
Upon a time, everything was already
Well-said to everyone well-read and now
Long dead. Now, no one knows what anyone
... is saying, and every stab at saying
... is a species of mock prayer, the bad bet
That someone who understands is waiting
Somewhere patiently out there. Thus, give every
Author hell: that's the art of reading well.
With unexpected kindness, pull out his
Eyes and generalize about his blindness.

xviii

Truth's guile is that you're the truth for a while
And show it. But despite the substance in
Your style, there's no way you'll ever be the
Truth and know it. Yes. You would surpass the
Frosted image in the looking glass. But
It looks too much like you. There's no bottom,

And no top, to the winding stair of your
Despair. But, yes, your last best hope will take
You there. New Jerusalem's a gleaming
Shack, the ramshackle reverie of the
Dreaming back, the propaganda of a
Particular hack, and that hack is you.
Therefore, if you will, give all you can give.
Death's never luckier than the life you live.

xix

The mask of your eternity is that
Greenest tree you look into the heart of
And say to yourself: *Oh, my God. That's me.*
Your masks, your secret sharers, whose burden
On you took their toll, were the unwitting
Barers of your soul. Your wrestling match with
Mask and anti-mask, your thankless task that
Does not end, costs more than your unlived life
Could ever spend. Masking what they reveal,
Your false faces betray the true, the one
Who, still struggling against your will, is you,
The one you cannot face but feel, the one who
You're destined to become without appeal.
Your last best chance to prove your worth won't last.

xx

The deeper the truth, the blanker is the
Vision. Eternity is imageless.
It is what you are at core. It's always
Precisely what you lack an image for.
Eternity is desire too large for your
Senses to touch, but just the right size
Of all those lies that would become your crutch.
Each image is a mask for a question
It may answer but never ask, and your
Eternity is an answer whose strange
Task is to predestine one and only
One question. Yes. There's a mask that is false
And a mask that is true. Eternity's
Task is to ask: which of these two are you?

xxi

Joy knows its cost is pain, knows that you are
Always lost in all that you hope to gain.
The rotted symbols, the knotted myths, you
Consumed their husks and discarded their piths.
You would cast away fear, cast away greed,
Cast away every everlasting need
Of the common day. But every unborn
Joy strives to have its say. No. You cannot
Cast away the scar of what you are. You
Cannot cast away the light of common day.
In heaven, there's a perpetual dearth
Of anything remotely resembling
Self-worth. That's why, of course, every angel
Covets, without remorse, the troubled earth.

xxii

There is no reverie untroubled, no
Narcissism unbubbled by its own
Stupor. The spirit you seek is every
Moment before your eyes, but your muddled
Self can only see what it sees as lies.
Eternity's calling card's the moment
That hands you a task too hard to do. It
Says: If you would ever be yourself, then
This, first and last, is what you must do. You
Must capture terrible beauty and make
It stay, to make the gleam on the beetle's
Wing seem like the fleeting light of common
Day. This, the life unseen, that's what your life
Must mean when it means what it ought to mean.

xxiii

No biography of small events could
Ever mock your dreams or prevent your life
From being more important than it seems.
If you pry open the brain of a cat,
Nothing beneath his skull can tell him where
He's at. He might as well be nowhere. That

Explains his purr. Stretching his toes, he knows
He's eternity relaxing itself
Inside his fur. Thus, put a pox on the
Orthodox. Unknit the knitted brow of
Every sacred cow and set it free. Yes.
If time be gone, all you are is shown and
Known. And all eternity would merely
Be: me watching you and you watching me.

xxiv

You studied the neuralgias and extolled
The gain you get from undeliberate
Pain. You plunged into the infinite, and
Your feet got wet. But you never got where
You thought you're going, at least not yet. You
Reap the whirlwind that most resembles you. And
You are that whirlwind through and through. You
Reap what you deserve, and what you deserve
Most of all is the fate of being you.
Your happiness happens by surprise. It's
Barely recognized in its usual
Guise. It goes unmeant, unseen, unnoticed.
In fields of clover, you mumbled: *Gee Whiz*.
No. You'll never know what happiness is.

XXV

At the end of a long and storied life,
They'll ask you what it means. Falling short of
Their test, you'll offer this last best guess. That
You have what you don't desire, and desire
What you don't possess: that's perhaps what leads
To all the mess. This long, long life, so you
Tell, this is the pattern of how you fell,
And in life to come, you keep on falling.
All that's left of you is only what your
Agony could tell. And this agony,
The way you fell, this is joy's blind angel
Calling. No nightingale can tell you why
It sings its song on the golden bough. But
What it sings tonight you hope will tell you how.

X. THE STUBBORN MIRACLE

For my part, when I enter most intimately into what I call myself, I always stumble on some particular perception or other, of heat or cold, light or shade, love or hatred, pain or pleasure. I never catch myself at any time without a perception, and can never observe any thing but the perception.
 – David Hume, *A Treatise of Human Nature* –

So that upon the whole we may conclude that the Christian Religion not only was at first attended with miracles but even to this day cannot be believed by any reasonable person without them. Mere reason is not sufficient to convince us of its veracity; and whoever is moved by Faith to assent to it, is conscious of a continued miracle in his own person, which subverts all the principles of his understanding and gives him a determination to believe what is most contrary to custom and experience.
 – David Hume, *An Enquiry Concerning Human Understanding* –

i

You're too indecently clear to hide your
Fear of what you seek but never find. Thus,
Your thought inspects, and common life rejects
What takes center stage in the theater
Of your mind. Rude ruminations challenged
Your good cheer, which never quite defeated
The folly of your melancholy. You're
Puzzled, shocked, amused by the condition
Of religious superstition. And yes.
For you, skepticism is justified,
But unlivable. Thus, as you advised:
Be human, all-too-human, if you can.
First, you must be a man. Then being a
Philosopher might be forgivable.

ii

You did a number on dogmatic slumber.
There's no self, no soul. What happens, happens,
As if you're in charge, but absent your control.

There's no just cause to believe in cause. No.
There are no clues empirical to the
Stubborn miracle of nature's laws. The
Evidence exceeds what philosophy
Thinks it needs. Your urge for survival calls
For common sense, and that's precisely what
It breeds. You rely on cause no matter
What you say. Logically, you scorn it, but
Believe in it anyway. Your patient good
Humor is a mask for those questions you
Could not answer, but now no longer ask.

iii

What you know is really very little.
Neither beginning nor end, do you know,
Only the rapidly shifting middle.
If each now you're in has a next-of-kin,
An equally lonely other, then each
Experience is a riddle that never
Meets its father, son or brother. What you
Say you know is always here and now, but
Never there or then. Yes, for you, one damn
Thing always follows another, and mere
Succession, you know, offers no cogent
Confession of self, substance or sin. And
The cause, you never know, never connects
With its effects because it has no claws.

iv

There's no greater inanity than the
Fallacy of misplaced vanity. What
You call consciousness is the jostling sea
Of your personal debris. To find the
Slippery self, you must show the impression
That catches it and fetches it out of
Chaos. You'd choose your own chaos, but the
Variants are infinite. Like the smell
Of old books, chaos, which gives the slip to
Each bridle, despite name, despite title,
  ... is, alas, always, always the same. You're the

Life you were and the life you are, now that
You're living it. You commit the sin of
Belief and live your life by forgiving it.

v

You revisit old prejudices and
Find them wanting, but necessary. You'll
Not the least bit be relieved to learn that
That you're both deceiver and deceived. You
Can't argue yourself into existence.
Your self, which does not exist, tricks itself
Into believing that it does. That self
Exists just long enough to realize
That it never really is or was what
It thought it was. Yet amid impressions
And ideas, you become quite devoted
To the self you thought they denoted. Then,
Your self, that illusion born threadbare, fades
And vanishes before you know it's there.

vi

If idea matches no impression, real
Or pretended, the relevant term lacks
Any meaning that could be defended.
Thus, you considered eternity and
Found it wanting, and you derided the
Superstition of all those it keeps on
Haunting. *God* and *eternity,* nonsense
Words, empty abstractions, irrational
Surds, not diamonds, but paste, can only be
Palpable in a pudding mixed with what
Passes the test of touch and taste. There's no
Secret power, no indiscernible
Cause. There's only that habit that must bow –
You don't know why or how – to nature's laws.

vii

Your senses provide no basis for their
Interpretation. Your impressions and

Ideas, that's your mind, and in your mind, there's
Nothing else to find. Apply logic to
Habits of belief, and all that you'd dare
To believe must come to grief. Thus, each fact's
A lonely orphan that can never be
Logically connected with other facts.
You believe without justification
That many things must be believed without
Justification. You have no reason
For your belief. You believe because you
Must. The unjustified need for belief,
That's the only thing that commands your trust.

viii

Your history's your immediate sense of
Change. Yes. You perceive continuity.
No moment's an island but always an
Isthmus connecting past and future. The
Solipsism of self and moment, that's
Your philosophic romance. And yet, the
Impact of your skepticism, clearly
Stated, has never quite abated. It
Still enchants. It captivates its victims
With its perpetual trance of sublime
Ignorance. If you don't know you're alive
In the continuous flow, there's nothing you
Can ever really know, and there's nothing
That logic alone would never let go.

ix

It's not the least bit odd that democracy
Demolishes God. All your perceptions,
With no discernible rank, waxed faded
And jaded before they slipped into the
Abyss of memory where they sank. If there's
No prevailing you, no bearer of the
Burden, no keeper of the promise, there's
Nothing and no one to betray or fulfill.
But the self you never knew, that's never
Still, is still for you that knot of dread and

Desire your fate must cling to. You can't live
Or die in a desecrated world. Not
Living, not dying, you keep trying to
Get what you think you ought to want, but don't.

x

You no longer remember how you came
To hate the ornate and love the simple.
With complexity, to lie is easy,
Straightforward, direct. With the complex, a
Lie quickly, lubriciously connects. It pays
False homage to truth and then defects. It's
Harder but still possible to deceive
With simplicity. If you add just a
Bit of spit and polish, you can make of
Simplicity a temple. Each person,
Each self, toward simplicity, is promise
And threat. Each person, the threat you cannot
Forget, is how the universe takes one more
Step toward complicating the simple.

xi

The simplicity you fell in love with,
You wanted so much that you enshrined it
In experience as you defined it.
Every now, every impression's always
Entangled with its priors and its next. No.
There's never any now you could ever
Know that could escape the briars of the
Complex. Only in fantasy, in self-
Deception, are there free-floating atoms
Of perception. Each perception's context,
Snaggled and jaggled, is already you
And the universe. To see otherwise,
That's to steer your imaginary glare
Toward what you want to see but isn't there.

xii

You'd unmask the unmasker. But which is
Greater: the answerer or the asker?

Paradox lures with awe those who admire
Its depth but overlook its flaw. The mind,
Your thought implies, is one wild-ass wit, that
Coddles the contradiction into which
It's split. It denies what it establishes
And establishes what it denies. It
Rummages for truth and traffics in lies. If
There's no one to betray or fulfill, then
Life's one triumphant skill is digging the
Hole you want to fill. Oh, yes. Paradox
Points to the missing shade of blue, to you,
To the sole exception that proves the rule.

xiii

Beliefs, you can't justify, ordain, as
It were, a salvific lie. These beliefs
You contrive not merely to thrive. You breed
Your self-deceptions to stay alive. For
The self, the cost of permanence is the
Promise of satisfaction. You begin
To crave what you cannot grasp or save. If
There's no self, there's nothing to preserve or
Save. If there's no self, there's nothing to make
You crave, and yet you do. To save yourself,
You pretend, like a sensible knave, that
You are you. Yes. Your dread, your desire, knows
Eternity by the skin of its fruit.
You're the self that stumbles in self-pursuit.

xiv

Miracle's what your history's all about.
The miracle continued in you is
Crowded by the self-proof of solitude's
Untruth. Thus, love it or abhor it: but
There's never any reason for it. All
You thought you knew can only be true, if
The universe, you thought you knew, somehow
Resembles you. You will suffer what you
Suffer, and suffer it for no reason,
For any time at all is suffering's

Season. Always, whatever's best suffers
The sternest test. What's highest falls faster,
Harder, deeper. There's no greater promise
Breaker than the would-be promise keeper.

XV

The promise, that great invention, gives birth
To avatars of human intention.
At the very next goal, you'll reach your bliss,
But again and again, what you want you
Miss. Joy, your desire for what's never clear,
Lives next-of-kin to fear of what you hold
Most dear. Joy, that priceless treasure never
Reached by pleasure, makes you want more and more
Of what you've always had before. Think then
Of joy as a special case of cause, one
That does not violate but confirms the
Wonder of nature's laws. With each joy, each
Miracle, God perfects his blunder. This is
The meaning of miracle, of wonder.

XI. AGAINST GRUDGING GODS

Very few things happen at the right time, and the rest do not happen at all. The conscientious historian will correct these defects. ... Man fears time; time fears the pyramids. ... If one is sufficiently lavish with time, everything possible happens.
— Herodotus, *The History* —

i

In every history, there's much to lament
And much that could never mean what you thought
It meant. Every thought is the likening
Of unlike things, and every history its
Unreliable, undeniable
Record. All the life you live, you live, as
If fate could never destroy the lust for
Human joy, as if your history could stay
Uncheckered by its tortured record of
Saying no to irony's woe. Before

The oracle fell silent, you pondered
Her word. Alone on the throne, you prayed. What
You yearned to hear, you heard. But the empire
You would destroy would be your very own.

ii

You strain at gnats to outlast the begats
Until you digest the good parts to your
Fill, and still, happiness, if it happens,
Can never stay. It fades too quickly in
The common light of the common day. Each
Honest historian, plain truth's story
Teller, is, alas, a glory-yeller,
Who selects what's worthy to record in
Vainglory's ever diminishing hoard.
In history, you marvel how there's famine
And also fun, how the starving, wild will
Run, with glee, through those bountiful stalls in
Tables of the sun. Yes. Time's ripening
Abundance may let happiness happen.

iii

You give imagination permission
To invent the myth that fits the facts. Thus,
You imagine yourself more than human,
As one whose luck could never change, as one
Whose happiness could never become a
Stranger to yourself. And you imagine
Yourself as wise, as that paradox, who
Welcomes change, but remains the same in a
Different guise. Such wisdom, like the future,
Cannot last. By the time it imagines
Itself, it's already past. This desperate
Wisdom, alas, is what even the wise
Forget. Yes. Forgetfulness is how gods
Try your patience and summon your regret.

iv

You walked north, south, east and west. Amateur

Voyeur on an extended tour of the
Known universe, you and your history did
Your best to face the truth and meet its test.
You would seek out origins, but when you
Think you reach the source you need, the veins of
Would-be truth bleed what they bleed, the blood of
Fantasy, myth and legend. You report
What dubious readers never believe,
And yet you don't expect them to, even
Though the reports they don't believe all come
From you. Oh, yes. Anyone who'd know the
Truth, you knew, should be able ... to discern
The honest truth in a well-told fable.

v

You're that journalist of a curious
Sort, who thought he had no obligation
To believe what he chose to report. For
You, the truth's always underwater; it
Never stays dry. For you, the truth only
Rises with the leavening of a lie.
Yes. There's truth beneath your lies. If you kick
Your history hard enough it cries. And what
It cries is: *Please listen to me. Believe,*
If you will, and know, as you disbelieve,
That I had no intent to deceive. Thus,
Your orbit toward truth encompasses an
Infinity of tries, and one person's
Truth questions every other person's lies.

vi

You wrote in naked prose, that scandalous
Poetry that shed its clothes. As Plutarch
Would suppose, there was malice in your prose,
Hidden but unbidden, like nettlesome
Beetles in a rose. Your history is told
Like the tale of a bard, who furtively
Throws away his true identity card.
Now that you are dead, there are one hundred
Million words between what you meant and what

You said. Now that you've had your say, there are
One hundred million questions about your
Intent. What really happened you cannot
Say. All that really happened is blinded
Now by the common light of common day.

vii

The oracles, you knew, spoke true, but you
Never could rightly construe what they meant
For you. When something has to happen, it
Always does. Then the oracle lets you
Know the future can never be what you
Thought it was. There's a balance of fortune
Between good and bad. The oracle lets
You know that you can never really get
Or keep what you think you've always had. You,
In your unwisdom, are in such a state
That you will hate what you love and love what
You hate. Every human paradox you
Try, but fail to state, poses the moral
Equivalence of this ambivalence.

viii

The oracle relies on the fact that
Everyone lies to himself and others.
Somewhere you stayed, somewhere you strayed on the
Continuum between the true and false,
Somewhere between the tempo of the two-
Step and the waltz. History is a matter
Of fudging the odds against grudging gods.
Thus, in your cosmic payback scheme, you try
To redeem, against all the odds, what no
One and nothing can redeem. You would make
Of chaos cosmos. You'd call it empire.
You'd call it history. Yes. You'd call it that
Puzzle, that mystery, that cannot be solved,
But only dissolved by time and patience.

ix

The scalps they took they used as napkins. Of

Skulls they made a drinking bowl. Some still say
That in it swims your murdered other's soul.
There is a god unhonored among gods,
A god without name, a god who bears the
Blame when everything that might have been so
Very different turns out to be the same.
History for you was a cul-de-sac that
Sucks in all the life you've ever had and
Never gives it back. There's ebb. There's flow. There's
The recurring tide of ignorance that
Drowns what everyone knows. There's wisdom, that
So soporific grows, that anyone
Still half-awake can lead it by the nose.

x

History is never in any shape to
Offer you escape. Just when you think you're
Out, it pulls you in. Just when you think it's
Over, it all begins again. History,
With nefarious wit, enters you, as
You presume to enter it. You would salt
That history with your own name and link it,
If you could, to those of greater fame. No
Truth about the past can last, for no truth,
In history, can ever start, lest it spring
From the honesty of one human heart.
History reaps what your promise never keeps.
Time's vapid vampire drains the blood from hearts
That never rise to champion what's good.

xi

History would, if it could, be eyewitness
To what happens, but it's not. It's always
The eye of blindness straining to see through
The darkness of its self-obscuring blot.
History is a reckless reveling, the
Drunken dance of novelty and chance, where
All that would be wise slumbers in its trance.
You were there at the beginning of your
Eternity's tours when you started to

Worship foreign gods and then made them yours.
Your history is your life, and your life your
History, a moldering, mostly unread
Book, into which you deign to take account
Of all the life you took but could not brook.

xii

The lust for novelty and nostalgia
Account for most of history's neuralgia.
When you become somebody, you lose the
Potential for staying inconsequential.
You were, though, you knew it too late, in the
Sway of ungrateful gods. Thus, everyone
Should reserve the right to offer up yet
Another thesis about Croesus. The
God behind your gods begrudges what he
Bestows. His resentment is far deeper
Than anyone suspects or knows. Oh, yes.
The gods resent that you are you, and you
Do too. Therefore, the gods can hardly be
Faulted for tearing down the exalted.

xiii

Every history of the other begins
With you, the looker looked at, the questioner
Questioned, the one who would ask and the one
Alone who is always taken to task.
For once upon a time ... that's how one of
Your many stories start, as you ferret
Out hidden motives of the human heart.
Your history of obsessive otherness
Makes clear your fear that everyone, far and
Near, is equally lonely and otherless.
There is just one way to meet another:
With the wonder of unmitigated
Blunder. Astonishment is how the far
Leaves on the near its everlasting scar.

xiv

Traveling from oasis to oasis

Gives you no basis for claiming that you
Are you. Each desert, each nowhere, is a
Desiccated sea. It's the ghost of a
Lost eternity. Self-identity,
A lonely crowd, is the motleyness of
A crew, the traces of many lonely
Others that conspire to make you you. Yes.
History happens at the border crossings.
The sleeper's nightmare goes nowhere till he
Starts turning and tossing, till he starts to
Wake where history happens, at the border
Crossings, the moment of clarity that
Confuses here with there, self with other.

XV

There's no story so grand it can stand the
Termite work of time and resentment. The
Saga of self and other is always the
Story of mutual disenchantment.
Each tale you tell is a border crossing,
An attempt at exile. You would exit
Yourself and become another. You would
Meet, greet and thus become your equally
Lonely others. And you do. The history
Of eternity is the history of
You becoming everyone else, and of
Everyone else becoming you. There is
But one book between us. It's mine. It's yours.
It's the history of eternity's tours.

xvi

All history's a struggle for coherence.
Such is the nascent impetus of each
Occurrence. Each part seeks its starring role
In the dreaded drama of the whole. You
Keep returning to what you throw away.
You keep blinding yourself in the common
Light of common day. You fear the dream of
Your cosmic payback scheme, that no one should
Trust us with its rough justice. You'd keep what

Promises. You'd promise what keeps. You'd dream
The dream that never sleeps. The more you'd stay.
The more you'd go. The more you'd go. The more
You'd stay. This is the sum of what you know
In the flickering light of common day.

XII. THE RAGGED BLINDFOLD

And so the ultimate or final purpose of all music and therefore also of the thorough-bass is nothing other than the praise of God and the recreation of the soul. When this is not taken into account, then there is no true music, only a devilish bawling and droning. ... It's easy to play any musical instrument: all you have to do is touch the right key at the right time and the instrument will play itself. ... The aim and final end of all music should be none other than the glory of God and the refreshment of the soul. ... If I decide to be an idiot, then I'll be an idiot on my own accord.
        – Johann Sebastian Bach –

i

Your music is a continuing prayer
That heaven is alive and well and that
You would, if you could, be already there.
There is in everyone anxiety
Over salvation. Nothing and no one,
Not even music, puts this dread to bed.
Yes. You're that strange relation that relates
Itself to its own self and gets twisted
Into a sham of what it was, before
It claims, as it does now, that it's always
Existed. Not to have been born at all
Might have been your considered preference, but
Now that desire's too late. You are what you
Are: this miracle of self-reference.

ii

There is a rightness to each note, deep down
In the sorrow of your throat. It begins
Where you are, with you. It begins with the

Pain unending, with the place where all the
Joy you want but miss is always tending.
There is behind the pain a love that dies.
Grief lurches into its moan of mourning.
It cries, and it tries, but it fails to swerve
Another way around this barren ground.
Again and again, you nudge yourself to dodge
What will not budge. Grief returns as jury,
As judge, until desperate, exhausted, you
Complete in self-deceit, the history that
Lets eternity go unaccosted.

iii

You're right from the first when you cursed and cried
That every love you've ever known has died.
Face the music, face the climax, and you
Face the facts. Plain truth appears, then summons
All your fantasies and fears. The music
Would, if it could, cleanse you in your tears, but
It offers what you must accept, even
As you trembled, even as you wept. It
Fulfills the promise that cannot be kept.
There's a love that lives in every death, a
Love that breathes in every breath, a love that
Burrows deep in the promise you would but
Cannot keep. When angels lift their wings with
Joy, this is the promise that makes you weep.

iv

Nothing now that you hear or fear tells you
How the music is both nowhere and now
Here. Nothing now tells you if or how the
Music is fantastic or factual.
Nothing now, no matter how you think or
Feel, tells you if or how the allegory
Or the actual is real. Your music,
As long as it lasts, suspends the real, and
The real for those moments is only what
You feel. You feel what it relieves you from.
You abandon the hive but hear the hum.

You will never reach the joy your music
Pointed to. No. You will never reach the
Joy that's there for others, but not for you.

v

The universe is not flat but deep. It's
That one long infinite promise only
God can keep. Though seemingly flat at first,
The universe is deepened by your thirst.
Somewhere vaguely down the line the dull plot
Thickens, a knot quickens, and suddenly,
Where once was nothing, there now is you. Yes.
What once was everything is now a who.
You stray from home and then return. And you
Must return, to apply and reapply
All the lessons that you learn. There's tension.
There's relief. There's desire that wills what it
Wills, and there is the tonic that would, if
It could, cure all your ills with feigned belief.

vi

Your music, you presume, is how God must
Speak when he made the world, made you, and then
Instilled in you the dream of a promise
Kept. Yes. There is in you a beauty and
A depth no playing can exhaust. There is
In you a thirst for satisfaction that
Overlooks the futility you lost
In the paying of satisfaction's cost.
There's but one music that's true, the music
That renders what's best, what's perfect in you.
Music is a sacred act. No use or
Abuse of it can ever change that fact.
When God shines his light on your soul's delight.
That's how you know you got the music right.

vii

The music makes you forget that God is
Dead. It makes you regret and then forget
All the philosophy you've read. It makes
You grieve for what you'd become but cannot
Be. It makes you believe with make-believe.
It makes of eternity what you grieve,
Makes you grieve and then believe. The music
Summons what you are and calls for what you
Ought to be. Its warning to the soul is
Stark. All else you do, no matter how wise,
You devise to blunt the lasting shock of
Eternity's spark. You and your music
Always have in view an eternity
That was meant for others but not for you.

viii

When the music is right, just right, it will
Reveal how you ought to feel. At least, that's
What you, in its moment, think it does, but
The music you feel never stays as real
As you thought it was. You dreamed that time, like
Your music, should take you somewhere, and yet
It never does. It always exiles you
To that nowhere where your emptiness is
And always was, but the music you say
You love has the tact to let you forget
That fact. Your music's arc of intent is
Always bent on disguising and praising
This lament. Music is how you connive
To satisfy your thirst to stay alive.

ix

The music of the universe is a
Never-ending ode, the existence of
All the gods is embedded in its code.
This then is your eternity. This then
Marks the time when time shall no longer be.
The apocalypse is a fairy tale

Come true. Every moment is a crisis
Of revelation for you. Music signs
Its secret signature as the scar, carved
In the near and the far, as the omen
Of what you fail to be and always are.
The music is neither here nor there. It's
Nowhere, and yet it's there. Music is now's
Enchanting presentiment of nowhere.

X

You were not content with despair's lament,
With the devilish blare, the hubbub and
Drub drub drub of boredom. You felt time and
Again its sting but summoned your talent
To make it sing, and you did. Into the
Heart of it, you chased your own chaos, and
In its harmony, you hid. Your music
Would, if it could, resolve time's enigma,
That your fleeting time is always time but
Heralds a time beyond the time, a promise.
The self you choose to be is not so much
A persistent presence as a gaping
Hole. Music is the knack for gilding your
Choice's lack with evidences of soul.

xi

You live in your own blind spot. You'd be what
You are, but you're always what you're not. Your
Music says what can't be spoken. It's the
Token of the promise that's promising
But broken. You live in the longing pulled
Taut between nowhere and now here, between
The dire and the dear. You live in fear of
Becoming to yourself far too clear. Your
Music's the only way you live now here
In the nowhere of here and now. Yours is
The music that tells you how. Near unto
Eternity, you're in the vicinity
Of what you'd be, but what cannot stay slips
Away into the light of common day.

xii

The promise, cynics say, is sentimental,
Even sappy. The legend of joy, they
Say, is a trick the malicious deploy
To annoy the unhappy. You defy
And deny the spirit because you fear
It. If there were no promise, you would not
Be haunted by the better part of yourself.
Music lets you know what you can't know. Its
Clairvoyance, its self-delusion, is the
Clarity of your confusion. You can't
See through all to what you are. You can't see
Through what you are to all. You only see
What you see. You only see yourself through
The ragged blindfold of eternity.

xiii

Your central sin is dread, your fear that you
Can't go on living like you're living in
Your head, your fear that you'll live your life in
Mediocrity's whoredom, that you'll live
Unclever forever in your boredom.
The notes that keep echoing in your head
Keep returning from the nowhere that they
Fled. You will live and live again in the
Never-ending stream of what's always been.
And before the beginning and after
The end, you'll say *Amen,* and then you'll do
It, you'll say it, you'll play it all again.
Nothing else you could ever do would do.
You've grown too much in love with being you.

xiv

Yes. It all begins back there in Eden
When snake philosophy gets it start, and
Does its con-man tricks on the human heart.
The pilgrim of the absolute is no
Longer resolute. But doing the best
You can, you play your own predestined part.

You waver, and you tremble. You pretend
To tell the truth, while you dissemble. With
Music well-made and well-played, you stave off
Boredom for a while with all the finest
Instruments of human guile. Your music's
Strains of joy, its rising repetition,
That's the goad to make you go, when goodness,
Giving all it's ever had, runs out of road.

XV

God, full-up on goodness, sated, lets you
Keep on doing what you've always hated.
Paradise is too comfortable, too nice.
Therefore, God calls in the fiery cherub,
Scorns you, banishes you, and then rolls the dice.
There was never any doubt that you'd be
Cast out. Exile from Eden was your deep
Defining desire, your desperate wish. Your
Not-so-secret trick was sin. You live your
Lust for life, get bored with the Lord, and then
You do it all again. Yes. Always, for
You, metaphysics is expedience.
Cynicism is prior to ethics,
To all the parables of obedience.

xvi

In deep distress, there's the cry, the moan, the
Trepidation that *sans* forgiveness you
Remain, without another, all alone.
Your eternity waits for your lonely
Other who would take you back, the one who
Would save you from the cosmic cul-de-sac.
Whatever's other will be you before
You're through. This irony is the way the
Spirit begins to deepen, by knowing
Not yourself, but others. In despair, you
Can still remember when you first began
To care about being there on cue, there
Where you wait for every lonely other,
And every lonely other waits for you.

xvii

All your music is a ritual of
Eternity. Again, again, it seeks
And cries for what always lives and never
Dies. All that would not yearn for what exceeds
Its needs bleeds in its rigid veins the blood
Of the stale and trite. All that only wants
What it thinks it gets is a parody
Of its own regrets. You were caught in the
Riddle of the middle, between too much
And too little, between what exceeds your
Needs and what is never enough because
Enough is never enough. Your music
Tattoos time's enigma on your heart. It
Scars that place where eternity must start.

xviii

You want what every time would hold. You want
Eternity, deep deep eternity,
Eternity that returns again and
Again in the ritual that repeats
It, in spirit made manifest in flesh,
In flesh made manifest in spirit, in
Beauty you desperately crave but never
Quite expect, in what always surprises
With more than all your senses can detect.
Yes. The enigma makes you want what you
Demand, but never understand. It makes
You hope against hope till the music of
Eternity starts and echoes its joyful
Noise in the hollowness of human hearts.

xix

What's true in music is dogma in speech.
The motive for joy that defeats the gloom
Will arrive unjustified to banish
Everything that's gone missing from the room.
Were your God not with you in your time, you
Would be lost. Were your God not with you in

Eternity, nothing at all would be
Worth the cost. To excel, you strive to reach
Where perfection might dwell. There you attain
That freedom no necessity could foretell.
There you break all the rules. You make all the
Sages seem like fools. There, the great, it will
Greatly annoy, that the heart of one so
Unspectacular, as you, is filled with joy.

— NINE —
PART SIX
DON'T STAY DAMNED

I. ITS HARDEST BONE

No one is going to thank us for what's underneath.
  – Balzac, The Unknown Masterpiece –

According to Swedenborg, an angel is the individual in whom the inward being has triumphed over the outward being.
  – Balzac, Louis Lambert –

Do you know the meaning of eternity? ... Is it God's part to stoop to you? Is it not yours rather to rise to Him? The Seer and the believer have within themselves eyes more piercing than are those eyes which are bent on things of earth, and they discern a dawn. ... To believe is a gift. To believe is to feel. To believe in God we must feel God. This feeling is a possession slowly acquired by the human being, just as other astonishing powers which you admire in great men, warriors, artists, scholars, those who know and those who act, are acquired. ... Do for God what you do for your ambitious projects, what you do in consecrating yourself to Art, what you have done when you loved a human creature or sought some secret of human science.
  – Balzac, Seraphita –

Our conscience is an infallible judge so long as we have not yet murdered it. ... To be in debt means that one no longer belongs to himself. Other men could call me to account for my life.
  – Balzac, The Wild Ass's Skin –

i

You're hated by your mother before you're
Born. You answered with your art, the sublime,
Surreptitious evidence of your scorn.
Your fantasies, avarice, rodomontade
Were self-advertisements of a would-be
Literary god. Yes. You were sure; the
Life of everyone, but you yourself, was
A caricature. You worked to excess
And, in excess, you rested. What would have
Exhausted anyone else, you matched and
Bested. No one else five feet two ever
Seemed as tall as you. Your genius lay not

In talent, but will. Life overdrew on
Your balance, and fate handed you the bill.

ii

Your ambition's vast, but the gist of it
All was terse, even perverse, as if you
Could distill into an epigram all
The complexity of the universe,
And insist that you'd let it contain, if
You could, nothing better and nothing worse.
You sketched humanity in every mode,
As if you had to know everything that
Could happen and be felt to break its code.
You knew to steal what's imagined from the
Real and make it seem more factual than
The actual. Shrewdly, you fake all the
Passions your characters must feel. The best
Realist sees fit to counterfeit the real.

iii

You saw yourself in a palace or a
Poor house, but never in between. Thus, you
Risked it all on literary poker
To stave off as long as you could the threat
Of the mediocre. Like Napoleon,
You'd conquer, you'd legislate. Never would
You settle for the sad and the second
Rate. You became more and more fecund as
The prospect of fame and fortune beckoned.
You engaged in a daily orgy of
Coffee. Only the magic of caffeine
Could make the drear and the drab mean all it
Could mean. Beneath your breath, you never ceased
To hum: *My day will come, my day will come.*

iv

There's a nightmare, you live in, that rankles,
Like a rude awakening unto death,
A shock that stops the clock, that makes you see

You never could have been what you thought you'd
Been then, as if you're now an insolent
Parvenu who has scorned and abandoned
The erstwhile heart of you, as if now you
Knew that the upshot of nature's laws was
This art of grasping after straws, as if
In grasping the absolute you grasped the
Least desirable particle of a
Second-hand article, as if you live
To despise what you can't refute, as if
You sell what you want to buy what you don't.

v

Your ruling passion, that's your absolute.
It plows, furrows, sows and tills and fills you
To the gills as it bears its bitter fruit.
For you, it's never too rash to do the
Slapdash thing for cash, your only idol.
Don't be demoralized by the second-
Rate. Whenever you encounter someone,
Like you, someone cheap, lie about the creep,
Exaggerate. You'd think of no one nicer
Than a shrewd self-sacrificer until
By one of them you're helped to death. Always,
It's your choice to become nothing, something
Or someone. If you don't know the difference
By now, it's your fate to be the dumb one.

vi

You will think yourself serene, pristine, but
One day you too will become this monster.
Debauchery, grimly sought, in orgies
Becomes nought, becomes the suicide of
Desire, becomes rebarbative, becomes
Desire that's as nice and as sweet as barbed
Wire. The more you want the less you get. The
More you try to remember the more you
Forget. Each struggle for remembrance is
A toxic orgy of oblivion.
Before it's all over, you will take one

Last, long-lasting sup from the vastness of
Life's last cup. And all you've done, you'll forget,
Except what you continue to regret.

vii

You'd repeat a joy you can't repeat, but
You're too astute about the absolute
To think it could be made cuddly or cute.
Whether you're alive or dead, the demon
In you keeps repeating your destiny,
The eternity of your desire that's
Implicit in all you said. You would, if
You could, purge the urge to purge, but it keeps
On humming in the midst of your failure to
Overcome your need for overcoming.
Genius arrives not second-handed, but
Only by doing what God has, of you,
Demanded. The work of genius is to
Do the work that you've been commanded.

viii

There's never any overcoming of
Overcoming. Any tune you carry
To its end keeps on humming. Yet you think
Against thought, against what you ought, as if
There is no terror, no sublime, as if
Everything that never works now will work
Out well in the happiness of a well-
Imagined time, a time that comes, as that tune
That never ends but always hums, as that
Overcoming that never overcomes.
You represent the absolute as the
Impossible aim of your desire, as
If its law must be smashed in the spasm
Of your relentless iconoclasm.

ix

Detail upon detail upon detail goes
Beyond the pale to give the illusion

Of the stubbornly real. You did what you
Did, not by genius, but by obsession,
By relentlessly doing it, and then
Screwing it to your own definition
Of eternity. That you could be what
You'd be was impossible, and yet you
Live, you existed, and defiantly
In all you said and in all you did, you
Insisted on what you just had to be.
You would, if you could, remain on the spot,
Becoming what you are forever and
Ever, never becoming what you're not.

x

The more your life tends to satisfy, the
More you die. Nowhere's now here each time you
Fear to make your meaning clear, each time you
Pray the moment will justify your lie.
That's when you'll – at least a little bit – die.
The talisman that would intensify
Your life will leave you less and less of it.
No matter what anyone thinks, you can't
Stretch out your life; you can never smooth out
Its stubborn kinks. You can only catch it
As you can on the rebound as it shrinks.
There is in your life a diamond, but its
Secret gets lost. Before you enjoy its
Luster, you're condemned to die of its cost.

xi

Bored with everything and everyone else,
You lapse into that last great refuge, the
Adventure no one but you ever knew,
The grand adventure of just being you.
In your time, you were all the rage; you're its
Foremost exemplar and grand exception.
You're the paragon of self-deception.
There's nothing you hid. There's nothing you failed
To say. Death dodger does his finest work
In the brightest light of the common day.

When value loses all stability,
What matters is the agility to
Change. When the age of what once mattered ends,
Change is what nihilism recommends.

xii

Your equally lonely other is your
Soul made visible. The faintest traces
Of emotions in your lonely other's
Heart are evidences of your own. You
Cannot love, you cannot live, you cannot
Die alone. You can only live and die
With others. Solitude's a moral void.
It's how you shun your loneliest other,
As if you could still be yourself and be
Only yourself and not another. In
Solitude, imagination peoples
Its loneliness with a crowd. That's why your
Solitude must lie to you in silence.
You decline to prevaricate out loud.

xiii

Solitude's that strange music that's first heard,
Like the nattering noise of a stammered
Word. It lets you believe you love more than
You love, and live more than you live. It's the
Music you remember, but the lie you
Never forgive. You were too impure to
Be anything other than unsure of
The lure of the infinite. The longing
Lasts as long as the music lasts. And then,
It stops and mercilessly recasts nowhere
Into now here, into that remorseless
Fate that's no longer far but all too near.
All that you ever wanted to be is
To be no longer nowhere but now here.

xiv

Your heart's an abyss that would, if it could,

Examine its own like, as if one depth could
Dive into another and drown into
What it deserves. Thus, there yawned before you
A dizzying crater. Tempted, you thought
You'd throw yourself in, but thinking better
Of it, you thought, of course, you can always
Do that later. And then you promise, and
The promise, like a talisman, once made,
   ... is full of magic. But the best played hands
Misplayed turn all too tragic. Promises
Always promise much more to come, but it
Never does. Therefore, the promising is
Never as promising as you thought it was.

XV

You knew how to master the genius and
The dunce. Thus, without missing a trick, you
Knew everyone and everything at once.
Your frantic perfection, always present,
But inscrutable, knew that your every
Suffering, every sorrow, every pity,
Was computable as a certain sum
Of money. That you could reduce human
Woes to cash was for you a joke, but one
That's not the least bit funny. The essence
Of your life is a compromise between
Cold hard cash and the folly that thinks of
Cash as the thin disguise for something that's
Always deeper, more beautiful, more wise.

xvi

The angel in you perishes as it
Loses what only unforgetfulness
Cherishes. An angel, any angel
You feel, must be remembered to be real.
You tried to live where you could not exist.
Some call that place ecstasy, joy, exile,
If you will, from all the gall and guile of
Human woe, from the misery of what you
Never quite believe in but claim you know.

Illusion uses as its shill tempting
Lusters of the real. If money won't buy
What you're looking for, then money isn't
Money anymore. You looked hard, but never
Found the better half of the golden calf.

xvii

You would, if you could, accept the fact that
Your life is obscure but bleak. You uttered
Strange languages to yourself you could not
Understand. And yet you still fear what you
Overhear. You imbibe the Latin of
It and speak the Greek, as if to seek what
You should seek. And yet, the devil answers
Every question. The only freedom he's
Allowed is the freedom to predestine.
But amid the violence of this abyss,
There's a tenderness that reaches and that
Teaches the infinite. No one ever
Suspected that you would be defined and
Then damned by what you've so long neglected.

xviii

You're not the least bit complacent, you tell
Yourself: your soul's not dead; it's intense; it's
Always full of heart; that's how you think of
Yourself when you hold yourself apart. Yes.
Every complacency, they say, should have its
Dante, its Rabelais. But when all your
Complacency goes away, no one can
Ever quite manage to see or say where
It goes in the light of the common day.
Like a sled, you glide on the snow of self-
Deceit. It takes only a bit of feigned
Intensity to make complacency
Complete. The sled of the spiritually dead
Keeps going, but only if it keeps snowing.

xix

Death, for you, was how your life, like water
Into water, pours all its lusterless
Emptiness into emptiness. But you'd
Be, like everyone, at once a dupe and
A duplicate of what you envision.
Duplicity is more prized because it's
Far more interesting than being honest
Or being wise. Bristling with energy,
With vision, you felt the need to scalpel
Your way through the belly of self-deceit
With your sly incision. Realism, your
Mask for a deeper and darker task, shines
The brightest light on the darkest night to
Answer everything anyone could ask.

xx

The steel point of the needle keeps moving,
Keeps proving you're alive, keeps hinting that
You'll keep on going the way you're going
Till you arrive. There is no species of
Intensity you would not connive to
Make you seem to others as one alive.
From everywhere you came, shunning blame, to
A nameless nowhere. Despair's deepest, they
Say, when it's in your hair, but you never
Know it's there. You circulate sans motion,
As if to dance on destiny's damn spot,
As if you can only be what you are
By becoming what you're not. Think then of
Now as bliss. It's all downhill after this.

xxi

Freedom allows you to be complicit
In the fraud of predestination. You
Would, of course, be far too many selves or
None. It's far too boring to be just one.
Your better angel eludes you, as your
Facile truth deludes you. Your life's never

Complete until you have made a public
Spectacle of your self-deceit. Yours is
An eternity of self-deception.
You always knew it. But if you use it
As a lens, you see quite clearly through it.
Between yourself and the absolute, there's
Just one hair. Only self-deception lets
You continue to think it's always there.

xxii

Your will to excess explains most of the
Mess, yet you know the error in what you're
Doing, and you keep doing it. You've got
A bone in your mouth, and you keep chewing
It. You got it, and you won't let go. You
Never live or act in accord with what
You know. You only trust what you can throw
Toward that mythical place where trust won't go.
The ungraspable was not answerable,
But askable. The merciless m.o.,
You never let go, was to denounce the
Ungraspable as a lie. False denial
Takes its toll. The body will not fail to
Be embarrassed by the presence of soul.

xxiii

If your heart's in the right place, it would be
Deep in the heart of now here, not nowhere,
Which, my dear, is where you always are, you
Fear. Yes. To others you're insane; only
To the one who loves you are you lucid.
Let us pretend not otherwise. Let there
Then be no confusion. With whomever
You share the same lucidity, with them,
You must also share the same delusion.
What you call the soul has its crossroads, its
Trespassing zone, where all your strangers, all
Your lonely others, meet and greet and love
Each other, and come back home. If soul has
A skeleton, this is its hardest bone.

xxiv

In the first half of your life, you create
Your dream guy, your lie, your fiction. Then the
Second half lives out your tawdry lack of
Conviction. And in the dissipating
Smoke, none but you could tell or care how your
Bank went broke. And none, but you, would pause to
Choke over the pain of your sacrifice.
Those noticing you will find you doing
Nothing, and the noticers knowing
That they're right will point it out to everyone
Else just for spite. But now you must do what's
Commanded and demanded. It's never
Too late to play your honest part. Give now
To God your genius and your troubled heart.

II. COMING BACK ... HARD

It is easy to go down into Hell; night and day, the gates of dark Death stand wide; but to climb back again, to retrace one's steps to the upper air – there's the rub, the task. ... Each of us bears his own hell.
         – Virgil, *The Aeneid*, Book VI –

i

With small desires and large disappointments,
You lived at the edge of fields you could not
Till, at the edge of lives you could not live
But only tell. Your voice, foreshadowing
Change, was first a whisper and then a yell.
Yes. You found yourself everywhere you looked,
But you did not like it. If existence
Were amenable to the author's pen,
You would identify your foulest sin
And strike it. But what your life has rudely
Written may be effaced, but not erased.
If you could make your past the future and
Your future the past, you'd take the time to
Better them both, and this time make them last.

ii

Your hero begins wishing he were dead,
For he carries, like you, the burden of
Memory in his head, the fate you hate and
Perpetuate, the fate that, without your
Permission, decided you'd be against
Yourself, divided. You end before you
Begin. And you depart before you come
Together. You reached the middle of being
And found it busted, broken, knowing all
You once trusted is now but a token
Of despair's own nightmare, a bad dream that
Never ends, but that slowly becomes the
Worst of what your foreboding portends. Thus,
You accuse what you pledged to honor.

iii

You were, it is said, the laureate of
Loss. You will reach out longingly for the
Farthest shore, chasing shadows of the dead
That were never shadows in the life that
You lived before the life you now deplore.
You wanted most that the record of the
Life you never enjoyed would be destroyed.
In the wrong road, you trusted far too long
Till at last your life became an error
You could no longer prolong. This is the
Futility you detect and can't neglect.
Yes. You need it, you heed it, and in the
Cryptogram that is the universe, you
Read it as the relentless book of life.

iv

There is, for you, no discernible way
Out of the woods. You're lost in the thicket,
Looking vainly for the flimsiest goods.
You were on the threshold of joy, but lacked
The will to go beyond it. All that you
Wanted, you wanted far too much. You would,

If you could, as if nowhere were something
To clutch, bend back both ends of the rainbow,
And bond it to what you would, but cannot
Touch. In solitude, you'll learn to adore
Your interior paramour. This frail
Loneliness, laid bare in you, you cannot
Bear. Its smallness, its if-onliness: All
That is the recipe for your despair.

v

Like any kindling, *The Aeneid,* yes,
Would burn and burn quickly, but what would its
Fiery finish start? What hope, if any,
Would its cruel demise replenish in the
Hollowness of your human heart? Thus, you
Must struggle to remember your latent
Oblivion, that ancient echo, that
Overtone, that you and you alone must
Own, that relic of your useless attempt
At resurrection, that final nakedness
Before death, when life, though still alive, has
Lost its artfulness and breath, when your soul
Sheds its self-deceit and readies itself
For the receipt of your eternity.

vi

The mediocrity that everyone
Hates, in the midst of the fraudulent best,
Yes, this is what buries. This is what drowns.
This is what inundates. But, if, as you
Say, each moment is blessed, each moment should
Survive the acid test of what is best.
No, there is no genius without applause.
Therefore, you must finish it before you
Burn it. Yes. You must burnish it with praise
Before you turn it into a relic
Of oblivion. Only what's really
Real, in ways not always clear, only the
Really real survives. And, then, even when
It pretends to be vanquished, it revives.

vii

In your puritan fantasy, you have
Altogether forgotten that there has
Never been a time that was not – through and
Through – altogether rotten. Yet the fool
In your heart never ceases crying peace,
When there is no peace, peace that's the symbol,
The pretense that death does not exist, but
It does, and the life you dreamed could be lived
Without it never really is what you
Thought it was. You dawdle in this ceaseless
Tension. There's really no other place to
Be. This, never going, never staying,
Never cursing, never praying, is the
Moving stillness of your eternity.

viii

The Day Star rises and by now it's seen
So much that nothing it sees surprises.
There will be love. There will be anguish. There
Will be ritual slaughter. The gods you
Would fear or revere stand off and scoff and
Let you bring all your troubles on yourself.
An exile by fate's decree, you would have
That fate default to someone else, but your
Honesty already had its only
Answer: *It must be me and only me.*
You are your own hope, or so you say. You
Know how slender that must be. Time's promise,
Unfulfilled, palters as it alters and
Tries the patience of your eternity.

ix

It's never clear what you love the most, the
Woman of flesh and blood or Dido's ghost.
Love, if it lasts long enough, always longs
To mate and then create with its lonely
Other. To this love you open your eyes:
You harken to its truth, yet labor with

Its endless, useless lies. Such love is the
Perception amid self-deception that
Upholds the promise. Those, *sans* perception,
Seek a quicker liquor than truth. Their strange
Intoxication will at once distract
And contract what they would be into the
Shabby remnant and everlasting scar
Of what now they must be and always are.

x

You, the wound in her fire and the fire in
Her wound, will love her, you say, as long as
Rivers run in the heat of sun, as long
As shadows play in the common light of
Common day. Wherever she would go, there,
You say, you would go and stay. This promise,
You say, you would never betray, and yet
You do. And you'll betray every other
Promise before you're through. No. You'll never
Forget her, you say, but you cannot help
But let her languish in her anguish. You
Cannot help but let her follow fate down
That road where suicide is the last great
Goad of troubled honor and tarnished love.

xi

You can't explain to your beloved why
You abandoned the one you love. You ask
Her to stay her step, to let you explain
The promise you kept unkept. You were trapped
In a destiny you didn't belong
To, a destiny larger and far more
Anonymous than you. You would, if you could,
Revere your household gods. And approving
Deities would thank you feebly with their
Feeble nods, but the emptiness of your
Suffering is deeper than the foundations
Of Rome. You would reject, if you could, that
Destiny now, but the golden bough can't
Tell you how; it can only lead you on.

xii

You were the hero of nowhere until
You found your gloried and storied somewhere.
This lust for home is a nostalgia you
Cannot shed until you're dead. You long for
An identity so deep it would put
Even your deepest dreams to sleep, even
Those dreams you dread. But to be what you are
Forever is not as comforting as
It seems. To be what you are forever:
That's to annihilate all your dreams, to
Live where wisdom's shopworn, and truth is shorn
Of the lie's first born, where truth that's hardest
Won will be poured through the self-annulling
Oblivion of the ivory horn.

xiii

Your epic rehashes the familiar
Fraud of ashes to ashes. No longer
Need you stand in awe when every law that
Rises crashes. Life, left alone in peace,
Would be a bore, if not for the savage
Futility of war. Everything, with
Unconscious cunning, conspires to boost the
Odds that the twilight of the gods comes as
It comes with the risk you're always running.
All you are takes its toll by complicating
History's rigamarole. Time no longer
Elapses. It accumulates in your
Synapses, like drifting snow. Your history
Gets tugged by eternity's undertow.

xiv

As you till the heavy earth, no matter
How you may turn the plow, there's always the
Question now of what it's worth, for there is
Always lamentation, always death, and
Both with bated breath strive to celebrate
The dearth of joy. What astonishes and

Terrifies is the appetite for life
That never dies. Look back too soon, and you
Lose the love you labored for. In death, you
Won't embrace what in life you could not face.
You play the role of a self-convicted
Thief when you fill the empty time with grief.
Oblivious of the obvious, you
Forget there's no just cause for grief ... but love.

XV

Each page, each leaf, each rage, each grief, each kiss,
Each kindness, each dream of sought-for bliss, each
Vision, each blindness, will insist that it
Can only exist as some ruggedly
Eloquent symbol of the soul in pain,
Its *sine qua non*. Your piety is
Patience, patience that's desperation in
Control, the strength to go on when there is
No reason for going on. This wound you
Could not heal, this is the pain you could not
Still, from which you'd seek relief, if there were
Not so vast a grief in the loss of true
Belief. Your last bad bet is that there's joy
You must have had but haven't remembered yet.

xvi

Only joy could make your heart forget to
Ache. And yet, you'll have none of it until
Everyone else who claims to have it is
Done with it. You'll calculate your final
Act of violence. You'll plot your own dismay,
Your pain. The burden of any task is
Greatest when you know in your heart you have
Nothing to gain. And yet nothing now can
Negate your lasting notoriety,
That the one who loved you will suffer for
Your piety. Guilt is self-awareness
Shoved into the sheath of self-hood to the
Hilt. In its glare, only the blind do not
Falter, do not wilt, do not admit their guilt.

xvii

Your worst thirst was for the superficial,
Yet your song was as long and deep as the
River of words that it was. Silent now,
It never sings of what it might have sung,
But what it never does, it never was.
Day by day, according to your will, you
Distilled in free rhyme the troubled time, what
History could thrill and chill but never quite
Completely dull or kill. You fiddle with
The second hand, as if you could abuse
The vicarious to understand what
You might have had first hand, if only the
Precarious had left undefeated
The life you never had but merely planned.

xviii

All the timelessness in your fickle heart
That stays never sings, but only stings. The
Cascade of history never pauses for
You, but whatever it must bring it brings.
Your ancient eyes were drunken, sunken in
Their sockets. Hard pressed for change, you rummaged
Through your pockets, and found not one single
Coin of the new and truly minted. You
Found only that negative miracle
That's you, desperate, dour and discontented.
When you're really old, everything that can
Hurt will. Of all your pains, you will keep a
Running score. And when of hurts, you've had your
Fill, there will, of course, before you're dead, be more.

xix

Even if you write on good paper, it
Will not last. Time's lechery will molest and
Destroy all that's past. It will not respect
Your neatly entered record of what once
Was. It will snicker, flicker and bicker
With all the other causes and then do

Once again what it always does. It will
Make the sum of what always is seem like
It never was. You do what you must do.
You do your duty, your task. That is the
Only task anyone should ask. Yet, the
God you do not heed asks far more, asks of
You to give far more than you have, far more
Than anyone could ever ask or need.

XX

Art, on rampant metaphor, runs, and life
On the literal, on its elusive
Perception of what it thinks it is. This,
The stigma of life's last enigma, is
The heart of eternity's fatal quiz.
Always, that damnable lie of deepest
Dye hides in its pocket the yellow eye
Of Prometheus. You worried even
Before the gods grew weak, when you failed to
See the gain in anything you seek. Please,
Now, anyone who still can see the use
Of the golden bough, let him speak. This is
The wound that left you scarred. Yes. In hell, the
Going down's easy, the coming back ... hard.

III. NIHILISM'S TRUMP CARD

Not time, but the moment, as that element in time which does not belong to it, communicates with eternity, in which alone perfect joy has its measure.
– Ernst Bloch, Traces –

We start out empty. ... So the darkness of nearness also gives the final reason for the melancholy of fulfillment: no earthly paradise remains what it is on entry without the shadow which the entry still casts over it. ... From early on, we want to get to ourselves. But we do not know who we are. All that seems clear is that nobody is what he would like to be or could be. ... What is to be fled, what is to be sought, this question must always most definitely be slept on. It is not as plain as day, neither in its individual parts nor in the whole, which comes later. Man

desires and wishes throughout his life, but if he has to say what he wants absolutely, what he wants at all, he is at a loss for an answer.
– Ernst Bloch, *The Principle of Hope* –

i

Long before your world started spinning, you
Suffered that damnable darkness in the
Beginning, when you and all your lonely
Others began happily sinning. Long
And hard, you kept preparing for the next
Mistake. You kept promising what in your
Heart you already knew you must forsake.
Why, you ask yourself, must you still do it?
It's the nature of life, you say. You must
Do what you do, just to get you through it.
You tell yourself that once upon a time
You had your chance, but, alas, you botched it.
Looking back, you see yourself just waiting
There, knowing you blew it, as you watched it.

ii

You start out empty; you end there too. Faux
Nothingness never made a larger hole
Than the hole it made in the heart of you.
You want most to reach the here and now, to
Brave its weather and at long last enter
What's but a gleaming shard, a splinter of
What you dreamed was there, but which never came
Together. You go on dreaming. You go
On scheming. You're always on the way to
The perfect moment, the place where you could
Honestly say: this is the life you were
Meant to live in the light of common day.
This is the life that makes you new. But your
Dream keeps shifting, and with it, you do too.

iii

You thought of bliss as home. You thought of joy

As the destiny of being whom and
What you imagined you'd be when you were
Just a boy. Only nowhere, only your
Utopia can ever be safe from
The reality of unbliss, unjoy.
You are damned to the distant gleam of a
Light that's never what it might seem but that
Shines forth its fatal gleam from nowhere. In
Joy, you find your only depth. In nowhere's
Moment, you find the only promise that
Ever deserved to be kept. Thus, nowhere's
Nothingness, big with itself, delivers
Unto you what can never come cheaply.

iv

You would, if you could, become beautiful,
More wise. But you tell yourself: you know what
Others do not know and never know. Your
Ugliness, your stupidity, is a
Put-up job, a jury-rigged disguise. And
Yes, behind the looking glass, you looked so
Very much better. For there, you'd become
What you are, a staunch forgetter that you're
An incompetent bumbler, an ass. That's
Why utopia, just like you, is best
Kept under glass, there where your trust in it
Laughs the loudest laugh it could ever laugh.
When trust, frustrated, goes on a binge, hope,
Which doesn't know its strength, has its revenge.

v

Movement's an entelechy incomplete.
All that moves seeks to justify itself,
And every stab at vindication is
An indication that you would, if you
Could, be what you are. That you'd be what you
Are, but can't, that's your most common complaint.
You're oppressed by longing, by your sense of
Belonging to what you think you want but
Don't. You're not quite like yourself. You never

Are. Your guiding image summons the dawn.
It's the lure that's sure to lead you on. It
Opens all you close. Never far from what
You think you are, it's always as near as
The end of your nose. And it's still too far.

vi

Each now's a night club with no future and
No past, and the band there, playing what it
Plays, plays as if your own perpetual
Perishing is the only thing to last.
There is, you surmise, a day club too, a
Garden party on the crowded, sunlit
Lawn, convened there just for you. That's what you
Proffer, what you boldly say. There must be
A place where the night life can go and dance
In the golden light of common day, a
Place where even the likes of you may come
And go, but never stay. The shrewdly wise
Are sometimes prone to say what they despise.
So they say what they're loath to say with lies.

vii

Conniving for consolation, you act
With unabashed metaphysical guile,
When you tell the moment: *Please stay awhile*.
You collect a prize for each new pleasure
You invent, but fiasco nonetheless
Exposes lies that the plainest facts could
Not prevent. You learn what happens when the
Varnish cracks. You look beyond the painted
Scene and behold that face that has no place,
No time, no tracks. And yet, despite your best
Efforts to exalt futility, all
That happens, happens as if desire's a
Vast conspiracy always tending to
Justify your sense of a happy ending.

viii

With the fatuity of the *horror*

Vacui, you fight futility with
Futility. You expose its lie. Into
Your emptiness, you pour more emptiness,
As if the will to will in the midst of
The utterly nil still wants to amount
To something. And it does. The emptiness
Into which you sneak a peek was never
As empty as you thought it was. Somewhere
Deep inside the emptiness of you there
Lurks the urge to make everything that's old
All new. Your myth of the other world makes
History. How strange that the nothingness
Of what's nowhere could engender such change.

ix

You dream that you could be made better, that
You could silence in you the regretter
And thus wake up the forgetter of what
Never counts. And yet, arising within
You, all that stumps your ability to
Be what you'd ruthlessly be ... mounts and mounts.
You hate to wait, but you do it. Then you
Wait for daydreams to vivify the wait
And thus help to get you through it. No now
On any of your tours is ever yours.
All you think, all you do is your effort
To renew it, to re-construe it, to
Reach where, if you could, you would arrive, where
There'd be no longer any urge to strive.

x

You would, if you could, relearn the art of
Entering paradise. But once in, how
Could you ever leave it? Once knowing joy,
How could you endure its absence and not
Endlessly grieve it? No one who exits
The theater still wants to act. Yes. Your
Exit betrays the fact that there is no
Now that is ever captured. You're always
Already beyond your sense of yourself

Enraptured, as though the only way to
Enjoy your joy is to perceive it as
Something you've never had, as if the one
And only way to be happy is to
Pretend you've never been the least bit glad.

xi

Utopia, you saw it everywhere,
And in everyone, in the salesman and
The professor, in the peasant and the
Prince, in the flowerpot, in the casserole,
In the superannuated spire, in
The congregation whose moral soul is
Still available for hire, whose dream of
Utopia surrenders before the
Hardest knocks and disappears from view as
the pistol cocks. Yes. Bloodshed, for you, should
Be a surefire clue that somehow your dream
Of bliss has gone askew. The fire bringer,
Who would bring salvation, brings a scourge. He
Brings the curse of your utopian urge.

xii

Hope seeks utopia's Mr. Fixer,
The one thing needful, the altogether
Elusive elixir that will soothe your
Anguish, that will ease your pain, that will calm
Your conscience, that will cleanse your guilt, that will
Remove the stubborn stain of all that you
Continue to scorn and to take in vain.
Only a new heaven, a new earth will
Let you shed your widowed skin and sagging
Spirit and let you quench your thirst in your
Unmitigated vision of self-worth.
Yes. You were there on the scene when the light
Of common day turned mean, when hope became
Principle, power, and domination.

xiii

You never learn to do without yourself.

You grab the dregs of you, drag them along,
As if to find that home where they belong.
Your desire for the authentic proves that
Self-deception is your normal state. You
Only seem complete in your blind spot of
Self-deceit. Every pretense of joy knows
In its heart of hearts that it's second rate.
You pay for what you want by getting it.
You enjoy what you get by regretting
It. Your pretended happiness, try as
It might, can never make itself seem right,
Can never quite muffle the lasting shocks
Of this reverberating paradox.

xiv

Who's there? so the start of *Hamlet* reads. The
Answer after that is all that follows,
All that proceeds. You never quite gather
Yourself in the now to do your bidding,
Without your conscience endlessly nagging,
As it keeps on kidding about what it
Says it needs. But then there's nihilism's
Trump card. Playing it's easy; living it's
Hard. You panic at the absence of the
Messianic, as if all the good of
You could be poured into a thimble and
Still leave room for the Atlantic. Yes. It's
Demoralizing, tragic, when the maestro,
Exposing his fraud, renounces his magic.

xv

The shortest line is sometimes crooked. In
Your banality, you'll lose all the sting
Of why you or anyone at all should
Become anyone or anything. The
Trace, the clue that's not nowhere or now here
Never wears a discernible face; it's
Never clear. The inconstruable is
Never reducible, and the vague is
Never screwable to one sticking place.

All around you, so much is there that must
Persist that you too, the inconstruable
You, insist on becoming something, but
You never do. To be what you cannot
Construe: that's the meaning of being you.

xvi

In the philosophy of history, it's
Hardly a mystery that the sense of your
Eternity abolishes history.
The revelation that is also the
Revolution promises that the *Ought*
Will be *Is*, and that the *Is* will be *Ought*,
And that history alone will provide all
The consolation you've sought. The world that's
Lost its core will still want more and more of
What it's never had before, as if it
Will at long last reach the promised scene and
Discover what it is that it's meant to
Mean. Your sense of history is how you learn
To use and abuse this news from nowhere.

xvii

If you don't awake on Monday morning as
One oppressed, then your fundamental
Sadness has not yet been fully expressed.
You never forget how the dog in the
Manger gets born in you when someone else
Has or does what you neither have nor do.
The kingdom comes with a little shift of
The world, with a little wobble of its
Adamant axis, as if the world that's
Now unshifted could be regifted with
A meaning that would no longer tax us
With its tyranny, as if there will come
A time, when all that is old becomes new,
When every dream you've ever had comes true.

xviii

Yours was atheism that continued

God by other means. In the wake of your
Murdered God, it happily thrives. But what
Dares the death of God and still survives is
Not worth surviving, and a God that would
Let himself die is not worth reviving.
Yes. The God you say is dead is the God
You can't regret because he's forever
The *no, not yet*. Thus, enamored of this
No, not yet, you fell out of here and now
Into nowhere and back again, into
That nowhere that confounds what still abounds
In God's little acre, where even the
Atheist still goes to meet his maker.

xix

Between the *not yet and the all-in-vain,*
You'd find the excluded middle and be
The first to make it plain. It was somewhere
In the middle of this nowhere's end where
All your desperate hopes were pinned. Anyone,
To be of value, needs someone with pull.
Only the gravity of others makes
Your emptiness full. The eternity
You saw naked was, yes, what it always
Was, indivisible into nothing
Other than its very own nakedness.
Your eternity has no face, no place,
Where it could ever be you. It's how what
You've always been and always are stays new.

xx

What's closest to you stands most in question.
Thus, you plowed through the moment to live what
It might predestine. You found it dark. And
Yet, you rummaged through the darkness, as if
To excavate eternity's spark. This
One moment tells you again and again
What you always knew: you are what you are
Forever, through and through. Watch now, if you
Will, how nothingness turns into something:

Stare at the darkness, and no matter how
Dark, beyond the shadows, you'll see the spark.
The God you can't believe in left in his
Wake, your hope, your hallowed, hollow trace of
His vast and everlasting act of grace.

IV. BET YOUR LIFE
"Everything is needed for the calling I follow," said Don Quixote. ... I remember who I am and who I may be if I choose. ... Too much sanity may be madness, and maddest of all is to see life as it is and not as it ought to be. ... "Do you know what I'm afraid of?" said Sancho upon this, "that I shall not be able to find my way back to this spot where I am leaving you, it is such an out-of-the-way place." ... And Don Quixote was born only for me, as I for him; he knew how to act and I how to write; we two together make but one.
   – Cervantes, *The History of the Ingenious Gentleman Don Quixote de la Mancha.* –

i

You could, if you would, die for your lady,
For your God, for your country, for your king,
And for the honor, as it were, of the
Thing, for all that it might, to you and your
Lonely others, bring. With left hand crippled
For the greater glory of the right, still
You summon the strength to fight, for you would,
If you could, make what's wrong seem right. Your self-
Delusion now regrets what sanity
Never quite forgets: how illusions of
Honor get caught and come to nought in the
Warp and woof of *Is* versus *Ought*. Against
This plainest fact, you stay defiant. The
Windmill's not a windmill, but a giant.

ii

Everything is what it must be and is.
Hence, comparison is an odious
Trifle. What it would illuminate, it
Must stifle. Among enigmas of your

Enchantment, there is an algebra of
Abracadabras, a magician's code
Of substitutions that captures in one
Of its phrases all that sadness bemoans
And happiness praises. You exalt what
You undermine, and you undermine what
You exalt. Your guilt, if that is what it
Was, was the gift of dreams. But now you know
It's no one's fault, if your life never was,
Never is, never could be what it seems.

iii

The obsession starts just as soon as you
Begin to care. You start to imagine
That what is never here is nonetheless
Somehow always there. You ask of your dream,
Not if it's true, but what the dream, if you
Could live it, would be like for you. The best
Lies catch the most flies. They win by doing
What the truth, always far too circumspect,
Never tries. With vigor, the best lies brag
Of that imagined rigor that's never
Won by appeal to fact, but that's always the
Offspring of egregious tact. Your history
Lost all of its clarity when its very
Best lies decayed into sincerity.

iv

Your life was mediocre, not really
That bad. It was the inanity of
Your sanity that drove you mad. You would,
If you could, be immortal, as if time
Offered you a portal to another
Time. And it always does. The sense of your
Eternity, for which you grieve, but which
You can never quite believe, tells you the
Value of the experience you had
But missed, when it became *what was*. And yes.
You always try, but never quite give up
To what you can't live up to. This lesson,

Always old, is always new when it does
All it can to make a fool out of you.

v

The trickster that's inside of you turns his
Unexpected corner. Reaching up your
Sleeve, he plays his stolen card. And yes, he
Imagines himself decent, even honest.
Others do too. To do so was never
For him very hard. Whoever wants to
Believe is always easy to deceive.
You will think of him, the dupe, as hero
Too. Think of him, if you will, as always
The better half of you. Fiction makes truth
Safe for your consumption. The logic of
Its plot hinges on the assumption that
The blood of fiction never bleeds outside
The text that nonetheless still bleeds in you.

vi

As far as you can tell, no one's yet learned
How best to dwell in a lifelong fairy
Tale. The chivalry you thought you knew was
Already dead before it found its way
Into all those books you read. Chivalry,
As it were, was dead before it started,
And your erstwhile world never really was
Whatever you thought you knew, but something
That instead grew colder and colder-hearted.
And yet, about all this, you would, if you
Could, tell an endearing fairy tale, so
You try to spin one. In the middle of
Telling the tale, you surprise yourself, when
With trepidation, you yell: *I'm in one!*

vii

The first part keeps promising the second
Part, and you keep forgetting the greatest
Fiction has the tact to remind you of the

Unforgettable fact, that you yourself
Are part of the act, that you too are part
Of its cunning art, which, of course, without
Remorse, lies at your heart. To know Quixote,
You must know who you are too. Despite your
Better efforts, that's something you never
Do. In the second book, your hero meets
His fame, his reputation. In the life
Of everyone, there is this possible
Second book, in which you're forced to greet the
Aftermath of chances you scorned, but took.

viii

Thus, your vanity is always prone to
Overrate the value of sanity, as
If, in one moment of lucidity,
You see it's never so bad to be mad,
If it lets you experience a joy
You've always wanted but never had. What
You mistake for joy is *joie de vivre*, bluff
Gusto that returns again and again
To itself and yet still knows how to grieve.
There's no seriousness, no tragedy,
No agony that cannot succumb to
The lure of play, that does not want to laugh
And sing, that does not want to make light of
The disenchanting light of common day.

ix

You were enamored of a romantic
Fossil, a humbug so colossal that
No beating or bruising could ever quite
Jostle you loose from the clamp of its grip.
But before the ghost of chivalry goes,
Your imagination will have restored
All the humbugs you once deplored. Now it's
Not so easy to say which illusion
You'd perpetuate and which you would sweep
Away into the light of common day.
Though suspicious of your ideal, it will

Be precisely what you think most real. You
Sneer at the gauziness of the ghost, yet
It will be the one that you love the most.

X

Your misunderstanders should thank you for
Your persistence. As the earliest and
Latest knight on chivalry's longest day,
You continue to say and say again
What they could never say. Ensconced within
You, there's that Sancho, that Don, who never
Understands the latest ideal until
You try it on. How often you cried when you
Should have laughed, and laughed when you should have
Cried, because your cynicism, yes, your
Idealism too, were both entirely
Justified. It's always necessary
To deceive, if you're to teach yourself and
All your lonely others how to believe.

xi

By dwelling on the familiar side of
The strange, you believed you'd keep the status
Quo the way it is and call that change. But
Desire lies to itself about what it
Wants. What the ghost of romance abandons,
It still haunts and taunts with protestations
Of its autonomy. You can never
Sit still with your restless will. You cannot
Abide the static. When you reach your goal,
Despair's disenchantment is automatic.
The knight, who would be a clown, at long last
Lets himself down. But, now, your erstwhile zeal
No longer seems the least bit real, and last
Year's nest can give to the new bird no rest.

xii

At the hub of your history's maze, there's a
Monster, like you, who shares what you cannot

Master, your obsession, your craze. You would,
If you could, make of this enemy your
Friend, so you study tales of his wayward
Ways, and thus heed what they portend. All this
Confirms your thesis that every story
Titillates with what it simulates, while
Betraying anagnorisis. In the
Deck of signs, there's always another ace
To play, another slant to the light of
Common day. There's always another face
Of you, always another face of God,
And of every other character too.

xiii

No two people meet the same Quixote,
And that Quixote who meets himself meets
Someone new. You're never quite yourself till
You become another whose loneliest
Other seemed much more like yourself than you.
Yes. Sancho and the Don were one angel,
One demon, one irrepressible, one
Impossible man. Those misbegotten
Two, as one profoundly hidden truth, lie
Coiled in the heart of you. What the fat man
Could not do, the skinny man can. What the
Skinny man tried to forget, the fat man
Always knew he knew. He always knew what
He'd never ever do and still regret.

xiv

There's you and the world as you see it, but
You never quite see it as you'd see it,
If you were able to free it of you
And your view. With one long elaborate
Lie, you speechify about what you're so
Enamored of, but cannot specify.
You keep on talking much, saying little,
Except to add more and more twists and turns
To endless curlicues of the riddle.
You know in your heart you believe in a

Fiction, yet your troubled history is the
Trauma of its arduous depiction.
More's the pity. You can dream but never
Live in the city of Señor Mitty.

XV

You believed in your immortality
Because you wanted to, because you must.
You believed what you had no reason at
All to trust. You believed because of the
Deepest cry of the human heart. That's where
All the damnedest dreams of humanity must
Start. One act of the counterfeit sublime
Will win for you that eternity that
Never knows the beginning or end of
Time. In the end, you were, by your madness,
Driven sane. And you saw your abandoned
Quest as childish, stupid, silly, vain. Your
Adventure was one long fatuous screech that
Taught you what dreams and dreams alone could teach.

xvi

Everyone's history, yes, everyone's dream
Recalls a paradise that no one can
Share. To reach for the impossible, you
Must dream of what's there beyond compare, but
That isn't there, a past or future that
Inhabits nowhen, but never now and
Never then, a past that's never here and
Now, but always just this side of nowhere.
Illusion creates the only sense of
The real you deeply feel. That, for you, is
Always illusion's deceitful law. All
The rest you assume is real is surface
Tension, an infinite onion in the
Raw, that keeps on shedding its peel. That's all.

xvii

Fiction faces the facts of life and will

Not budge. Against those facts, paranoia
Still holds its longest grudge. Daydream's fingers
Touch the deepest part of you, revive the
Myths and make them new. Here, dear journalist
Of suspicion, is the honest scoop. Yes.
You fear your lonely others and you too
Are, just like the Don, a dupe in the void,
Utterly unredeemed by the paranoid.
In every masterpiece, there's a blot. Look
Always for the trace of what it tried to
Do, but, alas, decidedly could not.
There, where something should be, but isn't, there
An imponderable X will mark the spot.

xviii

If you and all your lonely others could
Assimilate the finer ironies,
You'd say: *How odd of us to imagine
Ourselves reading history when we're reading
Herodotus.* History can only be
Read, if you assume that all the facts it's
About are dead, no longer true to life.
The irony here is thick, but still it
Lacerates, like the edge of the keenest
Knife. To your wager about whatever's
False, whatever's true, there can never be
Any reliable clue. And yet, the
Eternity, that's never through with you,
Whispers in your ear: *You must bet your life.*

V. OF ETERNITY'S SARCASM

Like his masters, since thought began, he was handicapped by the eternal mystery of force – the sink of all science. ... Every man with self-respect enough to become effective if only as a machine, has had to account to himself for himself somehow, and to invent a formula of his own for his universe, if the standard formulas failed. Then, whether finished or not, education stopped. The formula once made, could be but verified. ... The effort must begin at once for time present. The old formula had failed, and a new one had to be made, but after all the object

was not extravagant or eccentric. One sought no absolute truth. One sought only a spool on which to wind the thread of history without breaking it.
   – Henry Adams, *The Education of Henry Adams* –

Yes! At last I have reached the end! We shall grow to be wax images, and our talk will be like the squeaking of toy dolls. We shall all wander round and round the earth and shake hands. No one will have any object in this world, and there will be no other. It is worse than anything in the "Inferno." What an awful vision of eternity.
   – Henry Adams, *Democracy* –

i

You were born already too old for school,
Too clever to study like the rest of
Your class, far too wise to be a proper
Fool, but altogether capable of
Becoming an ass. In the end, you were
Stunned to learn more from what you write than from
What you read. You get the education
You deserve, but never the one you need.
You were naturally too stupid ever
To understand that it's natural to
Be too stupid to understand what you
Think you know. Yet by misunderstanding
Though, you create what you never planned, the
Secret meaning you never understand.

ii

You were in your time the ashes of your
Grandfather's wishes, an altogether
Promising failure. Your salient fault is
The everlasting scar of what you are,
The history of what you were and when, the
Parable of miseducation that
Despairs of what was never there, never
Then. Jeremiah of enchantment and
Entropy, you were American through
And through, solid, bought and sold. You sought to

Warm the ashes of yourself gone cold, as
If the manikin on which you'd drape the
Trendiest clothes could let you forget the
Dismal, disordered fact that you are you.

iii

The tailor retailored denudes himself
And then deludes himself with the false hope
Of new clothes. Yes. You're the sum of all your
Accidents, of all your chances, of all your
Misunderstood necessities, and
Backward glances. You become in sin the
Sum of what you've always been: you become
The pattern of your mistakes. There are those
Who steal, and there are those who are stolen
From. This dictum which, for you, has little
Curb appeal nonetheless makes the whole world
Hum. You learn its hardest lessons against
Your will. The surest education is
Always swallowing the bitterest pill.

iv

There's always the little matter of your
Calling, whether your vocation was a
Lifelong vacation from destiny, or
Just another way to keep on stalling.
Yes, the buttonhole in the shop-window's
Dummy keeps flaunting its loud begonia.
Whatever you opt to do, then do, or
Do not do: that, of course, you confess, is
What will own ya'. Enough, for you, is not
Enough. You would, if you could, go further
And father what your forefathers could not
Father. It is for the infinite that
You aspire. Thus, you try but fail to keep
Your balance on ambition's highest wire.

v

Long-held dogmas, once thought righteous, brave and

True, tremble before they begin to fail,
And then, at last, turn tail before they do.
That's how the drip, drip, drip of degradation
Goes. It trickles at first, suspiciously
Slow, before it conspires to flow, then run.
How it starts, why it stops, no one ever
Really knows. But all that purports to be
New again looks old in the evening sun.
Decadence is history's tedious law.
There's no need for astonishment at it,
No cause for awe. Wisdom's seven pillars
Crumble, topple, and tumble down. In its
Ruins, you see what wisdom never saw.

vi

At its birth, love foreshadowed its end. Yes.
Sometime ago, the business of the rose
Went bust. There are those who still want to love,
But they no longer have the will to trust.
The blessed Virgin had her own motives
For admiring her prodigal sons and
Daughters. But the history that forgot her
No longer tries to save what it slaughters.
Then, you spoke of love by man for woman,
Or by woman for man, but now you speak
As much as you care to, or can, but all
That's been transcended. Sometime in the twelfth
Century, love exhausted itself as
Soon as it began, and then it ended.

vii

There, under time's blunt ax, love despaired of
Itself, lost its head, betrayed the facts, and
Then sought to revenge itself with ugly
Scenes. Even with the vaunted luxury
Of retrospection, no historian
Could ever tell you what it means. Every
Age that becomes old enough always yearns
To retire to remorseless satire, to
That last great suffocating incense of

Negative sanctity. There was never
A hollow in you large enough to hold
Your heart. There was never a hollow in
You that did not want to be filled, never
An ideal that never longed to be killed.

viii

You keep searching in vain for knowledge you
Cannot attain, as if your boyhood hopes
Insisted that there's someone who's always
Existed, perhaps some local stiff, who'll
Now unwrap the mystery gift. But to know
The secret of the universe would be
Perverse. Any secret you come to know
Would make everything, not better, but worse.
The eloquence of the secret would be
Like toy dolls squeaking: You'd be astonished,
But could never understand the truth they're
Speaking. Thus, blow eternity a kiss,
For ignorance, they say, is bliss. You can't
Be horrified by the horrors you miss.

ix

In reverie, you can return, as you
Yearn, to times long dead. Only in you can
It revivify its long lost youth in
Your history-intoxicated head. You
Keep fantasizing about the past that
Never was what you thought it was till you
Too are dead. From jongleur to juggler to
Outright smuggler of the ridiculous
Into the sublime, you search for truth that
Frees the time. You know the now's no longer
Fulfillable, yet always killable,
And so are you. Any historian,
With the slightest clue, must still be able
To manage blue, if he can manage you.

x

Chaos is law. Order is dream, charming

Fiction. You're in turmoil. Thus, you obsess
Over its depiction. From unity
To multiplicity and back again,
The turnabout's left the troubled monad
Feeling sad. He yearns for unity he
Dreams of but fears he's never had. The lust
For the supersensual is always
Like forced sex, never consensual. It
Never asks permission from the lives it
Wrecks. Eternity, which you never knew,
Never stays at rest. It moves. It proves. And
Then it reconnects. It is the force of
The new in you that makes you eternal.

xi

Intellectual arrogance always
Lords it over the latest religion,
Over which it likes to ride roughshod. But
The lust for unity always sidesteps
Skepticism to satisfy itself
With some eloquent synonym for God.
Thus, you hunt for a replacement dogma.
But nirvana, a possible prey, was,
Alas, for you, never in season. You
Had tarried too long in the light of the
Common day. Or perhaps there was for you
Some other reason. And yet, to that vast
Fraternity of hearts that ache, you sought
For solid truths that you'd never forsake.

xii

Utopianism, that moldy old
Reliable, is no more willing to
Try the tryable. No longer extolled
And trusted, it is through and through weather-
Beaten, dog-tired and busted. Its remnant,
A tepid morality, still mourns the
Sacrifice of youth. Back in the day, it
Would look at itself and say: *oh yes, it's
Hard but still possible to guess the truth.*

Thou shalt not doubt: this, the commandment to
Yourself, you say, then break it in every
Possible way. You never quite agree
There's truth. To believe in it, while never
Pretending otherwise, seemed too uncouth.

xiii

*By now ye know why there's no such thang as
Walden Pond.* It's that phase woolgatherers
Wallow in to get beyond. Nothing could
Ever be more detrimental than a
Nihilism made palatable and
Sentimental. Corruption corrupts and
Connives for power to perpetuate
Corruption. Corruption pluralizes
The single and makes age-old wisdom a
Tawdry jingle. Unity succumbs as
It must to chaos, and chaos goes all
Thumbs, and it too succumbs. The virgin and
The dynamo are one, lewd signs of the
Same affinity for infinity.

xiv

Troubling doubt over what your history is
About provokes the recurring spasm
Of eternity's sarcasm. Thus, you
Could trust in no one's word, least of all your
Very own. That's why you're never in the
Best of company when you're all alone.
In the beginning, there was the void, and
The void with its own emptiness grew quite
Annoyed, craned its neck, as if to nod, and
Then said to nothingness: *Let there be God.*
You and your loneliest other belong
To the universe. The other is the
Exception. You're the proof that proves it's true
Through the miracle of self-deception.

VI. YOUR COMMON DAY
Hast thou seen what the ancients of the house of Israel do in

*the dark, every man in the chambers of his imagery. [8:12]
... Therefore prophesy against them, prophesy, O son of man.
[11:4] ... Thus saith the Lord God; Woe unto the foolish prophets, that follow their own spirit and have seen nothing! [13:3]
... The days are prolonged and every vision faileth. [12:22] ...
Thus, Ezekiel is unto you a sign: according to all he hath done
shall ye do. [24:24] ... Then said the Lord unto me; This gate
shall be shut, it shall not be opened, and no man shall enter in
by it; because the Lord, the God of Israel, hath entered in by it,
therefore it shall be shut. [44:2]*
 – From *The Book of the Prophet Ezekiel* –

i

There are forces strong and weak that in the
Darkness seize the chance to speak. They choose to
Speak through you. There's no way out, no escape
From your task. You do now whatever the
Whirlwind might ask. You do the will of your
Loneliest, onliest other. Your wife,
The apple of your eye, will die. There will
Be no time to cry, no time to mourn, no
Time to scorn the day that you and she were
Born. Her absence will be unto you a
Parable of absences to come, and
Under every tree gone green, you'll practice
There the lowest of the low, the basest
Of the base, and the meanest of the mean.

ii

Wheels, replete with eyes, turn as they promise
What you fear the most, yet will least surprise.
Wheels within each wheel are too grotesque to
Let you do anything other than fear
What you feel. You fear the fire that burns at
Its most dire in you. You fear the motion
That never lets you rest. You fear each new
Hour that arrives, as if to pose just one
More test. You fear what in your heart you know
But try in vain to suppress. You fear what
You know, that you've never done your best, for

You could not keep the promise. There's a God,
You fear, who seeks comfort in your suffering.
Your terror will be his consolation.

iii

Wheels within the wheels turn like cogs in the
Terrible machinery of God. Each cog
Moves like an angel whose motion is meant
As an endless act of devotion. As
His machinery churns and churns, to you, he
Turns, as if to seek assurance that he,
Like you, is the fire that burns. Wheels within
Wheels, that's the emblem of eternity
In motion, that steels the heart of what it
Moves and thrills but never seals. Each wheel, with
Starry-eyed wonder, stares down in awe at
Your perpetual blunder. Ten thousand
Eyes blink as they think what they always knew:
This, poor fool, is how you get to be you.

iv

Every house will have its cryptic law, will
Treasure its wayward pattern, and you will
Search in vain to find its flaw before the
Gate gets shut, and you see at last, as if
You saw what no one saw, as if you saw
What's holy, what's profane. In the dark
Of the common day, you saw it plain. You
Saw abominations in chambers of
Your imagery. For the charlatan and
The cad, for the virgin and the slut, for
The sinner and the saint, the way back to
Paradise is shut. Knowing all this, you
Rebel. You will not rest content with hell.
You'll trumpet the justice of your complaint.

v

In the midst of the fog, there's always the
Dreaded Gog, the mystery of what you fear

The most. There's that dark and dreadful angel
That's hid in deepest dregs of the truant
Id, that mercilessly makes its bid to bless
And repress what you won't confess. It is
Not in yourself but in God that you see
All that you see in you. It is not in
God but in you that you see all that you
See in God. You keep looking for yourself,
Keep failing to find it, keep telling tales
About yourself, as if yet another
Tale about yourself will not reveal it,
But forever blind it from what you are.

vi

There's that idiot questioner in you
Who undermines all your spirit finds. Thus,
Your imagination casts its shadow
Of self-doubt. All you loved, feared, and hated,
All you've struggled for, all you've endlessly
Debated, all those truths you're told not to
Question or doubt, that's not what your life has
Been about. The false angel deceives with
The truth. It's a parody of itself
That purports to reveal a truth it wants
To conceal. There's an angel false and an
Angel true. You must choose the angel that's
Meant for you. But to mistake false angels
For the true, that will be the ruin of you.

vii

The angel of the fiery sword blocks your
Path toward the tree of life, or perhaps it
Preserves it from the likes of you, for you
Would bring to it your cruel contagion of
Imitation and limitation. You
Would bring to it this cruelty merely
Through the act of being you. He who blocks
The way to Eden is the anointed
Guard of what becomes for you too hard. What's
Holy, what's infinite, eternity

In motion, is not bound or diminished
By the doubt that diminishes you. Thus,
Every day you must pray to make your way
Through the blinding light of your common day.

viii

Your task was to restore the hope of joy.
This was the essence of your vision, which
The sorrow of its aftermath could never
Quite destroy. When God went, the joy went too.
When God abandoned joy, he abandoned
You. It's the mourning that destroyed the joy
Of dawn. Before mid-afternoon, the God
You enjoyed was almost gone, and later
In places high, places low, all succumbed
To the weight of evening woe. If you'd cherish
Joy, you must do so before it's gone, for
When it's gone, when you have lost the hope of
Any savior, you'll blame, not yourself, but
His absence for all your bad behavior.

ix

You lie on your left. You lie on your right.
You endure in exile the insomnia
Of never-ending night. You told what you
Saw, as if the telling could ever be
Enough. And yes, you had to yell because
Even telling everything could never
Be enough. What you saw athwart the throne
Melted your idolatrous heart of stone.
Your own death, you fear, will be abundant,
But redundant. And yes. The denial
Of grief accelerates the conditions
Of freezing. Those who survive the frost will,
In their despair, no longer care about
The cost of surviving or appeasing.

x

When truth has perished, there will be nothing

Worshipped, nothing honored, nothing cherished.
For eons now, humanity has wept
Over the anguish of the promise it
Keeps unkept. Yes. Idolatry makes a
Guilty bystander of every craven
Misunderstander. Abominations
To come will of course be worse. Evil, which
Does all it ever could to masquerade
As good, grows more and more perverse. Thus, you
Will get what you expect and then regret.
All that was once worthwhile you now forget
With the guile of one sly smirk. In the guise
Of goodness, evil does its finest work.

xi

You obsess over the past even though
Your prophecy foretells it cannot last.
You stared deep into history's whoroscope,
And in its narrow span, you witness the
Suffocating death of woman and the
Death of man. For a long time now, Adam
Has honored the remembrance of Eve by
Wearing her perfume on his sleeve. But whores
Of perception can only be cleansed by
Self-deception. Thus, the God, who loved you
Dearly, loved you best, when he made sure you'd
Never be able to see too clearly.
Even now the watchman's words admonish
Those whom his visions fail to astonish.

xii

Go on that way, you say, and you'll throw your
Soul away. It won't return, even if
You have an eternity to learn what
You've never learned. If you still have the grit
To care, you're destined to earn your fair share
Of despair. The desperate don't imagine;
They fear. To the desperate, the mystery is
Always all-too-clear. Despair's that portable
Hell, that carry-on luggage, you use to

Travel on the cheap. Despair's the constant
Reminder of the promise you made but
Cannot keep. The wheels keep turning, and all
The while you keep learning what it's like to
Connive as hard as you can to seem alive.

xiii

The ecstatic liar's greatest lie is
That there is ecstasy that has no cost.
If you've never yet had yours, then there is, some
Say, no purpose at all to all your tours.
The vast progeny of these sayers still
Celebrate Energy, Delight. Despite
The legend of everlasting night, they
Have the gall to mimic joy. But ethics,
Others say, is not a toy. And though you
Know it would be quite nice, there will, there can
Be, no sacrifice of sacrifice. The
Promise promises promiscuity,
The nostalgia for all that's lost, and the
Dread over what regaining it would cost.

xiv

Illusions, your necessary angels,
Perform, as they must, their sacred role. They
Lead you where they lead, for they remain as
Always the symbols, the sounding brass of
What you think you need. Yes. The nature of
Self-knowledge and self-deceit are so close
Akin that the line between them must be
Very thin. This is the line you would not
Cross, but always do, the line you cross each
Day in every moment of common day.
There should, of course, by now no longer be
The slightest doubt. Yes. Persons perceiving
And misperceiving persons, and persons
Deceiving themselves: that's what it's all about.

VII. THE INVERSE AVATAR

Not I truly, who am a sinner, for I never drink without thirst, either present or future. To prevent it, as you know, I drink for the thirst to come. I drink eternally. This is to me an eternity of drinking, and drinking of eternity. ... Let the devil take him. Say amen. And now for a drink.
    – Francois Rabelais, *Gargantua and Pantagruel* –

Draw the curtain. The farce is over.
    – Francois Rabelais, Reputedly on his death bed

i

Do as thou wilt. If anything gets in
The way of that, let that be the only
Cause of guilt. You robbed Peter. You paid Paul.
And when no one else was there to help, they
Said, indeed, they lied, that you did it all.
You believe in sex, in piss, in dung, and
You believe in dice. And, yes, sometimes, when
You're itching to scratch, you believe in lice.
You're bitten by your own bug, smitten by
Your own self-hugging hug. Yes. Farce is that
Genre of a desperate kind. It says to
The reader: Please don't mind. Don't worry. Be
Patient. You'll know you're through, when the farce has
Finally made a total ass of you.

ii

You faced the extremity of pain, of
Cruelty, of torture. You would, if you could,
Undermine it with evasions. And you do.
Your humor would, if it could, burrow down
To a joy that's deeper than pain. But the
Lower you go the deeper the snow. Life
At its lowest is always life at its
Snowiest. Life at the very bottom
Of everything that it's tried is always
Showiest about what it wants to hide.
The world that others bemoan and deplore,

That world for you is an ecstasy at
Its core. The deeper you dive the more you
Enjoy the splendor of being alive.

iii

The undying child within you never
Grew old enough to know what he thought he
Knew. Circumstance almost killed it, but your
Humor, with each joke and adolescent
Trick, always thrilled it and brought back to life
The child you seek in you. Thus, you find it,
You pamper it, you exploit it, and you
Expect everyone one else to let it do
What it will and never mind it. You let
Your misery become a mystery to
Yourself. Hence, you try to explain it. You
Keep explaining as fast as you can. But
You can't sustain it. Yes. You always go
Wrong, if you try to keep it up too long.

iv

You took your nonsense seriously, and
You had the nerve to practice it with verve,
Yes, quite deliriously. The secret
Of the infant giant in you is the
Untroubled certitude of a child who
Knows that life is and only can be what
It is. All questions about it all are
Just a noisome, needless quiz. They arise
Only when the ideal now you strain to
Venerate has lost its fizz. The logic of
Either/or's a perpetual bore. Thus,
You demand to practice the Narcissus
Logic of *always can and always now*.
It's the law of *both/and* that tells you how.

v

Heaven perhaps does not exist, but hell,
Which never did before, now certainly

Does. Hell, the inverse avatar of joy,
That's the logical absurdity of
What you once thought the reality of
Heaven was. Thus, on earth, as in heaven.
In heaven, as it is on earth. And, now
Surprisingly, in Hell too. Wherever
You are with lonely others, wherever
Your lonely others may be with you, there's
No congregation that's never riddled
With politics through and through. In hell, have-
Nots have, and haves have not, and both obsess
Over what both still want but haven't got.

vi

You can't escape into Eternity
Or Nirvana, but, then, neither can you
Escape into confabulated joy,
Into that golden moment you believe
You can treat as your grown-up toy. Life will
Not liberate you from life. Yes. From one
Eternity to another it goes
On. And just when the sun is about to
Set, there is always yet another dawn.
To steer toward utopia in any
Wind that blows is to exalt the folly
Of every idiot who would, if he
Could, know better, but always insists on
Being the forgetter of what he knows.

vii

Eternity stirs in the gonads, in
The gullet, in the bowels, and when the sheets
Are in the wind, it roars, it howls. This, as
They say, is what is happening when the
Bottom of your belly growls. Or you feel
It in the knees when you're about to sneeze.
All these eternities of the nether
Regions naturally abstain from any
Pompous cerebrations of the brain. Yet
In underwear they leave their lasting stain.

You would, if you could, on nothing at all
Depend. You'd live, if you could, on wind. Thus,
Let the devil have his honest share, for
If you live as you should, then you won't care.

viii

A mob of fools is one of the tools of
Wit, as you surmise. They would, like Bozo
And Socrates, converse among themselves
As though they were clever, witty and wise.
There is nothing absolutely certain
That you've ever known; alas, you've only
Guessed, like all those idiots you detest.
Like a scrivener's dog-eared almagest,
Your life's the catalog of the worst and
Best, and poses the riddle of all that
Twiddle in the middle you can't digest.
You're never quite clear whether certainty
Or skepticism has the most to fear.
But this you mumble as you bumble on.

ix

A turd's only a piece of excrement
To those who lack your wit to see what lies
On the brighter side of shit. This brighter
Side, they say, is always in the way you
See. That's the proverbial clue, some say,
To your sense of eternity. The test of
Every book is its size, not its length or
Breadth, but the distance between its lows and
Highs. Bridge that gap with a book, then you can
Call yourself wise. There's an open secret,
But it's lost in the cosmic smile's deepest
Dimple. Yet you must celebrate all the
Complications of life. That is, if you
Will, the only way to keep it simple.

x

To deny the anguish you can flee from,

But never defeat: that's the paragon
Of self-deceit. Yes. Every age has an
Aquarian tinge, a utopian
Urge that makes even the wisest among
You cringe. You and your lonely others kept
Wanting to believe. But now, almost no
One does. The nowhere you thought was there and
Then is not now here and never was. You
Believed that everything's true except for
The belief that there's just one truth about
Everything. All has all to lose and nothing
To gain, if you should distill into just
One drop all the varieties of rain.

xi

Your giants were born too tall to be small,
Too tall to listen to littleness at
All. To every axiom you applied
An ax and cleaved apart the so-called facts.
Your attitude toward every platitude
Was to stop it in its tracks and reward
Each cliché with forty whacks. You loved not
One or two but every urge that sprang from
You, and through the bawdy masquerade, you
Begin to sense what you barely knew. The
Laughter was always after you, laughter
That let you pierce the blindness, laughter that
Let you make of uncommon charity
An infinite splurge of human kindness.

xii

You accept the world as it is because
You must. Anyone who does not accept
The world as such you do not trust. You would,
Even if you could, never bother to
Refute the absolute. You would, even
If you could, never abstract quintessence
From a fact. You'd leave the absolute and
Fact alone. You'd live your life knowing you're
Lucky you're not yet gone. You'll rejoice that

The life you can't ignore could be your own.
And, yes, of course you contradict yourself.
Anyone or anything consistent,
That's a yawn. Thus, please ask your loneliest
Other to wake you up when they are gone.

xiii

There's a deeper soul in you forever
New that stays in touch with you through all you
Do. But the logic of the lie it tries
To refute ends up by refuting you.
And yet, you would, if you could, forsake all
The wrong turns you take on the road toward
The promises you're bound to break. At the
End of the road, there will be one final
Dodge. Therefore, the eternity you seek
Deviates from you with one last mirage.
This, the mercy of time, the gift of your
Eternity, is self-deception. There's
Nothing in the universe to stem it.
Its power of forgiveness has no limit.

VIII. AN HONEST-TO-GOD HYPOCRITE

Whatever I say or do, there's always one part of myself which stays behind, and watches the other part compromise itself, which laughs at and hisses it, or applauds it. When one is divided that way, how is it possible to be sincere? ... One wants to deceive people, and one is so much occupied with seeming, that one ends by not knowing what one really is ... The true hypocrite is the one who ceases to perceive his deception, the one who lies with sincerity.
– Andre Gide, *The Counterfeiters* –

It is in eternity that right now one must live. And it is right *now that one must live in eternity.*
– Andre Gide, *The Journals (Numquid et tu?)* –

i

It's a story now quite old, that's rarely,
If ever, told, but never quite new. That
Story rarely told is the tragedy
Of being you. The devil designs all
The characters. God writes the plot. It's the
Entanglement of the two that makes the
Play a drama of who's the fraud and who's not.
Irony thus corrupts and absolute
Irony corrupts resolutely. Once
It begins it never knows when to stop.
You may think all of this is terribly
Twisted, but as a latecomer, you hold
Everyone but yourself to account for this
Confusion that has always existed.

ii

In your dreams, you cohabit with extremes.
And you flaunt your most flagrant assumptions,
Thereby giving no apology for
Ideology. You will double down
With fervor on your brute presumptions. Yes.
Your God neglects to disclose why he failed
To shorten Cleopatra's nose. If he
Had, then what's bad might never have been that
Bad, and all that's sad would be a life you
Might have imagined but never had. But
You live the life you never imagine,
And imagine the life you never live,
And all the life you live will be stressed and
Pressed, strained and drained through history's drastic sieve.

iii

You sought the best in yourself but couldn't
Find it. If only someone else could do
The job for you, then you wouldn't mind it.
All that you assumed would sharpen you keeps
Blunting your edges. All that you thought would
Simplify you keeps getting lost in your

Hedges. Dullest vagueness, your paradigm
Of infinity, thus reminds you, as
Always, of God's shapeless divinity.
When your assumptions burn off, you breathe in
Their dissipating vapor, that sense you
Have of life as a meaningless caper.
Perhaps another counterfeit coin
Will more than suffice to keep you going.

iv

You never are. You keep becoming. The
Rainbow that arcs from now here to nowhere,
You keep on strumming. To live sincerely,
You would forsake all you hold most dearly
And dive deep into the life you've never
Lived. You'll never be and see what you are.
If you could be it, you would not see it.
If you could see it, you would not be it.
Your sense of truth is the nerve to preserve
Your contradictions, and your loyalty's
Knowing how to swerve from your convictions.
Nothing good ever lets you do what you
Would, but only what you won't. When they say
Be yourself, the best you can do is: don't.

v

You wanted to paint a self-portrait you
Could admire, cherish, and revere. But that
Picture of yourself could never quite come
Together, never quite cohere. You were
Always too unstable to take a stand,
Too mercurial to stick with any
One demand, too fickle to meet any
Of the goals for which you planned. Therefore, you
Always resent what you represent. You
Have fervor but no durable faith. Your
Perpetual unease was incurable
Disease. For you and your lonely others,
The last sting's the ironic tease urging
You now to welcome only what would please.

vi

Your destiny is the death of you. It's
What you become when all else is through. You
Live your life as if you could live it up.
But now you know that you can never live
It down unless you give it up. Only
For a while can you pretend that you have
No guile. And when you think of what it would
Be like to be always sincere, it makes
You sneer with a counterfeit smile. Alas,
In the history of the universe, there's
Never been the slightest, single act of
Unadulterated sincerity.
You can take this to the bank. That is the
One and only eternal verity.

vii

Alas, sincerity is always a
Put-up job, the last ditch fraudulence of
A moral snob. And, yes. In every act
Of sincerity you forget the sin.
Perhaps, one day, you were sleeping, and then,
Some villain full of mischief slipped it in.
You take back your life to give it. You give
It to take it back. And in the give and
Take of it, God will forgive it, even
As you live it, and make what you make of
It. Eternity, for you, came with each
Act of forged sincerity. But each such
Act was always precisely that: an act.
If you'd have a heart, you must act the part.

viii

You're too much troubled by the recency
Of the latest indecency. In the
Midst of your conniving, the scandals keep
Arriving. They never really stop. The
Scandals keep occurring, despite your sly
Resolve to keep preferring something else.

The universe gives no deference to your
Preference. But you never quite give up your
Dream that one day all the indecency,
All the violence, all the banality
Of rampant evil will lose its steam. But
It never does. Yet it creates in your
Heart the nostalgia to return to the
Nowhere that never is and never was.

ix

High noon, you might say, is God's masterpiece.
That every moment is high noon means the
Challenge to become what you are must never
Cease. If every moment's high noon, you would
If you could, become what you are, but you
Must do it soon. To accomplish all this
Requires only a little effort for
The fraud in you to coax itself into
Perpetrating that ancient hoax called peace.
Nowadays, you lack the moral standards
And the wit to make you the least bit fit
To be an honest-to-God hypocrite.
If life were not so cryptic, you'd never
Be tempted by the apocalyptic.

x

You wish everyone had the decency
To become what you claim they are. But just
Like you, everyone else, you knew in your
Heart of hearts, is the still uncaptured light
Of a distant star. Till they have faces,
You wait, while imagination tempting
Fate, names its latest, greatest numen. Yes.
That's how you learn to love the inhuman.
You imagined that death's near miss would sweep
You clean, that it would purify you of
Every lie, and then tell you what your life
Was meant to mean before you die. But now
You know that every confession is just
One more stab at faking another try.

xi

You wanted a masterpiece not tender,
But cruel, one to people your fervor
With exhausted fuel. Your many moods were
An undisciplined squad, as you sought sans
Mercy to take full advantage of God.
You ask him to oversee your desperate
Spree, to unshackle time's undeserving
Prisoners and set them free. But he answers,
Saying: *Oh no, dear boy, that would be to
Quash your eternity and kill your joy.* This,
You say, to God, is something you've never
Understood. He says: *I never asked to
Be understood. I only ask you to
Love what you never could and live the good.*

xii

Your boredom, like demon rum, dribbles first
At your thirst and drubs you till you're numb from
The dreaded rhythm of its drum. You passed
Your exam with honors, yet no one's there
To sneer or care. The last step in being
Tried is that you get yourself certified.
All this, you ask yourself, is all for what?
In the thrall of sin, nagging futility
Kicks in. *If you'll see the angel, they say,
You'll see her then.* And of course you do. She'll
Whisper in your ear: *Let me walk with you.*
You exhale a moan, and as you go, you
Glimpse traces of angels in faces of
James, Simone, Michelangelo and Joan.

xiii

Eternity starts right here, right now, and
Never stops. Eternity is how you
Make what is nowhere here and now, how what
You revere makes nowhere not nowhere, but
Now here. In the far spent night, in the all-
Too-breezy headiness of the common

Day, you were deceived into the truth and
Then with mercy led astray. Again and
Again, you'll seek, you'll find, necessary
Self-justifications for your troubled
Mind. The God you never knew, but wanted
To, would never dwell on sin; he was far
Too kind. To see yourself too clearly is
Punishment. It's more blissful to be blind.

xiv

Always the prodigal son, you prided
Yourself on stealing other people's fun.
But then, you're asked to kill the Minotaur.
And, yes, this monster, which you fear is you,
Most certainly will be you before you're
Through. It's then that the miracle that should
Never happen, that never stops, makes bold
To start that tremor of happiness in
Your heart. The miracle you never wanted
Will come without warning to bother you.
You'll never start anything new until
The miracle finishes what it must do
To you. In the light of that uncommon
Day, even the atheist learns to pray.

xv

You saw what no one else could see, because
No one, except you, wanted to see what
You see. It was on the far horizon,
Alone, invisible, everlasting,
And free. That's when reality dropped its
Stubborn curtain. That's when you, nearly dead,
Summon your failing strength to look ahead.
When you're suddenly certain, that's when you
See eternity. The self you see in
Time is never you, but you, the seer, in
Eternity, are what the self in time
Has yearned to be and feared to learn. You now
Have one last chance to be sincere, to make
Eternity that's always nowhere now here.

IX. SEEING IT OTHERWISE

Death is not an event in life: we do not live to experience death. If we take eternity to mean not infinite temporal duration but timelessness, then eternal life belongs to those who live in the present. ... The solution of the problem of life is seen in the vanishing of the problem.
   – Ludwig Wittgenstein, *Tractatus-Logico Philosophicus* –

The honest religious thinker is like a tightrope walker. He almost looks as though he was walking on nothing but air. His support is the slenderest imaginable. And yet, it is possible to walk on it. ... What is ragged should be left ragged.
   – Ludwig Wittgenstein, *Culture and Value* –

i

You sought to assert what you wanted to
In a language logically perfect. Each
Saying, you thought, should mirror the shape of
The fact it states. You conjured away all
The problems you confronted and were quite
Relieved that, despite the brilliance of your
Vanishing trick, so little was achieved.
To give this moment a name would traduce
The rules of your game, the one you soon stopped
Playing, the one that kept dismaying those
Who never knew they were always only
Saying that *all is all* or that *small is
Small.* The puzzle you're in is a game that
You're never supposed to win. That is all.

ii

Or perhaps, it's not. For enough's never
Quite enough. And all is never quite all.
Or perhaps, your game is without a bat
And without a ball, without a goal, and
Without any rules at all. You assumed
Clarity could be absolute. In the
Light of such clarity, all problems, you
Thought, would simply vanish. To speak of what

You should not speak would be like a bull frog
Attempting Urdu or reciting Spanish.
To bring back everything to everyday
Means the profound gets lost in the light of
Common day. And the profound's not just what's
Hard, but what's quite impossible, to say.

iii

You lost your way in the light of common
Day. Not knowing your way about: that's what,
For you, philosophy's all about. Most
Philosophers, you knew, practiced nonsense
In disguise, while always pretending what
They did and said was wise. Philosophy
Can never answer what you would have it
Answer, even though again and again
In vain, it desperately tries. Life's always
The larger task to do what philosophy
Would never answer and never ask. To
Convince yourself of what is true for you,
You must find yourself where you are, and where
You are, is nowhere. You must start from there.

iv

Life, your life, everyone's life, is always
A desperation in search of peace. No
Theory, no explanation, no ode to
Joy, will suffice to make it cease. It keeps
On going. And your imagination
Keeps on snowing on the briars and brambles
Of the real. There's no emotion, there's no
Commotion, there's no act of devotion,
That could ever make the motion of your
Eternity keep still. Logic that leads
You nowhere is, for true belief, too hard,
Yet too cogent to discard. Dropping the
Common day's disguise is looking at what
You've always seen, but seeing it otherwise.

v

You wanted to practice philosophy
Like a businessman, to seal the deal, to
Get the transaction all settled, but you
Forgo satisfaction and find yourself
Decidedly nettled. It would put your
Sense of heaven in a rage, if you took
No time to stage yet another scene of
Faux sincerity, depth, and suffering.
Each time you heard foolosophy's shrillest
Dog-whistle, you felt the danger then of
Becoming even more superficial.
But the one moment you became sincere,
You never knew, because you can only
Become sincere by never wanting to.

vi

You'd be a genius, or you'd be nothing.
You studied genius, and you practiced it.
Thus, to be genuine, you must start out
First by being your own best counterfeit.
You worked on yourself, honing your focus,
Until solving the riddle was easy
As hocus pocus. Affectation was
Your finest art, your path to genius, the
Wayward path of your calculating heart.
Always in you a geyser's about to
Spew dregs from the very bottom of you.
And this fountain of hard truth tells you what
You already knew: if you fear to die,
You know, in your heart, that you've lived a lie.

vii

Yes. You would, if you could, elicit the
Clarity of the spirit and make it
Explicit. And you imagined clarity
Would shine, as if it should glow with the sum
Of what you know. But into the fog bank
Of a murky concept, you now know, is

About as far as the clearest thought can go.
You would, if you could, remove the blindfold
Of the common day. Again and again,
You say what you cannot say. And, thus, in
Doing so, you unwittingly show what
You can never know. The cure of all this
Nonsense is deliberate, painful, slow.
But you'll never quite stop doing it though.

viii

Questions that spur your hunger ask for what
Can never satisfy. So again and
Again, you ask yourself the question: Why
Try? What's most important you understand
The least. But the fact that there is famine
Will always show the value of the feast.
You can't help but wince, when you realize
There's nothing you can do to purge yourself
And your lonely others of the urge to
Practice nonsense. Thought, obsessed with its own
Foundations, founders. But every other
Thought does too. It's never a question of
What's the matter with your thought. It's always
A question of what's the matter with you.

ix

There will be no sign, no wonder. There will
Be only you and your blunder and what
You make of it. You walk on a tightrope
Of a promise that cannot be kept or
Broken. With all you believe, this tension
Pulls taut in you, but remains unspoken,
And if you will, as you must, surrender
Your tenuous trust, then all you claim to
Believe goes bust. There is no lucid fact
You may cite. Your sense of eternity,
That is the only token of seeing
The world, unspoken, as it must be seen,
Of seeing the darkest night suddenly
Aright in common day's uncommon light.

x

There's no error, no miscalculation,
No botched try, that's so deep as the promise
You should, but did not keep. All the deepest
Problems are not problems at all, but just
Promises that are much too tall, much too
Steep to keep. That there's a world, that there's you,
That there's meaning at all, is a gift, a
Covenant, a promise. If you could keep
Any promise that you make, this is the
One you should not break. But you do. Doing
So, at times, seems the essence of you. But,
No, you only resemble what you do
Or do not do. Lacking any essence
At all: that's the very essence of you.

xi

The one thing needful is the one-sided
Diet that nourishes. In the midst of
All your confusion, it still flourishes.
The way you speak echoes the life you seek.
You're driven to say what cannot be said.
This source of all your puzzles, your logic
Tries to silence what it never muzzles.
You would, if you could, get out of the fly
Bottle by going, engines racing, at
Fullest throttle. But you can't and don't. And
Yet, by never getting what you want, you
Learn to live with what you should want, but don't.
It's never the least bit fair, but God tempts
You most with what he knows you least can bear.

xii

Your pilgrim's progress toward the absolute,
That's a sham, for you think to yourself: *How
Can I become what I already am?*
But there's a value absolute that all
Your relativities fail to refute.
There's that sacred gesture, the miracle

That splashed upon the empirical the
Cold-water shock of seeing what is and
Seeing it anew. Until you see your
Way through to the splendor of the new, the
You, you thought you were, is never really
You. Therefore, be grateful for the gift of
Being. But the greater gift is the gift
Of seeing everything as miracle.

xiii

Don't look too hard. Don't see too clear. Don't do
What's barred. Don't try to mean what you cannot
Say. Don't try to say what you cannot mean.
Don't try to make the ragged neat or the
Muddied clean. If you'd stay, don't go. If you'd
Go, don't stay. There can, for you, be nothing
More obscene than to obscure the ragged
Light of the common day. If you'd sneak through
Logic's keyhole and take a peek, you would
Perhaps still be able to speak, but no
One, not even you, would understand. Yes.
Solipsism's slippery fly bottle is
Hard to flee. And yet every thou is a
Challenge to the loneliest part of thee.

xiv

There's God, there's self, there's world beyond world, where
The value of fact lies cunningly curled.
God, self, world, these are the sources of your
Confusions. You bump against the limits
Of language and then perversely cherish
Your contusions. You should purge yourself of
Your urge to make God, self and world converge.
But you never do. For the vanishing
Of this problem is the vanishing of
You. The true life is the new life, and the
New life's the true life of the present, whose
Eternity's sufficient unto the
Day thereof. It's never quite logical,
And yet never quite wrong to call it love.

XV

There is, for you, too much one-sidedness
In the decidedness of anything.
Eternity is how simplicity
Imagines it exists. Your time is thus
Complexity made manifest. First, you
Do not die, your sense of eternity
Insists. Then your forgetfulness of the
Monstrous facts of time will do the rest. But
After death, there will be no time, and there
Will be no death, for there will be no time
For you to be dead. All will be shown; and
Nothing will be said. God, with infinite
Mercy, will let your timelessness begin.
That's how the living God forgives your sin.

xvi

There is wonder; that is the gift. There is
Guilt; that is the debt you cannot forgive
Or forget. And there is that baseless sense
Of safety, you thought absolute, until
You face the threat you haven't met with yet.
To be in the eternal now is to
Make nowhere now here. It's to live without
Fear, without the persistent fear that you're
Insincere. You felt safe, invincible,
Then guilty. Both passions, though this may sound
Supremely odd, are evidences of
Eternity, of God. You now know what
History has to do with thee. You know the
Undying sense of your eternity.

X. THE CHRISTMAS KILLING

Perhaps it is on the instant that we realize, admit, that there is a logical pattern to evil, that we die, he thought, thinking of the expression he had once seen in the eyes of a dead child, and of other dead: the cooling indignation, the shocked despair fading, leaving two empty globes in which the motionless world lurked profoundly in miniature.
– William Faulkner, *The Sanctuary* –

They were trying to write down the heart's truth out of the heart's driving complexity, for all the complex and troubled hearts which would beat after them. What they were trying to tell, what He wanted said, was too simple. Those for whom He transcribed His words could not have believed them. It had to be expounded in the everyday terms which they were familiar with and could comprehend, not only those who listened but those who told it too, because if they, who were that near to Him as to have been elected from all that breathed and spoke language to transcribe and relay His words, could comprehend truth only through the complexity of passion and lust and hate and fear which drives the heart, what distance back to truth must they traverse whom truth could only reach by word of mouth?
– William Faulkner, *The Bear* –

"Christmas?" he shouted. "Did they say Christmas?"... Then he saw Christmas. ... But he has seen now the other face, the one that is not Christmas.
– William Faulkner, *Light in August* –

i

Every design must fail. The tragic, the
Comic, is the tail end of a tale that
Cheers on what it fails to quell. That's how you
Revoke what you evoke and evoke what
You revoke. On this paradox, you and
Your lonely others choke. Now here wants to
Be nowhere, and nowhere now here. All you
Fear, that's precisely what you hold most dear.
The nature of intent is to prevent
The fruition of intent. And design's
Defined by how it's undermined. You would,
If you could, explain what you can't explain,
But you can't. Thus, you try to say what you
Can't say anyway, yet you say it slant.

ii

In the life you live in, you don't belong.

There's something about you that seems all wrong.
There's no place to go, no place to stay, no
Way to hide how much you've lied in the light
Of common day. Thus, you would, if you could,
Relinquish your heart's last darling, that bright-
Eyed hobbledehoy, that latter day trace
Of long lost joy, that you imagined you
Were when just a boy. Yes. Your sanity's
Served, but still unnerved, when illusion is
Challenged, and, after a little trouble,
Gets preserved. Solving the problem of you
Becoming you is the easiest and
The hardest thing that anyone can do.

iii

You could, of course, always relinquish your
Darling. But you don't, for naturally you
Continue to want whatever you want.
The return of the repressed is always
A dreary déjà vu. Memory eludes
You, and impatiently you wait for its
Return. On the lineup into hell, you,
On tenterhooks, wait and then greedily
Yearn for your turn to burn. You wait in vain
For damnation to lift, but it never
Does. Thus, your life is now and tomorrow
Just as damned as it ever was. The door
Of your fate claps to on you. You're stuck in
Fate's pattern now no matter what you do.

iv

You wait for the sense of doom to lift. It
Never does. It keeps on coming like the
Keep-on-giving of a gift that arrives
To stay on the longest day that ever
Was. Death, your last unwelcome chore, a cup
That passes from the hand of the Lord, was,
For you, like the sawing of a very
Hard board. When it's about to happen, there's
No time to expound on the meaning of

Its rasping, grasping sound. In the chaos
Of cosmic noise, you're bound to lose, not just
Your poise, but everything you thought you found.
You've only time enough to deplore the
Prospect of death's vast, everlasting snore.

v

When you die, you won't know you're dead, but your
Spiritual flesh for a time will tarry
Wherever the trend of your life has led.
If you're wounded, your blood will flow till there's
Nothing you care to know. And if you die
Unwounded, and haven't said and done all
You could have done and said, your veins will still
Be gorged with blood you otherwise might have
Bled. Your world's not your world. Your life's not your
Life. Homesick for eternity, you let
The loose abandon of your life run free.
You're afraid you'll go crazy, crazy as
A bat. But when the time comes, you'll go much
Further than that. You'll go to Tennessee.

vi

Your greed for more and more life will tease with
Its promise of more and more unease. And
The spirit that craves the sanctuary
Of a temple nevertheless nestles
In the body's nasty, squalid dimple,
In the crease caused by a fat man's lap when
He sits, or in the tobacco-scarred cleft
Of a toothless maw when it hawks and spits.
That's what soul is like, an accidental
Tourist on an ugly spree that hates what
It's like to be, that fears, that loathes, the lure
Of its eternity. Yes. You confess:
Nihilism's normal, universal,
And there's now no chance for its reversal.

vii

Thus, all your expectation succumbs to
Expectoration and continues to
Try to shock what it only numbs. In the
Face of this futility, even the
Best of your ability becomes all
Thumbs. Blind fate's vision will never trust us.
That's what makes it blind. It wants to mete out
Its own brand of justice, which is never
The least bit kind to your befuddled mind.
All that once came alike to all is no
Longer familiar or comparable.
And, now, though you can barely bear to care,
Even a modicum of kindness makes
Humankind's unkindness almost bearable.

viii

Dead eyes that once looked upon the world now
Reflect its emptiness. When you can't live
Down the fact that you can't live it up, you
Know in your heart it's time to give it up.
Your would-be sanctuary despairs that
There is no sanctuary. That nowhere
That should be now here, you fear, isn't there.
After scandal, after shocks, there'll be a
Return to apathy. But the nature of
Your new despair is that you must care
That you don't care. Let that be your lasting
Paradox. To say that you care that you
Don't care is idle chatter. It doesn't
Really matter that it doesn't matter.

ix

There will be a promise of light in the
August rush for fall. That early morning
Light, you saw, you hoped would point the way to
The meaning of it all. But it never
Did, and from its rising noonday glare, you
Hid. Yes. When you were a kid you really,

Really did all those odious things you
Say you never did. If truth came easy,
It would never make you queasy when you
Find it. If truth were a consolation,
It would never sear your soul, and if it
Did, you would never mind it. But it does,
And you do. Thus, as long as you live, you're
Never through with what truth can do to you.

X

It's damnable the damned don't stay damned, that
They'll at last be saved, that the hitherto
Undamned become more and more depraved, that
Last will be first, and first last, and, yes, that
This lie's the history of everyone's past.
You were, you thought, a self-born man, one whose
Say-so started at the beginning, there
Where the cosmic excrement first hit the
Fan. But then life's hardest knocks taught you to
Disbelieve this monstrous paradox, that
You're not self-born, but created out of
The lust of two lost souls who mated, who
Sent you, thus, merrily on your way toward
Becoming now what you've always hated.

xi

Everyone, you knew, resembles what he
Writes before he's through, just as all you wrote
Resembles you. Thus, your prose, just like you,
Was often inebriated through and
Through. The act of naming was primitive,
Then cynical. Some sad sack had her way
And gave John Doe the name of a pagan
Holiday. But every day you knew in
Every way is just one more chance to dread
The common day. Thus, you sought instruction
In self-destruction and sanctuary
In a bottle. And yet the dullness of
The common day, which made no sense, was a
Bugbear that you tried, but failed to coddle.

xii

The character of Christmas can hardly
Be believed, unless, like the holiday
Itself, that character becomes a feast
For the all-too-happily self-deceived.
Perhaps, you're black, perhaps you're white. Of what
You are, you're never quite sure, but neither
You nor any of your lonely others
Can share the fantasy of being pure.
An outcast who survives on the outer
Rim of what's barely believable, you
Embody the cruelty of life that loves
To live not now here but nowhere, of life
That clings now here, now there, in vain despair
To the hell of hurt that's unrelievable.

xiii

Christmas, for you, is that appointed time
When history echoes eternity's most
Melodious rhyme. Christmas, the outlaw
Holiday, commits its crime, by stealing
Away the August light from the drib-drib-
Drabness of your common day to make that
Feast you cared for most become the feast that
You care for least. There's no way to say it
Nice: you let the Christmas killing be your
Self-defining sacrifice. Yes. This is
That damnable thing you always do. You
Make the brutal murder of Christmas, not
About him, not about the holiday,
But forever and only about you.

xiv

It all begins with the deed, with change's
Perennial seed, with history's dog-eared
Certificate that something that's been long-
Looked-forward-to has just happened. Yes. You're
Deep inside the unsayable when all
The moldy old reliables are no

Longer tryable, but still playable
And betrayable. You're never prepared
For your childhood to stay just what it is:
Unimproved. Somewhere in the past you're stuck
On something you thought could never last, but
Somehow, reaching where you arrived, you held
On fast and never moved. Despite your pain,
Your life never proves what you think it's proved.

XV

History, you don't want but need, pauses long
Enough to bleed into your character.
You, like your lonelier betters, were born
To bleed. You were born to need what you do
Not want and to want what you do not need.
The story of yourself and your world you
Tell over and over, as if getting
What you want is getting over what you
Don't. But you want what you never get, and
You get what you never want. Thus, every
Common day you learn to end this way, with
Your slyest and wryest taunt: there is no
Getting over getting over, and that,
Alas, is all that you're allowed to want.

xvi

The connivance and chicanery of
Conscience, good and bad, makes you think perchance
That honesty is a nasty virtue
Or a vanity you never wanted
And never had. The honest truth is an
Impossible thing, a fact too complex
To bring about, or to cling to, what it
Reluctantly, but desperately neglects.
Time stomped on you its stamp and gave you the
Style of your guile, your genre. And then all
The blame you tried to escape howled and scowled
With gall and glee as it bounced back on ya'.
Human fate always needs a knot to cling
To. More often than not, that knot is you.

xvii

Time hands you again and again this sharp
Rebuke: every would-be dynasty you
Would build is, of necessity, a fluke.
The grandfather's watch keeps ticking. And each
Moment that goes by keeps sticking to the
Past. The son's second-hand to the father,
And the father, once a son, is second-
Hand to another man. There will be spite;
There will be lust; there will be envy. And
Not one of these is new, but merely the
Repetition of a will to revenge,
Once, twice, and thrice removed, of the past you
Obsessed about over and over, but
Never got over and never improved.

xviii

To be fatherless is to be without
Roots. But when the father's there, he arrives,
As it were, from the middle of nowhere,
A stranger, an intruder, with whom you're
In cahoots in the art of what it means
To be a talented self-deluder.
You dream the nightmare twilight of fathers,
That you're the lonely other that no one
Bothers. The nostalgia for a lost world,
You prolong, as if the mutilated
Swan, as he lay dying, had time enough to
Sing his song. And he does. But he sings of
The world as it might have been, not of the
World as it always is and always was.

xix

The father's silence speaks in his son. If
Anyone now is going to speak, then he
Must be the one. You never outlive your
Father nor he you. In history's circular
Labyrinth, you repeat all that's happened and
Call that new. You become what you feared, what

You now abhor. You know childhood isn't
Childhood anymore. The petty pace of
Common day creeps in, with the haggard look
Of a young man's long lost hope and an old
Man's dream of what he might have been. You keep
Your promise by breaking it. You save what's
Sacred by killing it and making it
Profane. Your heart once full is now inane.

XX

What can't matter doesn't matter but must.
This, the last sanctuary in which you
Put your trust, you hoped had the power to
Renew misbegotten avatars of
You. But, by now you've known nakedness so
Long it seems like clothes. All in the main of
Light you now expose. That now here's nowhere,
And that nowhere's now here is either a
Tautology or a contradiction,
And both prospects you fear. That smoking hole
In your heart means you're getting ready to
Restart the whole damn schmear. The solution
To the problem of desire's not to end
It, but to bend it toward eternity.

xxi

Eternity's the *is* that always is,
And the *was* that always was. It's how you
Handle the death of Christmas, the day that
Promises to bring you presence, but it
Never does. No. You never quite get used to
The *never is* or *was* of *is* and *was*.
You killed the joy in the heart of Christmas.
This, they say, is how you betray the light
Of common day. Cruel is this parable
Of the hollow-hearted, but you never
Stop what never started. Eternity
Cannot be killed or stilled. You can only
Fill it with what you've always willed. You fill
It, as you will it, with woe and wonder.

XI. ETERNITY'S SHREWDEST PRETENDER

If I think of the storm of my heart, the terrible tenacity with which, against my desire, it would cling to the hope of life, and if even now I feel this hurricane within me, I have at least a quietus which in wakeful nights helps me to sleep. This is the genuine ardent longing for death, for absolute unconsciousness, total non-existence. Freedom from all dreams is our only salvation. ... As I have never in life felt the real bliss of love, I must erect a monument to the most beautiful of all my dreams, in which, from beginning to end, that love shall be thoroughly satiated.
 – Richard Wagner, Letter to Franz Liszt, December 16, 1854 –

I am sick of finding
Eternally only myself
In everything I achieve.
 – Richard Wagner, *The Valkyrie* –

Once more we have the promise, and – we hope.
 – Richard Wagner describing the prelude to *Parsifal* –

i

You act, as if you and you alone are
Excepted from all that everyone but
You has always known and thus accepted.
Everything you said and you did in the
Way you did it and said it seems to have
Insisted that you're the only one in
The universe who ever existed.
Yet you were off-and-on dejected that
You were everywhere and by everyone
Rejected, and yet you saw yourself, not
Merely as one of the elect, but, most
Surely, as the only one elected.
Therefore, you, who became quite bothered that

You were never fathered, fathered yourself.

ii

You would abolish history's longstanding
Contracts, abrogate moral codes, axe all
The moldering facts, and then annihilate
Joy's most brazen odes. You would resurrect
Rhapsodies of the unattainable
And unsustainable. All this you strive
To do. You revisit strategies of
Malice and presume they're new. Sooner or
Later, you peek under the bed. You see
The alligator. You encounter truth
That's too hard to take. All you once believed,
Once cherished, you know in your heart is fake.
But the last thing you do is fret about
The crime of never having paid your debt.

iii

You will what you suffer, and suffer what
You will. The longer you live, the finer
You're able to hone this tedious skill.
You had no time to be good, because you're
Driven to do what a good man never
Could. You trespass the taboo, the darkly
Forbidden, do all the demon in you
Has bidden. In one brief span, everyone
Becomes you, and you become everyman.
Like gods who perished, you'd throw away all
You are and fetch it back, as if repeating
Your mistakes could atone for what you lack.
But it's a matter of quite low odds that
You'd live up to the standard set by gods.

iv

You will the end, your end. You become that
Toward which you bend. You're nowhere, everywhere,
Then someone somewhere. Existence itself,
That's your crime. You commit it when you have
The unforgivable gall to live in
Time. There were gods before the gods you know.

These gods gave up, gave in, before the gods
You know decided to begin it all
Again. History always begins at the
Beginning and ends at the ending. But
The tension is where, against its will, it's
Always tending. It ends as it begins,
As they always say, in myth, in the death
Of the erstwhile gods you're no longer with.

v

To your equally lonely philistines,
Your music sounds like screeching, like screams of
Those who keep beseeching gods for release
From the wisdom it's teaching. Your music,
A parable of insomnia, would,
If it could, unknit the careless sleeve of
Sleep to make another promise you can't
Keep, as if you, oblivion's ally,
Could learn to live and love the lie, as if
To die were to defy the death you choose
To die, as if your insomnia could
Endure in silence derisive shocks of
Paradox, as if passion reaching closure
Would not die the death of its exposure.

vi

In music's pseudo-mathematical mesh,
You're entangled by the lyrics of the
Will's wily metaphysical hysterics.
You would, if you could, overmaster in
Time the dread of desire's disaster, but
What you cannot master in time, you must,
As eternity's shrewdest pretender,
Take in stride, as you swallow your wounded
Pride and surrender to the splendor of
The naked sublime. A conspiracy
Of desperation between you and your
Lonely others, will thrive, as if ritual
Could revive the spiritual and thus
Breathe life again into all it smothers.

vii

The maestro says, all ends in ecstasy,
But could anything be wronger than the
Promise of another eternity
Monger? Music that's not misunderstood
Could not possibly be any good. Thus,
Your music's so exceedingly clever
That with each new work you were always more
Misunderstood than ever. And, yes, of
Course, your salvific motto, *Redeem the
Redeemer,* is the call to arms for every
Schemer who's drowned all that's profound in the
Shallowness of snobs. That's what happens when
Honest men and women fail to pay their
Debts, keep their promises and do their jobs.

viii

There is, yes, the decadent thrill in the
Transgression of taboo, as if there's no
One and nothing anymore who can say
To you: *this is what you don't, and this is
What you do.* There's that nameless stirring that
Marks the fatal moment when you begin
Preferring what cannot happen to what
Keeps recurring. Art, you thought you knew, would
Come to the rescue of you and religion
Too. But it never did. And so, in the
Vagueness of its glitzy metaphors, you
Hid, as if music's chalice could heal the
Perpetual wound of human malice,
And redeem the world of woe with one swift blow.

ix

Your latest refuge is yet another
Ark in yet another deluge. This is
Your irresistible lure, your desperate
Flair that makes of exalted death a bliss
You say you want, but want to miss, a bliss
So bright, so fair, it lets you embark on

The fatal risk of eternity's kiss.
Thus, you populate the other side of
Now on the desolate plain of nowhere.
You imagine what isn't there is there.
You let the glamor of impossible
Love stare down despair. Thus, the plain chant of
Your lyrics says in lurid prose what your
Music proves that no one any longer knows.

x

For you and for the prophet you followed,
The phenomenal is the fountain of
All pessimism. Life made visible,
Thus, is a dreary, tragic affair, or,
So it seems, while the noumenal is the
Persistence of the shame, blame and guilt of
Existence continued by other means.
The longing comes up short. It always does.
And desire that never keeps its promise
Remains what it always was. The eros
You explore is lust become thanatos
That you say you want but deplore. When you've
Had it, you are, against your will, sad it
Was never enough. You always want more.

xi

Your music wants what it wants, keeps wanting.
The tension that's never resolved becomes
Involved in prolonging the riddle that
Can't be solved. Your music knows more than you
Know, suffers more than you suffer, enjoys
What you cannot. It summons all the lives
You knew you never lived, but then forgot.
It's the story of storytelling you've
Told that you keep telling. Words are, for you,
Mere whispers your music keeps on yelling.
Yes. It is your music that remembers
Your forgetfulness, but you don't. You no
Longer remember that you want what you
Do not get and get what you do not want.

xii

Love that would save the world destroys it. And
Happiness that would redeem is the dream
Of one who never enjoys it. Everyone
And everything is exchanged for something
Else. In the quivering shallows, the trout
Unplagued by doubt, swim through substitutions.
Only in the deeps can you play for keeps.
Love is the eternity of what you
And your lonely others will. For the sake
Of that, there is no time, no truth, no fact,
No faith, no fake, no fate, you will not kill.
In the disaster that's the end of days,
Your love claims its eternity in one
Remorseless, everlasting psalm of praise.

xiii

Your dream insists on the fact of a bliss
That you've always missed. Throughout your despair,
You'll continue to sniff the *as if*, the
Fragrance of a moment you imagined,
But that was never there. But if you do
Not live as if there's redemption, then there
Will be none. If you do, and there is an
Exemption from the crime of existence,
Then perhaps it's you who'll be the one. This
Moment is how the impossible, the
Sacred, like love, inhabits the time of
The possible, how the love you'd exalt,
Accepts the fact of death and knows that the
Crime of your existence is not your fault.

xiv

You wait for the lies and delusions to
Be admonished and extinguished, but they
Keep lying and deluding. Into the
Frail honor of truth's troubled solitude,
They keep intruding. You're alone with truth,
And truth's alone with you. And the truth you

Think you know is known by you and only
You. No one ever knows why, but truth, in
Fear of publicity, is shy, for no
One gives a damn about what you are and
Why. Your heart's hot flesh will melt before the
Eternity you always felt was real.
From whatever it is that makes you you,
There is, alas, no final court of appeal.

XV

Lovers dream of what their love could never
Redeem in an ecstasy beyond flesh.
The will has its fill when lovers die in
Love to the tune of this ecstasy of
One will. Therefore, you lean toward what you want,
And you mean toward what you say you mean. But
Getting there, the revelation of your
Ecstasy's despair, comes from hankering
After the impossibility of
Nowhere. If nowhere ever had a place,
Its place would be the cherished face of the
One you claim to love. Disenchantment, like
Any mystery, has its charms. But no one
Would want to rest forever in its arms.

xvi

Music's an artifice that inhibits
What it never quite exhibits. Thus, it
Moves not with the will, but manhandles it.
And artist and audience are both its
Victims. Music would make of love's distress
A rapture it cannot capture, and make
Of the death-devoted heart of death in
Love, that still hopes to redeem, a scheme that
Does not exhibit the will, but relies
On what the will must manufacture. There's
Always for you that indissoluble
Chord that marks the destiny of desire
As a standing note. This is the music
That again and again you play by rote.

xvii

You lie, cheat and damn to hell ideals you
Could not live, but pretended only your
Music could tell. Your music, it's said, is
Better than it sounds. It toughens the heart
And softens the brains of those it pounds. The
Myth of unadulterated joy, that's
A story, you've again and again been
Told. But there is, for you and your lonely
Others, no innocent gold. You yearn for
Annihilation, as if death solves what
Life could not, as if the burden of each
Memory repays what time forgot, as if
Life did not make you more and more involved
In what death leaves forever unresolved.

xviii

After death, there is, for motion, nothing
That can block or stall. Mountain, boulder, wall,
The dead, it is said, go unimpeded
Through it all. Nowhere is thus for the dead
Everywhere, and everywhere nowhere. If
Everywhere were now here, and if now here
Were everywhere, there'd be no where at all.
For each and every one of your instants,
You'd be able to traverse any distance.
Nothing that is, for the nothing you are,
Could offer any degree of resistance.
Joy is never where you are, but that toward
Which you tend. Bliss is your devotion to
Eternity's motion that does not end.

xix

The hero in the noonday sun will be
Sacrificed, as if he were the one and
Only one, and he would be you, except
That you're no hero, but the one whose whole
Life adds up again and again to the
Exorbitant sum of zero. Therefore,

You live afraid of the music your life
Has made and played, as if the scarecrows of
The sacred could chase away your hatred
Of what it meant to live your life. Thus, your
Music, like your life, tells you how to make
And break every promise, every vow. There's
Time before you die to break another
Promise. Thus, go ahead, and do it now.

XX

You scare away love, scare away joy, scare
Away suffering. You scare up a brand new
Toy that promises to deliver what
Can only annoy, and you welcome, with a
Smarmy hug, the smug and pompous wit that
Trades unhappy truth for its egregious
Counterfeit. All this, of course, you do. Yes.
Your quest for pleasure is the death of you.
In life there's never really any fun.
The ring's the thing that makes it clear that the
Fate you're dying to love is at one with
The whole damn schmear. What others abhor and
Deeply deplore you bravely sang. *Now ye
Know there's such a thang as the whole shebang.*

xxi

As long as it lasts, the music lets you
Believe, that you, not it, know how to deceive,
That you, not music, are the master of
The lie, that the will, to save itself, must
Deny itself and die. You cannot solve
The problem of desire by killing it
Or fulfilling it, but by willing it
To last, by the trick that lets you keep wanting
And loving. Therefore, find that wand of love
And want and hold on fast. The pernicious
Notion *that to exist is wrong* is wrong.
To be alive with desire forever
In your own eternity, that is where
You and all your lonely others belong.

XII. THEORY OF EVERYTHING

In a certain sense everything is everywhere at all times. For every location involves an aspect of itself in every location. Thus every spatio-temporal standpoint mirrors the world. ... Religion is a vision of something which stands beyond, behind and within, the passing flux of immediate things; something which is real, and yet waiting to be realized; something which is a remote possibility, and yet the greatest of present facts; something that gives meaning to all that passes, and yet eludes apprehension; something whose possession is the real good, and yet is beyond all reach; something which is the ultimate idea, and the hopeless quest.
  – Alfred North Whitehead, *Science and the Modern World* –

There is no entity, not even God, 'which requires nothing but itself in order to exist'.
   – Alfred North Whitehead, *Religion in the Making* –

Completion is the perishing of immediacy: 'It never really is.' No actual entity can be conscious of its own satisfaction; for such knowledge would be a component in the process, and would thereby alter the satisfaction. ... All the 'opposites' are elements in the nature of things, and are incorrigibly there. The concept of 'God' is the way in which we understand this incredible fact – that what cannot be, yet is.
   – Alfred North Whitehead, *Process and Reality* –

i

That all things flow is the first thing that you
Begin to know. Time would, if it could, stand
Still, but as long as it lasts, it never
Will. It's bemoaned in a thousand hymns, in
The psalms. Time's passage never starts, never
Stops, never calms. Eternity's motion
Wants to stay, but still must go. Its history,
That's all you really know. Whatever is,
Flows. But no one who buys this adage can
Tell you where it goes. Into you, into
The burgeoning world, it flows, or so you
Say, or into the future that's always

Not quite yet, but which you nonetheless bet
Gives birth to the light of the common day.

ii

You're in that club in which everyone and
Everything else is a member. You're that
Society of lost occasions that's
Nonetheless always found. There's no one and
Nothing alone. You need all that is to
Be all you call your very own. You're in
History; history's in you. You're in the world;
Your world's in you. You, your world, your history,
And every lonely other are in each
Other through and through. There's a piece of all
In all you say and do. Nowhere's everywhere.
No matter where you go, it's there. Though you're
Somewhere's philosopher, its poet, you're
The child of nowhere, but never know it.

iii

The efficient cause, that's the push, and the
Final cause, that's the pull, the promise of
Self-creation, the parable of how
Emptiness makes of itself something full.
Each actual occasion lures itself
To become what it must become and be.
And what it is, is a fragment ripped from
The organ music of eternity.
Led by lures of desire, each occasion
Has already died at the moment it's
Been satisfied. The universe, akin
To pop and fizz, can only become. The
Truth is that it never is or can be
What it never is. It can only hum.

iv

Time's passage is never at an instant,
My dear, but always a smudge, a blur, a
Nudge, a smear between nowhere and now here.
You're, alas, a minor player in the

Spectacle of the great receptacle.
There are no clear divisions in the air,
In the earth, in the fire, in the water.
There are no clear divisions anywhere.
No. There are no clear divisions between
Somewhere and nowhere. If hard won truth gets
Lost in this puzzling mix, you can train your
Pet delusions to do all your favorite
Tricks. The wisest of the wise always know
How best to pick the proper, slyest lies.

v

The present moment's pseudo-solipsism:
That is the kaleidoscopic prism
Reflecting the sum of all that is. In
The vastness of the universe, you will
Be awed by the immensity that keeps
You reeling. As you traverse the route of
Frail occasions, you aim for the feeling
Of intensity. For satisfaction's
Sake, you seek an intensity that would
Make the real seem fake. But that's a piece of
Elegant fakery, a tasty pastry
Concocted in the metaphysical
Bakery. What you think you perceive is
Thus a higher species of make-believe.

vi

As you evolve, you pursue puzzles you
Can't understand or solve. But the lure of
This impossible urge vivifies your
Propensity for intensity, your
Search for a harmony of contrasts that
Never fails, but that forever lasts. Yes.
All experiences matter. The dim,
The deep, the vague, the vivid, the blithely
Serene and the obscenely livid. All
Those moments, you thought trivial and long
Since justly discarded, come back in spades,
As if to say they never departed.

Vague intent's your melancholy baby,
Your halting step toward some lasting maybe.

vii

Attention flickers, emotion bickers
With emotion, and suspicion sneers and
Snickers at what you used to believe. As
Your civilization advances, it
Grows more and more enamored of its most
Cynical romances till the latest
Excuse no longer proves to be of use.
You, with one and all, will vulgarize the
Spiritual and turn this degradation
Into a persistent ritual of
Value's vainest vultures. When liars tell
The truth, logic, humiliated, totters.
And those ancient denizens of erstwhile
Certitude surrender to the squatters.

viii

There's discontent with the prevalent gods.
Thus, idolatries begin to topple.
They always do. And yes. Before you're done
With the past, you're startled by something new.
When the last at last arrives, the middle
And the first no longer matter. You try
Over and over to be satisfied,
But the outcome you strive to reach could not
Be any sadder. The perpetual
Tide of eternity in motion is
A treacherous ride. And every moment
You live, but never fully know, harbors
Within itself the irony of your
Overthrow. All you want to stay must go.

ix

Your theory of everything always stubs
Its toe on how much you fail to imagine
And how little you ever know. Thus, no

Theory of good and evil could suffice
To explain why God prefers the risk of
Tossing dice to the troubled certainty
Of always playing nice. You defied the
The false ideal of clarity, because
Complexity's the rule. Simplicity's
A rarity, and, more often than not,
It's the self-deceit that makes the vague seem
Clear and the messy neat. The fraud of the
Familiar relents when you perceive the real
Ontology of events and non-events.

X

Again and again, you settle for the
Mediocre glory of the likeliest
Story. Whatever's true has for a long
Time now been out of reach for the likes of
You. All that's ancient is lucidity
Lost. The history of eternity keeps
Paying its cost. Dogma's story is the
Decline of the sacred, how religion,
Thus considered, becomes a synonym
For hatred, how the mystic zeal you no
Longer feel achieves the emasculation
Of mere acceptance, how the fact that your
Conscience is an act is what you shun, how
Desperately in point of fact you blindly run.

xi

Even in the faintest feeling, you grasp
How many becomes one. In this epoch,
There's no cosmic weather where elements
Of chaos, no matter how raucously
Separate, fail to coalesce perhaps
Unwillingly, but thrillingly together.
Each event's a smear, a smudge, a nudge of
The real, that takes its own good time to peel
Away from the gregarious universe.
Each thing is an event that goes on long,
And each event is a would-be thing that

Comes up short. A moment's satisfaction,
Yes, that's what tells the event it's time to
Abort and become the past of others.

xii

All that changes, changes in relation
To you, as you, enduring as you do,
Change too. And yet, even as you change, you
Do not, and you cannot die. But you live
Forever before and beyond any
Moment that could satisfy. Yes. Every
Becoming keeps becoming. There is no
Now that never goes, no now that always
Stays. The eternity you imagine
Stands still keeps moving as it keeps proving
That you are alive, but relentlessly
Unforgiving. The appropriation
Of the dead by those still living is how
Your life gives the gift that keeps on giving.

xiii

You require the whole universe and all
Your lonely others in order to be
You. And the universe and your lonely
Others require you too. If you scratch at
The itch of common sense, you're bound to stir
The hive. Then, senses you've had, but never
Noticed, come alive. You would, if you could,
Accept what common sense can deliver, but
Imagination gets stunned by the force of
Stubborn fact, and this, your most reluctant
Forgiver, must then forget what's always
Promised, but not yet. Experience, that's
Satisfied nowhere, my dear, is gulled by
The lure of being satisfied now here.

xiv

Every quantum leap is an epoch of
Becoming. The lure of desire is what

Keeps the universe humming. From epoch
To epoch, the laws of nature change. There's
Nothing that you now know, no prevalent
Sanity, that some future will not look
Back on and think deranged. The world's not as
You find it, but how you imagine it,
For each fact's abstract, but you don't mind it,
Because abstraction's how you engender
Your sense of the real and blind it from the
Sum of all the facts you vaguely feel. That's
How you remind it of the deeper true
Discernible by God, but not by you.

XV

What you are is always emerging, or
You might say, always verging on the edge
Of desire's ruthless urging. Ecstasy,
The joy you say you seek, is a step beyond
Wakefulness, beyond sleep, a step beyond
Any promise you could ever keep. Once
You've become, you cannot *not be*. Once you
Step into being, you can't step out. You're
Part and parcel of eternity. To
Feel what's there is to make it here. And what
There is that is, is what it always is
Everywhere, and at every time, and in
Every way. That's what it means to see through
Everything to the light of common day.

xvi

Every actual occasion is defined
By its own moment of satisfaction,
Which exists only in that moment that
Was now here, but now is always nowhere.
Each occasion creates itself and the
Universe. God is what makes them matter.
All that arises must arise because you,
Your God, and your lonely others decide
What's important enough to emphasize.
To exist is to be of value for

Yourself, for your lonely others, and God.
There's no us, no them. God envisages
Anything and everything you do as
A possible embrace of her or him.

xvii

Your satisfaction is never now, but
Always in another moment. No. Your
Satisfaction's never in yourself, but
Always in another person. You would
Like to get there yourself to enjoy your
Satisfaction here and now, but nothing
You're experiencing now can tell you how.
All you've thought, you've dreamed, you've felt, yes, all that
Made you you, was desire made real, a dream
Come true, a cruelty or tenderness which,
Like the sugar, took its own sweet time to
Melt before the debt you owe yourself comes due.
Your metaphysics is a reminder that you're
Not the great unwinder, that you are you.

xviii

You could never be what you are, if you
Were all alone. There'd be no single thing,
No occasion you'd call your very own.
You are made of your lonely others, and
All your equally lonely others are
Made of you. You're what you are, never in
Isolation, which can never be, but
Only when you make your mark and bequeath
Your lasting spark to the lives of others.
To be you is not to repeat what you've
Always been. That's the unpardonable
And impossible sin. Yes. A seed must
Die to bear its fruit in the flower of
Others. To be you is to make a difference.

xix

In yourself, you see all else, all others
Reflected, and all else, all others, in
Themselves, see you. Yes. To be is to be
Related, and sooner than expected
To be belated. To be anything:
That is to become; and becoming what
You are, is your rattle of death: it's always
All over before you get your breath. There
Are no fundamental things; there's only
Process, motion, movements. That's the only
Way God can make improvements. Yes. There's a
Little bit of all in everything. And
Yes, there is the spur of unasked-for love:
That's what life makes you an example of.

xx

What's gone is nowhere and also now here.
Again and again, you've tried to make that
Clear. The passage through the flux of time to
Eternity is a blur, a smudge, a
Smear. You're never altogether nowhere,
Never altogether now here. Joy is
Your passage through time to eternity.
In the joy that fills eternity from
First to last, there's never any room for
The crack of doom. Eternity's sunrise:
That's the dawn that thrills in what's forever
Given, though still gone. Therefore, give your joy
A flying kiss: that's how to live and live
Again in the joy you only fear you miss.

— TEN —

CHOOSE ANOTHER POISON

Being believed is no sin. Believing is.
Michelangelo

I. THE THREAD OF TRUTH

i

Eagerly you breathe its brown aroma
To shock you out of Monday morning's coma.
But coffee kindles not light but darkness.
Should you choose another poison, you'd suffer
A scent as sweet as the sweat of children,
As if feigned innocence could still embrace
Five long, languishing decades of disgrace.
You dreamed reality with nothing added,
But your perception is always padded
With self-deception … with some faint or fat
And fulsome faith. Thus, renegotiate
Your fierce routine. That familiar stranger
… still crowing…the canon of lean caffeine
Must believe in nothing it can't demean.

ii

Tested and detested by small-breasted blondes,
You've grown quite fond of sneering at beyonds,
Of slow pain burning in the greenest wood.
Shall you go with the gods you worship?
Or is it time to cast off counterfeiting?
Give the metaphor of the root … the boot:
A speed bump on the road to nirvana,
That narrow fellow in the body of
Your knowledge widens into wisdom.
And wisdom dreams with its eyes wide shut.
Yes. If only you could blow yourself out,
You'd become as calm as a cucumber.
But prophets of grief can't stop their bickering:
You're the unsheltered wick still flickering.

iii

Language … is that robot wound inside you,
Long imitated by your ancestry,
Copied by your fathers, whose rotted names
You resurrect in praise of famous games

You no longer try because they exceed
Your strength and wisdom. Become a vulture:
Then, be raped by someone else's culture.
What is meat? Flesh. What is flesh? Meat ... a word
That guiltless vegetarians could eat.
Dare you repeat clichés of settled truth?
You can neither toil in its tedium
Nor swim in the antiquated medium
Of pallid eternity. Yet ... you're born
Rehearsing what you want ... but yearn to spurn.

iv

Giants erected ... slouch disconnected:
Dumb, dissembling limbs then bend before ghosts
Of abandoned bodies ... integrities
Leeching lies – little, white, black and large,
As large as belittled bodies of death
You thought you buried. But death's immortal,
An open sepulcher, a cave of secrets
Sealed by sin's cynical disclosures.
Fallacies of abstraction seek contrition
In novel strategies of suspicion.
Each capillary action is a faction
In the battle of the unbecoming
Principalities of remorseless law.
And the flaw in the law is your one and
Only chance to preserve your difference.

v

O... Inexcusable man ... you come
Before the rabble to babble. And what
Will you say? Shall you quibble, or propound,
Or declare that you found in the oriole
A feathery sound of ruffled repetition?
Closed is the closet of your confessions,
Echoes in chambers of your imagery.
Nothing that is not new will do, for you
Sought the mercy of difference and found
Folded in multifarious secrets
Many mediocrities of the same.

Yes. You were enfolded in the first man,
And your secret – your secret – is revealed:
Reluctant, but luminous in the last.

vi

Silent ... the church before the church begins
Welcomes the sign-languages of your sins.
Your life becomes occasion for parables.
Your history, an agreed-upon fable,
Can't justify the dubious label
Hero, nor exclaim: "What a word is this!"
Only he who hopes craves plainness of speech.
Only he who's had his certainty can teach
Neighborhoods of nattering naysayers.
Author and finisher ... sans conviction,
You strum the instrument of false diction.
And the music you make prolongs the fake,
Perpetuates cruelly your indistinction
With woollier mammoths of extinction.

vii

Who are you that you should be magnified
By the cracked lens of imagination?
You held her starlight in your waiting arms
As if to capture the unexpected,
Or swaddle your shriveling hope with love.
Yes. She stirs this dithering qualm
In you ... that life can be comprehended
By life ... Is art more than a dying patient's
Cup of things unsaid, undone, of measures
Untaken? Of distrust in foundations
Unshaken? No, you'll have no rest, no quiet,
No safety. Trouble comes in miracles
Of perilous trust, time's whispering doubt
That shouts: love is now, nowhere and forever.

viii

The thread of truth is unreeling into
Feeling... a fragment of eternity:

It must produce. It must release. It must
Transmit. No poem ... no prose ... can ever twang
The strain of it. You were steam, you were perfume,
You were nerve-glow's friction, a fame lit up
On the track of your own trestle, a train
Never needing riders or deriders.
Or to refute your brothers in a sentence:
Revenge against yourself is not repentance.
Yes. Those who say that sin has died have lied.
All your differences dissolve in rhyme.
You wait too late if you wait till your change
Can come. Now is the acceptable time.

ix

You dreamed Eternity because you feared
To live. You shared fantasies of Mercy
Because you were afraid to give ... what can
Only ... now ... be given dangerously.
Out of the moment's dwindling thimble,
Summon your courage and then assemble
The list of your emptiest important truths:
Indiscreet ... you're the sum of what you eat.
Live what you must live. Hum what you must hum.
Give what you must give. Be what you become.
All this ... you say ... is mere tautology.
All else is ... idle ... ideology.
Seek simplicity ... and then mistrust it:
Your god, your death, your now ... eternity.

x

You were courageless ... as the cowardly world.
But you were clever ... as though you had furled
Roads of experience on your back and
Called that freedom. As you die your death
Ten thousand others will still be brawling
Beneath your most rebellious solitude.
Slowly, you catch on: how casual fact
Becomes causal. How common blood touches
Uncommon blood. How your history's
Universal fate betrays a typo.

How a sad self-knowledge, still dithering
Still delves with the elves of self-improvement.
How becoming what one is ... is ... simply ... this:
Forgetfulness ... forgetting ... forgetfulness.

xi

The sad empyreal umpire that cloys
Negates premeditated ecstasies and joys.
Time's grinding imagery too soon becomes
Whatever whistles, dances, taps, or hums
Unpardonable songs of imitation.
To *be* ... or *not:* ... to be unshakeable
Unforsakeable ... unmakeable ... man.
You dwell: ... in a basement of abundance.
You exit: ... the door swings shut behind you.
You enter: ... blithe spirit ... a scape of endless scope.
You touch: ... the ungraspable ... touching you.
Is ... this ... then ... eternity? ... Will it do?
The spear of sense has shaken into farce.
What you'd throw away ... now ... you cannot throw.

xii

Watch how joy commits the fatal error
Of choosing time as its greatest terror:
You will have your fill of love till morning.
You will solace yourselves with many loves.
Faded roses ... that slavery of poses ...
Conceals your jaded lust then discloses
Your fears about what flesh will do to you.
You dwell on the underside of overcoming.
Yes. You stare in stupor at your shadow,
Yet forget what cast it out of Eden.
Lust only lusts for what it cannot trust.
Faith in suspicion is superstition:
There is no rule to assess your fitness.
Whatever's perfect endures no witness.

II. COVENANTS OF CHAOS

i

Necessity cavorts on wobbly heels:
You can no longer think what reason feels.
Lest every event with a cause should link,
Your hard-won axioms must learn to wink.
Euclid's strict home of simple connections,
Now swerves with error in all directions.
And errant particles ... future's bastards
Give time a chance to fall away backwards.
Observer ... observed so close-connected:
There is no separate world detected.
Everything solid is now so porous,
There is no *at once* to sing a chorus.
Unless your words cut nature at its joints,
Everything you say always disappoints.

ii

Imagine a poem that never reaches
Words, and you imagine no poem, but dream
That you defeat what you repeat with your
Imaginings. If you'll take the trouble,
Apply Ockham's razor to the stubble.
But whiskers of complexity cannot be
Shaved from the stubbornness of fate or fact:
Thus, no prediction without the friction
Of appearances that cannot be saved.
Your best forecast is unreliable.
Who, if any, can believe your report?
If indeterminacy should exist,
Then it begins at home, where neither you,
Nor others know what meaning really means.

iii

What chaos does understanding foretell?
Hear towers peal in the Fall, then recall
Eternity's mimes, as if you could tempt
Rude chaos into chimes. But rhymes know no

Season, and your strangest solitude swaps
Echoes for failed treason. Hang tough, enjoy
Anew the sad refrain of Autumn shadows.
Forget time's bark, that dark penumbra of
Substitution ... forget each leaf of your
Deciduous brain has peeled ... another
Bit of infinity congealed ... your own
Abscission zone of flesh and bone and spirit.
Only who bravely fails can be bereft.
Love ye therefore the stranger in yourself.

iv

You must reexamine your resentments.
All-too-soon, you'll have no more gall to bitch
  ... About whose more beautiful or more rich.
You must reexamine your resentments.
Yes. Your self-delusions were deemed so wise,
You became whatever you'd fantasize.
You must reexamine your resentments.
All that ancient wisdom seemed so jaded,
You waded through muddles they created.
You must reexamine your resentments.
You cannot shake off shackles that are yours:
Those lesser lessons taught by cut-rate tours.
So much yearning ... and so little power:
You must reexamine your resentments.

v

You are the lyre of a 1000 strings,
And strings you pluck compose your universe.
Return again to infancy and seek
Evergreener myths of self-improvement.
Alas, what good will your green life do you?
What will you save from your own impatience?
Walk the dizzy drunkard's walk of mind in
Bellies of noisy stars. For starry
Emotions are near to the whimper you are
And afar from the bang you left behind.
If space and time are words in the sentence
Of your world, then no space, no time: ... no world.

Or none that can utter its own meaning.
You'll be saved (or numbered), despite yourself.

vi

A tiny instant becomes a larger
Moment, still much too small to call its name.
A day, an hour, a month, a year, a life
Add fear to fear, killing them with sacrifice.
Your digital golems will overtake
All those occupations you must forsake.
The difference engine that you are
Inhabits the passage but leaves no scar.
Receive strong delusions. Believe a lie.
Rediscover covenants of chaos:
How every *you* becomes at last an *it,*
A final cause you cannot counterfeit.
The instinct of the mediocre is
... always stronger than the exceptional.

vii

If you knew what you sought, you cannot gain.
For the prize you searched for you had in tow.
Not knowing what you want, all search is vain.
For whatever you grasp, you'll never know.
Thus, you practiced arts of losing yourself
Methodically. That clown's jest is best
That never conspires to inspire a laugh.
You never met a physics you didn't scorn:
Becoming much too shrewd by more than half,
You might as well be dead or never born.
Ask not how long, how long, how long, how long:
Must you play out melodies of this song?
Forget how long you've striven to be wise:
Your end is your beginning in disguise.

viii

You can't escape the everlasting snow
To see the low in the light of the high,
To know the high in the light of the low,

Or flee the mimesis of mutterhood.
Eternity is the burden of God.
But eternity's free, its gift to you,
Your freedom, has now already happened,
Happening always, happening at once.
In your quaint forgetfulness, then confess
How you must mourn the loss of large in less.
Each lie, if you should choose to call it that,
Beggars bigger camels, swallows the gnat.
The door to conscience still swings uncatched
In solitude where you live, no strings attached.

ix

Ought God really to demand our best toys?...
Yes, indeed Lizzie... Yes, again, confess:
The book of life always opens at pain.
Pleasure refuses to pay attention.
Confused by circuitries of churning winds,
You will be filled with your own devices.
Darwin, fishing, anesthetized his worms.
No prophet has been more honest ... and yet
... what all life thinks it wants it must forget.
Likewise, sanitize terms of your sentence.
Fail to grasp the logic of repentance.
You must plan your debaucheries with care.
Hurry slowly: Grate the cheese of wisdom.
You will be had by what you do not have.

x

You were angry in noble solitudes,
That children should bear broken bodies,
That brokenness should be their destiny.
Sans dollops of blessedness, you sang your
Hollow, caustic anthems of wretchedness.
Fateless fact and artificer of fact,
You were guest of honor at creation.
Yes. Everyone was once the universe.
With cheer, be insincere about your fear.
You're neither casualty nor cause: you're free.
Yes. God made you free for eternity.

Therein lies cause for all terror and
All happiness. You must spend your time, and
Your times are wages of eternity.

xi

Needful it is for you to act rightly,
And to act rightly is the sole path of
Sincerity, if paths are possible.
To be sincere is to feel sincerely.
But all's fraudulent without right action.
Repetition is a formula for
Salvation. But ritual without right
Action is meaningless, and right action
Without ritual is impossible
For anyone, save a saint, whose entire
Life is a ritual of right action.
This then is the terror of your freedom:
Sincerity ages faster than sin,
… and sin itself is almost eternal.

xii

Penniless, you live between two treasures
Of darkness, and if their raging silence
Should speak, then could you buy their cheap report?
Thus, keep mishearing what's already said.
Practice misunderstanding till you're dead.
Time's a trump of the eye, a horse's trot
Between oblivions, a cicatrice
Of the brain, mute interchanges of chaff
On the rudderless raft that's eternity.
If preserving integrity's the goal
Of salvation, then saving yourself means
Always staying stubbornly what you are.
Grayness is failure of moral insight.
Be what you are: black veins in white marble.

III. APOLOGIES TO HIEROLOGIES

i

Some say the world arose from more, some say
From less. Lest you be conned, you must confess
Neither more nor less could explain the mess.
Starting somewhere, as you must, you hang hope's
Hat on one loose peg, as if reasons for
Life could be invented ... or prevented
From extolling those consoling lies that
Populate your hooks of convenient truth.
Your logic, of course, is quite defective.
Cartesian wells of certainty run dry.
You are plainly wrong, but still effective,
As fecund as an eye that greets an eye.
Your affinities are you ... through and through.
Icons you seize—to see the world—seize you.

ii

But before the foundations of the earth,
Before all that could ever be before,
Before you knew what life and death are worth,
There was no *then*, no chart for keeping score.
There was no *time*, for there was no never.
There was no *past*, no thirst for *first,* no *last,*
No asterisks for seeming so clever,
No deal, no scene ... to steal, no dice ... to cast.
But hoarding the body's pangs of pleasure,
Forgetting you are you, then you must do
What others do. Always ... then ... you measure
Some beginning toward some end. Then, it's true:
Your history is a parable of sin
Continuing a game you cannot win.

iii

Your lust for novelty, that vice of quick

Change artists, seeks perpetually newer
Simulacra, as if ever paler
Copies could somehow transmute marginal
Matters into miracles of meaning.
Your lust, served, became custom, and custom,
Unresisted, became necessity.
Thus, chaos huddled together becomes
A cosmos, that confusion you call the
Universe. You marvel at mongrel gods
Of every kind. ... *Resist this history.*
Meddle not with them who are prone to change,
For they that spread nets upon the ether,
They that weave networks ... shall be confounded.

iv

History is a few repeatable
Patterns. The master storyteller knows
At best only a few essential plots.
Novelty disguises your limited
Repertoire; the story of your stories
... is repetition. Repression of time's
Repetition is how you swerve from
What you are, from what you've said, and from what
You've always been. You swerve to prick a nerve,
To move yourself to keep moving ... Self-pity's
That commotion of emotion ... the master
Moved by himself, the victim, echoing
Vibrations of a nerve, the slave's summary
Of its sharpest pain into a dictum.

v

Yes. You skid ... on time's algebraic grid,
Trading one lost icon for another.
You'll seek your earliest satisfaction.
For the sake of realism, you may add
Blurred backdrops of extraneous detail,
But your focus remains the foreground,
The captive bird of your heart's desire, and
Your blueprint invariably bleeds toward the
Violence of explosive climax ... Yes. Your

Whorehound and your whore will cheat, complete, and
Re-repeat that ancient chore, rewriting those
Fables that starve you more, reliving fates
Relived before ... You begin to see how
Nothing's more repetitive than novelty.

vi

There can be no end to mythic chatter.
Mythology's that gossip gone grizzled
And chiseled into your fretwork's famous
History. You are that mosaic cobbled
Together out of moments untainted
By time's notorious forgetfulness,
By the body's melancholy labors,
By the body's giant over-belly and
Under-brain, by the body's bodiless
Hankering for what haunts it, by phantoms
It cannot hold, not taste, not touch, by what
It can neither consume, nor exhume from
The grave dimness that never vivifies
Its fatal wills and wants in imagery.

vii

Deaf hands that blindly grasp are the brain's most
Visible, vain and voiceless instruments.
You traced chill peripheries of spirit,
Rehearsing cruel cadences of time that
Disable your sense of eternity.
All pleasure palls. Pleasure—but not pain—knows
How varieties ... of ... false pieties
End in one gasping self-satisfaction.
Hell, that quaint, unquenchable pantheon
Of pain, cuts closest to your concept of
Eternity. But neither you nor your
Eternity is a concept. You failed
To grasp what your pain stands under. You could
Not put your concept into an image.

viii

Classification's gasifications

Turn all categories into bubbles.
From low to high to lower latitudes,
Down dead-end paths you're led by platitudes,
Phantasmagories of antique troubles.
With apologies to hierologies,
Meretricious clarity lulls the mind,
Repeats that rendezvous of rose and axe:
Elegant theories slain by sordid facts.
But in a world that's deaf, you have to scream
If only in dreams that are too extreme
To sidestep the infamy of a freak,
Crippled by those muscular emotions
Of poets who dare not know what they speak.

ix

You are always here, not there, always now,
Not then. All histories of eternity
Are episodes of tact that fantasies
Make famous. They praise, but never blame us.
They tease, they flatter, but never shame us.
Spirit is the body's coldest climate ...
... weather that cannot warm itself with words.
Renewing ... or un-renewing ... the new,
You cannot cause the cause that causes you.
Welcome the aftershocks of paradox,
The mental pout that shouts an anti-shout:
All that lives contradicts itself. Quiet
Consistency is the consolation
Of the dead who dare not speak what they know.

x

Brisk vomit of black hellebore was once
A prized remedy for insanity,
As terror is perhaps now your only
Surefire cure for inanity. You live
In the epoch of profanity, whose
Common stock is the ever feebler shock
Of its shocking images. But the trite
Turns tail in the face of terror, chased by
The false salvation of another shock.

That golden age of terror you live in
Now will produce nostalgias that only
An unimagined future can claim to
Understand ... if there should be a future
That resurrects the will to understand.

xi

Rivers run, they keep on running, until
The climate changes to icy cunning.
Nothing ... to those who fear to be duped ... could
Be more pleasing than sly suspicion that
Exults in the conditions of freezing.
Can you disobey orders not issued?
Can you avoid a siren that's not there?
Delusions strong or weak, loudly, softly,
They condescend to speak, then tweak your grasp
Of reality. This is how error
Becomes part of your truth, a genetic
Mistake that congeals before its break with
Eternity. Only rankest reasons
Justify: causes do not ask for reasons.

xii

There is a poem of matter, a field
Of gravitation, not seen, not felt, but
At least deduced. But being blind, there is
Nothing you want so much as those abstract
Languages of smell and touch. No, it is
Never too late to experience joy.
The infinitely visible denied
The blind is always graspable by the
Invisible organ of endless life.
But the devil that still dares to exist
Brings despair and deceit to defeat what
Eternity alone has introduced.
It's better to confess your death than to
Continue to pretend you're still alive.

ELEVEN
THE COMIC BOOK OF CHANGE

I. THERAPY IS TYRANNY

i

More than a thousand winter mornings you
Had seen, and hundreds had been robbed by frost
As thick as snow. You'd learned to love the light
Before that hot, fat Sol could warm the sky
Beyond grizzled hills, humped, though unhumbled
By the horrors of their ages, and you
A pre-schooler — never a single day —
And only occasional nights away
From home. You were at a place before wrath,
Before folly, before fatal error.
And in your unlettered state before books,
Before you had mastered the alphabet,
You had shivered ... not at the knee-deep snow
But at deeper terrors ... e.t.e.r.n.i.t.y ...

ii

Your echo mocks your original with
Ambitious reverberation. Always
You begin with exaggeration's
Mythology, major songs in minor
Keys. Only lower case can leave your line
Unbroken. There will be a perishing
Of persistent newcomers angling for
Lost minnows of unexhausted time.
What your line can't catch is not a fish,
Merely the farce of a wish that falters.
Abandon yearning, then abandon rhyme:
Seeing difference between now and then
Is perhaps the first beginning of sin,
Or at least the last of its earliest altars.

iii

Dictate memos to the easily startled:
Announce reorganizations, new worlds.
The chief cause of problems, your solutions,
Confounds your holiest institutions.

Decry ... traduce, the hoariest taboo.
Fetch a freedom you're not entitled to.
Nestle in novelty, then preach with zest:
Yea, verily, it's true. Incest must be best.
Unbottle the sham pain. Then try ... undo
The ugliest screw-ups you can't unscrew.
Trade in tawdry cant; mint counterfeit coins.
The higher the brow, the lower the loins.
The greater the spirit, the more perverse.
Why shouldn't this axiom be reversed?

iv

All therapy is tyranny, the lewd
Nihilism of change ... promising all ...
Fulfilling nothing. Your medicine chest
Of manufactured consolations
Bristles with ruse, excuse, and self-abuse.
Change is shrewd revenge on the status quo,
God's great gully where images flow
In whorls ... violent, cruel, holy ... awful.
All is permitted to the brilliant-witted.
Thus take care ... in doing nothing lawful.
Greatness begrudges mediocrity.
But eddies of eternity bear no score.
Eternity's what you lack an image for:
You never get over ... getting over.

v

From your sixteen ounces of flesh extract,
Another imageless, imageless act.
Then utter a sentence without repeal
And learn the lessons learning cannot heal.
Hum foreign songs. Keep those fingers strumming.
Yes. Keep overcoming ... overcoming.
Do ... tell. Do ... tell. Stability's so frail.
Get a little stale ... *and ye lands in jail.*
Go loiter where brittle, big lies can't reek.
You're always different from what you speak.
Promulgate poetry's omphalic eye,
And recover your past, the reason why

Your readership is a universe of one:
You cannot be misread until you're dead.

vi

Word lust smears the shill of the real too thin,
Thin as rainbow glints on slithering skin.
Justify the beauty of the taper.
Rape invisibles with blotted paper.
Confession comes like strutting fraudulence
To commit ... what you lack the wit to admit:
Yes. That you can only know what changes,
You can only believe what's eternal.
Your week begins weakly ... with the small,
Exceedingly small demands of yet another
Exceedingly small day. The history
Of your eternity begins with
Your forgetfulness of Eternity.
Nothing is costlier than beginning.

vii

Contrived in next week's answer section is
The simulated creativity
Of a crossword already bravely solved.
Culture keeps on recycling the givens:
Spidery moonlight, death, religion, fear.
The bridle on wordless flux keeps slipping.
Vocabularies of value keep tripping
Across your tongue in haste for the aftertaste.
Language, your brazen lie, is your first stab
At robotics, history's long curtsy
Before the narcotics of novelty.
Thus, seek in books safe harbors of defeated
Wisdoms. Truths shall be your perplexity.
Yes. The emptiers have emptied them out.

viii

Erstwhile knob-twisters discover truth is
Culturally tuneable, a channel
Changer, compact, exact, a fantasia

Of fact you contract into your armchair
Aleph. The timeless is dimeless expense,
A coinage far too cheap to phone for help,
That cannot screech the lion-hearted whelp
Of noisome knowledge... that cannot embrace
Your outcome in dispute and suffering.
No Buddha scolded into plump relief
Can smile, or help thou ... now ... thine unbelief.
Tautologies crave strongest narcotics
To mask discovery and stanch admission.
You are what you are ... without remission.

ix

Hell is the labyrinth of your imperfections.
From last to first, the sum of your reflexes
Unsettles and then unsexes what you are.
Your last thought, the seal of ultimate sin,
Will rule ruthlessly over what you've been.
You cannot go guiltless in the cruelty
Of being right ... as if light falls free of
All it floods. Around each bend in your self-
Similar woods, you're a wild ass alone.
Your abominations are as you love.
You will suffer the macropsia of
Ecstasy. Neither dwarf nor giant shall
Be your measure, and your treasure will be
The lonely heart you lost in amazement.

x

With every single theory you refute,
Stubbornly, you are you ... beyond dispute.
You're what you are, an event in the life
Of another self. Yes, the universe
You know, is a vast system of persons
Perceiving one another, perceiving
What you are ... and what you have always been —
Characters in an endless alphabet.
You are alpha's unteachable omega.
You are an infinite series in sum,
An uncertain slant of dawn: still, mute, and numb.

Before all the eulogies of despair proclaim:
No dice. Then respectfully put on ice
Your dark and brightest dreams of paradise.

xi

The dead keep visiting you on the way
Toward your own goodbye. Listen, if you will,
To wind song in mulberries. But good action
Rarely gets traction in the muddled ground
Of past and present. You must look then for
A quiet place to make a lasting stand …
… to stay still where all else has turned to go …
There where flies of a summer sleep in snow.
Wiser than the wind is the knell that clangs:
No. There is no emperor of diet.
Just the best of bad advice: Don't buy it.
Your future drinketh damage from the past.
You become a monument of your mistakes:
Characters in the comic book of change.

xii

There should be a Last, something after which
Nothing can be produced: this is Evil.
Time no longer rhymes with eternity.
That blaring strumpet wickedness begins
To admire herself. Take, therefore, a dim
View of vividness. Bad philosophers
Disparage mirrors because they fear to
Own what cannot be known … but only shown.
Become a fixture in your picture of
Dorian grayness. All satisfaction
… is abstraction. Your world repeats itself
Because character is habit-forming,
And repetition … without conviction
… is addiction … to the logic of sin.

II. NOMADS FROM NOWHERE

i

You were one face caught in many mirrors,
A thousand thrilling echoes from elsewhere.
Do what they did in darkness. Do what they
Did in harsh disdain. A chittering soul's
Robot apprentice to wisdom's sorcery,
You wait upon habits of conscience.
You must begin and end as all moral
Choice begins and ends ... by damning yourself.
From meritless grace to self-improvement:
How far you've fallen from all hope of help.
But the damned will not stay damned forever.
No, the damned will not stay damned forever.
You and your thousand lonely, unmet mates
Shall speak what eternity indicates.

ii

Behold breaking waves: one impersonal
Amplitude overtakes another. Push
This formula to infinity and
You have an image of calmness, that drowns
The terror of drowning. You will not answer
Light to light, nor right to right, for coiled within
Immortality's despotic logic
Are wrongs that are stronger than death or flight.
The windsock sage and rain will succor not.
Almost always, there will be a maudlin
Decomposition of the ultimate,
And this final breakdown will be a lie
As indigestible as the last breakfast
That the condemned can never choose to eat.

iii

Each morning you stumble on passages
To later experience until at
Long last, the past understands the future.
The line's drawn before you start to chalk it.

The road's closed before you start to walk it.
You crave the narrower simplicities
Of abbreviated, imagined worlds.
Though laboring in epistemic gyms,
Every founder is confounded by whims
Of those feeble hyperboles you call
Images, by faith in the first falsehoods.
Then metaphysics sets a final task.
Your idiot questioners itch to ask:
Can you become your unbecoming self?

iv

It was a clear crisp blue October day,
When you first realized that you no longer
Wanted transformation or translation.
You were caught in the fatness of autumn,
A rotund, post-sunburnt satisfaction,
Before the final chill sets in to kill.
You want to be free flesh, bound and braced by
The physical, not chased by quizzical
Phantoms of eternity. Begin with a
Clean slate: *Nashamah, ruah, and nefesh,*
An ethereal law encased in flesh.
Begin by reemerging from nowhere:
You relearn again how pragmatic is
The stimulus of the enigmatic.

v

It's not been long since the crustacean shell
... was cracked. Watchmaker blind, composer deaf,
Isn't there anyone left with the heft
To heave a sigh of profundity and
Meaning? Brothers and broken cisterns hold
No water. Yes, you still want a wisdom
That lets you laugh at this calamity.
Your day's edge deepens into night, nearing
The vast visibility of darkness.
On this cusp, fireflies flicker and crickets
Snicker at prospects of another end.
Folding unhappy tents of godless guiles,

All nomads from nowhere go quench their thirst:
Everything is the way nothingness smiles.

vi

You lived your life complete, from paraclete
To parakeet. Pirating and parroting
Pale images of other people's pain
And sundry pleasures, you succumb to the
Slow virus of cannibalistic rites.
Heed warning signs of sin and cinema:
Your constant unsteadiness of stance, your
Loss of coordination, your startled
Response of exaggerated alarm,
All symptoms of gorging on gray matter,
Amplify the continuous chatter
Of kuru's gurus: latter day prophets
Of your vicarious and viciously
Virtual unreality machines.

vii

You were there before your bliss broke up, but
You lost faith in the first page missing
From your book of life. Each specter is a
Defector from that cryptic origin.
The fossil comes before the flesh: no first,
No last, no future, no past, only thirst
For the vastitude of now's forever.
You were accused, yet you denied your guilt.
Go home. Go stay. Let your resentment try
    ... to tackle forgiveness without a lie.
To live is to know without an image:
Imagine imagination can stop ...
Its restlessness at the line of scrimmage
   ... that you can live your life without a prop.

viii

Your origin out of nowhere on an
Endless skid augurs destiny in the
Id. Bargain hunters keep rummaging for
Cheaper varieties of nakedness.

Old-fashioned pornography can't suffice.
Even coffee, your alibi, reflects
The fierce tyrannosaurus rex of sex.
Conscience goes naked and negligible
Before the blurring reign of blind instincts.
Clichés, coined by cut-flower culture's chieftains,
Make love a conspiracy of eunuchs.
No. What you want is a macho excuse
For tenderness. What you settle for ... is
... machismo in motion sans devotion.

ix

Home economics rearranges red
Letters in drab pigeonholes of brittle
But tidier truisms. You re-file
Familiar facts, forgetting stranger acts
Of compassion's crueler compensations.
An insider turning you inside out,
The local mimics the universal.
An outsider turning your outside in,
All change is relentlessly rehearsal.
Cruelty must precede each festival.
You require time and place to remember
Eternity. Your history genuflects
Next to this feared index of what you are
    ... without idols for its astonishment.

x

Recall how your soul once felt, then forgot
Its worth, how creature comforts breed a dearth
Of jejune joy, how you copped the chill in
The inner feel of the erstwhile real, how
Value is virtue vandalized, a vice
Vended by emasculated Visigoths,
Who vie to vaunt what you cannot practice,
Who find no succor, no succulence in
Bashing cactus, in the better beauty
Of bitterness, only the glitterness
Of greedy glamour that must clamor for
... acclaim. ...But, no, it was never your own

Ambition to lose your way. You accept
Responsibility, but not ... the blame.

xi

You and your equally lonely others
Are self-images you cannot escape
Because, if you did, you would not be you.
A speck ... a primitive streak, you begin.
At first, a ghostly snow-crystal, you spin
Out of coldness's thin air and nowhere.
You must fall to earth, then slowly, quickly,
Suddenly, massively, you begin to
Accumulate: images and scars and
That ever-present feeling that keeps you
Reeling, snowballing toward oblivion,
Through the random, genetic drift of strife.
In death, there is no good; in good, no death.
You become warm enough to waste your life.

xii

Before your breakup, you're that body in
Which all your moments belong as members.
Your future always comes and never goes;
Your past, never passing, always arrives
In standing waves of never-ending joy.
Nothing's misunderstood or mistaken.
Nothing is there ... that's lost or forsaken.
Sin ... is but the grin of a toddler's glee.
Yes. Eternity says: ... Remember thee.
Yet this basket in which everything falls
Welcomes the casket of forgetfulness
That appalls ... your lust to be immortal.
Here below ... or there above: The way you
Live with your loss of ecstasy is love.

TWELVE

IMITATIONS OF THE HUMAN

i

Lust has forgotten all its images,
But pale religious lechery still wants
What it wants…wants desecrated innocence:
… Wants to remain in its own energy
… Wants to burn with desultory camphor
… Wants elfin tricks of ancient metaphysics
… Wants to break time's coveting conscience
… Wants savagery, wants plainness in plain things
… Wants violence that's still sacredness to some
… Wants to purchase what it no longer buys
… Wants the botched appliance of self-reliance
… Wants time for the mercy of eternity
… Wants to pay the price of experience
… Wants songs of regret for what slips its grasp.

ii

The clocks are all correct but none agree:
Too late, too soon, between midnights, noons,
Shrieks the hapless schlock of six o'clock.
There are many times. And many voices.
No time is of one choice. No choice, one time.
Daily, you die daily, in dull rounds
Of repetition becoming reputation's
Reprehensible hold on character,
Forging by virtual habits of escape,
A machine for eternal recurrence.
Your world lines fatten into snarling worms
Of a fate too late to leap backwards.
Yes. What's last will be first, and what's first last.
You cannot fall in love with your own past.

iii

Spite stems the slandered, shallow stream, forgets
            … Automated fantasies of regrets:
Forgets its fatherhood in what becomes …
… Forgets bruises of its bruited mother
… Forgets its schadenfreudian thirst
… Forgets it cannot change into another

... Forgets to repeal its enamored curse
... Forgets dark religions are departed
... Forgets the imagoes of early snows
... Forgets to unfurl its nets in mourning
... Forgets to take its sacred bliss: *O Man*
... Forgets everything is its own vortex
... Forgets to stay alive in what can't die
... Forgets the fire's unfinished ... forever.

iv

Circling each being-here's a dead-eyed there,
Where folly's poets or puppets to despair
Preach persistence as insistence on wisdom.
Glum and guttural, clucking kites, devour
The unlonelier carrion of song.
Yes. All you feel is what a poet feels.
Yet what he says defames the feeling,
Makes vultures notoriously articulate.
Prick wizened stumps of amputated pain.
Drink poisons from many, squatting waters.
Then perhaps you'll regret what manhood was
Before your retreat to the invisible:
No sin without the law, no tenderness
Without the claw of concept to clutch the flesh
                                      ... of recurrence.

v

Envy regrets it could never father
A better lie to best its lonely betters ...
Regrets wagering what it never was:
... Regrets the cynic's death of exposure
... Regrets mystic ciphers in roots of fame
... Regrets parasitic paracletes of thought
... Regrets decoys of assignable blame
... Regrets guilty wisdoms it never sought
... Regrets what only a fool remembers
... Regrets the shabby experience ... joy
... Regrets it undergoes what cannot be
... Regrets the lie it calls ... eternity.
Regrets that shallowness in deepest grief

Unlimbers the muscles of true belief.

vi

No veins you breach can educate your kind.
No deeper mine can bleed the blind unblind,
Nor undim benighted praise with damning phrase.
Your words, you say, are a kind of action,
Inviting disbelief and vagrant grief in
Stultifying covenants of the game.
Poetry exhausts itself in pantomime.
Action alone can heal your wounded name.
When the ore's played out, when all's extracted,
You'll know you've grieved but never acted.
Defiantly, you searched the rainbow's end,
And found in its sinless bend no corners.
But jealous angels grin their wicked taunt:
Yes. All you can't forget is what you want.

vii

Uses dead to melancholy robots
Perpetuate false prayers of regret
For the superstition of traveling
Too far … from where – eternally – you are.
Yes. Hiss the myth before the myth begins.
Squeeze your squeezeboxes of popular song.
Crank your image pumps at demonic pace.
Worship imitations of the human,
Not understanding, but standing under
Unrefuted legacies of blunder.
But, as if time's lilting alibi had lied,
You recall an exuberance crucified.
That rumored giant, your squandered brother,
Mimicked the great last man … Be not another.

viii

If rhapsodies reply, give rhapsodies the lie.
Go to sleep, go weep in the warmest beer,
As if thirsting for authenticity
Could quench your quisling fear of the insincere.

Let flesh hoppers leaping from ice to life
Liberate the locust of lust in hives
 ... of your eternity's unhappiness.
Use that lie. Burrow into solitude
And find fluttering there nothing feathered
But your own despair. Yes. Yours was a lie
Interrupted ... Otherwise corrupted
By monotonies of one recurring scar.
All you are ... turns with the twist of one screw.
Yes. Everything recurs ... but prefers not to ...

ix

Love kidnaps a thousand identities,
Procuring stand-ins for another's sins.
Love trims the edges, divides the hedges ...
... Makes a covenant ... with riveting eyes
... Makes puppets ... happy hearts of wooden things
... Makes for a troubled midnight ... as it dies
... Makes stale ... the dread of its imitations
... Makes bright casualties ... of the darkest blight
... Makes unpardoned sins ...sin's intimations
... Makes joyful noises ... defies the thunder
... Makes each one ... a miracle of oneself
... Makes unwiser ... ones with widest wonder
... Mistakes oneself ... as one for all in all,
Then dwarfs the great and magnifies the small.

x

Unfathered ... unmothered? Whom must you hire
To re-inspire your changeling fantasy?
Deeper yawns under depth: She's not in you.
Keeper fawns over kept: No gift is new.
Speak mummeries ... of mutterhood. Let bloom
Your origin's womb, your first and final tomb.
Go home, go pray ... as if words, changing you,
Undo the consequences of a screw.
In eternity, old news travels faster
... faster than promises of disaster.
In her keys ... no order, in her throat ... no C.
She could only sing the tune she was:

A would-be, wayward woman from Tennessee,
Loved by the last good man, loved perfectly.

xi

Joy wills its other's afterworld, wills pain,
Wills foolish mastery of repetition,
Wills gleanings of its unattended gain:
... Wills to live in perpetual mourning
... Wills the knife that dissevers life from life
... Wills the paradox of prepared surprise
... Wills brave symmetries of catastrophe
... Wills literal letters of letting be
... Wills to enamel its binge of fate intact
... Wills all that's willable must be willed
... Wills all that's killable must be killed
... Wills all its fantasies revert to fact
... Wills wave on wave of clashing ocean foam ...
Wills what it wills ... a short stay in its long home.

xii

Lying nakedness next to nakedness,
Joy reveals how innocent lies arose.
Truth murders truth: honesty is Babbitt.
Her grace is verse, and yours the bungled prose
Of a wiser world you can't inhabit.
Her heart is home, hold candles toward her suns:
Eyelessly, behold in wonder plainest day.
Remembering what you were, you cannot stay
Alone with her savage enlightenment.
In solitude's demise, you'll be reborn.
Go ye thus into her world. Yes. Plainly tell
Her chronicles with taciturnity:
How time was defenseless against revenge
Until you armed each now with her eternity.

xiii

No poem, music, or art's advancing guard,
No doctrine, dogma, theory or frenzied guile
         ... can practice eternity as a child.

Travel afar from the banishing crowd,
Or sail the salient seas of lost commands:
Determine which is the greater violence.
Wait in sorrow ... till imagination
Grants its mercies ... those lions snoring loud,
Or these fleas that stray from dogs in silence.
Love the only law that's within your heart,
For your heart's the only art that never dies.
Know you'll never know why you're so clever:
Your image of your greatest ecstasy
Becomes what you are, unfinished, forever.

ABOUT THE AUTHOR

Mr. James E. Winder was born on June 16, 1953, in Athens, Tennessee, and graduated *summa cum laude* from Vanderbilt University in 1975 with a B.A. in philosophy and literature. He earned an M.A. in philosophy from Purdue University in 1980.

James Winder spent the lion's share of his career as a mid-level manager and intelligence analyst for the National Security Agency (NSA), where he retired in 2013 after 30 years of service. At NSA, Mr. Winder's most noteworthy assignment was in 1991-1992, when he served as Assistant Director of the President's Foreign Intelligence Advisory Board (PFIAB). During that time, he co-authored a report for President George H.W. Bush on intelligence lessons learned during the first Gulf War and provided extensive research and documentation on a wide range of other matters of great interest to the PFIAB board members. In a special commendation, then Acting PFIAB Chairman, Admiral Bobby Ray Inman, cited Mr. Winder for his "expert advice to the President of the United States" and for his "extremely incisive and timely contributions on some very complex issues."

During three decades at NSA, Mr. Winder produced three classified, book-length studies, most notably including a comprehensive report, which won NSA's annual Cryptologic Literature Award. He also wrote a wide variety of other in-depth reports on Soviet intelligence, terrorism, and technical threats to U.S. telecommunications.

Mr. Winder is the author of *The History of Eternity,* a series of philosophic meditations in poetic form, which is, according to Mr. Winder, the cryptic story of his life and the lives of many others. There is – in the history of philosophy or literature – no other work that is akin to it in nature and scope.

Printed in Great Britain
by Amazon